The Workfare State

AMERICAN GOVERNANCE:
POLITICS, POLICY, AND PUBLIC LAW

Series Editors: Richard Valelly, Pamela Brandwein,
Marie Gottschalk, Christopher Howard

A complete list of books in the series
is available from the publisher.

The Workfare State

Public Assistance Politics from the New Deal to the New Democrats

Eva Bertram

UNIVERSITY OF PENNSYLVANIA PRESS

PHILADELPHIA

Copyright © 2015 University of Pennsylvania Press

All rights reserved. Except for brief quotations used
for purposes of review or scholarly citation, none of this
book may be reproduced in any form by any means without written
permission from the publisher.

Published by
University of Pennsylvania Press
Philadelphia, Pennsylvania 19104-4112
www.upenn.edu/pennpress

Printed in the United States of America
on acid-free paper

1 3 5 7 9 10 8 6 4 2

Library of Congress Cataloging-in-Publication Data

Bertram, Eva, author.
　The workfare state : public assistance politics from the New Deal to the new Democrats / Eva Bertram.
　　　pages cm.—(American governance : politics, policy, and public law)
　Includes bibliographical references and index.
ISBN 978-0-8122-4707-7 (hardcover : alk. paper)
　1. Welfare recipients—Employment—United States—History—20th century.
2. Welfare recipients—United States—History—20th century.　3. Public welfare—Political aspects—United States—History—20th century.　4. Welfare state—United States—History—20th century.　5. United States—Social policy—20th century.
6. United States—Politics and government—20th century.　7. Democratic Party (U.S.)—History—20th century.　I. Title.　II. Series: American governance.
　HV95.B456 2015
　362.5'840973—dc23

2015008539

CONTENTS

Introduction	1
Chapter 1. Democratic Divisions on Work and Welfare	15
Chapter 2. Welfarists Confront Workfarists: The Family Assistance Plan	43
Chapter 3. Building Workfare: WIN II, SSI, and EITC	67
Chapter 4. The Political Economy of Work and Welfare	97
Chapter 5. The Conservative Assault and the Liberal Retreat	126
Chapter 6. The New South and the New Democrats	160
Chapter 7. Showdown and Settlement	180
Chapter 8. The New World of Workfare	210
Conclusion	242
Notes	257
Index	319
Acknowledgments	327

Introduction

Gripped by a severe recession in late 2007, the United States suffered the most sustained and extensive wave of job destruction the country had seen since the Great Depression. Over the next year and a half, unemployment topped 10 percent, and the number of Americans facing long-term joblessness set new records. Poverty rates climbed above 15 percent, and the Census Bureau reported that more Americans were poor than at any other time in the nation's history.

The recession ended in 2009, but the hardships did not. By the end of the decade, the median American family had lost twenty years' worth of accumulated wealth and drew an income more than $5,000 below the median a decade earlier. Five years into the recovery, six in ten Americans said that the recession continued to affect them personally; four in ten said that someone in their household had lost a job.[1]

Americans confronted these hard times with a reconfigured social safety net. Decades in the making, it was the product of intense political battles in Washington that saw policymakers replace core elements of the New Deal welfare state for poor families with a workfare system designed to more actively promote and reward employment among the poor.[2] The modern workfare state was built piecemeal, beginning in the 1960s and culminating in the welfare reform legislation signed by Bill Clinton in 1996. At the time, policymakers and poverty experts were divided over workfare's likely outcomes—and the early evidence was mixed. But the system went largely untested until the Great Recession of 2007–9 and the slow recovery that followed. The experience of American economic hardship in these years is therefore not only the story of a particularly severe and sustained downturn. It is the story of the failings and flaws in the nation's new work-conditioned safety net.

Media accounts of the Great Recession focused on the rising economic insecurity of middle-income families faced with the loss of jobs, homes, and savings. Less attention was paid to the population of poor and near-poor

Americans who confronted far harsher circumstances. Their numbers were disturbingly high even before the recession. By 2010, the Census Bureau reported, approximately one in three Americans (100.5 million) were poor or near-poor—and four years into the recovery, the numbers were no better: 32.5 percent of Americans (101.8 million) were poor or near-poor in 2013. Roughly half of these (52 million) were in families with incomes above the poverty level, but by less than 50 percent. It is these near-poor families (more than one in six Americans) who are often a single medical emergency or jobless spell away from poverty.[3] Many were already struggling in low- or median-wage jobs, and the recession hit them the hardest: blue-collar unemployment increased at nearly three times the rate of white-collar unemployment.[4]

The collapse of the labor market in the recession left many families with nowhere to turn. In the Great Depression, images of unemployed Americans standing in line for bread captured the depth of need. Where were the "bread lines" of the Great Recession? They were formed by the millions who could not find work but had exhausted or failed to qualify for unemployment benefits, who waited in line (or online) to plead their cases.[5] They included the hundreds of people lined up at the county fairgrounds in west Tennessee for boxes of free food, and those in upstate New York and elsewhere who attended "grocery auctions," where food past its sell-by date was sold off at steep discounts.[6] They included the one in three Americans in 2009 who could not afford to comply with their medical prescriptions.[7] They included young people attending church youth groups in the Rio Grande Valley, who asked why they should finish school if the best they could hope for was low-wage work—and their parents, who told local priests during weekly confessions about the economic pressures straining their marriages, as partners blamed themselves and each other for the failure to make ends meet.[8] And they included parents dropped from the welfare rolls in Arizona, who described the measures they took to put food on the table and keep the lights on: "They have sold food stamps, sold blood, skipped meals, shoplifted, doubled up with friends, scavenged for bottles and cans and returned to relationships with violent partners—all with children in tow."[9]

During the Depression, bread lines formed not only because jobs had disappeared but also because there was no federal safety net for those left stranded. The New Deal response to this collective experience included the creation of unemployment insurance and limited federal public assistance programs for certain categories of poor Americans, under the 1935 Social Security Act. Seventy-five years later, poor families in the Great Recession could turn to a combination of old and new programs stitched together into a safety net that was increasingly conditioned on work.

The story of a Delaware family profiled in a *New York Times* piece illustrates how this new safety net fails to protect families when work fails.[10] Well before the recession, Joe Parente found himself unemployed after a serious back injury forced him out of his job as a pipefitter. He successfully completed a state-sponsored retraining course in computer repair, only to find there was little demand for his new skills. He sought disability benefits, but could not qualify without undergoing a magnetic resonance imaging (MRI) test he could not afford; nor did he qualify for Medicaid. The family of five got by thanks to his wife Kristen's job as a waitress—until she was laid off in January 2009, when the recession hit Wilmington. She had always been able to find a new job quickly, but not this time. Nor was she eligible for unemployment insurance under Delaware's rules.[11] The Parentes had long viewed government assistance as something for people who "didn't want to work." Now they found themselves seeking food stamps and cash assistance from Temporary Assistance for Needy Families (TANF), which had replaced the New Deal entitlement program Aid to Families with Dependent Children (AFDC). TANF provides temporary cash support to parents who meet the program's work requirements, but there is no guarantee that an eligible family will receive that aid. After a long wait, they received an allotment of food stamps and $475 a month in cash assistance. TANF's work requirements meant that each parent had to apply for forty jobs a week and Kristen had to attend "job readiness" classes—even though the family's poverty had nothing to do with the will or readiness to work. Because no work was available, Kristen was also mandated to volunteer at a community agency. She was fortunate enough to receive a job offer at the agency, but they still needed a "small stipend from the government" to make ends meet. Even then, the family's resources were not enough to solve their housing problems.

The Parentes' experience captures many of the dilemmas of the workfare state. The family diligently pursued various forms of assistance, from unemployment benefits and cash assistance to job retraining and readiness classes. Time and again, despite their best efforts, they fell through the gaps in the work-based safety net. Although the Great Recession heightened the challenges faced by millions of families like the Parentes, the underlying problem pre-dates the downturn. It is rooted in the conjuncture of a deteriorating low-wage labor market in the United States and a work-based system of social protections. For many poor and near-poor families, the experience of poverty and economic insecurity is a three-sided trap, defined by a lack of assistance for the nonworking poor, inadequate support for those in low-wage jobs, and few exits from the low-wage sector to middle-class jobs with more robust social protections. How did we end up with a safety net that provides so few buffers against a crisis like the Great Recession?

The shift to workfare is arguably the most significant transformation in the U.S. welfare state of the past fifty years. Yet its dimensions, causes, and consequences have not been fully explored. *Workfare* is often narrowly used as shorthand for programs that require work of welfare recipients, but these policies are part of a much deeper shift in the approach to federal aid for the poor. Public assistance programs created in the New Deal had always been restrictive and inadequate, and many families combined wage-earning and welfare—but federal aid for the poor was not conditioned on work. Welfare provision rested on the logic of need-based entitlement for certain vulnerable groups unable to fully support themselves through employment. And over its first three decades, the policy trajectory was toward gradually expanding coverage and increasing benefits for eligible poor families.[12] With the turn to workfare in the 1960s, a formal link was forged between work and public assistance in federal policy, and higher levels of aid began to flow to the working poor while aid for those outside the labor market diminished. By the end of the 1990s, the logic of federal cash assistance for the poor had shifted. The majority of the nation's income assistance was now conditioned on employment, and the aim was to promote, require, and reward work among poor families in the low-wage labor market.[13]

* * *

This book is about the politics of the transformation to workfare. Its central argument is that the policy change was driven by a political split and struggle within the Democratic Party over the ends and means of antipoverty assistance. The outcome was a system of social protections that tied most public income assistance to private employment—precisely at the moment that deindustrialization and global economic competition made low-wage jobs less effective at providing income security and stability. Three core claims in this argument link developments in the Democratic Party, in Southern politics, and in the U.S. labor market. Together, they explain how and why political leaders rewrote the social contract for poor families between the 1960s and the 1990s. And they place these decisions about public assistance squarely in the context of the rising job instability and wage stagnation that began in the mid-1970s and continue today.

The first claim is that workfare was fundamentally a Democratic project. It grew out of divisions within the party over the trajectory of public assistance. New Deal welfarism was always contested, even among Democrats; it was a product of political compromises, and was circumscribed by the patchwork character of the 1935 Social Security Act. New Deal public assistance programs for discrete categories of poor Americans (the elderly, blind, single mothers with children, and later, the disabled) emerged as the weakest link in the chain of social protections provided under the act, both institutionally and politically. Unlike social insurance programs (such as Social Security and unemployment insurance), public assistance programs were designed for certain needy groups deemed "unemployable." Institutional authority and funding obligations for these programs were divided between state and federal governments. Public assistance thus embodied a thin concept of entitlement—always qualified, often distorted by state-level program administrators, and politically vulnerable. Yet within these constraints, New Deal welfarism nonetheless defined a role for the federal government in public assistance and established a basic framework for providing aid as an entitlement. Many liberal advocates during and after the New Deal hoped to expand this need-based welfarist ideal into a broader social safety net over time.[14]

In the early 1960s, however, a conservative faction of the Democratic Party began to construct a workfare regime alongside New Deal welfare programs. By the 1990s, workfare would eclipse New Deal assistance for poor families. Although Republicans were important allies at key junctures in the decades-long process of change, both the policy models for workfare at the federal level and the political decisions to adopt new workfare policies were crafted primarily by Democrats.

The book's second claim is that Southern Democratic leaders in particular played a pivotal role in constructing modern workfare in these years. This is a story of how the South—the region with the nation's highest levels of poverty and inequality and least generous social welfare policies—won the fight to rewrite America's family assistance policy in the decades between the Great Society and the 1996 welfare reform.[15] The role of Southern legislators in constraining New Deal welfarism at its creation in the 1930s is familiar to historians.[16] What is striking in this study is the role of subsequent cohorts of Southern conservatives and centrists in constructing a workfare regime on the remnants of the old welfarist system at the end of the twentieth century.

Many and various factors contributed to workfare's ascendance. Institutional arrangements strengthened the hand of workfare advocates and weakened the position of welfarists.[17] Public backlash against welfare curtailed the scope of debate.[18] Organized economic interests weighed in at important points, including business leaders who saw advantages in expanding workfare over welfare.[19] Southern leaders, in short, did not engineer this change by themselves. But they were positioned to powerfully influence the direction of social policy at key junctures. And they repeatedly used the opportunities presented to them—including shifting institutional advantages, changes in the national political balance of power, and heightened public opposition to welfare—to advance a workfare agenda.

My third claim addresses the paradox of imposing workfare on poor families in the context of a declining low-wage labor market. I argue that workfare reversed the logic of income security for poor families inscribed in the New Deal welfare state. Rather than shielding families from the market's vagaries, its effort to promote, require, and reward work tied assistance to jobs in an unstable labor market. What made this shift so consequential was not primarily the move to encourage employment. It was the fact that workfare policies were imposed in the context of sweeping economic changes that made low-wage work an increasingly unreliable path from poverty to economic security.

Conceptions of work within U.S. social policy were also changing in these years. Work has always held a vaunted role in American political culture, and this has shaped policies toward poor families since the nation's founding. Expectations about what work should provide, however, have varied over time. Debates over workfare have embodied deeper political and ideological contests over work as a moral imperative, a social obligation, and a source of economic security.[20] Since the New Deal, federal policies (from the Fair Labor Standards Act to the Social Security Act) affirmed the notion not only that work was a social obligation but also that a job should deliver a basic livelihood. Wage and workplace regulations and job-based social protections sought to ensure workers a measure of security in a volatile market. Yet the principle that government should define and enforce minimum job standards was always contested and unevenly applied.[21] And from the New Deal through the 1990s, the battle lines over work and welfare were drawn and redrawn in a political struggle over the appropriate roles of markets and government in providing income security for poor families. The conflicts were not simply over work requirements for poor mothers in the AFDC program. More fundamentally, they engaged questions of who should be expected to work, when, and under what terms; what counts as work and whose work counts; what low-wage jobs can be expected to deliver; and what government owes the most vulnerable Americans when markets fail. The triumph of workfare required a retreat from the New Deal's more ambitious responses to these questions.

This argument challenges much of the standard account of modern public assistance.[22] According to the conventional story, New Deal and Great Society Democrats promoted and expanded federal assistance from the 1930s through the 1960s. After the 1980 election, the tide turned. Conservative Republicans—led first by Ronald Reagan and later by Newt Gingrich—pursued an agenda of retrenchment and rollback, through budget cuts, eligibility restrictions, and escalating work requirements. Their efforts culminated in the dismantlement of the core New Deal welfare program for poor families, AFDC, in 1996. Although they did not achieve all they wanted, they ushered in a conservative era in welfare politics. Embedded in this familiar story is an unambiguous account of "who did what when": liberal Democrats led expansions of the welfare state until 1980, with their most ambitious visions thwarted by the conservative coalition in Congress; Republicans then brought contraction and retrenchment, backed by conservative Democrats and ultimately the Clinton White House.

Yet neither the cast of leading characters nor the timing of events in the conventional account is quite accurate. The decisive struggles took place not between the parties, but within the Democratic Party: the conflict ran between those seeking to expand or defend the New Deal welfarist vision of public assistance and those advocating a contending workfare approach, most prominent among Southerners. The turning point toward modern workfare was not the 1980s, but the late 1960s and 1970s, as Chapters 1 and 2 explain. And although there were many forces pressing for work-based reform, the central architects of the initial shift were not Republican advocates of retrenchment, but conservative Southern Democrats in Congress who sought to redefine the purposes of public assistance in ways that preserved the political, economic, and racial order of the South.[23]

The 1970s thus brought a decisive but largely unrecognized phase of *conservative* welfare state building, described in Chapter 3. Although expansionary, it marked a turn away from New Deal–style income supports toward programs to formally promote and enforce work. Southern leaders quietly passed federal initiatives to require work from the welfare poor (who received AFDC), to provide welfare to the working poor (through creating the EITC, the Earned Income Tax Credit), and to exempt from work only those unable to earn wages due to old age or disability (through creating SSI, Supplemental Security Income). The outcome of these new work-based approaches to public assistance would be determined not only in the policy realm but also in the context of a changing labor market, as Chapter 4 argues.

When conservative Republicans brought an agenda of welfare retrenchment and labor market deregulation to the White House in the 1980s, the work of these Southern Democrats paved the way, enabling Republican leaders to build new coalitions and compromises. Conservative Republicans were able to leverage earlier Democratic agreements on work and welfare to restrict and weaken AFDC and to fend off more fundamental labor market reform, as Chapter 5 demonstrates. Pressure for conservative reform in the 1980s and 1990s came, once again, from many sources, yet Southern Democrats played a pivotal role.

The final act in the turn to workfare, examined in Chapters 6 and 7, was orchestrated by a new centrist cohort of Southern Democrats in the White House and Congress in the 1990s. Led by Bill Clinton, these Southern centrists forged compromises with Southern conservative Republicans in Congress to rewrite the terms of public assistance for both the welfare poor and the working poor. The core political conflicts and alignments on work and welfare were thus defined well before the Republican ascendance in the 1980s. The new political settlement that emerged in the mid-1990s—embodied in a major expansion in the EITC and the demise of AFDC—was constructed on the groundwork, and largely on the terms, established by leading Southern Democrats beginning in the 1970s.

Quietly replacing the New Deal political settlement on federal income support for the poor, workfare has governed policy and politics ever since. Shifts in party control of Congress and the White House have tested the durability of the workfare settlement under a wide range of political configurations. The years from Clinton's reelection to Barack Obama's second term also tested the effectiveness of the work-conditioned safety net under some of the best of economic times (the late 1990s) and the worst of times (the late 2000s) in the postwar era. Workfare, the evidence suggests, often functioned best in the years of robust economic growth and worst in years of downturn and economic hardship. This turbulent period nonetheless saw the consolidation of workfare as the dominant approach to public assistance for poor families, as Chapter 8 demonstrates.

* * *

There are many ways to study the politics of work and welfare. This book draws on scholarship addressing the political and institutional origins of social policy, and on studies of post-1970s economic and labor market transformations.[24] Too often, these scholarly conversations are conducted separately, even as the effects of social policy and labor market conditions become increasingly reciprocal.[25] In addition to grounding an account of public policy development in its labor market context, this book seeks out the political and institutional roots of workfare, to understand both the sources of policy change, and the persistence of a work-based approach despite evidence of its shortcomings as a safety net.

To existing literatures on welfare state retrenchment and economic inequality, the story of workfare offers analytical leverage in understanding late twentieth-century changes in the U.S. welfare state and their implications. Recent comparative scholarship on models of social provision has posited an affinity between workfare and the new political economy of contemporary capitalism, with its increasing demand for "flexible" labor.[26] Few of these works, however, focus attention on the political development of workfare in U.S. public assistance—on how, when, and why this turn took place. This book suggests that the origins of workfare in the United States may have as much to do with the local and highly stratified Southern labor markets of the past as with the "flattened and flexible" global labor market of the twenty-first century.

Other scholars have leveled compelling new challenges at old assumptions about U.S. welfare-state retrenchment, with a focus on the 1980s and beyond.[27] Recent works have pointed to patterns of expansion in some policy areas even in periods of fiscal constraint, and to trends toward a new market-oriented "enabling" paradigm for social provision.[28] This account seeks out earlier architects of the conservative turn in U.S. welfare policy, and it examines the interaction effects between social programs to better understand the transformation. It demonstrates that conservatives in the 1980s and 1990s relied on programs developed by Southern Democrats in the 1960s and 1970s to build the political compromises and coalitions needed to achieve their aims.

This approach redefines the relationships between antipoverty programs. The EITC, for example, is conventionally seen as an exception to the retrenchment in public assistance exemplified by AFDC's dismantlement: it expanded even as other programs faced serious cutbacks.[29] In fact, the enactment and expansion of the EITC enabled conservatives to win moderate support for cuts in AFDC, and the EITC was thus used politically to facilitate AFDC's decline. Implicit here is the notion that retrenchment and reconfiguration may be two sides of the same coin: one model of income assistance was dismantled as another was constructed, offering one explanation for why some programs grew and others declined in a period of conservative ascendancy. Although opponents of the New Deal welfare state have at times undermined social welfare programs by cutting budgets, they have also achieved their aims by creating new programs, or turning the purposes of existing programs toward conservative ends.

The story of workfare's origins also speaks to recent debates on the political sources of economic inequality. Prominent accounts have focused on the role of voters and political parties, arguing, for example, that low-income Americans have fared better when elections yield Democratic rather than Republican administrations, based on income distribution data under varying conditions of party control.[30] But this metric may miss a deeper story. Workfare illustrates how particular Democratic-led social policies have reinforced or even exacerbated inequality over time. Other scholars in the inequality debate focus on the role of organized interests and institutions in policymaking. They argue that policy choices affecting income distribution are shaped more decisively by mobilized economic interests and structural advantages in the political environment than by the actions of individual voters or parties.[31] The complex role of different factions within the Democratic party, and their alliances with organized interests and like-minded Republicans in the development of workfare, lends evidence to this claim.

The case of workfare also engages larger theoretical debates about the sources and mechanisms of institutional change and stability. By showing how incremental shifts in the operation of public assistance over time came to redefine and undermine the original purposes and trajectory of social programs such as AFDC, for example, this analysis broadens conceptions of "path dependence."[32] The workfare case also sheds light on recent debates over "submerged," "delegated," "hidden," and "shadow" policymaking in American politics. The development of workfare relied on the use of tax incentives and other pro-market policy tools to win passage of favored social programs by centrist or conservative Democrats—from Louisiana Senator Russell Long to President Clinton. These "submerged" or "hidden" policy tools arguably undermined support for broader redistributive efforts at key moments, in part by obscuring the role of government in providing benefits.[33]

In focusing on federal policy and the role of work and labor markets, I do not mean to deny other frameworks for understanding the politics of public assistance. This book focuses on a significant, untold story about policy-making over time; as a result, the spotlight is on the role of political elites, mainly at the national level. Other actors have played vital roles in welfare politics, including welfare recipients, the civil rights and women's movements, business interests, and state and local officials; though not the focus of this study, their contributions to the politics of public assistance have been established in numerous accounts.[34]

Particularly on the subject of AFDC, there are rich literatures on the gender and racial politics of reform, and this book is indebted to many of these works. Gender analyses have exposed the ways welfare policies have been fueled by attempts to regulate and control the behavior of single mothers eligible for AFDC. Welfare has not only failed to provide adequate income for their families, but it has also been used systematically to undermine their rights and liberties regarding marriage, reproduction, and child-rearing. Race-centered scholarship demonstrates how welfare restrictions, rules, and cutbacks not only targeted nonmarried mothers, but were often racially motivated. My account argues that historically, welfare reform has been driven by political-economic factors in addition to and often in conjunction with race and gender.[35] Preoccupied with preserving regional labor markets with social hierarchies intact, Southern lawmakers led the charge to rewrite federal policy in the 1960s to impose work requirements on poor single mothers in AFDC, for example; this was a critical turning point in the gendered struggles over welfare rights and work obligations. They also provided the decisive template (the EITC) in the 1970s for addressing problems in the low-wage workforce, one that circumvented rather than challenged the deep racial and gender disparities in rates of unemployment, job tenure, wage mobility, and access to job-related social protections that continue today.[36]

* * *

This book has been animated by more than the scholarly conversations it engages, however. From the outset, my central interest has been to understand the staleness of the contemporary political debate on poverty and public assistance. For more than thirty years, the poverty debate has been framed largely by the question of how to move single mothers from welfare to work. Declining numbers on the welfare rolls are still used, by conservatives and liberals alike, as evidence of the success of federal antipoverty policies.[37] This book recasts the debate to focus on the economic security of families under the workfare system. Doing so demands attention not only to welfare families, but to the far larger population of poor and near-poor families who are the targets of workfare.

For politics and policy, the questions raised by the workfare state are pointed. Federal policy now seeks to address family poverty by tying income assistance to employment. How successfully is it achieving this aim? Is a strategy of conditioning the social contract for poor Americans on employment the best way to ensure basic economic security for these families?

The evidence to date is not encouraging. Viewed in the context of other wealthy nations, the record of the United States in addressing poverty is abysmal. Poor families with children put in more hours at work than their counterparts in any other rich country. The United States also leads these countries in the number of workers who hold low-wage jobs. At the same time, the United States does far less than other wealthy nations to reduce poverty through social expenditures and tax policies. In countries such as France, Germany, Italy, Belgium, the United Kingdom, and Finland, government transfer programs and taxes reduce the poverty rate by more than 20 percentage points. In the United States, it is a mere 9.7 points. So poor Americans work more, but more remain in poverty than in other wealthy nations (17.3 percent of Americans were poor a decade into the 2000s, measured by the shared international standard, compared with an average of 9.9 percent in twenty-three of the wealthiest nations). Comparisons of rates of poverty among children are particularly disturbing. As a percentage of national income, the United States spends about half as much as other wealthy countries on programs for nonelderly families with children. And our child poverty rate (23.1 percent using the international standard) is more than double the average rate in those countries.[38]

Political leaders point proudly to the number of Americans who have left welfare and to the growing reach of workfare programs. The EITC, for example, lifts some five to six million people out of poverty each year. But another three million are in poor families entirely outside the new system, receiving neither wages nor assistance, and some forty million Americans

Table I.1 Rates of Relative Poverty, Child Poverty, and Poverty Reduction Through Government Policy in Select Wealthy Nations, Late 2000s

Country	POPULATION IN POVERTY		CHILD POVERTY		POVERTY REDUCTION THROUGH TAXES AND TRANSFERS	
	Rank[a]	Percentage Poor	Rank[a]	Percentage Poor	Rank[a]	Percentage Points Poverty Reduction
United States	1	17.3	1	23.1	23	9.7
Japan	2	15.7	5	14.9	17	13.0
Australia	3	14.6	11	10.9	19	12.6
Spain	4	14.0	2	17.1	16	13.2
Canada	5	12.0	6	13.3	18	12.7
Italy	6	11.4	4	15.9	5	21.9
New Zealand	7	11.0	9	11.7	21	11.4
United Kingdom	8	11.0	8	12.1	8	20.2
Greece	9	9.8	3	16.0	7	20.3
Belgium	10	9.4	12	10.2	4	22.0
Switzerland	11	9.3	15	8.1	22	10.6
Germany	12	8.9	14	8.5	2	23.6
Luxembourg	13	8.5	7	12.3	9	18.4
Sweden	14	8.4	16	7.3	10	18.1
Finland	15	8.0	22	5.3	3	22.1
Slovenia	16	8.0	19	6.3	12	17.3
Austria	17	7.9	17	7.3	6	20.9
Norway	18	7.8	20	6.1	14	16.0
France	19	7.2	13	8.8	1	25.4
Netherlands	20	7.2	21	6.1	13	16.9
Slovak Republic	21	7.2	11	11.2	11	17.5
Iceland	22	6.4	23	4.7	20	12.6
Denmark	23	6.1	18	6.5	15	16.0
Average		**9.9**		**10.6**		**17.1**

Source: Elise Gould and Hilary Wething, "U.S. Poverty Rates Higher, Safety Net Weaker Than in Peer Countries," Economic Policy Institute, July 24, 2012, Figures C, D, and F.

Note: The United States is a standout among wealthy nations for its high rates of poverty in the population as a whole and among children. These figures represent rates of relative poverty using the common international standard—the percentage of people in households with less than half the median household income. The United States also does less than other wealthy countries to reduce poverty through government policy. The last column indicates the degree to which relative poverty is reduced by taxes and transfer programs; in these twenty-three countries, government policies reduce poverty by an average of 17.1 percentage points.

[a] Ranked highest to lowest.

receive poverty-level wages.[39] National poverty levels have remained stubbornly high over the past fifteen years, and tens of millions of Americans balance precariously just above the poverty line.[40] These trends have continued even in the wake of major declines in the welfare rolls, historic increases in the number of poor adults working year-round and full-time, and investments of more than $500 billion in the new workfare strategies.[41] Like "body counts" tallied in military conflicts, both the diminishing number of welfare recipients and the rising number of workfare participants are less indicators of progress than they are indictments of the deep structural weaknesses in the U.S. low-wage labor market, and the failure of social policy to address the problem.

CHAPTER 1

Democratic Divisions on Work and Welfare

Two eras command attention in the historical development of both the U.S. welfare state and the modern Democratic Party: the New Deal of the 1930s and the Great Society of the 1960s. Both were launched by liberal Democratic presidents backed by sizable congressional majorities, and the social welfare programs and policies they created came to be seen by supporters and detractors alike as among the defining legacies of the party. Yet the Democratic Party of the 1930s and 1960s was not only the party of Franklin D. Roosevelt, John F. Kennedy, Lyndon B. Johnson, and their liberal supporters. It was also the party of Representatives Robert Doughton and Wilbur Mills, Senator Russell Long, and their conservative colleagues from the South.

Southern Democrats held nearly 40 percent of the party's congressional seats in 1932 (38 percent in the House; 44 percent in the Senate) and more than 35 percent of them in 1968 (36 percent and 33 percent, respectively). Most were more conservative than others in the party, and they shared a distinctive approach to work and welfare. Several occupied some of the most powerful positions in Congress on social and domestic policy in these years. As debates unfolded over the shape and size of public assistance programs for poor families, the role of Southern Democrats in Congress proved decisive. During the 1930s, intraparty conflicts defined both the limits and possibilities of New Deal welfarism in federal policies toward the poor under the Social Security Act. And in the 1960s, Southern leaders would help execute an unmistakable rightward turn in welfare policy, even as scores of new antipoverty initiatives were launched by party leaders in the White House and social welfare spending spiked to new heights.

The origins of New Deal welfarism lay in the crisis of the Great Depression and the response of the incoming Roosevelt administration. The 1935 Social Security Act created both social insurance programs for workers (such as Unemployment Compensation and Social Security) and public assistance programs for discrete categories of poor Americans, including Aid to Dependent Children (ADC) for single-parent families. The new public assistance system was more comprehensive than the patchwork of state and local programs that preceded it. It created an unprecedented new role for the federal government and provided a new entitlement to certain vulnerable groups of poor Americans. Yet New Deal welfarism was constrained at its inception—not only by the limited scope of assistance, but also by an institutional structure that delimited federal authority over public assistance, and by a fractured coalition of political support within the Democratic Party. Even as the programs expanded in the decades that followed, these limitations left New Deal public assistance vulnerable to attacks by later critics, as the first section of this chapter demonstrates.

The turn from New Deal welfarism to modern workfare at the federal level began in the 1960s with a series of political skirmishes over ADC (later renamed Aid to Families with Dependent Children, AFDC). The transformation would, in time, encompass a range of other programs and expand well beyond work requirements for AFDC recipients. As the chapter's second section explains, it was in these years—on the watch of John Kennedy and Lyndon Johnson, and in the midst of the largest expansion of social welfare programs since the New Deal—that federal cash assistance for poor families began the slow-moving shift to a work-conditioned safety net that would culminate in the 1996 repeal of AFDC and its federal entitlement. Presidents Kennedy and Johnson pursued a series of liberal expansions of AFDC between 1961 and 1967. The strategies they chose backfired, however, creating opportunities for Southern conservatives within their own party to seize the initiative to pursue a workfare agenda.

New Deal Welfarism: A Thin Entitlement

The Great Depression was entering its third year and unemployment levels approached a staggering 33 percent when Franklin Roosevelt assumed office in 1933.[1] The attention of the nation and the new administration was trained on prolonged joblessness and the need for immediate relief for the tens of millions facing destitution. Ten weeks after his inauguration, FDR signed into law the Federal Emergency Relief Act, authorizing matching grants to states to ease acute and widespread poverty through the Federal Emergency Relief Administration (FERA). From the outset, both Roosevelt and FERA administrator Harry Hopkins were determined to provide work to the unemployed—rather than relief through direct cash assistance—wherever possible.[2] "Direct relief was merely a temporary emergency expedient," explained FERA assistant administrator Josephine Brown. "It was necessary to keep the unemployed from starving until work and wages in some form could be provided."[3] Public works programs soon emerged as a central component of the response to the Depression, with more than four million workers employed by the Civil Works Administration by January 1934. Federal relief flowed at unprecedented levels as well, reaching more than eleven million people at the beginning of 1934, and more than eighteen million by the fall.[4]

As the emergency began to subside, the president turned his attention to creating a permanent program of social protections designed to provide Americans with "security against the major hazards and vicissitudes of life."[5] He appointed a high-level Committee on Economic Security (CES) in June 1934 to study and prepare legislative recommendations for a comprehensive program of federal social provision. Their efforts would yield the landmark Social Security Act of 1935, which included both social insurance programs for current and retired workers and public assistance programs for eligible categories of poor Americans. Within the U.S. context, FDR's vision for economic security was a bold one, and it rested primarily on the promise of social insurance. "The President wanted everybody covered for every contingency in life—'cradle to grave,' he called it—under a social insurance system," said Labor Secretary Frances Perkins, who had been tapped to head the CES.[6] Social insurance programs were designed to shield workers from economic hardship when they were unable to earn due to circumstances beyond their control, such as temporary unemployment, illness, or old age. Unemployment insurance and, later, old age insurance emerged as priorities for the CES.[7]

Although envisioned as a "second line" of defense against destitution, behind social insurance, public assistance was regarded as a necessary "supplement" for certain populations facing poverty but unable to earn their own support.[8] Aid would be provided under the Social Security Act to three categories of poor Americans: the elderly through Title I (Old Age Assistance), single-mother families with dependent children through Title IV (Aid to

Dependent Children), and the blind through Title X (Aid to the Blind); a program of Aid to the Permanently and Totally Disabled (Title XIV) was added in 1950. For varying reasons, each group was considered "unemployable." As one FERA official explained, "An 'unemployable' person is one that is incapable of performing a day's work on account of age or physical disability, or where home and family duties will render it impossible for the individual to work."[9] Assistance to people in the three categories would be provided through federal grants-in-aid to match expenditures by the states, which would administer the programs. Planners reasoned that aid to the poor had long been handled at the local and state levels, and primary responsibility should remain there, particularly as the federal government was now assuming a major new burden in confronting unemployment and creating social insurance programs on a national scale.[10]

Differences arose, however, over the purposes and parameters of public assistance. The most robust of the main contending visions was articulated by the CES Advisory Committee on Public Employment and Relief and key leaders within the FERA.[11] The Advisory Committee lobbied for a dense and broad safety net that would provide both a larger public works program and income assistance for all those in need who could not participate in it. The committee urged a sober realism about the limits of employment to ensure adequate economic security and the resulting need for public assistance on a permanent basis, arguing that "the social hazards to which millions of persons and families are subjected, are too varied and too complicated to make it safe to assume that work would remove the need."[12] It also advised against a limited, categorical approach to determining who among the poor deserved assistance. The Advisory Committee argued instead for a unified program with appropriate federal authority, to address, in Josephine Brown's words, the needs of "the 'employables' who would not fit into the practical work programs" and the "unemployables" who did not fit into designated categories.[13] This vision of a broad program of federally supported general assistance to all poor Americans would surface repeatedly in subsequent decades.

The leading women activists at the federal Children's Bureau, who were tasked with submitting recommendations for assisting children in poverty, held a different view of public assistance. The bureau had championed the development of state-level "mothers' pensions" during the Progressive Era and saw New Deal public assistance as an opportunity to expand these programs. The aim would be to assist and enable eligible single mothers to provide proper care for their children in their homes without an undue burden of wage-earning. The bureau's vision emphasized a casework approach that combined income assistance and counseling by trained social workers.¹⁴

The CES was charged with crafting the administration's draft legislation, and many of its leaders—including executive director Edwin Witte and technical director Arthur Altmeyer—held a third position. Witte and Altmeyer were economists from Wisconsin who had helped create that state's pioneering social insurance programs. Along with other prominent New Dealers, they wanted to make federal social insurance the centerpiece of the proposed legislation. They embraced the need for a more comprehensive, fair, and equitable system of public assistance for the poor, but they had a different assessment of its trajectory—one that would later be exploited by critics of public assistance. They were convinced that the need for public assistance would diminish as employment and social insurance grew. They therefore sought to keep the public assistance programs limited, in part to ensure that the new social insurance initiatives gained broad popular and congressional support.¹⁵

Despite their differences, these three positions shared significant common ground, and New Deal welfarism ultimately reflected elements of each.¹⁶ As the CES drew up recommendations, it adopted the more limited, categorical approach to federal public assistance (providing aid to those in the three categories of "unemployables") rather than its Advisory Committee's recommendation for a unified program of general assistance for the poor. The CES was persuaded, according to its report, that if all of its recommendations were adopted, this categorical approach would be adequate because the relief problem "will have diminished to a point where it will be possible to return primary responsibility for the care of people who cannot work to the State and local governments."¹⁷ The CES plan did affirm the need for a more extensive and fairly administered system of aid for the poor—one with federal funding and oversight, however. In the case of poor families with children, the CES report stated bluntly that a "large group of children at present maintained by relief will not be aided by employment or unemployment compensation. There are the fatherless and other 'young' families without a breadwinner." For these groups, "increased State appropriations and Federal grants-in-aid are essential."¹⁸

The CES's proposed ADC program would provide cash assistance to help eligible poor single mothers support their children at home. The programs, according to the CES report, "are designed to release from the wage-earning role" these single mothers.¹⁹ This principle was amplified in testimony before Congress by Grace Abbott, one of the authors of Title IV, who served on the CES Advisory Committee and had directed the Children's Bureau. Because a "mother's services are worth more in the home than they are in the outside labor market," Abbott testified, she "should be enabled to stay home and take care of the children, and we expect she will have to do so until the children reach working age."[20]

As the ADC provisions moved through Congress with the other public assistance proposals, they quickly became the victim of intraparty conflict, as historian Linda Gordon and other scholars have documented.[21] Disagreements between the Northern liberal and Southern conservative wings of the Democratic Party emerged in both the House and Senate committees charged with producing the legislation, chaired by Representative Robert Doughton (D-N.C.) and Senator Pat Harrison (D-Miss.). Southern committee leaders ultimately rewrote the terms of assistance, including benefit and eligibility rules, in ways that radically curtailed the scope and reach of the program.[22]

The administration's original legislation provided benefit levels that sought to ensure adequate (if minimal) support, defined as "a reasonable subsistence, compatible with decency and health, to dependent children."[23] Southern Democrats in Congress opposed this provision, however. According to Abbott, they "feared that northern standards might be forced on the South in providing for Negro and white tenant families," and the clause was stripped from the bill.[24] Instead, the final legislation stated only that ADC was to enable each state "to furnish financial assistance, as far as practicable under the conditions of the state."[25] A similar clause was eliminated from the program for the elderly poor, Old Age Assistance. But the committee leaders' particular disregard for the ADC program was revealed when final benefit levels were determined: ADC benefits were the lowest of the three categories. Edwin Witte, executive director of the CES, later acknowledged that this may have been a mistake, but he "did not feel that it was wise to raise this point, lest we lose this aid altogether."[26]

The original administration bill also contained a broad standard of eligibility for ADC. Following recommendations by the FERA, the administration initially defined dependent children as those for whom there was "no adult person, other than the one needed to care for the children, able to work and provide a reasonable subsistence." This definition arguably would have laid the groundwork for federal assistance to virtually all poor children under working age, including those in two-parent families, and it would have exempted the caretaker parent—usually the mother—from waged work. Josephine Brown explained, "'Aid to Dependent Children' as conceived by the FERA meant general relief or assistance on a family basis to all families having children under sixteen."[27] However, Doughton's House Ways and Means Committee removed the implicit work exemption for the adult caretaker. The Senate Finance Committee further circumscribed eligibility by asserting that the children must have been deprived of parental support "by reason of death, continued absence from the home, or physical or mental incapacity of a parent."[28] These changes not only limited the program's reach. They also left unsettled the question of work obligations. The final federal legislation did not require work of poor mothers and was intended to support caregiving, but it did not explicitly prohibit states from imposing work rules. Moreover, the program's low benefits would force many families to combine welfare and work to make ends meet.

Conflict also arose over what appeared to be an unobjectionable bureaucratic clause in the administration's bill that provided for federal regulations "necessary to effectuate the purposes of this title." Perceiving this as a threat to state control and patronage jobs, the House committee scaled back the provisions, and the administration assented. The removal of this provision and federal oversight over other specific standards limited federal administrators to approving or disapproving state ADC programs in their entirety, rather than demanding piecemeal changes. Federal officials would have to choose between accepting a flawed state plan with objectionable restrictions on aid, or rejecting the plan altogether and thereby denying federal aid to all poor single-mother families within that state.[29]

The new system of public assistance was thus attenuated by compromises demanded by Southern legislators—concessions that would leave it vulnerable to subsequent workfare initiatives. New Deal public assistance still rested on a welfarist foundation, though a fragile one. Eligibility was based above all on need. There was no federal requirement that poor families earn wages in order to receive aid. Although states could determine their own standards of need, a federal guarantee ensured that matching funds would be provided to meet each state's need as it fluctuated with economic conditions. Some federal standards also remained in place. To receive funding, each state was required to submit an administrative plan for its ADC program, to be approved by the federal Social Security Board. Plans had to meet certain requirements—affirming, for example, that the program was available throughout the state and administered by a single statewide agency. States also had to provide for fair hearings for those denied assistance, a principle federal administrators saw as essential to defending the individual entitlement to aid.³⁰ As the Social Security Act became law, the question was whether the thin welfarist foundation of the new public assistance programs would be challenged and undermined, or shored up and strengthened over time.

* * *

The years following the Social Security Act's passage brought a marked expansion in the new program for poor families. ADC's growth was troubled and uneven, however, leading to frustration among its welfarist advocates. Jane Hoey, who led the Social Security Board's Bureau of Public Assistance (BPA), was anxious to see the program fully implemented as quickly as possible. Central to the agency's welfarist vision was an immediate goal of securing the involvement of all states, and all counties within them. Hoey calculated that ADC was likely "still caring for only a fraction of the needy children for whom Federal funds might be made available" in 1939, and she was impatient.³¹ The BPA wanted states to build ADC up more rapidly, and to adopt more generous and inclusive eligibility criteria.

For their part, many state administrators saw ADC largely as a source of federal funds to support—but not reform—their existing state-run mothers' pension programs. Deep-rooted state interests often ran against the expansionary vision of federal administrators. Most states faced serious fiscal constraints and worried about their funding obligations under the new assistance programs.³² Many officials wanted to keep programs small, affordable, and under their control. This trend was widespread in the South, where economic elites expected to maintain unfettered control over local workforces, leaving racial hierarchies at the heart of the region's labor relations unchallenged. Increased public assistance threatened to disrupt these long-standing social and economic arrangements by providing an alternative income source to poor families with current or potential workers.³³ State and local officials thus jealously guarded their administrative prerogatives, and throughout the South, state public welfare commissioners coordinated their efforts to limit federal oversight.³⁴

As federal funds began to flow, Southern states displayed a distinct pattern of policy preferences, illustrated most clearly in the size and scope of the three assistance programs. Between the 1930s and 1960s, Southern states built up programs for the elderly poor that were among the largest in the country by rate of recipients (per 1,000 elderly residents). Their programs for the blind

Table 1.1 Southern States' Old Age Assistance (OAA) Programs, 1960 and 1961

State	RECIPIENT RATE (PER 1,000 ELDERLY)		TOTAL RECIPIENTS		TOTAL PAYMENTS ($)		STATE POPULATION
	Rank	Number	Rank	Number	Rank	Total Amount	Rank
Louisiana	1	510	3	126,661	3	9,372,642	20
Mississippi	2	418	9	80,236	22	2,766,118	29
Alabama	3	374	5	100,301	7	5,950,078	19
Oklahoma	4	352	8	87,243	4	7,230,064	27
Georgia	5	326	6	94,087	12	4,360,273	16
Texas	7	292	2	219,445	2	11,988,021	6
Arkansas	8	285	15	55,884	20	2,888,359	31
South Carolina	12	207	25	30,001	30	1,277,494	26
Kentucky	13	189	14	56,173	18	2,984,082	22
North Carolina	18	151	20	46,992	24	2,312,504	12
Florida	25	122	10	70,323	15	4,208,718	10
Tennessee	27	118	17	52,707	23	2,330,103	17
Virginia	43	50	33	14,408	33	786,385	14

Source: Total recipient and payment data are from "Current Operating Statistics," Table 11, *Social Security Bulletin* 25, no. 3 (March 1962): 33; these data are for November 1961. Recipient rate data are from "Current Operating Statistics," Table 10, *Social Security Bulletin* 24, no. 9 (September 1961): 40; these data are for December 1960. The *Statistical Abstract of the United States, 1962*, 83rd ed. (Washington, D.C.: U.S. Bureau of the Census, 1962), reports similar OAA recipient figures in Table 403, page 298, and provides population rankings, page 10.
Note: Southern state public assistance programs for the elderly had the highest participation rates in the country. Many of their programs were among the nation's largest, measured by number of recipients as well as total monthly payments, even as Southern state population levels ranked mostly in the midrange nationally.

and disabled poor were also sizable.[35] Yet Southern states' programs for poor families were quite small, in terms of numbers of families supported and program costs, despite the region's high family poverty rates. Although benefit levels in all Southern public assistance programs were meager, the region's ADC programs were more restrictive in their reach, and they provided the lowest average benefits in the nation.[36]

Early studies in the 1940s confirmed what federal administrators suspected: a number of states were using their discretionary authority under the Social Security Act to serve local interests by restricting access to ADC.[37] One widespread strategy was the use of vague and ill-defined "suitable home"

Table 1.2 Southern States' Aid to Dependent Children (ADC), November 1961

State	Recipient Families Rank	Recipient Families Number	Payments ($) Rank	Payments ($) Total Amount	Average Family Benefit ($) Rank	Average Family Benefit ($) Monthly Aid
North Carolina	8	28,093	11	2,425,493	43	86.34
Florida	10	25,008	18	1,547,254	46	61.87
Louisiana	11	22,635	13	2,196,114	38	97.02
Tennessee	12	22,522	17	1,588,850	45	70.55
Kentucky	13	21,826	14	1,968,555	40	90.19
Alabama	14	21,210	32	875,362	49	41.27
Mississippi	15	20,533	34	740,866	50	36.05
Oklahoma	17	19,085	12	2,356,980	26	123.50
Texas	18	19,048	20	1,482,213	44	77.81
Georgia	19	16,411	21	1,431,822	42	87.25
Virginia	24	10,676	27	1,057,913	37	99.09
South Carolina	27	9,157	37	539,786	48	58.95
Arkansas	34	6,478	38	383,978	47	59.27
				National average		**121.29**

Source: "Current Operating Statistics," Table 14, *Social Security Bulletin* 25, no. 3 (March 1962): 34; the data are for November 1961. Similar data for recipients are reported in *Statistical Abstract of the United States, 1962,* Table 403, page 298; similar data for average family benefits are reported in Table 404, page 299.

Note: In contrast to the Southern programs for the elderly and disabled poor, Southern state ADC programs did not rank high nationally (by recipients or payments), and their average benefits were the lowest in the nation.

restrictions, a holdover from Progressive Era mothers' pension programs. These state rules—regarding a mother's home life, child-rearing practices, and sexual relations—left significant discretion to caseworkers.[38] Many states used the restrictions to refuse or limit aid to unmarried mothers. "Suitable home" rules drew prominent early criticism from Winifred Bell, who wrote a classic firsthand study of ADC in its initial decades.[39] Extensive scholarship since then has exposed the ways that suitable home rules were used to exert social control over poor women.[40]

Another strategy, and an important precursor to workfare, was to use employment rules to govern eligibility and benefits. States often granted local officials the discretion to determine a mother's "employability."[41] Many women were denied ADC assistance on the grounds that they were in fact employable and should be earning wages instead. Many others were instructed or compelled to earn wages to supplement their ADC grants, through temporary suspensions of aid or the provision of insufficient benefits.⁴² Decisions to deny or limit aid were sometimes made regardless of whether mothers were actually able to secure jobs or sufficient wages.⁴³ Though it is difficult to assess the numbers who were working, studies of closed cases in the 1950s and early 1960s showed that around one-third of ADC mothers worked for wages, either full-time, part-time, or seasonally.⁴⁴

Like suitable home restrictions, employment rules were more prevalent in the South and disproportionately used to exclude black families. A Southern public aid field supervisor observed:

> The number of Negro cases is few due to the unanimous feeling on the part of the staff and board that there are more work opportunities for Negro women and to their intense desire not to interfere with local labor conditions. The attitude that "they have always gotten along," and that "all they'll do is have more children" is definite. . . . Communities . . . see no reason why the employable Negro mother should not continue her usually sketchy seasonal labor or indefinite domestic service rather than receive a public assistance grant.⁴⁵

An investigation of complaints about ADC in Louisiana reached similar conclusions: "In some areas, it is contended that public assistance results in reducing the unskilled labor supply in employment where women and older children form a principal part of the labor supply . . . The fact that roughly two-thirds of the children receiving ADC are nonwhite influences attitudes toward the program."⁴⁶

Federal administrators pushed back against these and other state practices that undermined the BPA's welfarist aims. The agency's institutional leverage was limited, however, and its primary response was to issue new regulations and guidance. For example, BPA officials issued a series of requirements in 1947 that state agencies not deny any individual the opportunity to apply for the program, and that they provide assistance to every applicant deemed eligible.⁴⁷ The BPA's *Handbook of Public Assistance* was eventually over five inches thick with federal guidance.⁴⁸ On the employment question, the *Handbook* stated clearly that the ADC program and staff should "make it possible for a mother to choose between staying at home to care for her children and taking a job."⁴⁹ Jane Hoey expressed serious concern about the failure to adequately realize these goals when recipients left welfare for work or combined the two due to low benefit levels. Inadequate assistance payments rendered "meaningless" any choice between work and benefits, she asserted.[50]

Recognizing that states faced fiscal pressures to limit aid programs, federal administrators also increased the federal financial contribution to ADC.[51] This strategy measurably helped to expand the program to cover more families. In a review of ADC's first twenty-five years, Ellen Perkins at the Bureau of Family Services (BPA's successor) would later note that increased federal funding produced a significant rise in state assistance standards in these years, which made more families newly eligible.[52] Federal funding also helped generate greater coverage of nonwhite families. Between 1937 and 1940, some 14 to 17 percent of all ADC recipients nationwide were black; by 1948, the proportion of nonwhite families was 30 percent.[53]

Overall, assistance for poor families thus saw a slow but steady welfarist expansion in its first three decades, despite resistance from a number of states. In Washington, meanwhile, intraparty differences over public assistance were only deepening. Several leading administration officials continued to defend and prioritize social insurance over public assistance in deliberations over policy reforms. More than once, major welfarist expansions and reforms to strengthen the New Deal framework for public assistance were considered— but federal officials drew back, instead repeating earlier assurances that the assistance programs would shrink as social insurance grew.[54] In Congress, the frustration of Southern Democrats over the trajectory of public assistance was rising. The sentiment was captured by Senate Finance Committee chair Walter George of Georgia, who insisted in 1950 that proposed reforms should simply replace public assistance with social insurance.[55]

Liberal Expansions and the Southern Reaction in the 1960s

The role of the post–New Deal generation of Southern Democrats is less familiar than that of the Southerners who shaped the Social Security Act at its origins.[56] Led primarily by Wilbur Mills of Arkansas in the House and Russell Long of Louisiana in the Senate, who entered Congress in 1939 and 1948, respectively, this cohort would spearhead many of the first major legislative efforts to introduce workfare reforms in public assistance. Like their prede-

Table 1.3 Congressional Committee Chairs, 1933–2015

House Ways and Means
Robert L. Doughton (D-N.C.)	*1933–1947*
Harold Knudson (R-Minn.)	1947–1949
Robert L. Doughton (D-N.C.)	*1949–1953*
Daniel A. Reed (R-N.Y.)	1953–1955
Jere Cooper (D-Tenn.)	*1955–1957*
Wilbur D. Mills (D-Ark.)	*1957–1975*
Al Ullman (D-Ore.)	1975–1981
Dan Rostenkowski (D-Ill.)	1981–1994
Sam Gibbons (D-Fla.)	*1994–1995*
Bill Archer (R-Tex.)	*1995–2001*
William M. Thomas (R-Calif.)	2001–2007
Charles B. Rangel (D-N.Y.)	2007–2010
Sander M. Levin (D-Mich.)	2010–2011
Dave Camp (R-Mich.)	2010–2015
Paul Ryan (R-Wisc.)	2015–

Senate Finance
Pat Harrison (D-Miss.)	*1933–1941*
Walter F. George (D-Ga.)	*1941–1953*
Eugene D. Millikin (R-Colo.)	1953–1955
Harry F. Byrd (D-Va.)	*1955–1965*
Russell B. Long (D-La.)	*1966–1981*
Robert J. Dole (R-Kans.)	1981–1985
Bob Packwood (R-Ore.)	1985–1987
Lloyd Bentsen (D-Tex.)	*1987–1993*
Daniel Patrick Moynihan (D-N.Y.)	1993–1995
William V. Roth, Jr. (R-Del.)	1995–2001
Max Baucus (D-Mont.)	2001–2003
Charles E. Grassley (R-Iowa)	2003–2007
Max Baucus (D-Mont.)	2007–2014
Ron Wyden (D-Ore.)	2014–2015
Orrin Hatch (R-Utah)	2015–

Source: Congressional Directory, 1935 to 2012; *History of the Committee on Finance, United States Senate* (Washington, D.C.: U.S. Government Printing Office, 1981), 141–53.
Note: Southern legislators (in italics) dominated the chairmanships of committees with jurisdiction over social welfare policy from the New Deal to the mid-1970s, a period in which committee chairs exerted a high degree of control over legislation. Southerners chaired the House Ways and Means Committee in thirty-six of forty years, and the Senate Finance Committee in thirty-eight of forty years, from the time of the Social Security Act to 1975. Their influence continued for some years afterward, though it was diminished.
Note: Lee Metcalf (D-Mont.) was Finance Committee chair on January 14, 1966, the day Long began his tenure. Grassley also served as chair from January 20 to June 5, 2001.

cessors, they derived their influence in part from the sweeping prerogatives afforded to senior committee members in Congress before the institutional reforms of the early 1970s. The House Ways and Means Committee and the Senate Finance Committee had primary jurisdiction over public assistance policy. In the four decades following the act's passage, Southerners chaired the House Committee in thirty-six of forty years, and the Senate Committee in thirty-eight of forty years.[57]

These Southern lawmakers' policy decisions in the first three decades of the New Deal system reveal clear priorities.[58] They wanted to increase federal funds for those they considered truly "unemployable" and permanently outside of the labor force—namely, those physically unable to earn wages. And they wanted to ensure that others—including most single mothers with caregiving obligations—would work: they were not persuaded that these families should receive aid on the same terms as other categories of the "unemployable" poor. These priorities translated into active Southern support for the programs for the elderly, blind, and disabled poor, and deep suspicion of the ADC program. On five occasions in the 1950s, Southern and Western congressional leaders led the charge for increases in public assistance funding—particularly for the favored categories of elderly and disabled poor—that were not requested by the Truman administration, and that were opposed (to the point of a veto threat) by the Eisenhower administration.[59]

Southern Democrats were successful in increasing aid for the elderly and disabled poor through the 1950s, but they were frustrated by the growth of ADC. Over time, they became convinced that the answer was to change federal policy to restrict aid to and require work of ADC recipients.[60] Federal policy, however, regarded poor, single-mother families as one of the original categories of "unemployables" eligible for public assistance. Southerners had little chance to challenge these categories—until the 1960s, and reforms introduced by the Kennedy and Johnson administrations.

* * *

Although they shared an ambitious antipoverty agenda, reforming the New Deal public assistance programs was not initially a high priority for either Kennedy or Johnson. Kennedy's early domestic agenda focused on controlling unemployment levels in the wake of successive recessions between 1957 and 1961, and many of Johnson's antipoverty programs concentrated on creating opportunities and services for employable Americans.[61] Kennedy and

Johnson recognized, however, that new policies were needed to reach those unable to earn wages in the labor market: fully three out of five poor Americans were under eighteen or over sixty-five years of age.[62] Both administrations pursued expansionary reforms in public assistance and sought to extend the core welfarist commitments of the New Deal programs.

As the Kennedy team prepared to take office in 1961, a task force charged with proposing reforms for the new president took a first step in this direction. It was chaired by Wilbur Cohen, who had staffed FDR's Committee on Economic Security and later the Social Security Board. Cohen's team called for welfarist measures such as securing federal funding for state general assistance programs, pressing for more uniform assistance payments across states, denying aid to states that imposed undue restrictions, and boosting federal matching funds as a means to increase benefit levels.[63]

But the welfare system, and particularly ADC, was under attack as the new administration began. The controversy was fueled by the rising costs and caseloads of the program—which were spiraling up, not down as promised—and more pointedly, by the changing demographic composition of its recipients. An increasing proportion of ADC mothers were nonwhite and nonmarried. Conservative critics were building support for efforts to slash welfare rolls and costs. Some demanded that suspected "cheaters" be rooted out; others argued that all recipients able to work for wages should do so. Attempts to purge ADC rolls and to restrict welfare use at the state level had begun to escalate, particularly in the South and Southwest.[64] The regional and racial dimensions of the welfare struggle were underscored months before Kennedy's election, when state officials in Louisiana issued a tough new rule denying ADC benefits to mothers who failed to maintain "suitable homes." More than 23,000 children instantly lost eligibility; 95 percent of the children were black, and 70 percent were born to nonmarried mothers.[65] Although the Louisiana crisis was resolved by a federal ruling the following year, the case drew national attention.

Confronted with a widening political controversy over welfare, administration leaders crafted a series of reforms between 1961 and 1967. The first was the 1961 ADC-UP program; it was followed by the 1962 Public Welfare Amendments and the 1964 Work Experience and Training program. They were meant to simultaneously meet expansionary liberal aims and mollify conservative concerns about ADC's trajectory. Ironically, reform strategies intended to strengthen welfarist commitments to poor families would backfire by 1967 and instead advance a workfare alternative.[66]

Kennedy made the case for his first reform in a February 1961 message to Congress. He proposed to broaden ADC by permitting states to assist certain two-parent families. "Needy children are eligible for assistance if their fathers are deceased, disabled, or family deserters. In logic and humanity, a child should also be eligible for assistance if his father is a needy unemployed worker—for example, a person who has exhausted unemployment benefits."[67] The reform, which Kennedy had championed as a senator, was called "ADC-UP," for "unemployed parent."[68] In addition to softening the impact of the economic downturn for poor families, Kennedy had another motive. Critics had long argued that ADC unfairly favored single-parent homes and unintentionally created incentives for the breakup of two-parent families. Many ADC supporters shared these concerns. In seeking congressional support for ADC-UP, Health, Education, and Welfare (HEW) Secretary Abraham Ribicoff emphasized that the reform would remove any rationale for unemployed fathers to leave their homes to make their families eligible for assistance.[69]

Advocates hoped that this approach would increase support for the expansionary measure among moderates and conservatives—and the initial signs were positive. Jurisdiction over the proposed changes lay with the House Ways and Means and Senate Finance Committees, chaired by Southern Democrats Wilbur Mills (D-Ark.) in the House and Harry Byrd (D-Va.) in the Senate. The House Committee produced a bill that largely reflected the administration's proposal, and the measure was eventually approved in both chambers by voice vote. The new law authorized federal ADC grants for two-parent families with a parent who was either out of work or working fewer than a hundred hours a month.[70]

ADC-UP's smooth ride through Congress obscured important differences over key provisions among Democratic leaders, however. Passage was eased by the administration's decision to make ADC-UP optional, not mandatory, for states; as soon became clear, Southern states had no intention of adopting the welfarist expansion. Both committees also added language to restrict its scope and toughen its provisions. Mills's Ways and Means Committee sought a more aggressive approach to work promotion for the newly eligible unemployed parents—adding, for example, a provision that aid would be terminated if the parent refused a job offered by a state employment agency "without good cause." This stipulation would become a staple of workfare reforms in the years ahead.[71]

Liberals heralded the reform as a major new expansion. Many welfarist reformers believed it had the potential to transform ADC from a program for a select group of single-parent households to one serving the broader population of poor families, and might even lead to a more universal approach to public assistance.[72] Hopeful liberals misjudged the reform's impact, however. Because the program was optional for states, it had a limited effect on family poverty. Fully half of the states chose not to adopt it throughout the 1960s and 1970s. The South simply opted out. By 1967, twenty-one states had established ADC-UP programs, with benefits going to 67,500 families (less than 6 percent of all AFDC families). Oklahoma was the sole Southern state with a program, serving only 590 families; this amounted to less than one-quarter of 1 percent of recipient families in the South.[73]

ADC-UP did, however, open a new front in the escalating political battle against ADC, one that altered its trajectory in ways the creators of the reform neither anticipated nor desired. It was the first of the 1960s reforms that overtly challenged the premise that federal public assistance was for the unemployable poor. As Wilbur Cohen and Social Security Commissioner Robert Ball later observed, "After the enactment of Public Law 87-31 [ADC-UP], the question of work relief came sharply into focus, as Federal participation in assistance was being provided for the first time to a group of individuals [unemployed fathers] who were, by definition, employable."[74] Although benefits continued to flow overwhelmingly to single-mother families, ADC quickly became more vulnerable to claims that it encouraged idleness. Among the loudest critics were Southern congressional Democrats. Even as they chose not to enact ADC-UP in their own states, several used its passage to level new attacks at ADC. In the name of helping dependent children, charged Senator Strom Thurmond (D-S.C.), the measure "merely make[s] payments to a man to enable him to live without working for a living."[75]

The following year, the administration unveiled its second and most ambitious reform. The Kennedy team wanted a way to pursue its broadly liberalizing agenda for ADC, but without increasing the size of a program under fire. The "solution" came from experts in the social work community: provide social services, in addition to cash assistance, to the poor. Advocated by HEW Secretary Ribicoff, the strategy aimed not to eliminate cash assistance, but to shift attention to problems that might keep families from achieving self-support. Preventive and rehabilitative services ranged from counseling and employment assistance to alcohol rehabilitation and legal advice.[76] The "services solution" to poverty problems had been advanced by social workers since the Progressive Era and had gained traction in the 1950s, but this was a new and more receptive political context.[77] The strategy promised to meet liberals' desire for a more comprehensive response to the poverty-related problems of welfare families. At the same time, it was designed to appeal to conservatives by targeting the trends that concerned them, from out-of-wedlock births to fraud. The Kennedy strategy was packaged as a way to solve all of these problems—and in the process, to reduce welfare costs and caseloads.[78]

The proposed reform had far-reaching implications for welfare policy. Although the Kennedy administration understood the structural sources of economic insecurity, the services strategy was not grounded in these assumptions.[79] The provision of "preventive, rehabilitative, or protective" services to the poor, however well intentioned, implied that the causes of poverty were, at root, individual problems requiring counseling and casework. Funds were aimed not at transforming the social or economic environments that confronted the poor, but at changing the poor themselves. Most important for the political development of ADC, the services-for-self-support strategy could be cast broadly enough to accommodate work promotion policies. If adding unemployed men through ADC-UP had created a new political logic for work requirements, the services strategy now provided a policy framework for introducing work and training obligations, as one of several "rehabilitative" services to encourage individual self-support.

Liberal reformers emphasized that the purpose of the modest work and training provision they proposed was not coercive or punitive, and that the main target was unemployed men in ADC-UP who needed assistance in reentering the workforce. They continued to see cash assistance to support caregiving as a central purpose of ADC. Work programs would not curb the welfare load significantly, cautioned a study requested by Ribicoff, noting that "approximately 90 percent of the persons receiving assistance are too young to work, too old to work, or are caring for young children and should remain at home."[80] But these caveats were lost as the new strategy paved the way for a larger shift in federal policy. Once self-support was accepted as an explicit aim of federal welfare policy, and work programs were accepted as one means toward this end, a new debate opened up about work and welfare. In time, the question would narrow from *whether* most recipients could and should work, to *which* recipients should work and on what terms, and, finally, to *how* to make them do so.[81]

The social services strategy was set out in proposed amendments to the Social Security Act in early 1962. Once again, the president hoped to win over moderates and conservatives by emphasizing its potential to solve problems perceived to lie at the root of the rapid rise in the welfare rolls. And once again, the proposal moved fairly smoothly through Congress.[82] As with ADC-UP, however, the apparent consensus hid a growing policy divide within the Democratic Party on the purposes of public assistance. One difference between Southerners and the White House concerned which poor populations should receive federal assistance dollars. Mills's Ways and Means Committee obligingly approved the key components of the Kennedy proposal—but then shifted the legislation's budgetary focus to reflect Southern Democrats' priorities: the committee quietly added an increase in federal benefit payments for the Southerners' favored recipient groups, the elderly, blind, and disabled poor. The increase had not been requested by the administration, and Secretary Ribicoff testified against it. It proved the most costly single provision of the law.[83]

The two wings of the party also held conflicting ideas and expectations about the services strategy, and Kennedy's marketing tactics encouraged the dual interpretation. On the one hand, the president took care to emphasize that social services were primarily designed to build on—not replace—the liberal commitment to income assistance, and liberals saw it as an expansion of the New Deal welfarist ideal.[84] On the other hand, Kennedy sought to satisfy conservatives frustrated by ADC's costs and caseloads.[85] Above all, it was Kennedy's pledge that the reform would lower the ADC rolls that conservative members of his party wanted to hear. Lawmakers seized on this point, and the nuances in Kennedy's message evaporated. Many expected the new strategy to replace cash aid: it "places emphasis on the provision of services rather than depending on welfare checks," noted Mills's committee approvingly.[86]

Kennedy signed the Public Welfare Amendments on July 25. The law authorized federal payments to defray state costs for rehabilitative or preventive social services. It also renamed the program "Aid to Families with Dependent Children" (AFDC). Within the legislation, a new Community Work and Training (CWT) initiative was a minor provision reflecting one approach to "rehabilitating" recipients. The initiative was optional: state or local governments could choose to create CWT programs to help develop welfare recipients' work skills.[87] The primary targets were unemployed fathers, but the initiative was also designed to serve some AFDC mothers on a voluntary basis and with adequate childcare support.[88] Like ADC-UP, the work and training program remained limited in practice: by 1967, just twelve states had implemented the provision, enrolling a total of only 15,300 recipients.[89]

There was thus little reason, in the early 1960s, for liberal Democrats to suspect that this minor provision would serve as the opening wedge for a new conservative approach to public assistance for poor single mothers. But the Kennedy reforms had created a new dilemma for the program, one that made explicit the tension between the New Deal welfarist aim and the emerging workfare agenda. Gilbert Steiner at the Brookings Institution identified the conflict soon after the amendments passed. Pointing to a memo used by Ribicoff to build congressional support by promoting a "family-centered approach," he asked: "Is the public policy enunciated by President Kennedy of training adults for useful work instead of prolonged dependency consistent with the public policy enunciated by Ribicoff of providing children with adequate protection, support, and a maximum opportunity to become responsible citizens? Is the focus on child welfare or on adult rehabilitation?" Steiner had identified "the great new ADC dilemma: whether the program should be preoccupied with the economic needs of dependent children and their families or whether its preoccupation should be with transforming adults into breadwinners."[90] Over the next several years, this dilemma would define the divisions and struggles within the Democratic Party over welfare policy.

* * *

Lyndon Johnson did little to clarify or resolve the dilemma after assuming the presidency. Johnson declared a "War on Poverty" in his first State of the Union address on January 8, 1964, and signed the Economic Opportunity Act eight months later. His position on public assistance largely reflected and extended Kennedy's vision. But the focus on self-support grew more explicit under Johnson, and the emphasis shifted to services designed to more quickly prepare individuals for the workforce.

Johnson's emphasis on creating opportunity became a guiding principle for the War on Poverty, and was intended to convey a new Democratic commitment to helping the poor help themselves: "Rather than fight poverty by means of the dole," explained one analyst, "we were to restore the poor to self-sufficiency through education, training and work—all in the spirit of the Economic Opportunity Act."[91] The focus on opportunity obscured more than it illuminated, however. The issues that divided Democrats in the 1960s, as in the 1930s, were not whether generating opportunity was desirable, but what if anything government would do to provide opportunities if they were not readily available in the private labor market, and whether programs promoting opportunity and self-support would replace or complement cash assistance for those who could not or did not support themselves.

Johnson expanded on the work components of Kennedy's Public Welfare Amendments with his own reform—the Work Experience and Training program (WET), under Title V of the Economic Opportunity Act.[92] Unlike the CWT program, WET was fully funded by federal dollars. Federal funding led to its adoption by all but one state, but its results were hardly more encouraging than those of CWT. Between 1964 and early 1967, WET enrolled only 133,000 individuals; even at its high point in this period, just 5 percent of adults in AFDC participated in the program.[93]

Meanwhile, political struggles over welfare were heating up. The 1964 election of the most liberal Congress since the New Deal had effectively split the Democratic Party in three over the welfare issue, with the Kennedy–Johnson reformers occupying the rapidly diminishing middle-ground position. To their right were the conservative Democrats, whose frustration with AFDC was growing. But pressure was also building to the left of the administration, generated in part by civil rights and welfare rights activists. They mobilized in poor communities and pressed for reforms that went well beyond the commitments of the New Deal and the promises of the Great Society. Many argued (as earlier welfarists had) that the Democrats should abandon the model of limited categorical assistance, to provide an expanded and more generous entitlement for all poor families. The concept of providing a denser safety net for all who needed it—perhaps through a basic guaranteed income—was also making headway among many government officials.[94]

Pressed from both sides, liberals in the Johnson administration continued to seek compromise positions that could appeal to all. This strategy, however, was slowly collapsing. With each reform initiative, administration officials had promised that the welfare rolls would drop—and yet the rolls continued to spiral upward. Between early 1962 and 1967, the number of AFDC recipients increased from 3.5 to 5 million. Costs escalated from $994 million in 1960 to $2.2 billion in 1967.[95] The successive Kennedy–Johnson reforms, meanwhile, had gradually shredded the always tenuous distinction between the employable and unemployable poor at the heart of the New Deal rationale for public assistance. Aid was now granted (through AFDC-UP) to employable AFDC fathers, and (under the CWT and WET programs) to mothers as well as fathers who were encouraged to work. If federal policy directed aid to employable as well as unemployable poor adults, what was the basis and what were the parameters of public assistance for poor families? Who defined how employable a recipient might be? By 1967, the party's conservative faction was ready to provide its own answers.

As the Public Welfare Amendments approached the end of their five-year authorization that year, the president sent Congress new plans for addressing poverty among children and the elderly. Despite public criticism of the rising AFDC rolls, Johnson argued for new expansions in aid, claiming that too few poor children were receiving the help they needed. He condemned states for meager benefit levels and for not taking advantage of AFDC-UP to expand the program, and also criticized states for failing to fully implement CWT programs.[96] Johnson sought to sustain the same political balancing act that he and Kennedy had throughout the 1960s—combining welfarist expansions with noncoercive provisions to encourage work through incentives and social services.

But social service proponents were on the defensive. Measured against a yardstick selected by advocates themselves—declining rolls and costs—the 1962 services strategy had yielded few results in five years.[97] At the same time, increasing numbers of nonwhite and never-married recipients had gained access to the program since its inception, and the backlash against the gains of the civil rights movement had generated new attacks on AFDC and its recipients. Women were entering the workforce in larger numbers, fueling demands that poor single mothers on welfare work for wages. And state welfare offices were clamoring for fiscal relief. Demands for conservative reform, in short, were mounting from many quarters.[98]

In Congress, critics were increasingly frustrated with the unmet promises of liberal welfarists within the party. "Witness after witness told the Congress over the years that if we would just do this and do that to improve social insurance, then public assistance would eventually wither away," Wilbur Mills explained to social welfare officials in Arkansas. "And this is turning out to be largely true for every cash public assistance program except the AFDC program."[99] Mills directed particular ire at the failure of the services strategy to produce program reductions and savings.[100] Welfarist advocates countered that there had not been the time or opportunity for a true test.[101] Politically, however, the services strategy had run out of time. Mills and other congressional leaders had had enough. When the Johnson administration provided an opening by proposing an expanded work support program as part of AFDC's reauthorization in 1967, they seized the opportunity to press their own agenda for conservative reform.

The break with the administration on welfare policy had been brewing for some time, as tensions rose between Southern conservatives and Northern liberals over civil rights and the Great Society. The 1966 congressional midterm elections had strengthened the Southerners' position, as the liberal wing lost its majority. Democrats retained control of Congress but gave up forty-seven seats in the House, and more than three-quarters of those losses were from outside the South. In the wake of race riots in Newark and Detroit in July 1967, Mills's committee finally moved to "kill a major proposal to liberalize welfare," reported the *Wall Street Journal*.[102] Instead of approving Johnson's plans for AFDC, the committee sent the House a package of reforms that would, for the first time, require states to enroll AFDC recipients in work programs, formally alter the program's stated aims, and effectively end its entitlement status by freezing the number of recipients. The proposals, developed by Mills's committee in executive session over months, caught the administration by surprise.[103]

Tougher work policies, Mills suggested, would solve the AFDC crisis. His proposals built on the earlier Kennedy and Johnson programs—but shifted their logic and intent. The Ways and Means Committee began by revising the preamble to Title IV of the Social Security Act (AFDC). States should now ensure "that each appropriate relative, child and individual will enter the labor force and accept employment."[104] The committee crafted a new section to be added to Title IV, creating a Work Incentive (WIN) program. States would be required to establish work-training programs for adults and children over sixteen receiving AFDC; they would also be required to set up day-care centers for AFDC parents with young children, making these parents eligible for work and training as well. All eligible recipients were to be referred to the programs by state and local welfare agencies, and the committee envisioned that the vast majority of adult recipients would be judged appropriate for work referrals. Refusal to work or receive training without "good cause," the committee suggested, could lead to termination of AFDC assistance.[105] Mills's committee also included a measure to reward employment by creating positive incentives for welfare recipients, a strategy supported by liberals. Expanding on an administration proposal, Ways and Means proposed a work incentive permitting working parents to keep $30 plus one-third of their earnings before any deductions were made to their AFDC checks. This effectively reduced the "tax" on earnings from 100 percent to 67 percent and was more generous than the administration's proposed earnings disregard.[106]

In a marked change from past practice, the committee otherwise rejected virtually every major provision of the Johnson administration's 1967 proposal for public assistance reform. The final WIN provisions were crafted largely by lawmakers rather than federal administrators: WIN marked the entry of Congress as a central actor in charting welfare policy. The committee's bill departed from existing federal policy in several ways. Perhaps the single most important shift was the explicit assertion that all AFDC parents, with limited exceptions, should be considered for work or training programs; participation for those referred would not be voluntary. Although requiring single mothers to earn wages remained controversial, the committee clearly stated its intention "that a proper evaluation be made of the situation of all mothers to ascertain the extent to which appropriate child care arrangements should be made available so the mothers can go to work."[107]

In a second departure, the committee emphasized that the work provisions were to be mandatory, not optional, for the states. The workfare agenda for public assistance trumped the traditional Southern Democratic commitment to states' rights for Mills: "For 5 years, this load has gone up and up and up, with no end in sight.... We want states to see to it that ... unless there is a good cause for them not to be required to take it, that [recipients] take training and then work.... That is what we wanted to do in 1962. We left it to the option of the States, and they did not do it. Five years later, today, we are on the floor with a bill which requires that it be done."[108]

A third significant departure was a direct challenge to the entitlement principle within AFDC. For the first time, Congress would set a limit on the number of AFDC families for which each state would receive matching funds.[109] The "freeze" applied to cases in which the father was "absent" rather than deceased. In a reflection of conservative concerns about out-of-wedlock childbirth as well as work, the legislation also authorized the states to set up programs to reduce "illegitimate births."[110] The proposed limit on matching funds directly undercut the core New Deal welfarist commitment to provide public assistance to all who qualified, as a matter of right.

Mills's proposed reforms were sent to the House floor in August 1967. Because the reforms were debated under a closed rule, and as part of a measure with a major increase in benefits for the popular Social Security program, House passage was assured despite liberal objections to key provisions. But the federal workfare proposals would not make their way to the president's desk without a pitched battle among Democrats. The House bill drew immediate and strong opposition from several liberal quarters.[111]

Members of Congress were confronted by organized opposition to various aspects of the reform. Welfare rights groups labeled the proposed WIN amendments "the slave labor amendments."[112] Social workers accepted the principle of encouraging work through incentives and training, but rejected the compulsory and coercive elements embodied in the bill in favor of a voluntary, individualized approach. "Mothers must have the right of choice as to if and when it is appropriate and desirable for them to work outside the home, giving the care of their children to others," insisted a representative of the Family Service Society of America.[113] A broad array of civil rights, labor, and religious groups also organized against WIN, focusing on the provisions imposing mandatory employment and a freeze.

As the bill moved to the Senate, organizers worked with welfarist Senate leaders—notably Fred Harris (D-Okla.) and Robert Kennedy (D-N.Y.)—to ensure that the Senate version was less punitive. But liberals in the Senate had to contend with Senator Russell Long. Long's prominence on the Senate Finance Committee had risen in the wake of the 1963 death of Senator Robert Kerr (D-Okla.), a conservative who had nonetheless worked constructively with the White House on Social Security expansions. Long had assumed the position of committee chair in 1966. He was a Louisiana Democrat, a staunch opponent of civil and welfare rights and a leading proponent of workfare. During hearings on the bill, Long made his views known on the issue: "People who can work ought to work," he announced. Poor mothers should not receive cash assistance for "filling up whole houses with children," then refuse to work when jobs were available. He railed repeatedly against the twin evils of idleness and out-of-wedlock births, both of which were fueled, in his view, by the AFDC program.[114] In September, Long confronted welfare rights activists during a Finance Committee session, and the exchange grew heated. When the women refused to leave until more senators arrived to hear their testimony, Long exploded, banging his gavel so hard that it broke. "If they can find time to march in the streets, picket and sit all day in committee hearing rooms, they can find time to do some useful work."[115]

The Senate ultimately produced a bill that was less punitive than the House measure. After significant pressure from liberal Democrats, Long agreed to permit some work exemptions for recipients who were ill or had very young children. And in a series of close votes on the Senate floor that clearly demonstrated the divide between Northern and Southern Democrats, several of the most restrictive AFDC provisions were scaled back.[116] Southern conservatives won the next round, however. When House and Senate leaders met in a conference committee to iron out differences between their two bills, the conference agreement reflected the harsher House version, rather than the more liberal Senate version, on almost every important issue.[117]

Opponents ratcheted up the pressure. The National Association of Social Workers (NASW) contacted every senator to demand that new conferees be appointed. Telegrams were fired off to President Johnson from George Meany, president of the AFL-CIO, and Walter Reuther, president of the Industrial Union Department, urging opposition and a veto if necessary. As Congress prepared to adjourn in December, liberal reformers became convinced that the best option was to postpone final action to allow for an extended debate in the next session. However, Long devised a legislative maneuver with fellow conservative Democrat Robert Byrd (D-W.Va.) and Republican Everett Dirksen (R-Ill.). They moved to call up the conference report reflecting the House language and win passage on a voice vote—at a time when the Senate chamber was virtually empty of the bill's opponents, thwarting liberal plans to filibuster the legislation. Furious, the NASW sent a telegram to the president asking that he eliminate the punitive elements of the bill.[118]

The Johnson administration faced a difficult choice: fight to retain the core New Deal conception of welfare developed and championed by party liberals since the 1930s, or accept the move toward a model of restricted and work-conditioned aid favored by party conservatives. Administration officials were not inclined to wage a decisive battle with Southern Democrats over welfare reform, and the administration accepted the turn toward workfare. HEW had not expected the freeze to be included in the final package, and many officials worried about the punitive orientation of the new law. But HEW leaders elected not to join liberal welfarists and labor leaders in publicly pressing the president to veto the legislation. Many in HEW agreed with the need for more work and training, even if they preferred the use of incentives rather than requirements to increase participation in those programs.[119] Others in the administration may have held stronger reservations, but were simply unwilling to expend further political capital on the issue. "The Johnson administration stretched a long way in civil rights legislation and its war on poverty," concluded historian Blanche Coll. "This much being done, and having offered the elderly and the poor generous medical care, the executive branch was not inclined to buck Congressman Mills and Senator Long in their drive to put AFDC mothers to work."[120]

Although the WIN amendments were signed into law, the freeze provision had drawn enough public criticism to persuade Johnson to delay its implementation, and it was ultimately repealed by Congress in 1969, before it ever went into effect.[121] There was no delay, however, in implementing the amendments' work-related measures. A program was created that sought to prepare AFDC recipients "for work in the 'regular economy'" and to restore their families "to independence and useful roles in their communities."[122]

* * *

At the outset of the 1960s, the political initiative on welfare had rested with liberal Democrats in the White House, and a newly elected John Kennedy had galvanized the nation for a battle against poverty. By the end of the decade, Southern Democrats in Congress were charting the course in public assistance reform, toward workfare and restricted support for AFDC families. In the intervening years, two liberal administrations had pursued expansionary strategies that ultimately helped drive welfare policy in a conservative, work-based direction. They had undercut the existing New Deal rationale for public assistance and the fragile intraparty compromise on aiding the "unemployable poor." They had developed and oversold reforms in the AFDC program that were expected to reduce the welfare rolls and that emphasized the importance of recipients' self-support, fueling the pro-work arguments of welfare critics. And through initiating work programs (however small) as part of their social services strategy for AFDC recipients, they had created a justification and opportunity for conservatives within their own party to develop a policy initiative (WIN) that challenged core aims of welfarist public assistance.

In the end, welfare politics in the 1960s yielded contradictory outcomes. Developments early in the decade (particularly the Public Welfare Amendments of 1962) were seen by many as the culmination of the liberal welfarism of the War on Poverty, and they were described that way by President Kennedy. Broader political developments in the late 1960s, moreover, made AFDC by the end of the decade into the closest approximation of a genuine welfarist entitlement in the program's history. Indeed, some welfare scholars see this period as the only one in which the program provided a meaningful entitlement to eligible families.[123] Welfare rights drives and Supreme Court rulings knocked down barriers to access, and the percentage of eligible families actually receiving assistance climbed dramatically, from an estimated 33 percent in the early 1960s to more than 90 percent by 1971.[124] AFDC benefits, though still meager in most states, rose steadily through the decade, and in-kind assistance, including Medicaid, low-income housing assistance, and food stamps, also expanded.[125] Yet precisely at this moment, Congress and the White House shifted the program onto a workfarist rather than welfarist track at the federal level, a track that would eventually lead to the elimination of the entitlement and its replacement with a workfare alternative.

CHAPTER 2

Welfarists Confront Workfarists: The Family Assistance Plan

As the 1968 presidential race took shape, welfare reform emerged as an unavoidable campaign issue for both parties. In addition to congressional complaints about AFDC's rising price tag, a growing chorus of opposition arose from state and local officials facing grave fiscal crises.[1] These included prominent Republican governors from states such as California, New York, Illinois, and Pennsylvania; more than one-fourth of the AFDC caseload burden was carried by these four states alone.[2] "If you were going to run for President of the United States, you had to have a welfare reform program," said Martin Anderson, who became research director for Richard Nixon's campaign in 1968. But if welfare policy was familiar territory for the Democrats, it was, he observed, a "somewhat treacherous issue for a Republican candidate."[3] Anderson and other staffers were charged with developing policy proposals to aid the poor. Nixon's team produced plans combining program improvements and work measures, and the campaign staff believed they had achieved their goal: "The Democrats lost an issue, the press seemed baffled, and Nixon was very pleased with himself."[4]

On November 5, with the long economic expansion of the 1960s slowing, Johnson standing on the sidelines, and the country divided over war in Vietnam and racial tensions at home, Nixon won a narrow victory against Hubert Humphrey. The limits on the new president's power were clear from the outset. Democratic majorities controlled Congress, 243–192 in the House, and 58–42 in the Senate. Nixon had run a carefully calibrated race, touting a long list of positions designed to appeal to the "forgotten middle" in American politics. These included law and order in America's cities and a peace strategy for Vietnam. On the social welfare front, Nixon called for returning power to state governments—a reaction to what he saw as the excesses of the Great Society—and a commitment to "liberate the poor from the debilitating dependence on government."[5]

The president's conservatism led many to assume that he would follow the path charted by congressional passage of WIN, consolidating a shift toward greater work obligations for AFDC recipients and further restricting the reach of public assistance. Instead, Nixon's advisers crafted a plan to expand cash support for the poor and take public assistance reform well beyond the confines of AFDC. The most striking feature of Nixon's Family Assistance Plan (FAP) was its radical proposal to guarantee an income floor for all poor families, including two-parent working families. After a three-year struggle in which the proposal came surprisingly close to passing, FAP died in Congress. A small avalanche of expert opinion and analysis followed, seeking to make sense of its rise and fall.[6] But with a few notable exceptions, much of the scholarly literature on U.S. social welfare soon came to regard the politics of FAP as a footnote to history, a story about the reform that never happened—an interesting tale, but one largely irrelevant to the development of American social policy.[7]

The political significance of FAP, however, lay not in the content or fate of the failed Nixon initiative, but in the *reaction* to the proposal, particularly among the Southern Democrats who had begun to assume a more assertive role in shaping federal policy on work and welfare. The battle over FAP triggered a broad conservative shift in welfare policy at the federal level, reflected not only in the defeat of FAP (1969–72) but also in the creation of new work-based initiatives in its wake (1971–75). The Southern conservative drive for reform began with the WIN amendments to AFDC in 1967. But it was during the struggles over Nixon's FAP that a coherent alternative to New Deal welfarism emerged, an American brand of workfare that would change the basic functions of public assistance for poor families.

The core features of and contrasts between welfarist and work-based models of social provision have been charted and assessed in comparative studies by a number of scholars, such as Jamie Peck.[8] But how and why does a welfarist system change into a workfarist one? This chapter and the next focus on the politics that produced such a shift in U.S. public assistance programs in the early 1970s. Two distinct approaches to U.S. public assistance had emerged by then, with different guiding principles, ends, means, and measures of success.[9] Under New Deal welfarism, the guiding principle was government entitlement. The end of public assistance was to provide a basic safety net for certain groups of eligible poor Americans; the means toward this end was cash and in-kind assistance. Work might be encouraged and supported (as in the Kennedy–Johnson reforms), but these were not central strategies at the federal level and, above all, were not to undermine the larger end of guaranteeing a safety net. The measure of success was the policy's ability to provide income assistance to those who were eligible. Under workfare, in contrast, the guiding principle was not government entitlement, but market incentives. The end of public assistance was to promote, require, and reward work among all poor adults who were physically able to perform it, and the means was mandatory work requirements and job training or preparation. The primary measure of success was the policy's ability to ensure workforce participation, reduce reliance on government assistance, and leave to the market the functions of job allocation and wage setting.

Both approaches had deep roots in Anglo-American poor relief policies. Welfarism was rooted in the principle that those who were poor and unable to provide for themselves should receive some measure of government assistance; workfare grew out of the English poor law principle that relief should not intervene in the logic or incentives of the market. It was welfarism that had formally governed federal public assistance policies since the New Deal. The WIN amendments had signaled a shift. Debates over the Family Assistance Plan would now clarify the direction policy would take.

The FAP debates concerned the relationship between welfare and work, and between public assistance and the labor market; they boiled down to two issues. Should the welfare poor work, and if so, what policies should be used to encourage or require this? And should the working poor receive welfare, and if so, what policies would ensure that they continued to work? It was in the struggle over FAP in the late 1960s that income assistance for the working poor was first placed on the national policy agenda, leading ultimately to the creation of the Earned Income Tax Credit (EITC) in 1975.[10] It was also in these years that aid to the welfare poor (through AFDC) was roundly discredited in favor of aid to the working poor, and the rise of the EITC became linked to the decline of AFDC. Driving both developments were the strategies of the Nixon administration in promoting FAP and the fervent opposition to its passage among Southern Democrats.

Strikingly, the origins of work-based public assistance in the politics of Nixon's FAP followed a sequence that would be replayed twenty-five years later, in a new round of political fights that led to workfare's culmination in the mid-1990s under President Bill Clinton. In each case, a president envisioned a broad package of reforms that contained a mix of elements for poor families, including liberal welfarist measures and work supports. He wrapped the package, however, in tough rhetoric about promoting work and ending welfare, and marketed it as workfare. Congressional conservatives seized on the rhetoric of workfare and recast it in tougher terms, both in public debate and in proposed policies. Core welfarist elements of the president's plan collapsed—and conservatives helped secure a further shift toward workfare. This chapter starts with the evolution of FAP's guaranteed income concept, then turns to the internal debate that took place within the Nixon administration over work and welfare, and to the heated political struggles over the proposal that unfolded on Capitol Hill and around the country.

The Political Origins of the "Income Floor"

The intellectual and political history of both the Family Assistance Plan and the Earned Income Tax Credit began with the notion of providing a "floor" under the income of the working poor. The proposal originated not with the Nixon White House but with earlier generations of economists, analysts, and planners, and it had conservative as well as liberal roots.

In 1943, while working briefly at the Treasury Department, conservative economist Milton Friedman observed that the poorest workers confronted a host of tax-related inequities and work disincentives.[11] Friedman later proposed that the working poor be permitted to claim a refund on their 1040 tax forms equal to the amount the family income dropped below a certain point. When a family's income rose measurably above this floor, they would pay taxes; but when income dropped below the floor, they would receive a refund from the government. Friedman believed that this approach would curb poverty more efficiently and less expensively than the existing welfare system. The concept, in short, was pro-work, anti-tax, anti-welfare, and anti-bureaucracy. The principle of a "negative income tax" was not new among economists, but it was Friedman's 1962 book *Capitalism and Freedom* that won it a place on the political map.[12]

Despite Friedman's credentials, most political conservatives found the idea of providing a government-backed income floor anathema, seeing it as another costly and misguided expansion of the welfare state. During the Johnson years, the guaranteed income principle was promoted primarily by liberal welfarists. Liberals came to the idea from a very different starting point, emphasizing the logic of entitlement and social rights that had gained prominence in the 1960s. Advocates advanced various schemes for providing a guaranteed income, from negative income taxes to European-style child or family allowances.[13] The Johnson administration's own poverty research, meanwhile, was turning up some disturbing facts that argued for a new approach. A large portion of America's poor was slipping through the cracks in the safety net. The Planning and Evaluation Unit at HEW concluded in 1966 that at least 60 percent of needy Americans received no benefits from the nation's main antipoverty cash assistance programs, including AFDC and Old Age Assistance (OAA), as well as Social Security. A sizable percentage of this group were working and poor—particularly families with children.[14]

By the mid- to late 1960s, a number of American economists and analysts were actively promoting income floor schemes. A 1968 petition urging Congress to adopt a "national system of income guarantees and supplements" was signed by some 1,300 economists from almost 150 institutions. Leaders in the social work community also signaled their support, encouraging "income as a matter of right . . . at a uniformly adequate standard of living" in a position paper released by a National Association of Social Workers conference.[15] Confronted with the problem of the working poor, many liberal economists and Democratic policymakers turned first to traditional minimum wage strategies—but the income guarantee idea was gaining traction among analysts within the administration, particularly at the Office of Economic Opportunity (OEO) and HEW. Prompted by his advisers, President Johnson appointed various task forces to examine the guaranteed income concept, and the OEO launched pilot programs to explore its effect on the incentive to work. In 1968, even OEO director Sargent Shriver endorsed a version of the idea.[16] But President Johnson was unconvinced.[17] By the end of his presidency, the proposition had not gained broad popular support, Congress was skeptical at best, and Johnson remained committed to his own Great Society strategy of providing opportunity and services to the poor.[18]

When Nixon entered the White House, there was thus little reason to expect the guaranteed income idea to command attention beyond academic circles or government research commissions, even less to expect that it would be elevated to the national political agenda by a Republican leader. The wheels were set in motion when Nixon decided to take on welfare reform, in part to score points among Republican governors, lawmakers, and middle-class voters (especially Southern white voters) frustrated by the welfare system and its rising rolls.[19]

Shortly after the 1968 election, he tapped Richard Nathan, a Brookings Institution researcher who had worked on pre-election planning for the Nixon team, to head up a Transitional Task Force on Public Welfare. The Nathan task force suggested that an income floor be created under AFDC families nationwide, to be fully paid by the federal government. This would mean higher benefits in poor states (particularly in the South) and relief for state budgets. Arthur Burns, the president's chief domestic policy adviser, objected to the idea, arguing instead for cutting welfare rolls and costs. But Nixon's HEW secretary Robert Finch and urban affairs adviser Daniel Patrick Moynihan, a former assistant secretary of labor in the Kennedy and Johnson administrations, convinced the president to back the idea of a nationwide guaranteed standard for AFDC benefits.[20]

This itself would have marked a significant welfarist policy departure, particularly for a Republican president. Yet the administration would go further. A task force of staffers from HEW (including John Veneman, the new undersecretary) and the Budget Bureau reached agreement on a more far-reaching plan as an alternative to Nathan's, then set out to win the approval of the president and his key cabinet members for what would become FAP.[21] Conceptually, the breakthrough made by Nixon aides was to take a radically welfarist proposal—a guaranteed income for both working and nonworking poor families—and market it as work-based welfare reform.

The outlines of the administration's proposal emerged gradually. FAP would extend a guarantee of income to all poor families—with one or two parents, working or nonworking. A family of four with no other income would receive an annual minimum federal grant (ultimately set at $1,600), which could be supplemented by the states. Those who worked would receive an earnings disregard for the first $60 they earned monthly, and then see their benefits reduced by 50 percent for each dollar of earned income. Able-bodied family heads, with some exceptions, would be required to accept work or training positions, or lose their portion of the family's benefit.[22]

Throughout the spring and summer of 1969, the debate within the administration was heated. Arthur Burns presented a more limited plan, offering fiscal incentives to states to increase benefit levels. Members of Nixon's cabinet and inner circle lined up on one side or the other. Moynihan was a vocal advocate of FAP, Burns its staunchest critic. HEW secretary Finch and Nixon aide John Ehrlichman supported the FAP approach. The Treasury secretary, CEA chair, and budget director preferred the Burns plan. This internal opposition to the plan, along with early reports of Republican objections in Congress, almost sank it—and forced various adjustments to the proposal after a protracted internal debate over the purposes of public assistance.[23]

Welfare, Work, and Markets: The Internal Debate

Much of the discussion within the administration addressed familiar issues of rising welfare rolls and costs, benefit levels, and the question of welfare reliance—issues that had been at the center of the debate since the 1967 WIN amendments. But administration officials were also grappling with new and more fundamental questions about the relationship between welfare and work. What were the implications of making poor families on welfare work, and of providing welfare to those who were working but still poor?

The New Deal welfarist model of assistance provided no guidance here, because New Dealers had drawn a line in federal policy between work and welfare, creating social insurance programs for employable Americans and public assistance programs for needy "unemployables." Yet AFDC was now providing assistance to recipients who were employable (through AFDC-UP), and states were required to refer eligible recipients to work programs (through WIN). The latter policy change concerned many liberals, just as the former worried conservatives. The FAP plan proposed a further breach of the New Deal distinction, by providing public assistance not only for the *employable* poor (including some AFDC parents)—but for the *already employed* poor.

Political leaders confronted a major juncture in U.S. public assistance. Recent initiatives threatened to violate age-old poor law principles governing the relationship between assistance and labor markets, posing new dilemmas for policy. The passage of WIN, combined with increases in in-kind assistance in the 1960s, created one dilemma. Various social welfare programs now offered recipients more economic security than many jobs in the low-wage labor market, even as WIN sought to move them into that labor force. This undermined the long-standing "less eligibility" principle, which held that welfare assistance should never exceed the gains from the lowest-paid form of wage labor.[24] Now, policymakers wondered how to restore this balance: by requiring work and cutting benefits to the welfare poor? By providing aid to the working poor?

The prospect of aiding the poorest workers posed its own dilemma. It violated another poor law imperative, against the provision of "relief in aid of wages," aimed at preserving the principle of non-interference in the market system.²⁵ The concern was that providing public aid to the lowest-paid workers would lead them to work less—or not at all. It would distort the market's ability to set the price of labor, by supplementing market wages. Nixon's advisers now debated whether assisting these workers would be an effective way to reduce their poverty—or whether it would only draw them out of the workforce and onto the welfare rolls, undermining market mechanisms.²⁶ FAP took a bold stance on these thorny issues, by simultaneously strengthening the entitlement to aid at standardized levels, adding work requirements for the welfare poor, and extending assistance to the working poor. Within the administration, both supporters and opponents of FAP recognized that the stakes were high.

An opening salvo in the internal administration battle over FAP arrived on the president's desk in mid-April 1969. It was a memo from Burns's deputy Martin Anderson about the consequences of aiding the working poor, and it began with an ominous quote from Santayana: "Those who cannot remember the past are condemned to repeat it." The remainder of the memo consisted solely of lengthy excerpted passages from Karl Polanyi's discussion in *The Great Transformation* of the controversial Speenhamland public assistance system, in effect in England from 1795 to 1834.²⁷ "The justices of Berkshire," the excerpt began, meeting in Speenhamland in May 1795, "in a time of great distress, decided that subsidies in aid of wages should be granted . . . so that a minimum income should be assured to the poor regardless of their earnings." Anderson underscored Polanyi's contrast between the previous Elizabethan poor law system and the Speenhamland arrangement:

> Under Elizabethan Law the poor were forced to work at whatever wages they could get and only those who could obtain no work were entitled to relief; relief in aid of wages was neither intended nor given. Under the Speenhamland Law a man was relieved even if he was in employment, as long as his wages amounted to less than the family income granted to him by the scale. Hence, no laborer had any material interest in satisfying his employer . . . [and] the employer could obtain labor at almost any wages, however little he paid; the subsidy from the rates brought the workers' income up to scale.²⁸

Anderson was drawing a parallel between Speenhamland and FAP's (and later the EITC's) provisions to aid the working poor. The memo drove home what he saw as the flaws within the Speenhamland system. Among other problems, it contained disincentives for employees to devote adequate work hours and for employers to pay adequate wages—and thereby "prevented the establishment of a competitive labor market" until it was abolished in 1834.[29]

Anderson's conclusion was clear: nothing less than the existence of a functioning capitalist order was at stake in the battle over FAP and its proposal to aid the working poor. The implications were troubling enough that the president requested responses from several of his aides, and a flurry of memos followed. Moynihan expressed annoyance: "It seems absurd to trouble you with controversies concerning the post-Napoleonic economic history of Britain, but if you like . . . ." He argued (with supporting evidence) that economic historians had rejected several of Polanyi's conclusions about Speenhamland.[30] More to the point, Moynihan and other FAP advocates acknowledged the issue of adequate work incentives for low-wage workers and assured the president that FAP addressed it.[31] Any program that reduced cash assistance by a dollar for each dollar earned in wages—as Speenhamland did—would indeed reduce the incentive to work by imposing too high a "tax" on earnings. FAP, however, would reduce benefits by only 50 percent of earned income, rather than by 66⅔ percent (as under AFDC) or 100 percent (as under the old AFDC or the Speenhamland system).[32]

Labor secretary George Shultz, a FAP supporter, echoed the point about the tax on earnings. He then sought to widen the debate, pointing out that the Anderson memo productively exposed "the deficiencies in welfare proposals that entirely overlook labor market forces."[33] Shultz wanted to shift the focus from workers—and the potential disincentives to earn—to FAP's potential impact on the actions of employers. Drawing another point from the Polanyi excerpt, Shultz warned that a wage subsidy, such as that under Speenhamland (or FAP), could distort the labor market in a way that encouraged employers to keep wages low. If wage subsidies induced workers to remain in jobs that paid too little, employers would not face appropriate market pressures to raise wages or restructure jobs. Speenhamland, Schulz wrote, "made it unnecessary for employers to maintain wages in order to compete for manpower."[34]

Shultz added presciently that this problem could be exacerbated by a plan that combined work requirements for welfare recipients with wage subsidies for low-wage workers, particularly in the absence of training and other measures to ensure workers' upward mobility in the job market. He made the case that the combination of compulsory employment and the absence of training programs was a potential trap for poor workers and boon for employers: it meant that the system would generate a steady supply of low-skilled, low-wage labor, with little means of exit through higher skills and job mobility. "Employers who paid substandard wages could be assured that their labor pool would not be depleted through the process of upward skill mobility," Shultz wrote. He challenged the position of many conservatives by suggesting that to avoid these problems, "welfare programs must maintain a principle of free choice with respect to labor force participation."[35]

Other memos exchanged in the internal debate over FAP reflected a different concern: administration officials worried about the negative reactions of low-wage employers to the FAP measures. If the federal government offered *too many* opportunities (through job training) for workers to move up to better-paying jobs, disrupting the low-wage market for labor, these employers would surely object. A draft report by Moynihan's Urban Affairs Council said, for example, that training programs must be voluntary, because "employers of these persons paying them low wages would greatly resent the government coming in and luring, to say nothing of forcing, these low-paid employees to training programs.... Thus, required training programs might create serious disruptions in local labor markets."[36]

White House officials also debated the likely costs of such a program. Many FAP advocates wanted to lowball the numbers. Others urged a candid and realistic assessment of the potential impact of assisting low-wage workers—pointing precisely to the consequences conservative opponents feared. Some workers, they argued, could indeed be expected to work fewer hours or to quit altogether. "The possible responses of the working poor are not really accounted for," wrote Shultz in one memo regarding cost estimates. "Those eligible for [FAP] earn income of about $3.3 billion, which they might choose to forego in some significant measure in preference for [FAP] payments or training allowances."[37] This prospect, of course, was what worried conservatives, particularly those from states with sizable low-wage sectors—such as Southern states.

Underlying but largely unaddressed in this internal debate were deeper issues about work-based public assistance and labor markets. Who should carry the burden of assisting the working poor—the government, through an effective wage subsidy (such as FAP or the EITC), or employers, through higher wages? What was the combined impact of wage subsidies and work requirements on the low-wage labor market itself? Would the supply of workers from the welfare rolls, combined with the wage subsidy from the government, artificially sustain and even increase the number of low-wage jobs in some local labor markets? Would these policies help construct and fuel an oversized low-wage labor market?

The Battle over FAP

Despite opposition from many in his administration and his party, Nixon ultimately approved the proposal, and administration advocates rolled up their sleeves to decide how to pitch and promote the initiative on Capitol Hill and in the press.[38] FAP's political legacy began to take shape with the strategic choices the Nixon team made.

On August 8, 1969, Nixon presented his new plan in a nationally televised speech. The president might have made many different arguments to promote FAP. Canadian leaders in the late 1960s and 1970s, for example, defended similar programs on the merits of aiding workers and meeting the needs of the poor through universal assistance programs.[39] In the U.S. context, this would have meant constructing a welfarist argument for extending public assistance to an entirely new needy population. But Nixon elected to build his case for FAP on the failed record of AFDC, and to try to convince liberal welfarists and conservative workfare advocates alike that his plan was better. The president began with a broadside attack on the existing AFDC system, calling it a "colossal failure," a small Depression-era program that "has become a monster in the prosperous sixties."[40]

Nixon captured the objections of both conservatives and liberals to AFDC, saying, "It breaks up homes [a shared concern of conservatives and liberals]. It often penalizes work [conservatives]. It robs recipients of dignity [liberals]. And it grows [conservatives]." The president's attack on AFDC then merged seamlessly into a new argument about the working poor.

> The present system often makes it possible to receive more money on welfare than on a low-paying job. This creates an incentive not to work; it also is unfair to the working poor. It is morally wrong for a family that is working to try to make ends meet to receive less than the family across the street on welfare. This has been bitterly resented by the man who works, and rightly so—the rewards are just the opposite of what they should be. Its effect is to draw people off payrolls and onto welfare rolls—just the opposite of what government should be doing.[41]

Honest labor and the working poor were thus honored as morally superior to cash assistance and the welfare poor. The solution? Pass FAP, and under the president's plan, "the program now called 'Aid to Families with Dependent Children'—the program we normally think of when we think of 'welfare'—would be done away with completely."[42] Criticism of AFDC had echoed through Washington for years, but never had the program been so condemned at the core by the nation's leader. Nixon's decision to use the presidential bully pulpit to excoriate AFDC in order to promote FAP would have a lasting impact: although FAP would collapse, AFDC would never recover.

In contrast to AFDC, the president emphasized, FAP would include working families: "For the first time, the government would recognize that it has no less of an obligation to the working poor than to the nonworking poor; and for the first time, benefits would be scaled in such a way that it would always pay to work."[43] FAP's work requirement was underscored for the benefit of conservatives, in part to distinguish between FAP and other guaranteed income schemes that conservatives loathed. What would FAP mean, Nixon asked, for those "who can work but choose not to? Well, the answer is very simple. Under this proposal, everyone who accepts benefits must also accept work or training provided suitable jobs are available."[44] The sole exceptions would be those unable to work and mothers with very young children. In fact, FAP's work requirement was hardly rigorous (as administration officials were quick to point out to liberals). Even if an able-bodied parent refused to work, the rest of the family would continue to receive benefits.

The core elements of Nixon's strategy thus emerged in his opening speech. He would promote FAP as a "solution" to the existing welfare crisis and sell the proposal using the language of work promotion and enforcement. Nixon believed that the plan's work requirements and incentives, along with the promise of fiscal relief, would appeal to business, to moderate and conservative policymakers, and to state and local officials. He expected the measure's new national standards and guaranteed support for the poor to appeal to a broad liberal coalition, including labor, the social work community, welfare rights activists, and civil rights leaders, particularly those concerned about conditions in the South. But political support would prove elusive.[45] In the short run, Nixon's strategy would fail, contributing to FAP's defeat. In the long run, the strategy would reconfigure welfare politics, strengthening the drive for a vision of workfare defined not by FAP supporters but by its opponents in Congress.

Few signs of FAP's fate were evident in the initial glow of public reaction following President Nixon's address, however. Ninety-five percent of editorials nationwide were "favorable" toward FAP, according to an HEW survey, and nearly all of the major newspapers in the nation's twenty-five largest metropolitan areas were "enthusiastic." The *New York Times* described FAP as "a bold attempt to transform" the welfare system. *Business Week* said that FAP "is far more than just an ingenious compromise of opposing viewpoints. It is a new and promising approach to a problem that never could be solved in the framework of the old system." And *The Economist* said, "President Nixon's television message on welfare reform and revenue sharing may rank in importance with President Roosevelt's first proposals for a social security system in the mid-1930s, which were the beginning of America's now faltering welfare state."[46]

Public opinion seemed to echo the editorial sentiment. Indeed, the permanent staff at the White House could not remember any domestic issue drawing a public response so enormous and unanimous. Some 2,757 letters and telegrams arrived between August 9 and September 10. More than 80 percent voiced unqualified support, and only 9 percent expressed flat opposition. A favorite among the White House staff was the telegram that read simply: "TWO UPPER MIDDLE CLASS REPUBLICANS WHO WILL PAY FOR THE PROGRAM SAY BRAVO." Gallup began polling public opinion a week after the president's speech. The results reflected strong bipartisan support for "President Nixon's welfare reforms." Of those familiar with the proposal, 65 percent were favorable toward FAP; 20 percent were not.[47]

On closer examination, however, an unmistakable pattern emerged. Press reports and polling data revealed that the strongest expressions of support focused on the president's promise that FAP would replace the existing welfare system—not on the reform measures contained in the plan. The enthusiasm was less a vote for FAP than a vote *against* AFDC and related welfare programs: FAP had been packaged, presented, and received as a "solution" to the perceived welfare crisis. The *Detroit Free Press* editorial expressed a prevailing sentiment: "The *status quo* is no answer—so the President's attempt, complicated and controversial as it is, is a better way to go." Similarly, the focus of the positive telegrams pouring into the White House was almost exclusively on FAP's promise to reform current welfare policies. "FAP was an extraordinary departure in proclaimed public policy, for which there was virtually no public demand, and with which there was no familiarity,"

Moynihan later observed. But "the president had one large advantage: he was proposing to supplant the existing welfare system, which was widely regarded as a failure and about which something had to be done."[48] Nixon's strategy played to this advantage. His pitch for FAP ensured that it arrived on the public agenda and seized the spotlight not on its merits as an innovative plan to aid working as well as welfare poor families, but as an alternative to an unpopular welfare system.

* * *

Before long, cracks began to emerge in the initial foundation of public support. Attacking AFDC's failures, it turned out, provided little basis for building consensus on what should replace it. Liberal welfarists saw AFDC as inadequate and degrading; conservative workfare advocates saw it as overly generous, too costly, and pauperizing. As a result, despite the president's efforts to ensure that FAP contained something for both conservatives and liberals, his repeated attempts to reach out to one side succeeded primarily in alienating the other.

The policy agenda of business leaders, policymakers, and others in the conservative camp focused on the need to limit benefits and tighten work requirements, rein in rather than expand the welfare state, and, above all, avoid a guaranteed income. After an extensive outreach effort by the administration, some business organizations pledged grudging and conditional backing.[49] But the strongest voices in the business community opposed FAP. It was not true welfare reform, in their view, and demanded far too little of the welfare poor. Karl Schlotterbeck of the U.S. Chamber of Commerce warned the House Ways and Means Committee that FAP contained "the beginning of a national guaranteed income arrangement," and Chamber members fanned out in Washington to lobby against it.[50] In testimony before the Senate Finance Committee, Paul Henkel of the Council of State Chambers of Commerce concurred: "We support welfare reform but not guaranteed income." He urged lawmakers to take steps to "[tighten] up work and training requirements for welfare recipients."[51]

Business leaders particularly opposed FAP's provisions for the working poor. They worried that any guarantees of cash assistance for these workers might lead them out of the workforce and onto the welfare rolls. The answer to the problem of working poverty, Schlotterbeck insisted in Senate testimony, was economic growth, not welfare-state expansion.[52] In a full-page advertisement in the midst of the congressional debate in April 1970, the Chamber of Commerce decried FAP as a tool for higher taxes and a plan that "would triple our welfare rolls. Double our welfare costs."[53] Many state and local government officials joined conservatives in expressing skepticism about FAP, objecting in particular to its projected costs.[54]

Above all, conservative leaders feared the plan was a "gigantic giveaway which could further reward the indolent," said Representative Lawrence Williams (R-Pa.),[55] and that it would "make the whole nation into a welfare state," according to Senator Russell Long (D-La.).[56] A number of conservatives felt particularly betrayed by what they saw as the administration's mischaracterization of FAP as a tough work-based program. Columnist James Kilpatrick spoke for many conservatives when he wrote in early 1970, "President Nixon served up his welfare proposals last August, wrapped in a package of pretty rhetoric and tied with a bow of conservative blue. Sad to say some of us who should have known better were fairly swept off our feet. I hereby repent." Although Nixon originally emphasized "the idea of 'workfare' instead of welfare," a closer look at FAP showed that of the nearly ten million recipients on the rolls, the vast majority would be exempt under FAP because they were children, elderly, mothers of preschool children, sick, or disabled. As a result, Kilpatrick said, "only 500,000 prospects remain for the work-or-starve demand" that was so appealing to him and other staunch workfare advocates. Worse yet, the plan to aid the working poor would double welfare rolls and costs. These newly assisted working-poor families, he argued, "would be the permanent poor feeding like parasites on the body politic unto the end of time."[57]

Liberals were also disappointed by FAP's plans for the working and welfare poor. Many were initially drawn to FAP by the rhetoric of expanded entitlement and the promise of an "income floor" under all poor families. FAP looked good "at first blush," acknowledged Frances Fox Piven and Richard Cloward in 1971, then at Columbia's School of Social Work. But as liberal reformers took a second look, they saw that its main initial effect was to assist the needy in some of the nation's poorest regions, such as the South, where existing benefits were quite low. FAP offered virtually nothing to welfare families in the industrial, high-benefit North and West—where recipients were most numerous and well organized—except a new work requirement. Liberal activists expressed their frustration with FAP's hollow promise of an income floor to their congressional allies, through an organized campaign of phone calls, letter writing, public hearings, and private meetings.[58]

FAP missed its mark with liberals in part because support for the working poor was not a top priority for the liberal welfare reform coalition in the late 1960s. In the politics of labor rights and social provision after the New Deal, much of the organizing and advocacy for workers remained distinct from advocacy for the poor on public assistance. And liberal activists who were focused on the economic conditions of workers—such as trade union leaders—had serious concerns about the FAP strategy of income guarantees.

Labor objected to the gains that might accrue under FAP to employers paying low wages, through the combined effect of the work requirement and a government wage supplement for the working poor. Just as business leaders shared Anderson's worries that FAP would diminish workers' incentive and imperative to work, labor leaders shared Shultz's concern that it would eliminate employers' incentives to raise wages. A week before Nixon released his plan, AFL-CIO president George Meany declared flatly, "The AFL-CIO vigorously opposes the use of federal funds to subsidize the employers of cheap labor." Three months later, the United Automobile Workers voiced concern that FAP would "freeze present wage levels, and subsidize the sweatshop employer."[59] Labor leaders were worried in part about the ripple effect of depressing wages throughout the nation's wage structure. As a political strategy, therefore, they preferred regulations aimed at business—such as boosting the minimum wage—over increased spending strategies aimed at poor and near-poor workers. Some labor leaders also wanted a government-backed employment guarantee, one that would make the federal government the employer of last resort for all those unable to find work. This, they argued, would aid workers and tighten the job market.[60]

Although their concerns about FAP's proposals for the working poor were pointed, the liberal coalition directed its strongest opposition at FAP's provisions for the welfare poor. Many in the social work community backed the principle of a federally provided income guarantee, but they objected to the administration's work measures as too punitive, and to FAP's benefit levels as far too low.[61] In its ninety-eighth annual meeting in June 1970, the National Conference on Social Welfare called for an adequate, federally financed income maintenance program for the poor—then sent telegrams to Senate members demanding passage of a plan with benefit levels more than triple those of FAP.[62]

Welfare recipients and rights advocates organized under the National Welfare Rights Organization (NWRO) were the most vocal in their opposition. After sustained mobilization against the 1967 WIN amendments, the NWRO became the leading critical voice on the liberal left in the FAP debate. The organization wanted a minimum income of $5,500 for a family of four (not the $1,600 income floor proposed in FAP). This would bring the income of a mother with three children to approximately 50 percent above the poverty line, though it would still leave them in the bottom quarter of family incomes.[63] The NWRO also objected to FAP's work rules for welfare recipients. There was a logic behind the organization's position. The NWRO's base was heavily Northeastern and urban, and its active core was composed of African American women activists. Two-thirds of its members were from nine industrial states, with a particular concentration in New York City. Not coincidentally, current welfare recipients were concentrated in the Northeast and California. Nixon's FAP offered little to this constituency. By one government estimate, the net income—in cash and in-kind benefits—of a welfare family of four living in public housing in New York City at the time was $5,665. The NWRO's demand of $5,500 therefore reflected, in the view of organizers, nothing more than a principled refusal to take a step backward.[64] This was a logical extension of the welfarist entitlement principle, but it smacked of unreasonable demands to the administration and to conservatives.

Liberal members of Congress shared the view that any proposed reform should ensure gains for families currently on welfare. The administration pointed out repeatedly that FAP would help the nation's poorest welfare recipients, particularly in the South, and that it would expand assistance to many new recipients. But the fact remained that it would only raise the benefits of approximately 10 percent of current recipients. This led Fred Harris (D-Okla.), a leading welfarist Democrat (and rare Southern liberal), to pointedly question HEW secretary Elliott Richardson when he testified before the House in 1970: "Apart from the ten percent of AFDC families now living in the seven states making the lowest welfare payments, will any existing welfare family be better off?" Richardson's answer confirmed many liberals' primary reason for opposing FAP: "No."[65]

FAP's work requirement, moreover, did not play well among liberals. If conservatives read less into Nixon's workfare rhetoric than the Nixon administration intended, then liberals read more into it—seeing a tough and punitive demand. Some used familiar arguments to challenge the premise itself, particularly for mothers of young children: these parents, they argued, were entitled to remain home to care for their children, if they so chose. Many of these advocates accepted the value of encouraging and creating opportunities for work—but like many New Deal welfarists a generation earlier, they believed work should be voluntary, and that any work obligations should not undermine the basic safety net. Testifying on behalf of three national religious bodies, John Cosgrove told Congress, "Mothers of school aged children should be given the choice of taking care of their children or accepting jobs or training."[66]

In addition to challenging FAP's work requirement, a number of liberal lawmakers and advocates demanded a debate on the consequences of pushing AFDC recipients into the existing low-wage labor market and the terms under which they would be integrated into it. It would be unconscionable, Representative Ronald Dellums (D-Calif.) argued on the House floor, to "provide an incentive for people to get off welfare" and have them join the "40 percent of the labor force in America who . . . earn between $5,000 and $10,000 a year and . . . are the working poor."[67] Incentives to work, they suggested, should come from better conditions and guarantees in the job market—not from punitive policies imposed by government. Abraham Ribicoff, former secretary of HEW and now a Democratic senator from Connecticut, pushed for "a strong program of public service employment" in jobs with good working conditions and "opportunities for career advancement."[68]

Liberal advocates concurred: "Persons should not be referred to jobs paying less than the Federal minimum wage," Cosgrove told Congress, and FAP should "be accompanied in special legislation by a higher minimum wage with broad coverage; renewed efforts to end discrimination, a fully-funded low-income housing program; and recognition of the Federal Government as the employer of last resort to ensure that there are in fact jobs for which people would be trained and to which they could be referred."[69] Absent safeguards regarding wages and conditions, the work requirement "would only serve to create a pool of cheap labor," testified other liberal and labor leaders, undermining wages and working conditions for all workers.[70] AFL-CIO legislative director Andrew Biemiller also demanded that Congress protect welfare recipients facing work requirements by including provisions stating that the employment must be suitable and that it must pay either the prevailing or the minimum wage, whichever was higher.[71]

The heated racial politics of welfare further undercut Nixon's effort to build support for FAP. The larger civil rights community wavered between quiet skepticism and open hostility toward the Nixon plan, swayed in part by the NWRO's staunch opposition. Leaders of black social service organizations such as the Urban League—already suspicious of the conservative president—were reluctant to support his plan.[72] The NAACP did not actively oppose it but would not actively support it, urging significant changes. The Leadership Conference on Civil Rights took a similar stance, underlining concerns about work requirements.[73] Black leaders sought to expose the implications of FAP's work requirements for disproportionate numbers of poor minorities. The black press, along with civil and welfare rights leaders, condemned the expanding effort to force welfare recipients into the job market. A columnist for the *Greater Milwaukee Star* summarized the concern: "What recourse would there be for Blacks who say they are too sick to work? Who will be the judge? . . . Why can't some mothers remain in the home to raise their own children? . . . What guarantee does the Black recipient have that he will not be forced to take all of the dirty and sloppy jobs available in the sweatshops of industry?"[74]

On the question of work requirements, as on other issues, Nixon thus faced a gaping divide in perception and political positions. Both welfarists and workfarists had coherent conceptions of how to combine work and welfare, but their strategies served fundamentally different ends. Conservative workfarists believed welfare recipients should be required to work in order to reduce reliance on government aid; liberal welfarists argued that recipients had an entitlement to cash assistance and that work should be voluntary. And for different reasons, neither side was drawn toward policy compromise for the welfare poor by FAP's proposals for the working poor. The Nixon administration's attempts to mollify both sides on the work question thus proved unable to win over either. On the one hand, Moynihan repeatedly insisted to liberals that the FAP work requirements were not onerous and did not undermine the entitlement of assistance for poor children. He argued that it was all that was politically possible at the moment, and should be seen as a critical step forward, holding out the prospect of building a new kind of antipoverty politics across lines of race and employment status.[75] On the other hand, President Nixon, in a speech before a conference of Republican governors in April 1971, highlighted the other side of FAP. Displaying his conservative credentials, he said:

> I advocate a system which will encourage people to take work. And that means whatever work is available. It does not mean the attitude expressed not so long ago at a hearing on welfare by a lady who got up and screamed: "Don't talk to us about any of those menial jobs!" . . . Scrubbing floors or emptying bedpans is not enjoyable work, but a lot of people do it—and there is as much dignity in that as there is in any other work to be done in this country—including my own.

Within hours, the NWRO had fired off a terse press release: "You don't promote family life by forcing women out of their homes to empty bedpans. When Richard Nixon is ready to give up his $200,000 salary to scrub floors and empty bedpans in the interest of his family, then we will take him seriously."[76] Welfare recipients and other liberals emerged more firmly opposed to the president's plan—and conservatives were no more convinced that his commitment to workfare was serious.

* * *

FAP's fate was ultimately decided in a protracted legislative battle that extended over two congressional sessions, from 1969 through 1972. More than once, FAP passed the House, and there was a point at which the measure seemed within a hair's breadth of winning congressional approval. The House Ways and Means Committee first held hearings on the proposal in the fall of 1969, and FAP won the vital (and in many respects surprising) support of Wilbur Mills. FAP was, in his view, a preferred alternative to the revenue-sharing proposals that were then under consideration, and the plan's work provision assuaged many of his concerns.[77] Once Mills threw his weight behind the bill, he steered it to easy passage when the House took up the measure the following spring. More than 80 percent of Mills's fellow Southern Democrats voted against FAP despite his support. Nonetheless, FAP passed the House floor by a vote of 243–155 on April 16, 1970, and prospects in the Senate looked good.

Two weeks later, however, the Senate Finance Committee brought the auspicious early progress to a halt. Chairman Russell Long (D-La.) led the opposition, joined by John Williams of Delaware, the ranking minority member. In a critical round of hearings in April 1970, committee leaders struck a conservative, workfarist position. Lawmakers charged that the plan contained particularly powerful disincentives to work, because it retained the automatic link created under AFDC between eligibility for cash assistance and access to the new and expanding in-kind programs such as food stamps and Medicaid. This automatic link meant, in effect, that when a family earned enough wage income to reach the "cutoff" notch, they immediately lost a significant source of benefits. The extra dollar of earnings that placed the family beyond the eligibility point cost far more than a lost dollar of cash assistance: it also meant the family would lose linked benefits such as health insurance and food aid. This created a logic to earn less than the cutoff point, the senators argued.[78]

This "notch effect" plagued the existing AFDC system as well. But conservatives worried that FAP was worse, because it threatened not only to persuade current recipients to stay on welfare but also to draw current workers onto the rolls.[79] Like Nixon aide Martin Anderson, lawmakers worried that the combination of FAP's cash aid and existing in-kind benefits might offer poor workers a better deal than they could find in the labor market. In response to the committee's concerns about this and other issues, administration officials reworked the legislation. Once again, the revisions earned little additional conservative support and turned liberals already troubled by what they saw as low benefits and harsh work requirements more adamantly against FAP.[80]

Throughout the summer and fall of 1970, the Nixon White House believed that it had the votes to win passage—if the bill could be moved out of the Finance Committee and onto the Senate floor. But Long and others strategically delayed the vote, and the bill stalled in committee.[81] Lacking the support of even a majority of Republicans, FAP needed Democratic votes to pass. Yet in the partisan atmosphere of the fall of 1970, as the nation geared up for a congressional election, few Democrats were in the mood to hand the president a legislative victory. When Vice President Spiro Agnew hit the campaign trail with stump speeches condemning "radical liberals," resentment surged among liberal Democrats—and FAP's prospects plunged further. By the time the vote was taken in the Senate Finance Committee on November 20, four liberal Democrats joined the conservatives in defeating the bill, 6–10. These included not only Eugene McCarthy (D-Minn.) but Fred Harris (D-Okla.), who was swayed by NWRO arguments, and Albert Gore, Sr. (D-Tenn.), who was one of the Democrats bruised by Agnew's attacks. A last-ditch effort to secure a victory on the floor of the Senate also failed, 21–49.[82]

Undeterred, Nixon vowed to make FAP a "major legislative goal" for the new ninety-first Congress. A reworked FAP once again passed the House, and, once again, stalled in the Senate.[83] The revised bill, called H.R. 1, offered some new attractions for both conservatives and liberals. But conservative objections were sharpened by an increase in the basic benefit level, and removal of the stipulation that recipients could be forced to take any job paying standard local wages, no matter how low.[84] And liberals were outraged by the elimination of the guarantee that recipients would not receive less under FAP than under existing AFDC programs, and removal of the provision allowing recipients to refuse to take jobs that were not "suitable." The NWRO, moreover, organized a more effective and far-reaching opposition to the bill among congressional liberals this time.[85]

In the Senate, welfarists and workfarists crafted alternative legislative proposals. Liberals lined up behind Senator Ribicoff (D-Conn.), who came forward with a more generous family assistance bill in October 1971 that shored up and strengthened the welfare entitlement. Senator Long of the Senate Finance Committee unveiled his own plan, billed as a true and tougher "workfare" proposal. The Finance Committee—still dominated by a conservative majority—rejected both FAP and the Ribicoff proposal, and approved Long's workfare plan.[86]

The bill was slow to reach the floor of the Senate, and as months passed, Nixon lost interest in the FAP campaign. When the full Senate finally turned its attention to family assistance in the fall of 1972, the nation was in the throes of another election season, including a vitriolic presidential campaign pitting Nixon against Senator George McGovern (D-S. Dak.), the standard-bearer of the Democratic Party's liberal wing. In the end, none of the three bills—H.R. 1, the Ribicoff plan, or the Long alternative—earned enough support to pass. The struggle over family assistance was over.[87]

FAP's Failure and Welfare's Future

One of the most remarkable conclusions about the story of the Family Assistance Plan is how close it came to becoming law. A legislative proposal that would have remade federal social welfare policy by extending aid to all poor families—working or nonworking, single or two-parent—cleared the House twice with strong margins. According to the White House's vote count, it may well have cleared the Senate had it been brought to a vote in the summer of 1970; even at the end, in the fall of 1972, FAP might have been enacted if the administration or the Democratic leadership had found the eight votes to reverse the 35–51 outcome on October 4.[88]

Despite its defeat, the battle over the Nixon proposal changed the terms of the debate and defined new political coalitions in the politics of public assistance. FAP had put the working poor on the national political agenda: both sides in the FAP debate agreed that the problem demanded attention. The welfare poor did not fare so well. The sustained attack on AFDC in the campaign for FAP had left the program and its recipients more discredited than ever, and proposals (by liberal Democrats) to broaden welfarist protections, or to defend the principle of choice in the labor market (as Shultz had argued), were rejected.

The dominant explanation for FAP's defeat was that the proposal was unable to gain adequate support from either liberals or conservatives. Strictly speaking, this is accurate, but it obscures two deeper factors essential to understanding subsequent welfare politics. First, by the early 1970s, the debate over work and welfare was not simply a debate between "liberals" and "conservatives." It had evolved into a struggle between two competing conceptions of public assistance, each with its own logic for work and welfare. One was welfarism, rooted in the premise of entitlement to cash assistance to all eligible families; a noncoercive approach to work could be accommodated within this framework. The other approach was a modern form of workfare. The idea at its core—that the poor must be made to work—was not new, of course; nor was the policy of work requirements for welfare recipients. But the concept of elevating work promotion and enforcement *above* and *outside of* the commitment to the traditional safety net against poverty, and the idea of replacing the logic of entitlement with the logic of work incentives, was just beginning to take form as a full-blown policy alternative to welfarism at the federal level.

The battle over FAP exposed and deepened the political divide between welfarists and workfarists. It also pushed workfarists to more aggressively articulate and advocate for their alternative. The defeat of FAP struck an ideological blow for their position. Workfare would not gain institutional expression until the passage of three legislative initiatives, described in the next chapter. It would not become the dominant approach to public assistance until the passage of the 1996 welfare reform. But it was during the political struggles over FAP that many of the core ideas behind U.S. workfare began to coalesce, along with the beginnings of a political coalition to support it, from state and local officials to Southern Democratic and conservative Republican lawmakers.

A second critical factor in the battle over FAP was the role of moderates and conservatives. The conventional wisdom on the defeat of FAP emphasizes the actions of liberals: the widespread perception was that liberals "lost" FAP in the quest for an even more far-reaching reform. Liberal defections gained far more media and scholarly attention, particularly from those partial to the reform. These observers aimed their harshest criticism at liberal opponents for being too "pure" in their position, or for demanding even more than FAP proposed—and more than was politically feasible.[89]

In fact, a close analysis of the votes undertaken by Lester Salamon showed that liberal support for FAP was extremely strong in the final vote tallies. The critical defection from FAP came from the absence of both conservative and moderate support in the Senate. In the face of a strong conservative challenge in the Senate led by Long and his Republican Finance Committee colleagues, there was a palpable lack of leadership to mobilize support for FAP among moderates. Senate Majority Leader Michael Mansfield (D-Mont.), for example, did not take a position. By the time FAP arrived on the Senate floor, moreover, even the president had distanced himself from it, giving moderates still greater reason to play it safe on the issue. So although more than 70 percent of moderates in the House voted in support of H.R. 1, for example, less than 40 percent did so in the Senate.[90]

The role of moderates and conservatives in FAP's defeat also supports a core claim of this chapter: by the time FAP came to a vote, there was little common ground in the debate over work and welfare. Policymakers and the public were divided between liberal welfarists and conservative workfarists. Each had moved toward a stauncher position through the late 1960s. The Nixon administration's strategy of appealing to each side in the FAP debate of the early 1970s only widened the chasm between them. Moderates, meanwhile, were left with little reason to believe that anything would work, and no new middle ground to stand on.

In the end, conservative Senate Democrats played the most decisive role in the FAP battles. FAP had the momentum of a nationally broadcast presidential address and easy House passage when it reached Senate Democrats in the spring of 1970. They tied it down and picked it apart until a successor version of the legislation was finally defeated in the fall of 1972. Southern Democrats then picked up select pieces of the wreckage they had made and fashioned the beginnings of a fundamentally different approach to welfare and work, as the next chapter explains. Their role in creating a workfare alternative was no accident: they had a deep stake in the debate over who received cash assistance, and how. In the process of defending these interests, they would permanently transform the national system of public assistance.

CHAPTER 3

Building Workfare: WIN II, SSI, and EITC

Senator Russell Long had headed home to Louisiana victorious when Congress adjourned in December 1967. He had regaled a crowd in Shreveport with the story of how his eleventh-hour maneuver on the Senate floor had foiled a filibuster planned by liberal Democrats, securing passage of the WIN amendments authored by his fellow Southerner Wilbur Mills and sealing the fate of the welfare measure proposed by President Johnson and Senate liberals. "That group of young turks," he concluded, "has a lot to learn" about how to run a filibuster.[1] Four years later, he was back before crowds in his home state to celebrate an even greater victory in blocking another president's liberal welfare reform proposal. This time it was Richard Nixon's Family Assistance Plan (FAP). Hand-scrawled in the margins of Long's March 1971 speech was his conclusion: "Last year FAP failed. Finance Committee and I as the chairman in particular was blamed.... Good thing."[2] Long would later call the defeat of FAP the crowning achievement of his legislative career.

With FAP's collapse, the campaign by conservative Southern Democrats against liberal welfare reform measures seemed to draw to a close. As it turned out, they were just getting warmed up. In the early 1970s, emboldened by their victories on WIN and FAP, Southern Democratic leaders in Congress shifted from a strategy of blocking liberal reform initiatives to crafting their own model of federal income assistance. They quietly spearheaded three legislative initiatives in quick succession that changed the landscape of public assistance: the Talmadge Work Incentive amendments (WIN II) were approved in 1971, Supplemental Security Income (SSI) passed in 1972, and the Earned Income Tax Credit (EITC) became law in 1975. Though not conceived or executed as a coordinated conservative assault on the New Deal system, the piecemeal reforms fundamentally altered much of the existing structure of public assistance. Their combined impact was to steer the ends and means of federal income assistance toward the principle of rewarding and enforcing work.

The three reforms are often overlooked in accounts of welfare policy change, or treated as distinct, unrelated developments. Many accounts move quickly from the (largely expansionary) 1960s to the (largely contractionary) 1980s. The 1970s were, in the words of one historian, years of "stalemate" in poverty politics, sandwiched between the liberal and conservative welfare state projects.[3] The Talmadge amendments are often raised only in passing, as a tightening of the original 1967 WIN work requirements. SSI is typically tacked onto the social welfare expansions of the Great Society period, mentioned as a consolation prize after the disintegration of FAP, or treated as a mere administrative change. And despite increasing recognition of the EITC's importance as an antipoverty measure, the politics of its passage are rarely incorporated into the larger story of welfare policy.[4]

Far from years of stalemate, the early 1970s saw a distinct phase of welfare state development led by antiwelfare Southerners, one that disrupts the neat demarcations between expansion and contraction, and between the respective roles of liberal Democratic welfare state "builders" and conservative Republican "retrenchers." It marked a conservative turn, but it was not an episode of retrenchment: it was a period of welfare-state building, and, in fact, it produced an expansion of programs for the elderly, disabled, and working poor. Far from a series of minor and unrelated initiatives, moreover, the three 1970s initiatives recast public assistance policies—to require work from those on AFDC, to reward work among low-wage workers, and to exempt from work only those too old or ill to earn wages.

Three conclusions emerge from a close study of the legislative and political history. First, the initiatives reflected a political response by Southern congressional Democrats to Nixon's Family Assistance Plan, which threatened to expand the welfarist model of public assistance. As this chapter will show, FAP triggered a counterreaction by Southern Democratic lawmakers, and these programs were its leading edge. To create the three programs, Southern Democrats moved to "hive off" favored elements of the Nixon FAP proposal, modify them as necessary, and secure passage through independent legislative vehicles. This had the immediate political effect of undercutting moderate and conservative support for FAP, carefully cultivated by the administration on the basis of precisely these provisions.

Second, although Southern Democratic leaders had many reasons to oppose the Republican administration's plan, their statements and strategies reveal that a core concern was the challenge FAP posed to social, political, and economic arrangements in the South. Key Southern leaders were convinced that Nixon's proposal threatened to destabilize local low-wage labor markets: by directing federal cash assistance to current and potential workers, FAP would provide those workers with an alternative means of livelihood and the ability to refuse low-wage jobs or reduce work hours. Each of their three favored legislative alternatives, in contrast, promised to leave labor market relations largely intact by ensuring that the able-bodied poor were compelled to enter the workforce and by subsidizing—rather than disrupting—low-wage labor markets. The initiatives were in this sense profoundly conservative, even though they marked expansions, and they protected traditional Southern economic and political interests.

Third, these initiatives, taken together, reoriented the purposes of federally supported income assistance. The struggle over public assistance has long been a debate over whether and how to aid three categories of poor Americans: (a) those who are poor *because they cannot work*, (b) those who are poor *because they will not work*, and (c) those who are poor *even though they are working*.[5] The New Deal framework sought to direct assistance to the first category and to withhold aid from the second category; those in the third category (working but poor) received no public assistance, though they benefited from other New Deal legislation.[6] FAP proposed to erase these distinctions by installing an income floor under all poor families. The Southern conservative counterreaction assertively redrew its own distinctions. The piecemeal reforms introduced by leading Southern legislators—such as Senate Finance Committee chair Russell Long (D-La.), House Ways and Means Committee chair Wilbur Mills (D-Ark.), and Senator Herman Talmadge (D-Ga.)—created a new public assistance model. It provided aid to a much smaller population judged to be *physically unable to work*, through SSI; imposed work requirements on those judged *able but unwilling to work*, through WIN II; and offered a new entitlement to those who were poor *even though they were working*, through the EITC. This established the foundation of the workfare approach. By the mid-1970s, programs for the poor had been expanded, but in ways that accorded new priority to the criteria and imperative of work.[7] This chapter opens with an analysis of the role of Southern politics in the rise of workfare, then examines the political developments leading to the creation of the three programs in the 1970s.

The Fight to Control Welfare in the South

Why would conservative Southern lawmakers, who were generally opposed to both a large federal role in public assistance and the creation of new programs for the poor, spearhead an expansion of the federal welfare state? Southern leaders' motives and interests in public assistance policy were neither uniform nor unchanging.[8] Their role in building a new workfare regime is best understood in the context of relief's place in the region's social and economic order, and of Southern leaders' reaction to FAP.

From the 1930s through the 1960s, Southern political leaders were largely successful in defending the prerogatives of state authority in public assistance programs. But by the late 1960s, Southerners were beginning to lose many of their traditional assistance-related means of control over their disproportionately black low-wage labor forces and the size and costs of state welfare rolls. The Civil Rights Act had banned discrimination in distribution of federal funds, limiting local and state discretion, and Supreme Court rulings had explicitly struck down several favored tactics for controlling welfare eligibility and benefits.[9] Welfare rolls rose quickly as eligibility restrictions were lifted. Many conservatives were feeling besieged and disarmed, and congressional leaders such as Long condemned court decisions that limited their states' capacities to restrict welfare.[10] The new cohort of younger leaders elected in the wake of the civil rights battles and hailed as representatives of the "New South," meanwhile, largely tracked the positions of political elders such as Long, Talmadge, and Mills on federal public assistance.[11] Even as the region's social order was transformed by black migration, economic expansion, and the extension of voting rights, welfare in the South remained controversial, tied to struggles over the region's low-wage labor force and persistent racial hierarchies.

When Richard Nixon unveiled his expensive new social welfare initiative in a televised address in August 1969, therefore, Southerners were watching closely, and other leaders were watching the South. As the Nixon administration awaited Congress's reaction, "the major question," recalled Daniel Patrick Moynihan, one of FAP's architects in the administration, "was how the South would respond." Moynihan was banking on Southern support. The South had changed, he reasoned, and political leaders might see FAP as an opportunity to bring billions in federal resources to address Southern poverty, and to bridge divides of race and region through an agenda of "economic liberalism."[12] Indeed, Moynihan had made the case within the Nixon administration that FAP could defuse racial tensions over public assistance. AFDC was losing public support in part because it was increasingly identified with African American recipients, he argued; FAP would change the equation by bringing millions of the mostly white working poor into the nation's aid system.[13] Robert Finch, Secretary of Health, Education, and Welfare, advanced the same argument in the administration's initial bid for support from Congress.[14]

But the administration's hopes for Southern support were never realized. The overwhelming majority of Southern lawmakers opposed FAP. Two aspects of the plan drew repeated fire. The first was the principle of a federally guaranteed income. The promise of federal aid to families on the basis of income levels would mean an enormous infusion of cash assistance to the region's poor through the federal social welfare system. The second was the principle that most family members would receive some aid whether or not the family head was working. Southern leaders worried that this would lead workers in low-paid sectors to work less—or not at all.[15] "Bluntly put," wrote analyst Kevin Phillips in a July 1970 column, as FAP sat in the Senate Finance Committee, "the program would strike at the rural socioeconomic and political power base of Dixie's conservative Democrats."[16]

If the stakes seemed high, it is because the numbers were striking. One-half of all poor families in the nation lived in the South, and two-thirds of poor black families did. Wages and working conditions for those at the bottom of the labor market were the worst in the nation, particularly for blacks. According to the Labor Department, the percentage of black workers forced to accept part-time jobs, poorly paid and irregular, was twice as high in the South as elsewhere in the United States.[17]

In this economic context, even the low benefit levels promised under FAP would have a sweeping impact. Of the nearly four million households that would receive FAP payments, more than two million were in the South: under FAP, the percentage of families with incomes less than $2,000 in the South would approach that of other parts of the country for the first time.[18] Estimates from the Nixon administration and members of Congress suggested that FAP would make more than one-third of Mississippi's population eligible for public assistance, along with one-quarter of Kentuckians and Louisianans and roughly one-fifth of the populations of Alabama, Arkansas, Georgia, Tennessee, North Carolina, and South Carolina.[19] FAP would triple the welfare rolls in thirteen states, railed Senator Harry Byrd, Jr. (D-Va.).[20]

As Southern elites recognized immediately, providing welfare assistance to six to seven million additional Southerners, primarily in working-poor families, would alter the economic choices available to workers, changing the character of the low-wage labor market.[21] In correspondence to Southern lawmakers, local business leaders reported difficulties in finding and retaining "unskilled labor," especially in food and service industries. They worried, as a business leader in Little Rock wrote, that "our inability to employ our labor needs" may be due not to "a shortage in the potential work force but perhaps an unwillingness on the part of many people to work, preferring instead to receive benefits from various places such as welfare, unemployment compensation, food stamps and the like."[22]

FAP also threatened to upset the balance of political power in the South by providing a new base of economic security for blacks. A majority of FAP benefits would continue to go to white families, according to administration estimates.[23] But, as an official of the anti-integration Citizens' Councils stated, FAP "would enormously increase the voting power of the poor people, and in the South an awful lot of poor people are Negroes."[24] Among other things, FAP's income guarantee would limit the effectiveness of economic reprisals—such as reductions in pay or loss of employment—that many employers used to intimidate blacks from voting. This meant, wrote Steve Van Evera in *New South* in the fall of 1971, that FAP could give black political power "the greatest boost . . . in the rural South since the Voting Rights Act of 1965."[25] When a 1970 survey of Southern opinion on FAP was published in the *Wall Street Journal*, the vast majority, the paper reported, "agree[d] with Senator Herman Talmadge, the Georgia Democrat, that the bill 'would undermine the best qualities of this nation'" and "bring significant changes in the Southern way of life."[26]

On Capitol Hill, lawmakers argued that increased access to public assistance would be a disincentive to work. Representative Phil Landrum (D-Ga.) told a reporter, "There's not going to be anybody left to toll these wheelbarrows and press these shirts. They're all going to be on welfare."[27] Long and others also worried about the larger labor market implications of FAP's guaranteed income, including potential upward wage pressures. Arguing for his own alternative to FAP, Long emphasized to fellow conservatives that unlike FAP, his plan would not disrupt the existing wage structure in the low-wage sector. He carefully listed forty-one distinct jobs in which a person might continue to earn less than the federal minimum wage under his plan, including in public sector positions, "small retail stores," "small service establishments," "agricultural pursuits," and "domestic service."[28]

In the face of FAP's challenge to the existing order, its modest work requirement appeared to be little more than a cruel joke to Southern conservatives. They saw quickly what Nixon aide Patrick Moynihan was unable to convey to Northern liberals who opposed FAP's work mandate as too tough: under the FAP requirement, guaranteed assistance would continue to flow to other family members even if the head of the family refused to take an available job.[29] The only penalty for refusing work was the loss of the breadwinner's share of the family grant. After decades of local work rules, Southerners were accustomed to more stringent controls on welfare recipients' labor.

Some in the Nixon administration believed Southern leaders' interest in maintaining cheap labor supplies fueled their dogged attempts to tighten work requirements. One exasperated HEW official questioned whether Long's devotion to the idea of imposing strict work obligations on welfare recipients had less to do with the alleged erosion of the work ethic among poor mothers—and more to do with the availability of domestic labor for the Southern elite. Regardless of costs or family circumstances, he emphasized, "[Long] will reply, 'That's okay, you can't put a value on those children seeing a mother get up at 5:30 to go to work.' Doing what? Picking armadillos off the highway? . . . I think that . . . what Long and others are really concerned about [is] that if this bill goes through they won't be able to get a maid down in Louisiana."[30]

Southerners' concerns about FAP's impact on employment helped fuel the protracted legislative tug-of-war over work provisions described in the previous chapter. Southern Democrats joined Republicans in stripping the caveat from FAP's work requirement that recipients were only obliged to accept "suitable" employment. Representative Joel Broyhill of Virginia drew the line in the sand, telling reporters: "I will insist that no one receive any assistance through the welfare program who is physically able to do work but refuses to do so. I don't want any provision limiting the requirement to 'suitable' employment. Any type of work should be considered suitable or reasonable to a person seeking public assistance."[31]

The Southern contingent lost a battle, however, when the Nixon administration reworked the original FAP bill (after it died in the Senate in 1970)

Table 3.1 House Votes on Nixon's Family Assistance Plan, 1970 and 1971

	APRIL 16, 1970	
	Yes (pro-FAP)	No (anti-FAP)
Southern Democrats	15 (19%)	64 (81%)
Northern Democrats	126 (86.9%)	19 (13.1%)
Republicans	102 (58.6%)	72 (41.4%)
	JUNE 22, 1971	
	No (pro-FAP)	Yes (anti-FAP)
Southern Democrats	25 (29.8%)	59 (70.2%)
Northern Democrats	116 (72.1%)	45 (27.9%)
Republicans	93 (52.8%)	83 (47.2%)

Source: Author's calculations based on vote totals reported in *Congressional Quarterly Almanac* 26 (1970): 16H; and *Congressional Quarterly Almanac* 27 (1971): 35H.
Note: On the two key FAP-related votes in the House, Northern Democrats were overwhelmingly in favor, Southern Democrats were overwhelmingly opposed, and Republicans were split. The first vote was on final passage of H.R. 16311, which passed 243–155 on April 16, 1970. The second vote was on a motion by Representative Al Ullman (D-Ore.) to delete the FAP provisions from the 1971 Social Security Amendments (H.R. 1). The Ullman motion was rejected 187–234 on June 22, 1971.

and reintroduced it as H.R. 1 in 1971. The original bill had stipulated that FAP recipients could be assigned to any job paying the "prevailing wage" and permitted states to administer the program. This provided latitude to Southern administrators seeking to preserve the existing hierarchies in the region's labor market, where the "prevailing wage" for domestic work in Mississippi was $4 a day.[32] But in an appeal to labor and Northern liberals, the revised bill mandated federal rather than state administration and asserted that family breadwinners had the right to reject any job paying less than $1.20 an hour (the federal minimum was $1.60 at the time).[33] These income levels would significantly force wages up throughout the rural South, which had the lowest average hourly earnings ($1.08) in the nation.[34] FAP would provide a federal income to a poor family, even if a parent rejected many of the jobs then available—unless local employers boosted wages for farmhands, dishwashers, domestics, and other positions not covered by the federal minimum wage, to reach the FAP minimum of $1.20.[35]

Despite numerous attempts by the Nixon administration to address Southerners' concerns, opposition remained strong. On the two direct votes on

Table 3.2 Senate Votes on Nixon's Family Assistance Plan, 1972

	OCTOBER 3, 1972	
	No (pro-FAP)	Yes (anti-FAP)
Southern Democrats	0 (0%)	17 (100%)
Northern Democrats	19 (63.3%)	11 (36.7%)
Republicans	14 (36.8%)	24 (63.2%)
	OCTOBER 4, 1972	
	No (pro-FAP)	Yes (anti-FAP)
Southern Democrats	1 (6.3%)	15 (93.7%)
Northern Democrats	22 (73.3%)	8 (26.7%)
Republicans	18 (46.2%)	21 (53.8%)
	OCTOBER 4, 1972	
	No (pro-FAP)	Yes (anti-FAP)
Southern Democrats	1 (6.3%)	15 (93.7%)
Northern Democrats	22 (71%)	9 (29%)
Republicans	18 (45%)	22 (55%)

Source: Calculations based on vote totals reported in *Congressional Quarterly Almanac* 28 (1972): 72S–73S.
Note: Key Senate votes on FAP in 1972 reflected divisions between Northern and Southern Democrats, and the fact that Southern Democrats often held the balance of votes in the Senate. The first vote was on a motion by Senator Long (D-La.) to table (kill) Senator Ribicoff's (D-Conn.) liberal version of FAP; the vote to table passed 52–34 on October 3, 1972. The second was on a Long motion to table a Ribicoff amendment to remove workfare provisions from a Social Security bill passed by the Finance Committee. Long's motion passed 44–41 on October 4, 1972. The third vote was on a motion by Senator Roth (R-Del.) to pilot-test competing welfare reform proposals rather than enact FAP or other alternatives; the motion passed 46–41 on October 4, 1972.

FAP in the House, Southern Democrats voted against the plan by large margins, with 81 and 70 percent opposed. Northern Democrats were 86 and 72 percent in favor; Republicans were nearly evenly split. In the Senate, the pattern was similar, though there were no direct up-or-down votes on the measure: on FAP-related votes, over 90 percent of Southern Senate Democrats cast votes that opposed the measure.[36]

Only a small percentage of Southern members of the president's own party, meanwhile, was willing to support him. Cast largely out of party loyalty, these Republican votes were costly to party stalwarts such as Representative

George H. W. Bush of Texas, who made a bid for a Senate seat in the November 1970 election—and lost. True to the Southern Democratic position, his opponent Lloyd Bentsen produced ads that criticized Bush's pro-FAP vote and the prospect of "14 million more on welfare," and described a vote for Bentsen as a "vote against big welfare" and higher taxes.[37] President Nixon wrote to Bush in late October: "I understand that you have been attacked by your opponent for your support of the Family Assistance Plan on the grounds that it is a 'guaranteed annual income.' This is a very serious misinterpretation of the goals of our plan."[38]

But, of course, it was not a serious misinterpretation, and Southern leaders knew it. Many feared, in short, "that FAP's guaranteed income would shrink the supply of cheap labor, bankrupt marginal industry, boost the cost of locally produced goods and services, increase taxes, and put more blacks into political office," concluded journalists Vince and Vee Burke in their 1974 study of FAP.[39] Little wonder, with these perceived stakes for his region, that Senator Long waged a pitched battle against FAP from his pivotal position as chair of the Finance Committee. FAP, he said with no trace of irony, made him "tremble in fear for the fate of this Republic."[40]

As it became clear that FAP was not simply going to go away after its initial setbacks, however, opponents realized that they needed to counter with their own alternative proposals. The twin commitments to defeating FAP and defending Southern political and economic arrangements created a powerful incentive to craft conservative—if expansionary—reforms.

Building Workfare Through Piecemeal Policymaking

Beginning in 1971, with the nation riveted on the legislative battle over the Nixon proposal, conservative Southern leaders in Congress began quietly passing legislation that would usher in a new era in public assistance. The three legislative initiatives shared several features. Each reflected elements of the conservative vision and regional interests of key Southern leaders. And each helped redefine the terms of public assistance for a distinct category of poor Americans. The Talmadge amendments targeted current welfare recipients, many of whom, in the view of conservative workfarists, were poor *because they would not work*. SSI restructured assistance for elderly and disabled adults, whom conservatives believed were poor *because they could not work*. And the EITC extended aid to families who, conservatives recognized, were poor *even though they were working*. In altering the terms of assistance, each of the initiatives advanced the core premises of workfarist public assistance—namely, require work from single mothers on AFDC, exempt from work only those too old or infirm to earn wages, and reward work among low-wage workers. Ultimately, each of the initiatives would facilitate compromises and coalitions in the 1980s and 1990s that helped erode and then dismantle the core welfarist entitlement for poor families.

The first move was made by Democratic Senator Herman Talmadge of Georgia. It took aim at the welfare poor, and in particular, at AFDC recipients. Under the New Deal model of public assistance, federal policy considered these recipients poor because caregiving obligations made them *unable to work* at sufficient levels to support their families.[41] Beginning with the push by Wilbur Mills to add a new federal work mandate to AFDC through the initial 1967 WIN amendments, conservative reformers began to assert, instead, that these recipients were too often simply *unwilling to work*, and therefore should be evaluated for referral to state work programs.

Talmadge was one of the harshest congressional critics of FAP. He shared the concerns of other Southerners about the sheer numbers that would be brought into the system of federal cash assistance under the plan.[42] And he believed that FAP did far too little to require work of all who were able. In hearings before the Senate Finance Committee in the spring of 1970, Talmadge grilled HEW Secretary Robert Finch and Undersecretary John Veneman.[43] He concluded that in many parts of Georgia, "we might have over half the people in individual counties on welfare."[44] Under Talmadge's questioning, Veneman acknowledged the low cash penalty a FAP family would pay if a family head refused work, confirming conservatives' worst fears about FAP.[45]

After the first version of FAP collapsed in 1970, Talmadge took action. He led conservatives in pulling the work requirement out of the FAP proposal and passing a version of it in separate Social Security legislation. The aim, in his view, must be a workfarist one—namely, to "make productive citizens out of nonproductive citizens."[46] Dubbed "WIN II" because they revised the initial WIN rules, the Talmadge amendments were signed into law in December 1971.[47]

As a political maneuver, the amendments had an immediate effect on the balance of forces in the FAP struggle. Passing the work requirement independently of the other elements of the FAP package significantly reduced FAP's appeal to conservatives when the administration came back with a revised version of the bill. The work requirement, as Representative John Byrnes (R-Wisc.) explained, was "what some consider the sweetener."[48] With WIN II, conservatives got the "sweetener" without having to swallow the rest of the package. Scheduled to take effect on July 1, 1972, WIN II was on the books during the Senate's final deliberations on FAP.

As a policy initiative, WIN II had a deeper and enduring impact on the politics of welfare. Work obligations of various forms had been imposed on welfare recipients at the state level for decades. But federal policy from the New Deal to the Great Society had not formally conditioned assistance on a work requirement.[49] WIN I had imposed the first federal mandate that states create work and training programs, and refer any "appropriate persons" to them. WIN II established a more sweeping standard, requiring *all* adult recipients, *except* those explicitly exempted, to register for work, under penalty of loss of benefits. By removing the reference to "appropriate persons" and eliminating state officials' discretion in determining who met this qualification, the law significantly widened the categories of recipients considered eligible for work and included mothers of school-age children.[50]

The new law also had greater enforcement power: states would lose a portion of their federal funds if they failed to refer at least 15 percent of their adult recipients to the program by mid-1974. Exemptions, loopholes, and lack of funding would limit the reach and impact of the Talmadge amendments, as they had with WIN I. Nonetheless, WIN II was markedly tougher than existing law, and its passage signaled the rising frustration in Congress over the performance of WIN I.[51] In the long run, WIN II would help facilitate the shift to workfare by affirming a new evaluative measure for AFDC's success: moving recipients from welfare to work. Once virtually all adult recipients were judged work-appropriate, and once states were expected to establish programs that moved recipients from welfare to work, policymakers began to focus increasingly on how well AFDC was meeting this aim.

WIN II signaled two additional trends, both of which prefigured the conservative position in the policy debates of the 1980s and 1990s. Programmatically, the measure took a decisive step toward equating the aim of encouraging self-support with being "tough" on work requirements. Among other things, this meant elevating "work-first" approaches over those designed to strengthen the long-term employability and earning power of jobless recipients. WIN I had been designed in part to encourage recipients to pursue formal education and training to improve their prospects for employment. In some cases, for example, it included support for recipients to attend college. In a move that foreshadowed the dominant approach to workfare reform in the 1990s, WIN II changed the emphasis from boosting the long-term employability and skills of welfare recipients, to immediate referral to available jobs ("work-first" plans). The shift was in part a response to studies indicating that immediate placement and on-the-job training were more effective at reducing AFDC caseloads. Under WIN II, states were to spend at least one-third of WIN funds on on-the-job training and public service employment.[52]

The passage of the Talmadge amendments also marked a trend toward escalating work requirements even in the face of policy failure. This would emerge as a defining pattern in the politics of welfare and work. Faced with evidence that previous attempts (such as WIN I) were failing to move recipients into the workforce, policymakers responded not by reassessing the strategy but by escalating it, imposing more and tougher requirements. As evidence mounted of WIN I's failures, members of Congress from both parties were largely silent on the obstacles posed by the weaknesses in the low-wage labor market and the characteristics of the recipient pool, electing instead simply to tighten the rules. Studies of WIN I showed, for example, that only a fraction of recipients were judged appropriate for work by local authorities. The remainder were ill, needed at home, without childcare, or considered otherwise inappropriate for training. Lawmakers' response in WIN II, however, was to impose further restrictions, in part by eliminating state and local discretion to determine whether recipients were appropriate for referral. Similarly, policymakers were confronted with discouraging evidence on training and placement rates. Some 400,000 people were enrolled in WIN I by mid-1972, when WIN II took effect; only about 25 percent of these finished training. In the end, only 52,000, less than 2 percent of the total pool, actually held jobs. Faced with this evidence, the response of lawmakers was to sidestep the challenge of training and education, and shift the emphasis and expectations to immediate job placement.[53]

WIN II thus put into place the first piece of the new workfare regime by strengthening work requirements for AFDC recipients, and established significant political precedents. The measure promoted self-support by being "tough on work" and elevated "work-first" approaches over those designed to strengthen recipients' employability and earning power. With the two WIN amendments, the central measure of AFDC's success began to shift decidedly from the welfarist aim of reducing family poverty through income support to the workfarist aim of moving recipients from welfare to work—and policymakers began to chart the program's less-than-impressive record in doing so.

* * *

The next major policy initiative pulled from the administration's FAP proposal and passed independently was an expanded program of assistance for the poor elderly, disabled, and blind. Approved in October 1972, the new Supplemental Security Income (SSI) program would appear, at first glance, to have little to do with a turn to workfare in public assistance or with the retrenchment of AFDC decades later. But SSI was essential for whom it excluded. The program broke apart the "trio" of New Deal public assistance programs and more narrowly defined which poor Americans should receive income assistance without work obligations. SSI wrote into law the conservative answer to the question of which Americans are poor *because they cannot work* and erased the New Deal definition.

Under New Deal welfarism, programs for the categories of needy Americans deemed "unemployable"—the elderly, the blind (and later the disabled), and mothers with dependent children—were inscribed in the Social Security Act.[54] The institutional relationship between these programs provided a measure of political protection for AFDC by linking the fate of its recipients to those of the aged and disabled poor. Federal administrators routinely developed reforms, rules, and expansions that would apply to all of these programs in the decades after the New Deal.[55]

SSI reconfigured public assistance by creating a new program for only two of the three original recipient categories, those physically unable to work due to age or disability. Poor families were left out.[56] SSI marked a significant expansion of the welfare state: the new program served greater numbers of needy within its specific categories, was federally administered, and provided a floor of assistance. But it also marked an exclusion of the largest and most controversial group of unemployables, dependent children and their caregivers.[57] Politically, this set SSI on the path of institutional growth in subsequent years—and AFDC on the road to contraction.

Conservative Southern Democrats in Congress again provided the primary impetus and strategy for "hiving off" of FAP the provisions that became SSI, as Jennifer Erkulwater's historical study of the program described.[58] Congressional support for the Nixon administration's provisions for the elderly and disabled poor emerged early, in both House and Senate responses to FAP.[59] Leaders of poor Southern states had a long-standing interest in increased federal assistance for these needy populations. As Mills observed in the 1970 FAP debates, "I think we would all agree ... that the adult public assistance recipients, the old, the halt, the blind, are most deserving of any additional help that we can give them."[60] Mills and Long differed in their approaches—Mills had consistently argued that aid to the elderly poor through social insurance was preferable to the traditional public assistance increases championed by Long—but both repeatedly pressed for additional support for the elderly and disabled poor, and Southerners backed the initial FAP provisions for these groups.[61]

From the outset, Mills's position in the FAP debate departed from that of many of his Southern colleagues. In principle, Mills advocated states' rights, limited federal government, the free market, and the work ethic. FAP's proposal to provide an income guarantee for the working poor troubled him, as it did other Southerners. He worried that it "would create tremendous disincentives to work in some states, like mine for example, where the wages are low."[62] All the same, Mills supported FAP and its proposed federalization of public assistance. He felt that these programs, and particularly AFDC, had been "sadly and badly administered" by the states.[63] It bothered Mills enormously that although the federal government picked up the bill for more than half of public assistance costs, it was constrained in its ability to control federal welfare spending because of the existing cost-sharing system. The New Deal structure of divided authority (championed by many Southern lawmakers) also made it too easy for states to evade federal rules—including the 1967 WIN work requirements. Mills sought to persuade skeptical conservatives that reducing state discretion would address WIN's failures and rein in costs.[64] His Republican counterpart Byrnes echoed Mills's concern, pointing to low state participation in WIN, and asserting, "Hell, we can't trust the states.... Look at what has happened to the WIN program."[65] In a Rules Committee hearing on FAP, Byrnes argued that "this new system has much better administrative potential than the present system ... [for] getting people into the economic system and going to work."[66]

Though Mills's main concern was with state administration of AFDC, he extended the logic to the "adult categories." For these programs, Mills proposed not only federal administration of matching grant programs, but also an increase in the income floor.[67] This concept became the basis for the provisions in FAP that would become SSI. It would not be easy, however, to convince other Southern leaders to support the federalization of public assistance for the elderly and disabled, as proposed in the 1971 version of FAP. For decades, the Southern position on public assistance had been to accept federal dollars but maintain state control over administration. In deliberations in the heavily Southern and Western Senate Finance Committee in the fall of 1972, members balked. The Committee wanted the adult programs to remain under state administration, and voted accordingly. "This motion was advocated by the 'states' rights types' on the Committee," explained a Senate staffer. "It took a big lobbying job by HEW to get the federal program approved by the House back into the Senate bill."[68]

In fact, it took more than "a big lobbying job" to win Southern conservative support. It took a shift in the political and economic interests of Southern elites, and the persistent pressure of one of their leaders in the Senate, Russell Long. By the early 1970s, demographic shifts had changed the logic of public assistance in the South, and Long understood this. Waves of migration beginning in the 1940s had brought primarily young African American workers and their families to the North. This was spurred in part, Long noted, by "mechanization of the farm," which had "cut back drastically on the availability of jobs."[69] Large numbers of elderly blacks remained behind, most of whom were no longer able to work for wages. Rural Southern counties were increasingly saddled with the twin burdens of a diminishing tax base and a growing public assistance burden. One Mississippi county, for example, saw its elderly population expand from 5 to 11 percent between 1940 and 1970.[70] In Long's state of Louisiana, roughly one-third of the elderly population received Old Age Assistance for the poor, and Louisiana's OAA program had grown to the third largest in the nation.[71] Indeed, of the thirteen largest OAA programs, eight were in the South.[72]

By the time SSI was considered in Congress, therefore, Southern leaders faced a new reality. Concerns over local control of assistance for the elderly and disabled poor had diminished or been superseded by the burden of increased payments. But if these demographic changes led some policymakers to see the proposed SSI reform as less of a threat, it required the political savvy of Russell Long to see in SSI an opportunity to advance the interests of conservative Southerners in defeating FAP and promoting workfare.

For two years, Long had used his power as Finance Committee chair to block FAP. During this protracted struggle, Long developed a parallel strategy to that of delay. He would defeat FAP by proposing a sizable expansion of funding for the two categories of poor he believed should receive public assistance: those physically unable to work, and the working poor.[73] The first would eventually become SSI; the second would become the EITC.

By 1972, with FAP languishing but not yet defeated, Long made a critical move. In September, his committee announced its support for the House proposal to federalize aid to the elderly and disabled—reversing its previous position and paving the way for approval of SSI.[74] As Long later explained to his biographer, he believed that supporting federalization of the so-called adult programs for the elderly and disabled would eliminate any chance that the "family support" provisions of FAP would ever be enacted: "To keep them from coming back with something that was going to make the whole nation into a welfare state, I felt that the way to spike their guns on that would be to take all the money they estimated spending on this family program and apply that to the aged."[75]

With Long and his committee no longer an obstacle, SSI was included in the omnibus Social Security legislation passed later that year. The creation of a major new federal assistance program, SSI, was thus due in no small measure to the divergent workfare campaigns of two conservative Southern leaders who had long been protective of states' rights: Mills's drive to impose work requirements on AFDC recipients, and Long's persistent attempts to scuttle the Family Assistance Plan.

Meanwhile, the Nixon administration's strategy on the adult assistance programs also helped secure passage of SSI. Support for the program within the Nixon administration came from John Veneman and Robert Finch at HEW (both FAP supporters), and from Social Security Administration commissioner Robert Ball. Their case for SSI on Capitol Hill was critical in shaping the nascent workfare regime in public assistance.[76] Administration officials sought not only to combine the adult assistance programs for the elderly, blind, and disabled into a single federal program, but also to shift the public perception of this aid from a form of welfare to an extension of social insurance. The new program was to be federally funded; it would be indexed for inflation and would provide more stable and generous benefits than the existing adult assistance programs. Above all, it was to be administered by the respected Social Security Administration. The program was initially titled "Assistance to the Aged, Blind and Disabled." Veneman pressed to rename the program "Supplemental Security Income." This eliminated the word "assistance" and made the program sound more like the popular Social Security program. According to a staff member of the Finance Committee, the committee concurred because members "didn't want SSI called welfare."[77]

Tying SSI to Social Security solved a troublesome political dilemma for the program's administrators. By the early 1970s, Social Security had ballooned in size and reach. Yet it had drawn some criticism from liberal policymakers and activists for failing to curb poverty among the poorest Americans, many of whom did not qualify for Social Security or received extremely low payments. Presented as a "supplement" to Social Security, SSI promised to help fill these gaps.[78] Packaging SSI as an extension of Social Security rather than an expansion of welfare also made passage easier on Capitol Hill: Mills, for example, touted SSI by emphasizing its support for the elderly.[79]

The efforts of Mills, Long, and administration supporters paid off. At the close of the FAP legislative battles in the fall of 1972, House and Senate members sat down in the conference session to see what they could agree to pass as amendments to the Social Security Act. The controversial family assistance provisions were eliminated. But members did approve increases for Social Security, Medicare, and Medicaid. And they passed SSI.[80]

In the short run, SSI was billed as the one program salvaged from FAP, the program backed by both sides in the debate.[81] And, indeed, SSI created a sizable new entitlement. Its eligibility criteria promised to extend coverage to 2.8 million new recipients, an increase of nearly 50 percent.[82] The benefit floor for elderly individuals of $140 a month exceeded benefits paid in more than half the states under the old public assistance programs, and Congress indexed SSI benefits to keep pace with inflation, as it had done for the Social Security program in separate legislation earlier in the year.[83]

In the long run, however, the decision to create this program absent other elements of the FAP proposal also had a conservative impact on the politics and debate over public assistance, particularly for poor families. It reconfigured the category of nonworking poor Americans deemed worthy of federal cash assistance. Confronted with political pressure to provide a "floor" under the income of poor Americans, Southern leaders responded with SSI—saying, in effect, that the only needy Americans who should be provided a guaranteed income were those too old or disabled to earn.

The House Ways and Means Committee clarified the new rationale for SSI, as an "effective assistance program" to complement Social Security benefits for those "who because of age, disability, or blindness are not able to support themselves through work."[84] The exclusion of able-bodied adults further paved the way for the shift to workfare. Recast as potential workers, poor single mothers were "written out" of the new social contract that was SSI, along with their children—a total of eleven million AFDC recipients by 1972—who had been part of the public assistance trio since the New Deal.

Politically, the move to delink AFDC from the other two programs would also facilitate AFDC's retrenchment in later years. SSI was explicitly designed and promoted in ways that eroded political support for AFDC. Like Social Security before it, the program was billed by its advocates as superior to the AFDC "dole," in this case as a "supplement" to existing social insurance.[85] This image further tarnished AFDC as a mere "welfare" program. The distinction was more than rhetorical: AFDC's demeaning approaches to means-testing, work requirements, and paltry benefits would now mark it as a less-favored entitlement than SSI.

One of the most important consequences of the distinction arose when SSI and other social insurance programs were indexed for inflation in 1972, and AFDC was not. AFDC benefits began to erode due to inflation beginning in the 1970s and would continue to lose ground after policy cuts in the 1980s, ultimately losing nearly half their value, in real terms, over twenty years.[86] The public and policymakers would see this as an indication that AFDC was not only failing to meet its new workfarist goal of moving recipients from welfare to work, but also proving markedly less effective at meeting its old welfarist aim of reducing poverty levels among recipient families. In contrast, SSI benefits, though never generous, would more than maintain their value in real terms (and increase more than threefold in absolute terms) over the same period.[87] The contrast would further enable conservatives to persuade moderates that AFDC was uniquely ineffective and ill managed, bolstering the coalition that opposed it. At the same time, the creation of SSI for the aged and disabled poor gave moderates the political cover they needed to support conservative cuts and reforms in AFDC while still claiming that the "truly needy" and most vulnerable populations would be protected under SSI.[88]

* * *

The third policy initiative by congressional conservatives was led by Russell Long. It addressed the final category of poor Americans—those who were poor *even though they were working*. This group had been categorically excluded from New Deal public assistance programs; they were not, by definition, "unemployable." Bringing them in expanded federal assistance to the poor and helped solidify the workfare paradigm.

Like WIN II and SSI, the Earned Income Tax Credit of 1975 had its origins in FAP. In size and scope as well as political support, the EITC would eclipse AFDC by the time that program was repealed and replaced by Temporary Assistance for Needy Families (TANF) in 1996.[89] But the deeper political roots and social policy impact of the EITC's development are not well understood.[90] Because the EITC was created in response to—and promoted as a solution to—the problems of AFDC, a fateful link was forged between the EITC's ascent and AFDC's decline.

The EITC program was conceived by Long as a political solution to what he saw as a problem of welfarism run amok in the AFDC program. Its political development can be traced through several phases from conception to passage. The progression reveals how Long, its chief architect, was prodded by Nixon's initiative to develop his own plan, and how he crafted one that would meet his simultaneous aims of blocking FAP, addressing the "welfare mess," and protecting Southern interests as he perceived them.

Long's critique of FAP's welfarism spurred the first phase of the EITC's development. The senator was convinced that work should be required of able-bodied welfare recipients, and that aid should not be disbursed to them as an entitlement on the basis of need. At the start of the Senate Finance Committee hearings on FAP in the spring of 1970, Long articulated his own workfare criteria for programs for the welfare poor: they should reduce "dependency" by moving recipients from the welfare rolls into the workforce. He maintained that this had been a central aim of Congress not only since WIN but since the 1962 Public Welfare Amendments, and that the measure of any proposed reform was whether it would finally achieve this objective.[91]

FAP, in Long's view, threatened to worsen existing problems. Its weak work incentives would do no more "than repeat the failures of the existing law."[92] The Committee questioned the Nixon administration on FAP's ability to meet the goal of limiting welfare and promoting work, and by the second day of hearings, Long was exasperated: "Why don't we junk the whole thing and start all over again?"[93] He suspended the hearings the next day, demanding that the administration revise the bill—in particular, to address the relationship between FAP and other means-tested programs such as food stamps and low-income housing assistance, and the problem of built-in incentives "for able individuals to reduce or quit gainful employment in order to qualify for larger welfare benefits" (the "notch" issue).⁹⁴ When the administration sent down a revised bill in June, Long dismissed it as "a worse bill—and a more costly one."⁹⁵

Long may have been unimpressed with the evolving FAP proposal, but he was concerned about its political momentum. FAP had spotlighted the problems of the working poor, and this group was drawing broad sympathy, creating both a political imperative and an opportunity. He responded with his own proposal, triggering the second phase of the EITC's development. Poor workers, he specified, should receive assistance when no work was available and wage supplements if their hourly wages were too low.⁹⁶ The proposal reflected Long's concern for the working poor, but it was also politically shrewd. Long saw that ensuring adequate rewards to low-wage work was essential to successful welfare reform, as he and other workfarists defined it. And he knew that some initiatives—including FAP's income floor for the working poor—posed serious threats to the Southern social and economic order. He needed something less threatening.

In committee hearings on July 22, Long began to articulate the heart of what would become the EITC. "The bill could include 'wage supplements' to public or private employers which would help increase salaries of low-income employees who would otherwise qualify for welfare assistance." The idea was straightforward: require poor adults to enter the workforce, and pay employers to pay them more: "Pay private employers to put people to work. That can muster a majority in this Committee right now."⁹⁷ These early Long proposals, offered in reaction to FAP's welfarist proposals, reflected three core workfare principles. Require work of all who were physically capable of it. Reward work for those in the low-wage labor force. And preserve market incentives for workers in the process, by bolstering the wage system rather than undermining it or reforming it.

Long's emerging workfare initiative also protected the interests of Southern economic elites, precisely where FAP would undermine them. Unlike FAP, Long's proposal provided no income guarantee that would allow able-bodied workers to opt out of wage labor and collect federal benefits. It imposed a tough, non-negotiable work requirement and shielded existing labor market structures while aiding the working poor. Rather than allowing the government to provide a non-wage income source to workers, it strengthened the wage relationship with a "supplement." There would be no increase in labor costs to employers. These costs would be subsidized by government. Nor would there be ripple effects as wage pressures pushed wage levels up through the market as a whole. Long's approach, in short, would have a deeply stabilizing effect on the Southern low-wage labor market. His efforts to defend the existing low-wage sector were further reflected in legislation he introduced in mid-1971 to provide a tax deduction to employers of household or domestic labor.[98]

FAP advocates in the Nixon administration recognized the many motives behind Long's obstructionism. The senator was more than once accused of opposing FAP to preserve elite control of the Southern economy and low-wage labor force.[99] Nixon staffers also understood the distinction between FAP's welfarist approach and Long's competing workfare approach. In a memorandum to the president, John Veneman, undersecretary of HEW, explained Long's preference for using the market (through subsidies) rather than government assistance to address the problems of the working poor: "The Chairman has an idea of his own which he seems very much wedded to. He accepts the concept that the working poor need help, but instead of giving them income supplementation from the government he wants to give them higher wages than they are worth by subsidizing the employer."[100]

As Long worked behind the scenes to develop his workfare alternative, he used his position repeatedly to stave off votes on the administration's FAP plan in the spring and summer of 1970—when Nixon officials believed they had the votes to pass their plan—until the first FAP measure died in Congress late that year.[101]

The next phase in the EITC's development began early in the new congressional session, after Nixon vowed to reintroduce FAP and to make it "White House priority number one until it is enacted."[102] Long rolled up his sleeves. His primary tactics remained obstructionist and dilatory parliamentary maneuvers. But he also took steps to build a coalition behind a full-fledged workfare alternative to FAP. In the process, Long made two critical moves. The first was to tie together proposals for cutting cash assistance to many AFDC recipients with proposals for extending aid to the working poor. This made his "welfare reform" appear at once generous (to the working poor) and tough (on the welfare poor). His second move was to design and package the bonus for the working poor as a Social Security tax offset, and to bill it as "tax relief." This increased its appeal, particularly among conservatives.

The basic outlines of Long's workfare plan contained several components. Families headed by an employable father or a mother with no children under age six would no longer be eligible for any cash assistance, including AFDC. This would force some 40 percent—1.2 million families—off the AFDC rolls and into the workforce. They would instead be eligible for federally guaranteed jobs paying 60 percent of minimum wage, or for federal wage supplements if they found low-paying jobs in the private sector. Long's rationale was that this would give the parents (mostly single mothers) "an opportunity to become independent through employment, including a guaranteed job and substantial economic incentives to move into regular jobs."[103]

Current low-wage workers, under Long's plan, would also receive a "work bonus." Family heads with income under $4,000 would receive a cash refund equal to 10 percent of their wages subject to Social Security taxes. This is typically seen as the earliest form of the EITC. Long argued that this "work bonus" would offset (recently increased) Social Security taxes, act as an earnings subsidy, and prevent the taxing of poor individuals onto the welfare rolls. It was, he emphasized, distinct from a guaranteed income or a general negative income tax, because it conditioned payments on work.[104]

Conservative support for this idea would not be easy to marshal or sustain. Some conservatives opposed expanding assistance to the poor in any form. Other conservatives, such as Nixon aide Martin Anderson (a vocal internal critic of FAP), particularly resisted the idea of aiding the working poor.[105] But Long reasoned, correctly, that a plan to provide tax relief for poor workers would resonate with most conservatives far more than one seeking (as FAP did) to give the poor a "handout."

Long's proposal, however, was above all designed to serve his workfare objectives for reforming welfare. Tax equity effects were secondary. A pure argument for tax equity for the working poor, after all, would demand tax credits for *all* of those whose wages and tax burden left them below the poverty line. The aim would be to prevent the taxation of people into poverty. Long's concern was narrower: he wanted to stop the taxation of people onto the welfare rolls. He would therefore provide the tax credit only to those who might otherwise seek public assistance.

By 1972, Long's evolving plan proposed expansionary new measures, but rested on solidly conservative principles—cutting the welfare rolls, requiring work, and providing tax relief. The senator proved adept at using a range of rationales and political premises to support the proposal. He maintained that the plan was developed as a way of "relieving low-income working persons from the social security tax," but he also argued that labor market conditions called for wage supports. As Long explained on the Senate floor: "One can look at this as he wants to. He can look at it as a work subsidy for those making low wages. He can look at it as a tax refund. We decided to call it a work bonus, because, whatever one calls it, it results from tax money collected as a result of the man's working."[106] Above all, Long saw his workfare plan as a repudiation of a failed welfarism. The Finance Committee concluded "that paying an employable person a benefit based on need, the essence of the welfare approach, has not worked."[107] His plan, Long said, was clear: "If someone doesn't work, he doesn't get the payments, and that's how it should be."[108]

The Social Security bill that had been approved by the House in early 1971, with FAP as its centerpiece, finally came to the full Senate for debate in September 1972. "A floor fight over the 'workfare' provisions appeared inevitable," *Congressional Quarterly* concluded, despite broad support for other measures. "The outcome of that struggle would determine the fate of H.R. 1, once labeled 'number-one priority' by President Nixon."[109] As the debate unfolded, it became clear that Long's strategy of packaging the wage subsidy as tax relief had indeed won over some conservatives and moderates. Those concerned with the prospect of "adding" the working poor to the welfare rolls and triggering a massive expansion in public assistance through a FAP-style reform now had another way to interpret Long's plan. The exchange between Long and Lawton Chiles, a moderate Florida Democrat, illustrates the point:

> CHILES: This proposal would not be like the present family assistance program, would it, where we would take somebody not now on welfare, who is employed, but give him a monthly check and put him on the welfare rolls? This would be a way of supplementing his earnings and getting around that; would it not?
>
> LONG: That is the way we view it.[110]

In the end, the Senate voted to "pilot test" three competing welfare reform plans.[111] All three proposals were then eliminated during the conference session with the House, and Long had achieved his goal. After delaying action on the bill for almost sixteen months after FAP first passed the House, Long had helped guide Nixon's plan to its defeat.

The final phase of the EITC's development came in FAP's aftermath. Long's proposal had had instrumental value in helping to defeat FAP, but he also wanted to see it enacted. He recognized its benefits, for his region and others, and believed that it would both address the welfare problem and help the working poor. Long tried unsuccessfully to win passage of his plan in 1973 and 1974. The proposal failed to muster adequate support, in part due to lingering congressional concerns that Long's tax credit still smacked of FAP-style income guarantees.[112]

The proposal would not win passage until 1975, when it was incorporated into a major tax reduction package developed to spur the economy in the wake of the previous year's recession. In this context, Long sold his workfarist reform plan as both tax relief and economic stimulus. Christopher Howard and others have examined the factors leading to the EITC's eventual passage, including the changed legislative context and the economic recession.[113] Particularly important to the development of workfare was the battle waged and won by Long over the design of the final initiative. In a confrontation with Representative Al Ullman (D-Ore.), Long ensured that the EITC was designed as a workfare measure.

When the House took up the Ford administration's 1975 tax bill, Ullman, a political moderate who had succeeded Wilbur Mills as chair of the House Ways and Means Committee, included an "earned income credit." Clearly modeled on Long's previous work bonus proposals, it was presented by the committee as a way to "offset the impact of the Social Security taxes on low-income persons."[114] Ullman, however, had structured the provision to address the broad problem of taxing low-wage workers into poverty, as Howard demonstrated. It would therefore be available to all earners within the income limits, regardless of whether they were married or had dependent children, and would cover an estimated twenty-eight million people.[115] Ullman reduced the benefit to 5 percent of income—half of what Long had been proposing—to rein in costs. With a larger eligible population, the program was estimated to cost $3 billion in its first year—an ambitious new federal assistance program for the working poor. Long, on the other hand, intended that the EITC serve as part of his workfare vision. The tax credit, he argued, should be aimed at the current or potential welfare population, not poor workers as a whole.

The defining struggle over the shape of the EITC took place when Ullman's proposal reached the Senate. Long's Senate Finance Committee fundamentally altered the measure by shifting the target to the welfare population rather than the broader working poor population. The ceiling on earnings eligible for a full credit was raised to $8,000 and the benefit rate was moved back up to 10 percent of income, but the credit was restricted to low-income workers with dependent children—precisely the population likely to end up on AFDC rolls. The effect was to dramatically reduce the number of possible beneficiaries, to cut the overall costs to $1.5 billion (even though benefits were higher), and to make it a measure designed to address what Long's committee called its "most significant objective, to assist in encouraging people to obtain employment, reducing the unemployment rate and reducing the welfare rolls."[116] The House–Senate conference committee, dominated by Long, abandoned Ullman's vision of a broad-based EITC for all of the working poor and passed the Senate version of the bill.

As a result of Long's victory, the EITC was enacted as a workfarist response to the AFDC program. The benefit was designed to exclude not only non-earners, but also the working poor without children. Long's measure focused squarely on the problem of moving and keeping people off welfare and in the low-wage labor market, rather than the broader challenge of improving the conditions of those who are poor even though they work.[117]

Closing the 1970s: Failed Reforms in Work and Welfare

Eight years after President Richard Nixon addressed the nation with his proposal to "end the welfare mess," President Jimmy Carter made good on his own campaign pledge to produce a plan for a "complete overhaul of our welfare system."[118] Like FAP, the Carter plan (the Program for Better Jobs and Income, or PBJI) sought to introduce significant changes in public assistance by combining expanded entitlements with new work-based measures. Carter's program would scrap major assistance programs—including AFDC, the newly created SSI, and food stamps—and create a new federal structure of cash benefits, public-sector jobs, and tax credits for the poor.

Carter proposed a two-track system that cut along the familiar divide of the "employable" and "unemployable" poor. Eligible families would receive a cash grant based on income, family size, and where they fell on this divide. Unlike FAP, the Carter plan had a jobs component. It emphasized placing recipients in private-sector jobs, but it also proposed the creation of jobs and training slots for 1.4 million people in the public sector. PBJI included an expanded EITC as well. Altogether, some thirty-two million people were expected to receive benefits under PBJI, including the working poor. This was two million more than were currently aided by AFDC, SSI, and food stamps.[119]

Despite Carter's attempts to develop a more feasible initiative—and steer it through a Congress controlled by his own party—PBJI ended up going the way of FAP. A special welfare reform subcommittee was created in the House specifically to consider the proposal; it held hearings in the fall of 1977 and approved the proposal with minor modifications in February 1978. But the plan got no further on Capitol Hill.

PBJI had strong detractors from the outset. Senator Long argued that the costs would be higher than the administration claimed, and he continued to push for additional workfare measures through the fall of 1977, including a program that would allow states to require that welfare recipients work off their benefits.[120] Liberals, such as Representative William Clay (D-Mo.), charged that PBJI "doesn't even scratch the surface" of the problem of inner-city joblessness. Meanwhile, Representative Ullman—whose Ways and Means Committee had primary jurisdiction in the House—objected to the measures for the working poor and to the size of the public jobs proposal, and chose not to advance the legislation.[121] By the summer of 1978, with action stalled in the House and Long unlikely to move the measure in the Senate, PBJI was effectively dead.[122]

Liberal attempts to revive and revise favored elements of the reform failed. The Democratic Party reiterated its commitment to a national minimum welfare benefit in its 1980 platform, but the Congress failed to act on the proposal in the wake of PBJI's collapse. Carter's welfare reform initiative did trigger the first major expansion of the EITC, however. Even as PBJI foundered, lawmakers lifted the EITC provisions from the plan and took steps to strengthen the EITC through the Revenue Act of 1978. The revisions simplified and expanded eligibility, increased the maximum credit, and made the program permanent. As the proposal moved through Congress, the congressional Joint Committee on Taxation hailed the EITC as an "effective way of providing tax relief for low-income families, while at the same time providing work incentives for these individuals." The Senate Finance Committee, meanwhile, continued to tailor the program's design to help reduce the welfare rolls by stipulating that EITC benefits would be counted as earned income in determinations about welfare eligibility and benefits. This was necessary, the committee stated, to ensure that the EITC provided an adequate "incentive to work and a disincentive for being on welfare."[123] Though still limited to low-income working families with children, the program was no longer dependent on Long's annual advocacy for its survival.[124]

Detailed accounts have examined the development and collapse of the larger PBJI.[125] For purposes of this study, two conclusions about the politics of PBJI are critical. First, the Carter initiative tried but failed to build consensus within the party by combining several competing Democratic reform priorities. The plan included work requirements, but also an improved safety net for those unable to work or to find employment, and public-sector job creation to pick up the slack. The jobs proposal in PBJI built on efforts by congressional Democrats to enact emergency job creation measures and expand public service employment in the 1970s. It aimed to provide employment for all low-income families supporting children, not just those receiving AFDC. According to Labor Department estimates, 57 percent of these positions were expected to be taken by people who were "working poor" but not receiving federal cash assistance under existing programs. Like FAP, this provision of PBJI triggered intense debate over possible labor market impacts. Members of Congress debated whether "employers might fire regular workers in order to hire cheaper, government-subsidized minimum-wage employees," or whether "the government would be indirectly subsidizing employers who would have little incentive to raise their employees' salaries above the minimum wage."[126] The divisions in the party over these and other issues proved too wide to bridge through a proposal such as PBJI.

Second, the struggles over PBJI established the EITC as a prominent card to be played in debates over welfare reform. Politically, it was championed as a favored approach to work and welfare by an increasing number of lawmakers from across the political spectrum by the late 1970s. Conservatives such as Long advanced the EITC alongside an agenda to restrict or eliminate AFDC. As Long sought to make the EITC permanent, he pushed his own workfare measures for AFDC recipients.[127] He also crafted conservative proposals for dismantling AFDC that closely resembled the welfare reforms of 1996. Indeed, in 1979, Long introduced legislation to transform AFDC into a fixed block grant to the states, and to allow states to require work as a condition for eligibility.[128] The plan won bipartisan support on the Senate Finance Committee, but went no further.

Moderates, meanwhile, sought to use the EITC not to replace outright, but to "fill in" for some of the more controversial welfare cash assistance. In response to PBJI, for example, Ullman developed a competing plan that would have retained food stamps, SSI, and AFDC, but phased out benefits at a lower level. He argued that the difference would be made up by the expanding EITC if the recipient were in a private-sector job. In the words of a congressional staffer: "They're getting the same amount of money but from an employer through the earned income tax credit instead of from the government. It reduces the stigma and saves going to the welfare office."[129]

Liberals, for their part, used the EITC to supplement existing aid and entitlements. In the fall of 1978, after PBJI negotiations ground to a halt, Senator Edward Kennedy (D-Mass.) introduced a liberal welfare reform measure that included a minimum national AFDC benefit level of 65 percent of the poverty level—and an expanded EITC.[130] The EITC program thus emerged from the Carter years with a wide range of supporters. Equally important to its development, however, was its evolving political relationship to AFDC. Only liberals saw the EITC primarily as a way to extend an entitlement to cash assistance to a new population of working families in addition to welfare families. For both conservatives and moderates, much of the EITC's political value lay in its potential to solve the problems—and reduce the costs—of AFDC. The EITC's broadening appeal and political strength thus hinged in part on AFDC's political weakness.

Also significant for the EITC's emerging role was the political and economic context of its early expansion. The program was becoming a favored stopgap measure to aid low-wage workers at a time of increasing economic hardship. When the EITC won passage as a minor provision of an economic stimulus package promoted by President Ford in response to the 1974 recession, it introduced a new (and narrower) policy response to the growing problem of economic insecurity.

Congressional liberals supported the EITC but many shared a more ambitious policy agenda in the early and mid-1970s. In late 1974, they had passed (and Ford had signed) an Emergency Jobs and Unemployment Assistance Act. It provided aid for workers not eligible for benefits under existing state and federal unemployment rules, and it included $2.5 billion to create short-term public service jobs through the Comprehensive Employment and Training Act (CETA) program created in 1973.[131] In 1975, Democrats followed up by passing a $5.3 billion jobs bill, designed to create more than a million new jobs, which Ford vetoed.[132] Seeking longer-term solutions, liberal policymakers revived campaigns to commit the federal government to achieving full employment (through the Full Employment and Balanced Growth Act of 1976, dubbed the Humphrey–Hawkins bill for its sponsors), and to raising the floor beneath wages (through increasing and indexing the minimum wage). They faced fierce opposition from conservative lawmakers and business groups on both fronts, and their legislative accomplishments fell short of their aims.¹³³ In the wake of these stymied efforts, the EITC emerged as a far more limited—but more politically viable—approach to assisting low-income workers in hard times.

* * *

The 1970s began and ended with bold presidential initiatives to overhaul American public assistance and extend government income support to working-poor families. The public assistance system created in the New Deal was remade in fundamental ways. But the transformation was not carried out by Presidents Nixon or Carter, nor by liberal welfarists in Congress, who had defined much of the welfare state's expansion since 1935. It was led instead by conservative Southern Democrats in Congress who opposed the presidential initiatives. And it was done, piece by piece, in a way that reflected and reinforced their commitment to promoting work, limiting welfare entitlements, and protecting Southern interests in maintaining control over local labor markets. In combination, the policy changes they introduced lay the foundation for a new workfare approach to public assistance in the United States.

The decade also began and ended, however, with a series of economic developments that altered the debate over work and welfare. In the early 1970s, the drive for welfarist expansion through Nixon's Family Assistance Plan was undermined in part by a recession that helped spike the AFDC rolls just as Congress was debating the proposal. In the mid-1970s, the need to respond to a sharp economic recession provided both the policy rationale and the political vehicle for the creation of the Earned Income Tax Credit. By the end of the decade, as the next chapter will show, deeper and more enduring shifts in the labor market had begun to change conditions facing both the welfare and the working poor—and the political trajectory of programs for each.

CHAPTER 4

The Political Economy of Work and Welfare

By the mid-1970s, successive policy changes had conditioned a growing proportion of federal public assistance on private employment. Only the elderly and disabled poor were categorically exempt from work. Others eligible for aid, through new programs such as the EITC or old ones such as AFDC, were either already working or increasingly expected to do so. Although the decisive battles over AFDC were still to come, these changes had begun to redirect public assistance. They had also eroded one of the defining distinctions between the social insurance and public assistance programs of the New Deal welfare state, by bringing core assistance programs for poor families into the broader ambit of employment-based programs.

Despite the growing link between aid and employment, the state of the labor market had triggered little serious policy debate in the battles over WIN I or II, FAP, or the EITC. Certainly, the initiatives had produced heated arguments over work and welfare. Would aiding poor workers lead them to work less? Under what conditions should welfare recipients be expected to work? The overriding focus of these debates, however, was the likely behavior of current and potential *workers*—rather than the constraints of *work* in the existing labor market, and particularly the low-wage sector in which most poor workers labored.

This limited debate reflected a deep ideological divide over the role and functions of work for poor families. For many workfarists, the principle that the able-bodied poor must earn their own support was a moral, not an economic, question and was not predicated on labor market conditions. Indeed, Southern conservatives had pursued reforms during the FAP debate precisely to preserve this obligation under the adverse conditions of the Southern low-wage economy, arguing in several cases that even under these conditions the experience of work would reform the character of the poor families that engaged in it. Southerners successfully fought for changes to the FAP proposal by asserting that no job should be considered "unsuitable" for a welfare recipient. And Senator Russell Long explicitly assured his supporters that unlike FAP, his proposed alternative would not alter the terms and conditions of the South's low-wage system. He and others promoted the EITC specifically as a means to supplement wages without undermining work incentives or the wage structure of the existing private labor market.

The welfarist position, in contrast, suggested that work should be both a moral obligation and a means to an adequate livelihood. Since the New Deal, the latter expectation was embodied in policies ranging from the federal minimum wage and workplace health and safety regulations to social insurance programs such as unemployment insurance and Social Security. These policies were designed to ensure that employment delivered a basic minimum of economic security and well-being, even in an uncertain market.[1] The moral obligation to work, meanwhile, was inscribed not only in the rules conditioning social insurance benefits on employment, but also in the understanding that those able to work for wages would not be eligible for public assistance for the poor.

Because New Deal public assistance was nominally reserved for the "unemployable" poor, welfarists had little reason to confront labor market conditions in early debates over aid to the poor. Since the 1960s, however, workfarists had pushed for and won policy compromises on the work question. Liberal Democrats in the administration (in 1967) and in Congress (in 1971) eventually accepted federal work requirements for the welfare poor, and growing reliance on the EITC for the working poor. Welfarists had reached such compromises in part because they remained confident that welfare-to-work goals could be achieved largely through carrots (services, supports, and positive incentives) without resorting to sticks (strict work requirements with benefit cutoffs). They believed that federal policy could support and promote work for recipients willing and able to do so, while still retaining the guarantee of a basic safety net for those unable to find or hold a job. Liberal Democrats also clung to the New Deal notion that those who did enter the labor market would find economic security through a combination of wages and access to social insurance benefits such as unemployment insurance and Social Security. Yet precisely as workfare reforms in public assistance took root in the 1970s, the character and promise of work itself began to change in ways that fundamentally undercut these welfarist premises, especially for workers in the low-wage labor market.

The central argument of this chapter is that beginning in the mid-1970s, structural shifts in the labor market limited the ability of work and related welfare-state programs to deliver the levels of social protection they were designed to provide.[2] This transformation not only created new sources of insecurity for large numbers of working Americans. It also undermined the logic of welfare-to-work reforms in AFDC and limited the ability of the EITC's wage subsidy to provide sustained economic security for the working poor. By the 1980s, employment conditions made welfarist compromises and strategies increasingly untenable in the low-wage labor market. And as liberal measures failed to move recipients from welfare to work, workfarists would push for tougher policies in the 1980s and 1990s— and win.

This argument demands a turn from the politics of public assistance to the political economy of work and welfare. It requires attention to the assumptions about the labor market embedded not only in the emerging workfarist public assistance policies, but also in the traditional work-based social insurance programs of the New Deal welfare state. The first section of this chapter steps back historically, briefly returning to the 1930s and 1940s to examine the New Deal system of social provision and its premise that economic growth and work-based social protections would meet the challenge of providing basic security to most Americans. The second section uses labor market and survey data to demonstrate that the core New Deal assumptions about the character of work were systematically undermined by new labor market conditions beginning in the 1970s. The analysis tracks changes from the 1970s first to the mid-1990s (when the demise of AFDC and the expansion of the EITC marked the end of welfare and the arrival of workfare), and then to the first decade of the 2000s (when the workfare regime was consolidated). Throughout the post-1970s period, the evidence suggests, labor market changes rendered many welfare-state programs less effective at meeting their own objectives of providing adequate social protections for working Americans. These effects were particularly damaging for the poor and near-poor, and programs such as the EITC and AFDC were ill suited to address the new economic insecurities they encountered.

New Deal Social Provision and the Limits of Growth

The broad system of social provision that emerged from the New Deal rested on the principle of work. Access to benefits within the core social insurance programs of the welfare state assumed that those willing and able to work would find adequate employment on reasonable terms. Yet government policies were not in place to ensure that this condition was met, for reasons explored by Margaret Weir and other scholars.[3] Their absence not only created income uncertainty and hardships for working families. It also left the New Deal system of social provision on a shaky foundation.

This was not, of course, the intent of New Deal planners as they prepared the outlines of the Social Security Act in 1934. President Roosevelt's Committee on Economic Security (CES) was acutely aware that their system of permanent social protections depended on the availability of jobs, and they focused great attention on the problem of unemployment. The logic of the New Deal system was that all who were able to work were expected to find jobs that would give them access to work-based social insurance (such as Social Security and unemployment insurance) as the economy recovered and coverage was expanded. Those who were poor and unable to earn (such as the elderly, blind, and single mothers with dependent children) would have access to public assistance programs as a safety net of last resort. The leading framers of the Social Security Act expected that public assistance would diminish as the economy and employment levels grew, social insurance increased, and poverty levels dropped.[4]

Central to the CES's vision was the notion of guaranteed employment. "As the major contribution of the Federal Government in providing a safeguard against unemployment," the CES report to the president stated, "we suggest employment assurance—the stimulation of private employment and the provision of public employment for those able-bodied workers whom industry cannot employ at a given time."[5] Initially, the Social Security Act's formulators envisioned extensions of New Deal public works and employment programs. By the late 1930s, many New Dealers were advocating social Keynesian measures, designed to combine steady and substantial levels of social welfare spending with macroeconomic stimulus to promote equitable growth with full employment. Their proposals included public job creation where necessary, robust social welfare programs (including national health insurance), and broader labor protections. Many economists also pressed for job policies to retrain and relocate workers after the war to ensure full employment.[6]

Such social Keynesian measures would have forged a significantly different relationship between social policies and the labor market, and generated a more expansive debate over work and welfare. But these proposals met fierce opposition from conservative lawmakers backed by private interests. In 1938 and 1939, Congress rejected President Roosevelt's proposed administrative reorganization—which would have enabled the president to carry out public investment, economic planning, and coordination—and his spending measures to stimulate the economy and boost employment. The spending bill fell victim to the newly emboldened conservative coalition of Southern Democrats and Republicans. The conservatives were united against Northern Democrats, who lost an astounding seventy-two seats in the 1938 House elections.[7] The same coalition hobbled New Deal plans for a stable new federal minimum wage by insisting that Congress—not an independent board—retain the power to set the wage level and determine subsequent increases.[8] Four years later, the conservative coalition defunded the National Resources Planning Board, institutional home of social Keynesian planners in the federal government.[9]

Cognizant of the stakes, business leaders fought alongside conservative lawmakers to restrict the scope and reach of New Deal initiatives ranging from temporary job creation (through programs such as the Works Progress Administration) and labor reforms (through the Wagner Act), to social protections (through the Social Security Act) and workplace regulation (through the Fair Labor Standards Act).[10] Employers recognized that the Depression had sown grave doubts about the capacity of the private sector to chart a path to growth that would meet the nation's employment needs and protect against widespread economic insecurity.[11] Led by groups such as the National Association of Manufacturers (NAM), business leaders launched a protracted public relations counteroffensive beginning in the late 1930s to persuade Americans that their interests lay with private-sector-led growth strategies, rather than with labor unions, government regulation, and the emerging welfare state.[12]

A major showdown over work and social policy came in the struggle over a proposed plan for full employment in 1945, perceived by proponents and critics alike as the cornerstone of the liberal social Keynesian agenda. The proposed full employment bill sought to establish that all Americans "able to work and seeking work" had the right to steady, full-time employment—and to commit the federal government to guarantee that right, through government spending or hiring if needed to close periodic gaps in national investment and employment levels.[13] When the bill passed with overwhelming support in the Senate in September 1945, Southern Democrats and Midwestern Republicans, backed by employer groups, mobilized to defeat or dilute the legislation in the House.[14] Representative Will Whittington, a conservative Democrat from Mississippi, teamed up with the Chamber of Commerce to produce a House alternative that stripped the bill of its commitment to public-sector investment and job creation. Whittington's substitute passed the House and ultimately prevailed.[15]

The defeat of the full employment bill signaled the beginning of a larger political retreat, leaving social Keynesians and their political allies on the defensive and disarmed.[16] What emerged in the aftermath was a more conservative commercial Keynesianism, acceptable to moderates in the business community, that advocated limited fiscal and monetary policies and deeper reliance on business to secure growth with minimal government intervention in the terms on which employers created jobs.[17] Subsequent efforts to commit the federal government to achieving full employment, notably the Humphrey–Hawkins legislation of the 1970s, also collapsed in the face of mobilized opposition by conservative lawmakers and business.[18]

The failure to enact employment guarantees left the ideological and institutional foundations of New Deal social provision vulnerable. The ideological vision of growth with equity was compromised. Social welfare policies were increasingly separated from pro-growth macroeconomic policies; by the 1980s they would be cast as impediments to economic expansion. Institutionally, the failure to win employment assurance left a gap between the intended aims of New Deal welfare-state planners and the system they created. In principle, the New Deal welfare state sought to provide modest federal guarantees of protection for those willing and able to work when they confronted circumstances beyond their control (such as old age, illness, or temporary layoffs). This was the rationale behind work-based social insurance, and it was reflected in policies governing access to, eligibility for, and benefits in core programs such as Unemployment Compensation and Social Security. But in the absence of employment guarantees, the system was precariously dependent on a strong private labor market to deliver on this promise.

At first, the limits of the New Deal system were obscured, as the social risks and costs of the system's dependence on labor market conditions were not fully recognized in the political and economic climate of the postwar era. The expanding economy brought job creation, high employment, and steady increases in wage levels and income equality, and pro-market business and political leaders insisted that the nation's social needs could be met largely through continued private-sector-led growth.[19] Policymakers across the political spectrum were eager to embrace economic growth as the best "solution" to poverty. Unlike other policy options, it demanded no difficult tradeoffs, no debates over the causes of poverty or the role of government in addressing these problems, no thorny decisions over how much help—and what kind—was most effective. The idea was captured by President John Kennedy's image—repeated by Ronald Reagan twenty years later—that "a rising tide lifts all boats."

If the Depression stood as the prime example of how economic collapse causes poverty to skyrocket due to high unemployment levels, the first three decades of the postwar period seemed to offer compelling evidence that growth drives down unemployment levels and poverty rates. The country saw its longest and strongest economic expansion to date between 1961 and 1969, a period in which the economy grew an average of 4.6 percent a year after inflation. The impact on poverty levels was dramatic: some 22 percent of Americans lived in families below the official poverty line in 1960; only 13 percent did by 1970. Although the War on Poverty and new programs such as Medicare and Medicaid transformed the economic circumstances of millions of low-income Americans in these years, leading economists agreed that rapid economic growth was the driving force behind falling aggregate poverty levels.[20] The presumed link between economic expansion and falling poverty rates was private employment: when the economy grew, the logic went, employers created jobs, and poverty and social needs declined. At the aggregate level, the solution to economic insecurity seemed to be growth; at the individual level, the answer was work.

Not until the structural economic shifts of the 1970s did it become clear that the link between growth and economic security was not as direct as it seemed, and that a system of social welfare provision tied to work created profound vulnerabilities. Even then, it took more than a decade for the findings of labor market economists to penetrate the policy debate, so strong was the confidence that economic growth alone could ensure adequate security for working Americans. In 1986, economists Rebecca Blank and Alan Blinder used historical data running from 1959 through the early 1980s to demonstrate that job expansion and falling unemployment strongly correlated with decreased poverty levels. On the basis of the evidence, they predicted a steep decline in poverty over the mid- to late 1980s, as the economy recovered from the severe recession at the beginning of the decade. But events proved the model wrong. For most of the 1980s (from 1983 to 1989), the U.S. economy experienced its second longest and strongest economic expansion to date, growing an average of 3.7 percent per year. Despite growth rates that approached those of the 1960s, however, poverty fell only modestly.[21] Blank, a senior staff economist for the Council of Economic Advisors in 1989, explained how difficult it was to recognize that the long-standing premise was flawed:

> One of our responsibilities was to produce short memos for the White House when major economic statistics were released, summarizing the implications of these data. In October, the Census Bureau released its annual report on income and poverty for 1988, which happened to be a year of very strong economic growth and rising average personal incomes. Oddly, however, the poverty rate fell by an insignificant amount that year. I wrote up my summary and brought it back to my boss for approval. He read it through, handed it back to me, and said, "Add a paragraph explaining why poverty didn't fall last year." I dutifully went back to my desk, sat down at my computer, stared at it a while, and realized I had no explanation to offer.[22]

In the 1990s, the trend deepened. A mild two-year recession in 1990 and 1991 triggered an expected increase in poverty. But the economic expansion that began in 1992 utterly failed to reverse this increase: poverty continued to rise in both 1992 and 1993, despite a growing economy. When the government released its official statistics on income and poverty in November 1994, the numbers revealed a further, inexplicable development: in 1993, when the rate of aggregate economic growth after inflation was a healthy 3 percent—and the unemployment rate was falling—the proportion of Americans who were poor actually *rose*.²³ For the first time in modern U.S. history, poverty rates were rising as they had historically in times of economic downturn—but were not reliably falling with economic growth. Subsequent years—both the high-growth late 1990s and the slow-growth 2000s—bore out the same trend, with poverty rates remaining in the 12 percent range through most of both periods.²⁴

The problem, as Blank and others discovered, was that the link between growth, employment, and poverty was not nearly as robust as assumed. A growing economy can bring higher employment, and employment levels do have an effect on poverty rates. But so too do the terms and conditions of employment, including job stability and wage and benefit levels. This made sense of the confusing trends. In the expansion of the 1960s, job growth was an important factor behind falling poverty rates, but so were wage levels, which rose for virtually all workers. Each 1 percent expansion in the economy during the 1960s was associated with a $2.18 increase in weekly wages (after inflation) for workers in low-income families.²⁵ As employees both worked more hours and earned more per hour, poverty dropped dramatically.

In the expansion of the 1980s (1983 to 1989), unemployment fell even more quickly and the weeks of work by low-income households rose at a faster rate than in the 1960s expansion. However, wages had entered a long period of decline and stagnation. During the growth years of the 1980s, a 1 percent expansion in the aggregate economy was correlated with a thirty-two-cent decline in weekly wages for the poorest 10 percent of Americans. Thus in the economy of the 1980s, falling wages offset expanding employment opportunities for many. The overall result was a drop in poverty in the 1980s, but a much slower one than in the 1960s. By the economic expansion of the 1990s, declining poverty rates could no longer be assumed. Even as the economy expanded starting in 1992, AFDC caseloads kept rising, reaching a record high in 1994. Wages for less-skilled workers continued to fall through the first half of the decade, and as late as 1997, the poverty rate of 13.3 percent was still higher than it had been at the end of the 1980s. Poverty levels finally dipped below 12 percent from 1999 to 2001, but then climbed back above that level through the expansion of the early 2000s and the slow recovery that began in 2009.²⁶ Another development further complicated the relationship between growth, employment, and economic security in the 2000s: growth resumed after recessions, but without bringing high employment levels. These were the so-called jobless recoveries that followed the recessions of 2001 and 2007–9, and they too suppressed wage increases for workers.

The evidence was in. Even in the context of a growing economy, poverty could continue apace, unemployment could remain high, and wage gains for working families could no longer be assumed.

Doors, Floors, Ladders, and Nets: Four Flawed Assumptions

These trends signaled a deeper, structural change in the character and conditions of employment beginning in the mid- to late 1970s. The growing economy did not yield an aggregate decline in poverty in part because work no longer delivered the economic security it once had. The sources of this transformation are familiar: in the late 1960s and early 1970s, many American businesses responded to a drop in profit rates and a rise in competitive pressures with strategies to reduce labor costs and increase workforce flexibility. These included downsizing and reorganizing internal firm hierarchies, outsourcing and offshoring production, imposing or negotiating reductions in pay and benefits, and increasing the use of part-time, temporary, and other contingent labor.[27] Employers' responses, in turn, created new conditions in the labor market that were in many cases beyond the scope of existing social policies. Declining unionization further undercut institutional sources of protection for workers.

The resulting labor market shifts not only affected the living standards of working families. They also distorted and undermined many of the social protections designed precisely to cushion their impact. The system of social provision created during and after the New Deal, I argue, embodied a set of core assumptions about the basic character and conditions of work. Each has since been unraveled by employer strategies and the larger structural economic shifts of the post-1970s period—and as a consequence, many welfare-state programs less adequately meet their aims of providing security against what FDR called the "hazards and vicissitudes of life."

Simply put, work under the New Deal system was expected to provide *doors, floors, ladders,* and *nets* for all who were willing and able to seek and hold a job.[28] Workers could expect to find, first, *open doors* to employment: the assumption was that adequate employment would be available for all who were willing to work, and that unemployment (or underemployment) in a growing economy was therefore, in most cases, voluntary and willful. The second assumption was that there were *stable floors* under most jobs: those prepared to work well and steadily could expect security and stability from their jobs over time. Third, work would provide *income ladders* for workers whose job performance was solid: they could expect adequate and rising incomes over the course of their working lives. For those starting out in low-wage jobs, the assumption was that steady work could earn entry to middle-class jobs. Finally, jobs would be equipped with *safety nets* providing protections against unavoidable hardships, such as illness, old age, disability, and temporary unemployment.

Significantly, these four assumptions applied not simply to the "best jobs" at the high end of the wage scale, but to the average job in the post–New Deal labor market. Likewise, the "model worker" of the New Deal welfare state was not expected to be highly skilled, educated, or exceptionally motivated—only to be willing to accept and hold a job, and to perform adequately and consistently on the job over time. This much earned the worker access to social protections. Benefit levels—for programs such as Social Security and unemployment insurance—were typically pegged to wages and/or longevity on the job, as time and effort at work brought rising earnings and job tenures. The welfare state, in short, was designed to support most workers in most jobs. And as long as its core assumptions held, the structure of the system appeared clear and compelling.[29] But by the late 1970s, fewer workers met the criteria for earning the welfare state's social insurance entitlements—not because there were fewer "model workers" prepared to work hard and steadily, but because there were far fewer "model jobs" that met the assumptions of the work-based welfare state. As a result, problems arose with each of the welfare state's core premises.

Labor market data illuminate the pattern of circumstances facing workers and current or potential public assistance recipients, including several subgroups that are overrepresented among the poor and near-poor (women, racial and ethnic minorities, younger workers, and workers with less education).[30] The data (including multi-year studies compiled in *The State of Working America*)[31] illustrate trends beginning in the mid-1970s as the shift to work-based public assistance began in earnest, and continuing through the first decade of the 2000s, when the workfare state was consolidated. As the numbers show, the trends were not fundamentally reversed by the high growth of the late 1990s; likewise, they were exacerbated by the historic recession of 2007–9 but were not resolved by the end of that recession.

Open Doors: The "Available Employment" Assumption

One of the central premises built into the post–New Deal welfare state was that those seeking work would find it. The decision to ground most social insurance protections in employment—rather than in a basic incomes policy or a family-wage system provided to all—meant that welfare-state programs rested on the proposition that work was generally available on a steady and full-time basis for all who wanted it. Lack of work was therefore voluntary or temporary, and it could be weathered with short-term unemployment insurance. This assumption was extended from social insurance to the public assistance realm through various workfare policies, which promoted or rewarded work based on the notion that it was available and offered a reliable route out of poverty.

Despite the failure to provide employment assurance, official unemployment levels remained relatively low for most of the postwar period. The unemployment rate in 1947 was below 4 percent, near the 3 percent rate that economists consider "frictional," reflecting the level of job switching and job searching that would occur in any labor market. Over subsequent decades, unemployment rose periodically, but a comparison across business cycle peaks demonstrates that over time, postwar unemployment rates were largely held in check, particularly through the early 1970s. The average unemployment rate between business cycle peaks rose in the 1970s and 1980s then trended down again in the mid-1990s, reaching a generational low of 4 percent in 2000. Unemployment hovered around 5 percent for most of the 2000s; it shot above 10 percent in the wake of the 2007–9 recession and remained elevated for years into the recovery.[32] On balance, however, the postwar unemployment record suggests that for most of the past six decades, most Americans seeking work have found it.

These indicators make the assumption that work is available (and that nonwork is therefore voluntary) appear reasonable. There are problems with this conclusion, however. The unemployment rate is an effective measure of the percentage of people *who are actively seeking work* among the total who are at work or searching for it. But it does not measure the population underlying the "work availability" assumption of the New Deal welfare state—that is, those who are *willing and able to work* but unable to find it.

To begin with, the unemployment rate measures those seeking work at a specific moment in time. If the metric shifts, to count all of those workers who experience unemployment at some point in a given year, the rate can be more than twice as high.[33] The unemployment rate also does not include several clearly identifiable groups that are seeking adequate work but cannot find it. It does not count "discouraged workers" who want to work but have been discouraged from looking by their failure to find jobs. Nor does it include other "marginally attached" workers—such as those who are neither working nor searching at the moment, but who indicate that they want and have looked for work in the past twelve months. Finally, it does not include "involuntary part-timers" who are working part-time, but want to work full-time. These descriptions apply to a significant number of EITC recipients (particularly those who are working but want more hours) and welfare recipients (particularly those who cycle in and out of welfare programs and unstable jobs).[34]

The total population of involuntary nonworkers and part-timers is captured in the *underemployment rate*, calculated by the Bureau of Labor Statistics only since 1994.[35] Although the rate rises and falls with the economy, the number of underemployed Americans has grown in recent decades.[36] The underemployment rate is often nearly twice the unemployment rate. It is a far more robust—and troubling—measure of the employment success of those willing and able to work, and it is this larger population that the welfare state arguably sought to protect from labor market failures.[37] Even when unemployment rates are low, widespread underemployment erodes the premise that adequate work is reliably available to those who seek it and poses a stark challenge to the effectiveness of U.S. social provision.

There is another problem with assuming the availability of work based on the official unemployment rate: it is an aggregate measure. If the aggregate rate hides deep and persistent differences in the employment prospects of different groups, it is a misleading indicator of whether all who are willing and able to work are finding employment. Evidence suggests this is clearly the case for two groups: racial and ethnic minorities (particularly African American and Hispanic workers) and workers with less education.

Unemployment rates for African American workers are consistently nearly double those of white workers; this held true even in the tight labor markets of the late 1990s, when unemployment rates for blacks began to fall. In 2008, the first year of the Great Recession, the annual unemployment rate for whites was 5.2 percent; for blacks it was nearly twice as high, 10.1 percent. For Hispanics it was 7.6 percent.[38] Unemployment climbed faster for blacks and Hispanics during the downturn, and remained elevated for longer: in 2009, black unemployment reached an annual rate of 12.4 percent, and four years into the recovery in 2013, it was still 12.1 percent, again nearly twice the rate for whites.[39] Even more daunting unemployment rates face workers with lower levels of education. In the mid-1990s, the unemployment rate for those with less than a high school degree was 15 percent—five times that of workers with a four-year college degree. The gap diminished with the tight labor markets of the late 1990s, but at the outset of the 2007–9 recession, and five years into the recovery, it was still more than three times as high.[40]

The data suggest that over a period of decades, the unemployment rates of minorities and less-educated workers have frequently been between two and four times as high as the rates for more advantaged workers. Underemployment rates have also been disproportionately high.[41] For young workers in these categories, the unemployment and underemployment rates have rivaled the general unemployment rate of the United States in the Great Depression. Even in the strong economy of the late 1990s, the unemployment and underemployment rates for young black workers with less than a high school degree were staggering: 21.3 percent were unemployed, and 32.7 percent were underemployed.[42] The fact that entire groups of workers who want to work are consistently unable to secure jobs—in good economic times as well as bad—casts further doubt on the assumption that work is available to all who seek it and that nonwork is voluntary.

The post-1970s period has also seen significant and troubling changes in the duration of unemployment. The average length of an unemployment spell rose from 8.6 weeks in 1970 to 12.6 in 2000, then climbed sharply and stood at 16.8 percent in 2007, before the Great Recession. The percentage of the unemployed who were "long-termers" (without work for fifteen weeks or more) has doubled over time, from 16.2 percent in 1970 to 32 percent in 1996, about where it remained a decade later, in 2007. In the recession month of September 2009, the percentage of long-termers reached an astonishing 55.9 percent, and it remained extremely high (47.6 percent) five years later, in September 2014.[43] Racial differences again emerge, under both strong and weak economic conditions. In both 1997 and 2007, unemployment spells for black workers were on average five weeks longer than those of white workers, a gap that remained in 2013.[44]

Table 4.1 Length of Unemployment Spells

Year	Average Weeks Unemployed	Year	Average Weeks Unemployed
1968	9.4	1992	16.1
1970	7.9	1994	18.6
1972	12.1	1996	16.1
1974	9.5	1998	15.6
1976	16.6	2000	13.1
1978	12.9	2002	14.7
1980	10.4	2004	19.9
1982	13.4	2006	16.9
1984	20.4	2008	17.5
1986	14.8	2010	30.3
1988	14.2	2012	40.1
1990	11.8	2014	35.4

Source: U.S. Department of Labor, Bureau of Labor Statistics, "Average Weeks Unemployed (Seasonally Adjusted)," Labor Force Statistics from the Current Population Survey (data reported in January each year).
Note: The average length of unemployment spells rises with recessions and falls with recoveries, but it has trended gradually upward in the post-1970s period. It rose steeply during and after the 2007–9 recession.

Some of the factors fueling these higher unemployment rates and spells are deeply rooted and familiar; race-based distinctions are enduring features of the U.S. labor market, for example. But long-standing discriminatory trends have been exacerbated by newer features of the labor market, resulting from the particular character of job creation and restructuring in recent decades. The demand for more educated and skilled workers in certain sectors of the economy, for example, marks a structural change in the labor market, and its impact has fallen disproportionately on less-advantaged workers.[45] The result, given the work-based eligibility and benefit rules of the welfare state, too often has been to leave less-educated and less-skilled workers not only without work, but without access to the social protections that work provides. Likewise, the rise of contingent labor represents a new and growing source of underemployment and diminishing access to social protections, particularly for low-wage workers.

Both trends complicate the effort to move people from welfare to work, and expand the pool of potential EITC recipients. Welfare-to-work requirements, absent a job guarantee, increase the pressure on workfare recipients to enter the labor force but do not diminish the limitations to job availability they face there. The EITC is based on a different strategy—increasing the work incentives of the poor by boosting the returns to low-income work—but it too fails to address the question of job availability.

Stable Floors: The "Job Security" Assumption

A second core premise of the New Deal welfare state was that those willing to work could expect to find and hold stable, regular employment over time. Most jobs came with solid "floors" beneath them, and as long as a worker performed adequately, that worker could expect to continue working and drawing steady earnings. This is a premise of modern workfare policies as well: adults who secure jobs are expected to remain gainfully employed.

The model that guided the development of welfare-state benefits was long-term attachment to a single employer; and the job security assumption was embodied in the welfare state in two ways.[46] First, specified job tenure periods became the direct path of entry to several social insurance programs, including government-provided unemployment insurance and Social Security, as well as government-subsidized health and pension plans provided by employers or unions. Typically, a worker is eligible for these programs only if he or she has held a given job for a certain period of time. Less directly, longevity on the job is rewarded through increased benefit levels for many programs, such as civil service retirement programs: benefits are calibrated in part to reward those who have held their jobs the longest.

Longevity seemed a reasonable and equitable basis for determining eligibility and benefits in the first few decades of the postwar economy. Failure to hold a single job over time was assumed to reflect the choices and actions of individual workers, not the limited time span or changing terms of the job itself. One of the hallmarks of the post-1970s economy, however, was the shift from secure to short-term or contingent work. Increasingly, there was no "floor" under the jobs created in the economy, no guarantee that a job would be in place as long as the worker was.

Job tenure (length of time on the job) is the most common measure of stability in employment. Tenure levels are generally divided by age group, to adjust for the inevitably shorter tenures of younger workers. From 1963 to 2008, tenure for men in all age groups fell. The median time a forty-five- to fifty-four-year-old male worker spent with his current employer fell from

11.4 years in 1963 to 8.2 in 2008. Women consistently have lower tenure levels than men of the same age, although their rates are rising. A woman in the same age group saw her tenure rise from 6.1 years to 7.0 years during this time frame; most of the increase happened before 1987.[47] The median tenure of *all* workers was 4.1 in January 2008, although rates vary significantly by age and industry. Among the major occupational groups, workers in the service sector had the shortest median tenure, at 2.8 years. This sector also comprises the single largest occupational category (accounting for more than a third) of low-wage workers.[48] A similar trend emerges in studies of the share of all jobs that are "long-term." Over the past thirty years, the percentage of workers who have held their jobs for a decade or longer has dropped, with the period from the 1980s to the 2000s showing significant declines.[49]

Guided by old assumptions about the longevity of jobs, some have argued that tenure levels may be falling simply because workers are choosing to change jobs more often to pursue new or better opportunities, rather than because they are facing layoffs and shorter-term jobs. The evidence suggests, however, that much of the drop has not been by choice. Rates of "involuntary job loss" rose in the 1980s, with "position abolished" more often cited as the reason for job loss, even during economic recovery years. From January 2005 to December 2007, some 8.2 million workers were displaced. Company or plant closings or moves accounted for 45 percent of the displacements; positions or shifts abolished was the second most common factor, at 31 percent.[50] During the 2007–9 recession, the number of displaced workers nearly doubled, to 15.4 million, with "insufficient work" cited as the most common reason for job loss. Displacements slowed after the massive job losses of the recession, but still affected 9.5 million workers from 2011 to 2013; closings, shift or position eliminations, and insufficient work were cited as causes of these displacements in nearly equal measure.[51]

These findings on job insecurity are reinforced by data from nationally representative surveys between 1978 and 2002. Except during the last years of the 1990s, workers reported declining confidence that their jobs would remain in place as long as their performance was adequate. Thirty-four percent reported that it would be "very easy" to find another job with the same pay and benefits in 1989, and only 24 percent did in 2002.[52] Evidence supported these workers' bleak assessments. Interview data covering the period from 1981 to 2007 show that when questioned one to three years after their displacements, more than a third of workers were out of work (with the exception of the late 1990s). Those who did find work drew lower pay and fewer benefits. More than a quarter of those who had health insurance in their old jobs were not covered in their new ones.[53] Of the 15.4 million who lost their jobs between 2007 and 2009, only 49 percent were re-employed in January 2010, the lowest level since the survey began in the 1980s. And more than half of those who were re-employed after losing stable jobs reported a cut in earnings in their new positions.[54]

The larger story behind these numbers has drawn increasing attention in recent years. The loss of jobs with certain characteristics (longevity and stability)—and the creation of new jobs with different ones (contingency and instability)—have fueled a basic transformation in the character of work. If the data on displacement document what has been lost, the spread of contingent jobs tells the rest of this story.

The rise in nonstandard and irregular work is another hallmark of the post-1970s economy, most prominent once again in the low-wage sector. By the mid-2000s, more than 30 percent of workers were employed in situations that were not regular full-time jobs. As with the unemployment rate, the definition and measurement of contingent labor can obscure important trends in economic insecurity. Contingent labor is generally defined broadly, to include nonstandard workers ranging from self-employed independent contractors to temporary workers and day laborers. Many therefore assume that these workers freely choose and prefer such arrangements, and much emphasis is placed on the desirable increase in flexibility provided through contingent work. The assumption is that the jobs are just as good, only more flexible and less permanent.

Many contingent workers do report that they enjoy such flexibility, but this is only part of the picture. In fact, contingent work is not only widespread but often substandard and increasingly involuntary. Nonstandard workers tend to be concentrated in low-paying industries and occupations. In addition, contingent workers generally earn less per hour (by approximately 20 percent) than workers with comparable skills and backgrounds who do similar work in regular full-time jobs.[55] They are also far less likely to receive employer-provided, government-backed health and pension benefits.[56] Among regular full-time workers in the mid-2000s, slightly more than 70 percent received employer-provided health benefits. Among nonstandard workers, just over 20 percent were covered. In 2005, 66 percent of full-time workers participated in employee-sponsored pension and retirement programs, but only 23 percent of nonstandard workers did so.[57]

Nor is contingent work a matter of choice for many workers in the post-1970s economy. The share of jobs that are part time, for example, rose from 15.9 percent in 1973 to 17.3 percent in 1989. This increase resulted almost entirely from a rise in *involuntary* part-time employment, which expanded from 3.0 to 4.2 percent of the workforce. By 1989, nearly one in four of those working part-time were doing so involuntarily.[58] Between 1989 and 2013, the rate of part-time work (voluntary and involuntary) continued to rise and fall with the economy, yet the most significant shifts were again in involuntary part-time employment. The number of involuntary part-timers increased to 6.4 percent of the total workforce in 2009 and 2010, and stood at 5.5 percent in 2013.[59]

Within the contingent labor category, moreover, certain types of jobs were being created more rapidly than others. Self-employment, including independent contracting, remained relatively constant in the 1980s and 1990s, at just over 7 percent of the workforce. But the share of workers employed through temporary help and contract agencies jumped from 0.3 percent of the total workforce in 1973 to 2.4 percent in 1997. In the narrower category of temporary help agencies, government data show that employment doubled between 1982 and 1989, and doubled again between 1989 and 2000, reaching 2 percent of the labor force, where the figure stood in mid-2012.[60]

Identifying where the increase in contingency is occurring is important, because the sweeping category of "nonstandard labor" hides a hierarchy with nontrivial disparities. Those most likely to do well in terms of pay and benefits are self-employed workers, including some independent contractors; those least likely to do well, temps, are in the fastest-growing category.[61] Men, moreover, are more likely than women to be self-employed. Whites are nearly four times as likely to be self-employed as African Americans. At the other end of the pay and benefit scale, women are three times as likely as men to hold part-time positions, African American workers are more than twice as likely as whites to work as temps, and Hispanic workers are almost twice as likely as blacks or whites to do "on-call" work.[62]

The overall trend toward declining job stability and security is striking. From the late 1970s to the late 2000s, job tenure dropped markedly (despite some increases for women) and is particularly low for younger and service-sector workers. Rates of involuntary job loss, involuntary part-time work, and surveyed reports of job insecurity rose, even in periods of low unemployment. And within the growing nonstandard workforce, women and minorities were concentrated in positions that compared least favorably to regular jobs in terms of pay and benefits.

Income Ladders: The "Adequate and Rising Earnings" Assumption

A third premise of the New Deal welfare state was that full-time work would secure the economic well-being of employees and their families by providing an adequate income and the opportunity to increase earnings over time. This was always a limited assumption. There was no implied guarantee of professional advancement or satisfaction within a worker's field: income ladders were not "career ladders." Nor was there any assumption of equitable advancement on the income ladder. Movement might be minimal and gradual for some, and rapid for others, particularly those with more education. But all could expect adequate and rising earnings and some advancement over a lifetime of labor, and with sufficient effort, many low earners could expect to work their way into the middle class.

The income assumption is built into the wage-based eligibility and benefit rules of the welfare state. A number of programs—from Social Security to Unemployment Compensation—peg benefits directly to wages, generally through a formula providing a fraction of a worker's current or average lifetime earnings. Even when formulas include a measure of progressivity (as in the Social Security program), they embody a premise about work and wages. The use of such formulas to determine a fair benefit level assumes both reasonable wages and steady increases over a lifetime, as a measure (along with longevity on the job) of effort and diligence. The same assumption guides welfare-to-work policies that seek to move public assistance recipients into the first available job, even if wages are low or irregular ("work-first" strategies); the premise is that workers will advance over time to employment adequate to sustain their families.

Again, the first two decades of the postwar economy made the assumption of adequate and rising wages plausible for most of the workforce. Wages increased for all workers in these years, including those at the bottom of the wage scale.[63] Throughout the 1960s, for example, each 1 percent expansion in the economy meant a weekly wage increase of more than $2 (after inflation) in weekly wages for workers in low-income working families.[64] By the late 1970s, however, a new pattern of stagnant and declining wages emerged. It continued steadily through much of the economic recovery of the 1990s. Even the wage increases of the late 1990s proved insufficient to offset the wage losses sustained over the previous two decades.[65] The 2000s brought very modest wage growth, most of which was wiped out in 2008 and 2009. By 2010, the real median income of working-age families stood at $6,300 below its 2000 peak, a drop of more than 10 percent.[66]

Two trends undermined the assumption that full-time work would provide adequate and rising earnings. First, a persistently high number of jobs paid poverty-level wages or less, leaving workers without enough wage income to support themselves and their families despite a demonstrated willingness to work full-time. The poverty wage level is the hourly wage that a full-time, year-round worker must earn to sustain a family of four at the poverty threshold ($11.49 an hour in 2013). From the late 1970s to the early 2010s, between a quarter and a third of workers earned poverty-level wages. Within this group, moreover, a rising number of workers had earnings significantly below the poverty level.[67] These wage conditions elevated the number of workers eligible for the EITC in the 1980s and early 1990s. They also reduced the returns to work for those on AFDC who sought employment in these years.

A second trend struck a wider range of working families in this period: many American workers experienced no real wage increases over time, in part because a significant percentage of new jobs created were in sectors of the economy that provide fewer opportunities for decent and rising wages. Many workers found that the bottom rung on the income ladder had dropped lower—sometimes below the poverty line—and that other rungs were simply missing, leaving them unable to climb out of low-wage work despite sustained effort.

An examination of workers at various points on the wage scale over the past three decades shows extended periods of wage stagnation or decline, interspersed with shorter periods of growth, for much of the workforce. Over the entire 1979 to 2007 period, real hourly wages for those in the bottom 10 percent of earners actually fell by 1 percent. Workers in the 20th to 40th percentile of earners saw slight increases (of 4 to 5 percent) in their hourly wages over the entire thirty-year period. Only workers in the top 40 percent or higher on the wage scale saw double-digit increases.[68]

Table 4.2 Long-Term Trends in Wages

					WAGE BY PERCENTILE: MEN					
	10th	20th	30th	40th	50th	60th	70th	80th	90th	95th
Year					Real Hourly Wage (2011 dollars)					
1979	9.39	11.94	14.37	16.72	19.13	21.73	24.37	28.30	34.46	41.32
1989	8.35	10.45	12.83	15.19	17.68	20.81	24.07	28.20	35.33	43.87
1995	8.05	10.16	12.08	14.53	17.03	19.91	23.39	27.97	36.46	45.60
2000	8.97	10.99	13.14	15.57	18.21	21.18	24.93	30.25	40.30	50.46
2011	8.52	10.16	12.45	14.95	17.72	20.76	25.00	30.93	42.58	55.61
	Percent Change									
1979–2011	-9.3	-14.9	-13.3	-10.6	-7.4	-4.5	2.6	9.3	23.6	34.6

					WAGE BY PERCENTILE: WOMEN					
	10th	20th	30th	40th	50th	60th	70th	80th	90th	95th
Year					Real Hourly Wage (2011 dollars)					
1979	8.14	8.82	9.58	10.68	11.99	13.63	15.18	17.66	21.98	25.98
1989	6.79	8.36	9.68	11.12	12.92	14.77	17.39	20.84	26.16	31.54
1995	7.10	8.46	9.89	11.38	13.07	15.06	17.89	21.86	28.10	34.92
2000	7.83	9.32	10.74	12.44	14.20	16.41	19.44	23.62	31.04	38.13
2011	7.95	9.25	10.81	12.70	14.89	17.37	20.64	25.29	34.20	43.33
	Percent Change									
1979–2011	-2.3	4.8	12.9	18.9	24.2	27.5	36.0	43.2	55.6	66.8

Source: Material adapted from Lawrence Mishel, Josh Bivens, Elise Gould, and Heidi Shierholz, *The State of Working America*, 12th ed. (Ithaca, N.Y.: Cornell University Press, 2012), 189–90. Used by permission.

Note: From 1979 to 2011, real wages were stagnant or declining for most male workers and many female low-wage workers. The trend was worse for those at the bottom of the wage distribution. (The data are distributed by percentile: 10 percent of workers earn less than the 10th percentile wage, for example, while 90 percent earn more.) The figures here are from select business cycle peak years across the period, as well as from 1995, the start of a brief period of stronger wage growth in the late 1990s.

Since the late 1970s, with the exception of a few years at the end of the 1990s, most workers could not expect the steady wage gains their counterparts experienced a generation earlier, regardless of how hard they worked. Nor could workers who started out at the lowest levels of the wage scale expect to move up significantly over the course of a lifetime.[69] These trends have contributed to a gradual but relatively consistent decline in overall income mobility rates since 1974, measured by a steady increase in the percentage of families that have remained in the same income bracket.[70]

As with unemployment, the measures typically used to assess wage levels and income—in this case, the reliance on aggregate weekly or annual income rather than hourly wages—hide an important part of the story.[71] By the mid-1970s, as hourly wages for most workers stagnated or fell, families tried to compensate by increasing the number of weeks worked per year and the number of hours worked per week: working families were laboring longer and harder simply to maintain their current income levels. One indicator of this trend was an increase in the share of workers holding multiple jobs, particularly in the 1980s and 1990s, which topped 6 percent by the late 1990s.[72] The slow-growth recovery following the recession of 2001 made securing additional work hours more difficult for many, and the combination of the downward creep in work hours and relatively flat wages produced stagnant or declining family incomes across the 2000 to 2007 period.[73] When recession brought increased layoffs and further reductions in work hours, median household incomes dropped by 3.6 percent in 2008, and continued to fall through the next three years before stagnating in 2012 and 2013.[74]

Disaggregated wage data reveal other trends and are essential to evaluate the familiar claim that jobs with low wages are acceptable because workers can eventually make their way up the income ladder. Though never equally achievable for all social groups, this was a more accurate characterization of the American workforce of the 1960s. Wage trends in the post-1970s economy do not support the claim, particularly for three overlapping groups: young, entry-level workers; workers with a high-school degree or less; and racial and ethnic minorities. In some cases, these workers earned *less* than their counterparts a generation earlier. The entry-level hourly wage for a young male high school graduate in 2007 was $11.79—a full 17.8 percent lower in constant dollars than his counterpart in 1973. Female entry-level workers in 2007 started off with wages 10 percent lower than in 1973.[75] Among African American workers, wage declines in the 1980s were reversed in the late 1990s; their wages then remained flat through the next decade.[76]

Taken together, the data indicate that the assumption about earnings no longer applied to large segments of the labor market by the early 2000s, even before the Great Recession. The sources and duration of this trend, like the patterns in job availability and security, suggest that it marks a structural rather than cyclical change. Wage declines are in large part a function of the types of jobs that are being created and destroyed in the labor market. Between 1979 and 2007, the nation saw the loss of about 2.8 million manufacturing and mining jobs, and an increase of 50.4 million jobs in the service sector. Most of the job growth was in retail trade and services, two of the three lowest-paying service-sector industries; together, they accounted for 78 percent of all net new jobs over the thirty-year period. The share of the workforce in high-wage sectors (both goods-producing industries and government) dropped 13.3 percentage points, while the share in the lower-paying service-producing sector increased 11.6 points in this period, pushing wages down over time. The 2007–9 recession accelerated the labor market trend toward replacing high-wage jobs with lower-wage ones. Longer-term projections (through 2020) suggest that the shift toward service-producing jobs is a durable one, and that the pattern of limited opportunities for adequate and rising earnings is likely to continue.[77]

The eroding value of the minimum wage has further contributed to the earnings decline for low-wage workers. In the absence of legislated increases to keep pace with inflation, the real value of the minimum wage has fallen steeply in recent decades from its high point in 1968. The drop was particularly sharp between 1979 and 1989, when the value of the minimum wage fell 29.9 percent. Modest, periodic increases from 1989 to 1997 restored some of the wage's value, but it was down 25.7 percent overall from 1967 to 2005. Even after increases passed in 2007, it remained at more than 20 percent below the 1968 level in real terms in 2013.[78]

The data on wage trends clarify that the assumption of adequate and rising wages no longer holds for large numbers of workers. In the post-1970s economy, a worker can work full time and remain unable to bring his or her family above the poverty line. A worker willing to accept a job at the low end of the income ladder may be unable to move up over a lifetime of labor. These developments have further eroded the logic and effectiveness of core welfare-state programs, which assumed adequate and rising wages, and set levels for wage replacement in periods of job loss or retirement based on workers' earnings. In the low-wage sector, these conditions increased the burden on the

EITC and complicated efforts to reduce AFDC rolls through policies that encouraged or required work.[79]

Safety Nets: The "Social Protections" Assumption

The fourth assumption of the New Deal welfare state was that work would provide access to a system of public and private social protections against unavoidable hardships. If a worker at any level of the income ladder fell off and was unable to work for reasons beyond his or her control (temporary layoff, disability, old age), a basic "safety net" would be there to help prevent the family from falling into poverty or joining the welfare rolls. Tax breaks for employer-provided health and pension benefits reflect this assumption, as do the core social insurance programs of the welfare state such as Social Security and unemployment insurance.[80] Likewise, workfarist public assistance policies generally assume that such protections are available to poor families seeking to leave or avoid welfare by supporting themselves in the labor market.

The initial post–New Deal decades saw steady expansions in the proportion of the workforce that received job-based social protections, in part due to policy changes and pressures generated by organized labor, and in part due to rapid job creation.[81] Employment growth was particularly strong in sectors (such as manufacturing) that provided jobs that were not only secure and relatively well paid, but also equipped with government-supported benefits. When this pattern of job growth ended in the 1970s, access to these protections suffered. An increasing number of jobs did not offer tax-subsidized, employer-provided health insurance and retirement benefits. Government programs such as unemployment insurance also provided less protection for many workers in the new labor market.

The trend toward reduced job-based benefits ran across sectors and wage levels, but the sharpest decline was among the very jobs that have historically provided few benefits to begin with. Current and potential workers in the low-wage sector—including EITC and AFDC recipients—were now *less* likely than before to receive social protections through their employers. From 1979 to 2006, the proportion of private-sector workers covered by their own employer-provided health care plans dropped steeply, from 69 percent to 55 percent. Most of the decline took place in the 1980s (7.4 percentage points) and after 2000 (3.9 points). The loss of coverage was widespread, although greater at lower wage and education levels. Whites and blacks experienced about the same rate of loss; Hispanics saw the sharpest drop in coverage, a loss of 23.1 percentage points. By 2010, the proportion of private-sector workers covered by their own work-based health plans had dropped to 53.1 percent, a drop of 5.8 points over the decade of the 2000s.[82]

The rate of private-sector pension coverage also slid precipitously in the 1980s, dropping from 50.6 percent in 1979 to 43.7 percent in 1989, before rising in the 1990s, then dropping again to 42.8 percent in 2010. Black workers faced declines of 8.1 percentage points, more than twice as steep as those for whites (3.9 points); Hispanics saw the most drastic drop, at 14.3 percentage points. Most workers with college degrees retained pension coverage on the job (though their rate of coverage fell from 61 to 56.1 percent), but high school graduates saw their rate of coverage fall 14.9 points (from 51.2 to 36.3 percent). For those in the lowest-wage quintile, pension coverage was rare and became rarer: 18.4 percent had pensions in 1979, but only 13.7 percent did in 2010.[83] Overall, these changes left almost half of all workers in jobs without health insurance and nearly 60 percent without pension coverage.

Another pattern emerged among workers whose jobs *did* provide social protections. Increasingly in the 1980s and 1990s, these workers discovered that their access to robust job-related benefits had been curtailed by changing labor market conditions. This trend is more subtle and multifaceted. In some cases, workers have been able to collect benefits, but at a value that has been significantly eroded by new employment patterns. Benefits are often tied to workplace performance, measured in wage levels and longevity. In the post-1970s labor market, many workers found that the amount they were able to collect from programs ranging from unemployment insurance to employer-provided pensions was affected by frequent job changes and stagnant or declining wages. Data on the average "benefit package" (including both payroll taxes for government welfare-state programs and employer-provided health and pension plans) capture the overall trend. The value of benefits grew rapidly (6.3 percent annually) from 1959 to 1973, and it grew 4.9 percent annually from 1973 to 1979 (adjusted for inflation). From 1979 to 1989, the average increase in the value of benefits slowed significantly, to just 0.8 percent per year. From 1989 to 2000, the average value fell 0.9 percent annually, before turning up again, though increasing at a much slower rate than in earlier decades (by 2.3 percent annually from 2000 to 2007).[84]

Table 4.3 Employer-Provided Health Insurance and Pension Coverage

	PENSION COVERAGE (PERCENTAGE)			HEALTH INSURANCE COVERAGE (PERCENTAGE)		
	White	Black	Hispanic	White	Black	Hispanic
1979	52.2	48.5	38.2	70.3	63.1	60.4
1989	46.1	40.7	26.3	64.0	56.3	46.0
1995	49.5	42.6	24.7	61.7	53.0	42.1
2000	53.7	41.3	27.5	62.7	55.4	41.8
2007	50.3	39.1	24.8	59.6	52.4	37.3
2010	48.2	37.7	23.9	57.8	49.5	36.3
	Percent Change					
1979–2010	−3.9	−8.1	−14.3	−12.5	−13.6	−24.1

Source: Material adapted from Lawrence Mishel, Josh Bivens, Elise Gould, and Heidi Shierholz, *The State of Working America*, 12th ed. (Ithaca, N.Y.: Cornell University Press, 2012), 42. Used by permission.

Note: Rates of employer-provided pension and health insurance coverage declined significantly after the 1970s. Coverage for African American and Hispanic workers, lower to begin with, dropped more steeply than for white workers. Data are for private-sector wage and salary workers ages eighteen to sixty-four who worked at least twenty hours a week and twenty-six weeks per year. The federal government supports these benefits by providing tax breaks to employers providing them.

In other cases, workers have been unable to collect their benefits because job displacements or other labor market conditions have made them ineligible under outdated policy rules. The trend toward shorter job tenures in the post-1970s labor market, for example, has made it more difficult for many workers to qualify for certain employer-provided benefits. The traditional "vesting" period (time worked on the job before gaining access to a traditional defined-benefit pension) is five years.[85] The median job tenure, however, had fallen to under four years by the mid-1990s (and to a mere 2.4 years for those in the service sector), and it remained in this range for over a decade, standing at 4.1 years at the beginning of the Great Recession. Even for those in their prime working years, median job tenure dropped below five years by 1998, where it remained through most of the 2000s, before edging up to 5.5 years in January 2014.[86] The retirement implications of these trends are sobering: a significant number of prime-age workers were unlikely to remain in their jobs long enough to fully vest in a traditional pension—if this benefit were offered by their employers.

Perhaps the clearest example of this pattern is unemployment insurance.[87] Unemployment benefits in the postwar period reached most unemployed workers. The percentage of the unemployed who received benefits peaked at 81 percent in 1975, and it stood at more than 50 percent for most of the late 1970s, then fell to under 40 percent in the early 1980s.[88] Over the next three decades, a significant proportion of unemployed workers either did not qualify for unemployment insurance—often because they had not worked in a position long enough due to job turnovers—or had exhausted their benefits despite continued efforts to find work. Part of the reason for this is that the character of unemployment has changed since the program was created. The post-1970s period saw widespread structural unemployment, which is generally longer in duration and often demands that workers change occupations to find new jobs. In 2007, only 36 percent of the unemployed received unemployment benefits, according to the House Ways and Means Committee. The percentage has largely remained in this low range since the early 1980s, except in the brief periods immediately following legislation to temporarily extend benefits in the recessions of the 1990s and 2000s. After temporary benefit extensions expired at the end of 2013, the percentage of jobless Americans receiving unemployment benefits fell to a low 25.9 in August 2014.[89]

Finally, as in the previous cases, the old and new features of the labor market combined to compound the impact of these changes on minorities and less-educated workers. Fewer of these workers were covered by employer-provided health and pension plans; fewer received government benefits such as unemployment insurance; and those who did received lower benefit levels.[90] As economic insecurity among low-income families increased, neither the EITC nor welfare-to-work programs were designed to address these labor market shortcomings.

* * *

In the wake of major structural economic shifts in the 1970s, work remained the primary mechanism determining access to and benefits within the welfare state, and work was increasingly the presumed route off of public assistance and out of poverty. Yet the character of jobs had fundamentally changed. Each of the transformations described above—from long-term to short-term employment, from stable to contingent jobs, from rising to declining wage levels, from expanding to contracting job-based benefits and social protections—altered the prospects for and rewards from employment. These changing conditions of work, in turn, redefined the patterns and possibilities of social provision for most Americans in the work-based welfare state. Until the mid-1970s, most (if not all) workers found the doors to some form of employment open. They found stable, secure floors under the jobs they accepted, the promise of adequate and rising earnings on the income ladder, and a reliable (if imperfect) safety net to shield them from unforeseen or unavoidable misfortune. By the 1980s and 1990s, rising numbers of workers found few, if any, of these conditions.

The work-based structure of eligibility and benefits has always been limited and exclusionary. But the changes of the past three decades mean that even on its own terms, the post-1970s welfare state no longer reflects or reinforces the work effort of growing numbers of Americans in the labor market. Both social insurance and public assistance programs rest on outdated assumptions about the nature and conditions of work. Even as Americans work longer and harder, more are subject to the uncertainty and volatility of the labor market, and fewer are positioned to draw the social protections designed to shield them from precisely such market hazards. Moreover, the American working population has not shouldered the impact of these changes evenly. By virtually every measure examined here, low-wage workers paid a heavier price throughout the 1980s, most of the 1990s, and the early 2000s. Ironically, it has been precisely those workers most likely to be affected by these structural economic shifts who are least likely to gain the job-based protections they need and have earned. The post-1970s economy marked the first time since the New Deal that work proved persistently less reliable in providing a path to economic security, particularly for low-income working families. This was the context within which the decisive political conflicts and policy decisions over the emerging workfare regime would unfold beginning in the 1980s.

CHAPTER 5

The Conservative Assault and the Liberal Retreat

In the years spanning the election of Ronald Reagan and the passage of welfare reform legislation under Bill Clinton, policy battles over work and welfare exploded onto the national political agenda. But welfare reform was only one act in a much larger struggle over social policy toward the poor. Two far-reaching policy questions were at stake in this fifteen-year debate. The first concerned federal income assistance for poor families, working and nonworking, with one parent or two: when and how should needy families be granted assistance, at what levels, and under what conditions? This issue had been at the center of a slow-moving political conflict for decades.

A second question now arose alongside the first: what, if any, responsibility did the federal government have to address the deteriorating conditions confronting poor families in the low-wage labor market? Job conditions were declining precisely as policies to encourage and require work were escalating. Beginning in the 1980s, policymakers were confronted repeatedly with evidence of diminishing returns to employment in debates over welfare and work. Conservative Republicans argued for relying on market incentives in a largely deregulated low-wage labor market. Liberal and moderate Democrats occasionally countered with a modest agenda of economic "fairness," with initiatives to "make work pay" and proposals to aid welfare recipients in the transition from welfare to work.

For the most part, however, the widening gap between the assumptions embedded in work-based antipoverty policies and conditions in the labor market received little serious or sustained policy attention. Instead, political leaders adopted piecemeal responses through policy decisions on the minimum wage, job creation and training, and workforce development. The verdict was in by the end of the 1980s and would be confirmed in the 1990s: the federal government would do little to change market conditions or employer strategies to ensure that year-round full-time work secured above-poverty wages or provided economic security or mobility for families. The government would instead provide limited subsidies and supports to those within it, through programs such as the EITC.

Accounts of welfare reform often overlook the policy developments on low-wage labor that unfolded alongside the drive to move poor families into the labor market. But it was the convergence of policy trends on welfare and on low-wage work that made the reforms of the 1980s and 1990s so consequential. Likewise, many studies of welfare reform focus on the role of conservative Republicans—led by Ronald Reagan and then Newt Gingrich—in ushering in a new conservative agenda. There is little doubt that Republican leaders moved welfare politics to the right in these years. But overstating the triumph of Republican ideas and strategies on welfare, work, and poverty in the 1980s and 1990s can obscure other (and earlier) sources of conservative policy change. In important respects, developments in the 1980s and 1990s reflected an acceleration of trends initiated by conservative Democrats in the late 1960s and 1970s, and the ideas and influence of a new cohort of Southerners would prove equally influential in these later years.

The argument in this chapter unfolds in four main claims about the 1980s. First, the conservative policy assault on welfare under Reagan produced a "hollowing out" of the welfarist system. The structure of the New Deal system—its broad principles and policies—remained in place, but its content was significantly diminished by the end of the decade. As welfarist programs were undermined, the nascent workfare system was gradually constructed on the framework established in the 1970s: the EITC saw a major expansion, and states were encouraged to experiment with work programs for welfare recipients.

Second, Republicans' ability to advance their version of workfare in the 1980s depended at key junctures on both the votes of contemporary Southern Democrats in Congress and the legacies left by an earlier generation of Southern leaders. Congress had changed: institutional reforms pressed by liberal House Democrats in the 1970s had reined in the power of committee chairs—a traditional lever of Southern influence—and increased the authority of the party leadership. But with party control of Congress more evenly divided than in previous decades, conservative Democrats were able to exercise considerable influence by forging a reinvigorated "conservative coalition" with Republicans.[1] Much of Ronald Reagan's social policy agenda could not have been enacted without the cooperation of these Southern Democrats.

Time and again, moreover, Reagan Republicans reached for the arguments and policies forged by Southern leaders in the 1970s—to build public support for their agenda, to deflect criticism of their policies, and to fend off policy proposals advanced by liberal Democrats. Above all, these earlier policy legacies created the conditions necessary for congressional moderates in the 1980s to abandon traditional welfarist commitments to AFDC and their alliance with liberals. To do so, moderates needed to embrace work expectations for welfare recipients, they needed to be assured that remaining public assistance programs would take care of the most vulnerable needy, and they needed to identify an alternative source of support for families who left welfare. Each of the major workfare initiatives championed by Southerners in the 1970s helped in this. The WIN work incentive programs made the case for work requirements, SSI promised to protect the "truly needy" who were unable to work, and the EITC offered aid to those forced to leave the welfare rolls—and Republicans used each to mobilize support for conservative reform.

Third, the expansion of workfare in the 1980s was as much a consequence of successive liberal retreats from earlier welfarist positions as it was a result of conservative advances. In the 1980s, the task facing the Democratic leadership was to keep liberals, centrists, and above all, Southern conservatives within the caucus. The price extracted by these Southerners for party unity included a series of major concessions on work and welfare legislation, from the minimum wage to AFDC reform.

Fourth and finally, deteriorating conditions in the labor market—and their political consequences—led conservative Republicans to support a more expansive system of workfare supports than they wanted. In the face of public and partisan attacks in the early 1980s, conservative Republicans were forced to compromise on their approach to the problems facing low-wage working families. Though many would have preferred no new policy expansions, they adopted a job training program and successive EITC increases, gradually building up a more far-reaching workfare regime through new supports for poor workers.

Work and Welfare: The State of the Debate

As the 1980 presidential campaign heated up, concerns about the nation's economic crisis topped the political agenda. The parties put forward radically different proposals not only for economic recovery, but also for addressing poverty and welfare in hard economic times. The Democrats' platform committed the party to addressing the needs of the working poor as well as "those not in the labor market" and to "provid[ing] an income floor" for both. For welfare recipients, the Democrats urged a work and training requirement for all who were able to work and not caring for young children, and they proposed to match this with assured employment "through the private sector and, if that is insufficient, through public employment." The Republican platform, in contrast, attacked "federally-subsidized poverty and manipulated dependency" generated by antipoverty programs dating to the Great Society. Republicans called for eliminating the "poverty trap" created by overly generous welfare benefits that competed with earnings from low-wage work.[2]

The election produced a landslide for the Republicans. Not only did Ronald Reagan win the White House, but the party seized control of the Senate and cut sharply into the Democratic majority in the House, gaining thirty-three seats (their largest increase since 1966), for a total of 192.[3] The Republican agenda flatly rejected the New Deal vision underlying most existing social welfare programs. However, it also departed from the workfarist Southern Democrats' position in significant ways. Conservative Republicans in the White House and Congress advanced what might be called a "market fundamentalist" perspective, one that incorporated a far more conservative version of workfare than had emerged in the national policy debate to date.[4] Reagan argued that unleashing market forces was the only way to revitalize and restructure the economy, and the key to doing so was to get government out of the market's way. As he famously put it in his inaugural address: "Government is not the solution to our problem. It is the problem."[5] The answer was to reduce public spending, lift the regulatory burden on employers, and allow markets to function with minimal government interference. In the labor market, this meant avoiding unnecessary constraints on the availability, price, and allocation of labor, and above all, avoiding policies that might allow current or potential workers to rely instead on public support.[6]

The approach to poverty, in short, was to let the labor market—largely unregulated and unrestrained—determine outcomes. Government policy should ensure that all able-bodied adults enter and remain in the workforce; once there, individuals needed to adjust to existing market conditions. In practice, this meant eliminating or curtailing nonmarket income. Such government assistance, while well intended, at best undermined or prolonged the necessary adjustment to market conditions that all workers must make; at worst, it produced an oversized public sector and created dependence on government support. Thus welfare led families to avoid work. Extended unemployment insurance led workers to stay out of the workforce longer than necessary or desirable. Even work supports could prolong or impede the adjustments workers needed to make to constraints and opportunities within the market. Reagan was consistent in applying this market logic to both the welfare and the working poor. Their problems may be different, but the medicine was the same: enter and adjust to the market.[7]

The conservative position drew broad public attention through two popular works in the early 1980s. George Gilder's *Wealth and Poverty* quickly became a favorite of the new president, who quoted it extensively in his speeches.[8] Gilder argued that assisting the poor made them dependent on government, and this extended to programs for the working poor. Jobs programs used government funds to subsidize work at decent wages—and this "deprives the poor of an understanding of their real predicament: the need to work harder than the classes above them in order to get ahead."[9] Soon after, Charles Murray's *Losing Ground* hit the bookstands. Government aid to the poor, Murray asserted, harmed those it purported to help by creating incentives to seek or stay on welfare rather than to enter and remain in the low-wage workforce. To change these incentives required eliminating most welfare programs.[10] The *New York Times* observed that officials in "agency after agency" of the Reagan administration "cite the Murray book as the philosophical base for proposals" to cut budgets.[11]

The contrast to the liberal Democratic position was clear. For welfarists, government had both a protective and a redistributive function. The federal government had an obligation to ensure a measure of economic security for certain categories of vulnerable and needy families. This meant shielding them from economic uncertainties and hazards in the labor market, through nonwage, nonmarket income alternatives such as public assistance. Conditions within the low-wage job market also needed to be reformed, through minimum wage increases, expanded unemployment insurance, guaranteed social protections (such as health insurance), and even public-sector job creation when private markets failed to provide adequate employment. Democratic leaders had occasionally pursued such measures in the previous decade, and they were often stymied by Republican and Southern Democratic opposition.[12]

By the 1970s, many liberals had come to support the idea of moving AFDC recipients into the workforce, as previous chapters have shown, but only on welfarist terms. Programs should be noncoercive for those with young children, should put poor families' economic security above work-related goals, and should provide supports to those seeking to enter or stay in the workforce. Liberals continued to promote core welfarist principles, including the entitlement to adequate and equitable assistance for all eligible families and an active role for the federal government.[13] The liberal position was expressed in the work of poverty scholars such as William Julius Wilson, whose book *The Truly Disadvantaged* argued that the roots of poverty lie in structural weaknesses in the labor market, particularly in urban areas. Contrary to the claims of Gilder and Murray, Wilson argued that the problem of poverty required attention to economic development, jobs, training, and education for the poor.[14]

Although the liberal position was dominant among the Democratic congressional leadership in the 1980s, many in the party's evolving Southern wing remained skeptical of New Deal welfarism. Some abandoned the party to support the Republican agenda on key issues. A more diffuse group of moderate-to-conservative Southern Democrats took a different approach, seeking to redefine their party's position on social welfare policy. Drawing on the workfarist policy foundations built by the previous generation of Southern leaders, they would stake out a third position in the work and welfare debate by the end of the Reagan years.

In the early to mid-1980s, the broad outlines of this centrist position were emerging. It was a pro-market vision, but it retained a larger role for government than the Republican position. It envisioned the government's role as pro-growth rather than redistributive, and it held that policy should compensate for but not alter labor market outcomes in the low-wage sector. This position counseled cautious opposition to minimum wage increases (which interfered with the market's wage-setting function), but support for the EITC (which compensated for the market's low wages after the fact). It advocated tough work requirements, but with some supports to aid in the transition from welfare to work. On balance, these workfare supporters strongly preferred market mechanisms to government action, and local or state government measures to federal measures, wherever possible. Unlike many conservative Republicans, they were not afraid to use federal dollars to achieve their ends.

Within the public debate, these moderate-to-conservative workfare advocates found support for their positions in the work of Lawrence Mead, among others. Mead's *Beyond Entitlement* recast the relationship between poor citizens and the state by suggesting that welfare should be not an entitlement but a matter of mutual obligation. He departed from Wilson's emphasis on the labor market by arguing that the "main impediment" facing the inner-city poor "is the permissive nature of welfare and employment programs, which have seldom seriously expected the employable to work as a condition of benefits."[15] Mead's work would have a profound long-term impact on policy.[16]

At the outset of the Reagan era, all three policy visions were in play. Conservatives held the advantage, however: the president had the political winds at his back, Southern conservatives saw new opportunities for brokering compromises, and liberals were besieged and in disarray.

Restricting Welfare, 1981–1982

Ronald Reagan's first year in office triggered an intense partisan battle over the future of social welfare policy, pitting a unified and energized Republican party against a divided and demoralized Democratic coalition. The Reagan team was focused and disciplined. A central aim was, as one observer noted, "to launch a blitzkrieg upon the welfare state before its creators could organize a defense." The administration was "single-minded in those first six to eight months," said White House Chief of Staff James Baker. "We kept our eye on the ball."[17]

With the Senate in Republican hands, the nominal leadership of the Democratic Party rested with the office of Speaker Tip O'Neill (D-Mass.) in the House. O'Neill and his circle were old-school, New Deal Democrats, but they were governing an increasingly unwieldy coalition, and some of the starkest differences were over social policy. In early March 1981, O'Neill counted no fewer than seven distinct factions within the party.[18]

On the left were liberal and progressive Democrats. They argued that the party should reorganize and recommit to its New Deal roots, including on social welfare issues. As a matter of principle, Democrats should brook no compromise and instead launch a full-scale campaign against Reagan and all he represented. These liberals and progressives were scattered among four identifiable groups—the Democratic Study Group, the Congressional Black Caucus, a group linked to Phil Burton (D-Calif.), and a group of younger, post-Watergate members.[19] In the political center of the party were two additional groups—one led by Gillis Long (D-La., Russell's cousin) and another composed of members on the House Budget Committee.

On the right were the Southern conservative Democrats, who came to be known as the boll weevils. They read the election returns as a vindication of their positions on social policy and other issues. Led by Charles Stenholm of Texas, they created the Conservative Democratic Forum (CDF), which aimed simultaneously to move their party in a conservative direction and to "barter their votes for a voice in the [Reagan] Administration," according to *Congressional Quarterly*. Forty-three out of forty-seven CDF members in the House were from the South, and eleven of fourteen members in a parallel group in the Senate were Southerners.[20] These conservative Democrats recognized that they now held the balance of power, especially in the House. "We agreed with a lot of the things Ronald Reagan said he wanted to do," explained Martin Leath (D-Tex.). "We agreed that the tax system needed to be reformed, that our defense effort needed to be strengthened, and that the Great Society programs should be cut back and eliminated."[21]

In the aftermath of the election, the conservatives wasted no time in meeting with Speaker O'Neill to demand greater input on Democratic policies and better committee assignments. Texas Democrat Phil Gramm fought for and won a seat on the Budget Committee, to the subsequent chagrin of party leaders (much of the Reagan budget would ultimately be put together by Gramm working behind the scenes with Reagan budget director David Stockman). It soon became clear that when this group voted with the strengthened Republican minority, the "conservative coalition" would have its way in the Congress. Indeed, the conservative coalition of Southern Democrats and Republicans would win 92 percent of the votes on which they allied against Northern liberal and moderate Democrats in Reagan's first year.[22]

O'Neill worried aloud about how to "keep all these groups under the same umbrella." And for the next six years, the liberal House leader would struggle to hold the Democratic coalition together while pursuing a broadly welfarist agenda on social policy. Early on, the Democratic leadership had a singular aim: to "save the House." O'Neill wanted to hold onto existing Democratic seats and increase their number in the 1982 congressional elections. The Reagan administration was committed to nothing less than "repealing the Great Society, the New Frontier, the Fair Deal and the New Deal," he warned. Pragmatically, he believed that holding the Democratic coalition together meant moderating the party's liberal positions, adopting an inclusive stance, and tolerating conservative defections.[23] As the 1981 legislative session began, O'Neill saw immediately that the new arithmetic on the House side had fundamentally altered the party's ability to pursue its own policy agenda or defeat the Reagan agenda. The Democrats had lost the "two or three dozen Republicans . . . whom we could always count on," along with the Southern Democrats. "As a result, the huge majority we had enjoyed during the Carter years disappeared."[24]

O'Neill and House Majority Leader Jim Wright (D-Tex.), a liberal Southerner, had little time to rebuild morale or mobilize a new coalition. Ronald Reagan laid out an ambitious and unyielding agenda in his campaign and inaugural address. He had endorsed the highly conservative Kemp–Roth tax plan (advanced by Representative Jack Kemp of New York and Senator William Roth of Delaware) with its 30 percent across-the-board tax cut. He now called for scaling back the size and scope of government, higher defense spending, and deep budget reductions. At the center of Reagan's plan were radical cuts in the core of the welfare state, including programs for the welfare and working poor. When skeptics asked how he planned simultaneously to cut taxes, balance the budget, and increase defense spending, he maintained that his supply-side economic plan would generate new growth and new revenues.[25]

Despite his bold rhetoric, congressional Democrats were not prepared for the budget Reagan sent down in March 1981. O'Neill expected a much more modest proposal for domestic spending cuts, then several rounds of negotiation to reach a consensus. Jim Wright thought the two House leaders could persuade Reagan "that some of his preconceptions were in error, or [to] moderate his more extreme views," Wright recalled. "To put it bluntly, we . . . got rolled."[26]

The president's plan called for a staggering $41 billion in spending cuts for the next fiscal year, much of which would come from programs for poor families. The breadth and targeting of the proposed cuts were consistent not only with Reagan's pro-market ideology but also with his longer-term political strategy of using social and economic policy to split the Democratic Party's traditional constituencies and win the support of white working-class voters.[27] Reagan's rhetoric on welfare had long been divisive and racially charged. In a series of presidential primary campaign events in 1976, Reagan had famously (and erroneously) told the "hard-working people" of southern New Hampshire about the "welfare queen" in Chicago collecting payments under eighty names, and the fancy subsidized housing units that are available if you are a "slum dweller" in New York.[28]

The Reagan team understood that they needed to win the support of moderates from both parties to secure passage. On social welfare issues, they calculated that moderates would be reluctant to support any plan that appeared to abandon the most vulnerable poor Americans. Their response was to leverage the distinction established by Southern Democrats in the early 1970s, with the creation of SSI. In the decision to provide coverage to two of the original trio of New Deal public assistance recipient groups (the elderly and disabled poor) while excluding a third (AFDC families), SSI's creators provided a convenient categorical distinction. The existence of SSI now allowed President Reagan to claim that he was ensuring aid for the "truly needy" in SSI—"those who through no fault of their own, must depend on the rest of us"—even as he imposed sharp reductions in AFDC. He singled out the SSI program, assuring Congress and the public that he would not pursue cuts in "supplemental income for the blind, the aged, and the disabled."[29]

For AFDC families, meanwhile, Reagan borrowed the logic of another Southern workfare initiative—the WIN program. WIN II established that virtually all AFDC parents should be expected to work and move from welfare into jobs. Reagan pressed WIN's workfarist aim to its logical conclusion, seeking to eliminate welfare assistance to those who had proved they were able to work. He also took steps to end the transitional assistance that allowed recipients to retain a portion of their earnings even as they continued to receive aid. (This "earnings disregard" had been included in the 1967 WIN amendments; it required states to disregard the first $30 and a third of earned monthly income when determining a family's AFDC eligibility and benefits.) The administration's logic was that poor families with an adult capable of working ought to sustain themselves without public assistance, and that "welfare is a safety net and not an income-supplement program."[30]

The administration masterfully tied Reagan's agenda for social policy change to his proposed budget cuts. The plan provoked sharp opposition from liberals, but support from conservatives and a number of moderates. Leaders in both parties understood that the Southern conservatives held the margin of votes. On April 28, the president spoke about the budget and tax debates then under way. O'Neill, sitting next to Vice President George H. W. Bush during Reagan's address, eyed the conservative Southern Democrats who stood to clap when Reagan lauded the budget-cutting proposal developed by

Representatives Phil Gramm (D-Tex.) and Delbert Latta (R-Ohio), which reflected the administration's priorities. "Here's your 40 votes," he whispered to Bush.[31]

The White House did not take that Southern Democratic support for granted, however. Administration officials—and the president himself—worked the phones and halls of Congress. Democratic leaders, for their part, used both warnings and entreaties to keep the party's Southern wing from defecting and to win over moderate Republicans. Budget Committee leaders offered horse trades on issues close to conservative hearts, including pledges to increase defense spending and to work toward a balanced budget. O'Neill tried to keep his members in line, bluntly warning those contemplating defection. "The Stockman program is going to falter along the line," and when it does, "I do not know how you are going to get yourselves off the hook," he said, before reminding them, "You have an opportunity to vote for an alternative program."[32]

In the end, however, O'Neill concluded that if the party was going to hold onto the boll weevils' forty-plus seats in the 1982 elections, they must be allowed to break party ranks on the Reagan budget votes. Others in the Democratic coalition were livid. The message to undecided Democrats, Leon Panetta (D-Calif.) said, was that they could vote for the bill with no fear of reprisal. The Democrats were in "disarray," reported *Congressional Quarterly*. One party whip admitted, "We have no game plan. We're just going to get killed. It's pathetic."[33]

When it came time to vote to determine the level of spending cuts, every Republican (190) voted for the Reagan-backed Gramm–Latta plan, as did sixty-three Democrats. Days later, O'Neill declared in a televised appearance: "From now on, it's Reagan's budget. From now on, it's Reagan's unemployment rate. . . . It's Reagan's ball game."[34] But of course, it wasn't. It took Democratic votes to pass the measure, and forty-six of them had come from Southern members, providing the margin of victory.[35]

The final budget resolution to match spending with revenues—the 1981 Omnibus Budget Reconciliation Act, or OBRA—was scheduled to come to the floor in late June. The Democratic leadership's strategy was to offer a number of amendments that would force members to take public positions on specific and unpopular budget cuts. But the Reagan team wanted to shield the boll weevils and other administration supporters from the political impact of these votes. Their ingenious response was to combine all of the spending cuts in a single enormous reconciliation bill. Members would be forced to vote the entire package up or down. It was a brilliant strategic move engineered, according to Wright, by "the President's forces, with the help of Southern Democrats."[36] Once again, the White House lobbied hard for the votes of conservative Democrats. Republicans were nearly unanimous (188–2) in backing Reagan's position on the measure, and Northern Democrats were nearly unanimous (3–157) in opposing it. But twenty-nine Democrats defected to vote with the administration, and twenty-six of them were from the South. The Reagan budget cuts passed the House on June 26 by a bare six-vote margin (217–211).[37]

The reconciliation bill was a watershed in federal poverty policy. It eliminated fifty-seven social programs by folding them into block grants, and it raised the eligibility bar for AFDC, food stamps, and unemployment insurance.[38] By 1983, some 408,000 families had lost eligibility for AFDC; another 300,000 faced reductions in benefits.[39] OBRA reduced federal spending for AFDC by roughly $680 million per year beginning in 1984. An additional $1.5 billion was cut from the federal food stamp program for fiscal 1982. Close to one million of the twenty million food stamp recipients were expected to lose all of their benefits. Through OBRA, the administration also succeeded in eliminating CETA, the job creation and training program created during the Nixon administration that had been used to support expanded public-sector employment under presidents Ford and Carter.[40]

A month after winning passage of OBRA, the president sent another shot across the bow, with a major tax bill. Called the Economic Recovery Tax Act of 1981 (ERTA), it imposed a sweeping cut in individual income tax rates and altered the structure of the tax code. The administration advertised the measure as an across-the-board rate reduction that would ease the tax burden on all American taxpayers. It was also advanced as a means of "restrain[ing] the growth of the Federal Government," according to the Senate Finance Committee, by reducing tax revenues available to finance federal programs.[41] Despite its billing as an evenhanded tax cut, it offered little to working-poor families. In reducing marginal tax rates, ERTA was skewed to provide the largest tax cuts to high-income earners. It delayed until 1985 provisions to index for inflation the personal exemption and zero bracket amounts, two of the most significant determinants of the tax burden facing low-income workers.[42] It did nothing to address the inflation-induced drop in the value of the Earned Income Tax Credit for the working poor. Together with the OBRA

Table 5.1 House Support for Reagan Budget and Tax Cut Measures, 1981

	JUNE 26, 1981, REAGAN BUDGET VOTE	
	Yes	No
Southern Democrats	26 (*33.3%*)	52 (*66.7%*)
Northern Democrats	3 (*1.9%*)	157 (*98.1%*)
Republicans	188 (*98.9%*)	2 (*1.1%*)
	JULY 29, 1981, REAGAN TAX CUT VOTE	
	Yes	No
Southern Democrats	36 (*45.6%*)	43 (*54.4%*)
Northern Democrats	12 (*7.4%*)	151 (*92.6%*)
Republicans	190 (*99.5%*)	1 (*0.5%*)

Sources: Author's calculations based on vote totals reported in *Congressional Roll Call, 97th Congress, 1st Session* (Washington, D.C.: Congressional Quarterly, 1982), 12; and *Congress and the Nation* 6 (1981–1984): 886.

Note: In the votes on the Reagan administration's spending cuts and tax cut in 1981, Southern Democrats provided Republicans with the margin of victory in the House. The first vote was on legislation (Gramm–Latta II, the House version of the Omnibus Budget Reconciliation Act of 1981) offered by Representatives Gramm (D-Tex.) and Latta (R-Ohio), to implement spending cuts backed by the Reagan administration. It passed 217–211 on June 26, 1981. The second vote was on the Economic Recovery Tax Act of 1981 (ERTA), on an administration-backed substitute offered by Representatives Conable (R-N.Y.) and Hance (D-Tex.). It passed 238–195 on July 29, 1981.

cuts for low-income workers and efforts to eliminate the AFDC earnings disregard, the ERTA provisions signaled that the Reagan administration sought to limit policy supports for the working poor.

Again, the House staged the major legislative showdown. Democratic leaders fashioned a compromise to hold together party liberals and conservatives. But Republicans voted 190–1 for an administration-backed plan instead, and Southern Democrats split nearly evenly, providing the margin of victory for the Reagan administration.[43]

The passage of OBRA and ERTA had long-term social policy consequences. The way they won passage (pushed over the top with votes from Southern Democrats) would have an equally significant impact on the *politics* of social policy—as liberal House Democratic leaders repeatedly scaled back their policy agenda in subsequent legislative battles to preempt further Southern Democratic defections.

Ronald Reagan wanted to do more than reduce the scope and reach of welfare assistance through cuts in programs and tax revenues, however. He also wanted to enact reforms in the public assistance system that would alter the structure of New Deal welfarism. In particular, he wanted to shift authority for programs like AFDC away from the federal government and national entitlement. His "New Federalism" proposal sought to reverse a fifty-year trend toward nationalizing and standardizing public assistance, a trend welfarist leaders had sought to advance since the New Deal.[44] The administration weighed proposals in 1981 to turn AFDC into a block grant to the states.[45] The Reagan team ultimately concluded that block-granting AFDC was politically infeasible, and instead sought a federal-state "exchange" of responsibilities to devolve more welfare administration to the states. The president also wanted to impose what he called a "workfare" program nationwide. Modeled on a California program dating back to his governorship, the plan sought to condition eligibility for welfare on a nationwide work requirement, in a bold escalation beyond the WIN program.[46]

By 1996, both of these proposals would be embraced by a Democratic president and would win bipartisan (though divided) support in Congress. But in the early 1980s, the Democratic position had not strayed this far from welfarist principles, and both of these moves were opposed by party leaders. In the end, the New Federalism initiative was not even introduced in Congress. Likewise, Democratic leaders balked when Reagan approached Congress with his proposal for mandatory work requirements, first in 1981, and again two years later.[47]

Though unable to enact these reforms through separate legislation, the administration identified a back-door vehicle to advance Reagan's objectives. Reagan officials struck a quiet deal with congressional leaders on the Senate Finance Committee in the wrangling over OBRA in 1981. In a nod toward Reagan's workfare agenda, committee members passed a number of amendments designed to give states "broad flexibility to experiment with alternative ways of encouraging work effort on the part of persons eligible for AFDC."[48] The Reagan team was assisted in this not only by Republicans, but also by Russell Long, now a member of the minority but still a major player on the Senate committee. Long's support for workfare, for state control of public assistance, and for "experimenting" with welfare alternatives, prominent in the battles over the Family Assistance Plan, now aligned with the aims of the Reagan administration.[49] The final version of OBRA ultimately included a compromise measure authorizing states to seek waivers from federal rules to "experiment" with ways to move recipients into the workforce—effectively creating a workfare "exception" to welfarist policies.[50] Many state officials had long preferred the flexibility to impose their own brand of work measures. Now OBRA was giving them license to do just this.

By 1986, approximately forty states had imposed some form of new work-related policy in at least some counties. The number of recipients in work-related programs doubled between 1981 and 1985, from roughly 400,000 to one million.[51] In 1987, President Reagan took an additional step, setting up an inter-agency Low Income Opportunity Advisory Board based out of the White House to streamline the process of approving waivers. The strategy was to encourage state experiments along conservative lines.[52] The effectiveness of the programs—measured in terms of successful work entry and welfare exit—was mixed at best.[53] But they enabled states to become central players in facilitating the turn to workfare in federal policy.

Reagan's first months in office thus brought a new and accelerated phase in the transformation in public assistance. The next steps toward workfare were not chosen by the president, nor did they reflect the conservative Republican view of workfare. Rather, they were forced on Reagan's administration and his party by declining economic conditions, increasing instability in labor markets, and the political fallout that resulted. The first step would produce a new federal job-training program, the second an expansion of the EITC.

Building Workfare, 1982–1986

In late summer of 1981, the Reagan administration was basking in its successive legislative victories. But some on the Reagan team, including budget director David Stockman, were worried. The administration's wins had not triggered the anticipated surge in the stock market, nor a burst of new economic growth. Stockman concluded that without additional deep spending cuts, the administration would face hundreds of billions of dollars in budget deficits. Meanwhile, Paul Volcker at the Federal Reserve was continuing to squeeze inflation from the economy with an extremely restrictive monetary policy.[54]

The Democratic leadership recognized the signs of trouble—and the opportunity they presented. "A recession brought about by tight money is at hand," noted O'Neill staffer Kirk O'Donnell in an eleven-page internal memo to the Speaker that August. "It is an ideal time to expose the weaknesses of the Reagan economic program." The strategy called for Democratic committee chairs to hold hearings in their home districts across the country to explain the impact of the administration's policies. Democrats needed to "identify where [the cuts] are going to occur and who is going to be hurt. . . . It is time to take the offensive."[55]

But to do so required holding together a splintered Democratic coalition. In a closed-door caucus the following month, party leaders again forgave the Southern boll weevil contingent for defecting and called for a unified party to go on the offensive. More than sixty hearings by various congressional committees were scheduled for the fall and winter in districts across the nation, with dozens in large media markets. And the public was ready to listen: a majority (52 percent) now believed that Reagan was primarily concerned with the wealthy, an increase of nearly 30 percentage points in five months.[56] By the fall, the economy had slipped into recession. When the *Atlantic Monthly* published an account of Stockman's doubts about the administration's supply-side economic strategy—and his assessment that Reagan's across-the-board tax cut was "always a Trojan horse to bring down the top rate" for wealthy taxpayers—O'Neill seized the offensive. "The architect of the administration's economic program is admitting exactly what I and other critics have been saying for six months," the Speaker said. "Mr. Stockman misled Congress and the nation as to the consequences of the Reagan economic program."[57]

In January 1982, the administration's own assessment was grim: "The job creation push of the tax cuts is actually far less than thought and will cause a serious shortfall in new jobs created."[58] The nation soon found itself in the throes of the worst downturn since the Depression. Unemployment rose to over 9 percent in the spring of 1982, and over 10 percent by the fall. Banks failed, farms collapsed, and small businesses folded at rates not seen since the 1930s. In the context of the structural shifts in wage and work conditions described in the previous chapter, the impact of the cyclical downturn was particularly devastating. In industries weakened by international competition and disabled by sustained high interest rates, many jobs lost in the downturn were gone for good. And new jobs created were disproportionately in low-paying sectors of the service economy.[59]

Reagan was both frustrated and flummoxed by headlines about job losses and plant closings: "Is it news that some fellow out in South Succotash someplace has just been laid off, that he should be interviewed nationwide?"[60] Democratic Party leaders pushed hard during the economy's relentless downward spiral, raising the banner of economic "fairness" to a more receptive public. By summer of 1982, White House staffers had grown to resent the attacks, and produced a lengthy "Executive Briefing Book" on the fairness issue.[61]

The downturn also created cracks in the conservative coalition. Traditionally opposed to large federal deficits, several leading Southern Democrats were skeptical of the administration's supply-side claims and worried about the fiscal impact of the large tax cuts planned over three years in the midst of a deepening recession. In late 1981, Russell Long and fellow Louisiana Democrat Bennett Johnston, along with other conservative senators, met with the president to express their concerns. Johnston argued for "some linkage between his tax cuts and the performance of the economy," to no avail.[62]

Reagan's commitment to his economic program was relentlessly sunny and unswerving. He entertained no mid-course corrections in policy, and he would not press the Federal Reserve to back off its high-cost battle against inflation. Politically, the president aimed to tame inflation and put the resulting recession behind him before facing reelection in 1984—and in this he would succeed. Congressional Republicans facing midterm elections in 1982, however, were not so sanguine.[63]

By February, polls reported that 63 percent of Americans disapproved of Reagan's handling of the unemployment problem. Congressional Democrats were hammering the policies of the Republican administration in the media and on the campaign trail. Their policy arsenal included short-term public job creation, a traditional liberal response to economic downturns.[64] Republicans seeking election needed their own response to the growing public demand for more and better jobs. In the months before the election, increasing numbers seized on a modest job training proposal then under construction in the Senate. The Job Training and Partnership Act (JTPA) was developed by Senator Dan Quayle (R-Ind.), chair of the Senate Labor Subcommittee on Employment and Productivity.[65]

JTPA was originally formulated as a replacement for CETA, the training and public jobs program Reagan eliminated through spending cuts. Republicans drew a sharp—and salient—distinction between creating public-sector jobs, which they staunchly opposed, and providing training for private-sector jobs, which they viewed skeptically. CETA did both, and most Republicans had roundly condemned the program.[66] But faced with the changed political logic of 1982, many embraced job training through JTPA. They conceived it in narrow terms—as a program to help ill-prepared workers into available jobs—and intended to commit few federal dollars to the effort. Above all, they knew they had to advance some solution to unemployment, and they saw job training as vastly preferable to public job creation.[67]

Liberal Democrats, for their part, supported job training as one element of federal employment policy, but they considered it inadequate to address the crisis. They had argued in previous years for measures such as stimulus spending, direct job creation (including expanded public service employment), and more permanent full employment policies (as in the original Humphrey-Hawkins bill). But liberals were no longer calling the shots. In the early 1980s, wrote Gordon Lafer in describing the history of JTPA, "the functional debate for congressional Democrats was not between public employment and job training, but between job training and nothing."[68] With Republicans adamantly opposed to public employment strategies, liberals resolved to get what they could from the JTPA initiative.

From the White House, meanwhile, the Quayle initiative drew repeated veto threats for undercutting the administration's pro-market, limited-government ethos. As the economy worsened and public outcry mounted in 1982, the Reagan team gradually began to change its tune.[69] The move was in part political. Unemployment and economic hardship were producing growing disillusionment among a valued constituency, blue-collar workers. Republican strategists had worked hard to win over these voters in 1980, and they did not want to lose them. They knew the Democrats were just as intent on winning them back. JTPA carried a small price tag, was packaged as a block grant to the states rather than a major federal program, and above all, promised only training, not job creation. The implicit argument was one the administration could accept: the source of the unemployment problem lay not in the lack of stable jobs, but in the failure of workers to develop the skills and capacities needed by employers in the labor market of the 1980s.[70]

If the president was slow to sign on to the new job training initiative, he lost no time in using it for the administration's political purposes once he did. The Democratic leadership was seeking passage of a small emergency jobs program to create 200,000 public works jobs.[71] Using JTPA to deflect the proposal, Reagan derided such "artificial programs that make for dead end and temporary jobs" and argued instead for JTPA's proposal to "train young people . . . for those jobs we know are there, and are not being filled. At the rate of a million a year, we think this is a good investment."[72]

The modest Democratic jobs bill passed the House but got no further.[73] The job training legislation supported by both parties, on the other hand, "gained added popularity as the unemployment rate neared 10 percent," reported *Congressional Quarterly*.[74] Passed in 1982, JTPA took effect in 1984 and remained in place until superseded by the 1998 Workforce Investment Act. Two years after its inception, the program was spending on adult training programs less than half of the funds that CETA had been projected to spend on public-sector employment, and over its sixteen years it had little measurable effect on participants' hourly earnings or mobility.[75]

The deeper significance of JTPA, arguably, was its role in building the nascent workfare regime. The JTPA struggle was fundamentally over the causes and appropriate solutions to joblessness and inadequate earnings among low-wage workers. New Deal Democrats had long argued that high rates of joblessness and slow wage growth were due to weaknesses in the labor market. They had responded over the years with a combination of unemployment benefit extensions, economic stimulus measures, periodic proposals for full-employment policy, and in some cases, public employment programs.[76] The replacement of CETA (which included a public jobs component) with JTPA changed the terms of debate about the causes of economic insecurity among poor families in the low-wage sector. The underlying premise of JTPA (and other job training programs) was that the root of the problem was not the labor market, but workers and their lack of appropriate skills. Economic insecurity was cast as an individual, not a structural or economic, problem. This assumption steered policy to the question of how to "fix" workers rather than how to reform the job market.[77]

The recession and the Democrats' job creation proposals had forced the hand of Reagan and congressional Republicans. But the larger victory belonged to the workfarists. By eliminating CETA through OBRA and then passing JTPA, the Republicans had furthered a rightward shift in the ends and means of federal employment policy. CETA was replaced with a job training program that limited government's role to helping workers address the shortcomings in skills or "job readiness" that hampered their progress in the labor market.[78]

* * *

The Republicans' defensive maneuvers were too little and too late to alter the electoral landscape of 1982, however. The Democrats won major gains in midterm congressional elections, picking up twenty-six seats in the House. Tip O'Neill's explicit agenda was to use these gains to defend the accomplishments of the New Deal and Great Society.[79] Combining critiques of Reagan's record on jobs and the distributional effects of his tax and spending policies, Democrats pressed ahead with their call for "fairness."

The numbers were on their side. Even as the employment picture slowly improved, evidence was mounting that the 1981 budget and tax cuts had compounded the hardships facing low-income working families.[80] OBRA had exacted severe cuts not only in programs for the welfare poor, but in programs on which many working-poor families relied, including food stamps and school lunches.[81] ERTA had increased rather than decreased the tax burdens of low-wage workers by neglecting provisions targeting low earners. A family of four with poverty-level earnings paid 1.3 percent of its income in federal income and payroll taxes in 1975. By 1985, this would skyrocket to 10.5 percent.[82] The Congressional Budget Office reported that families with incomes under $10,000 a year lost $240 worth of benefits from OBRA, while those with incomes exceeding $80,000 benefited on average $15,130 from the tax cuts.[83]

As preparations began for the president's reelection bid in 1984, Republican strategists again found themselves fending off Democratic attacks on Reagan's tax policies. The result would be a bipartisan tax reform plan that included major new assistance to the working poor, including an increased EITC.[84] The EITC expansion would be the next major building block of the workfare regime, again constructed by the Reagan administration on foundations laid by congressional Southern Democrats in the 1970s.

The reform originated with a 1982 proposal by moderate Senator Bill Bradley (D-N.J.) and Representative Richard Gephardt (D-Mo.). The plan would simplify the tax rate system, eliminate many loopholes and tax breaks, and increase the standard deduction and personal exemption in order to remove many low-income families from the tax rolls.[85] The proposal drew the attention of both parties as the 1984 election neared. Democratic frontrunner Walter Mondale considered campaigning on a version of the Bradley–Gephardt plan, but backed away. Worried that Mondale would seize the issue, however, and facing pressure from supply-siders in his own party, Reagan called for a study of tax reform in his 1984 State of the Union address. The Treasury Department was charged with meeting the president's call for "an historic reform for fairness, simplicity, and incentives for growth."[86]

Treasury officials faced a number of challenges in this mission. Among these was the fact that inflation had eroded tax protections for poor and near-poor Americans. More of them were paying taxes than in the past, and in some cases doing so dropped their incomes below the poverty line. Treasury needed a way to address the problems of the working poor without undermining core conservative principles. One solution, following Bradley-Gephardt, was to increase the personal exemption. The value of the personal and dependent exemptions (the limited amount of income excluded from taxes) had plummeted over time, even as Social Security taxes had risen, and the Treasury plan addressed this.[87] The second solution came courtesy of Russell Long's 1975 creation, the EITC. Faced now with the need for greater tax fairness for the working poor, the Reagan administration made a case for a sizable increase in the program.

This was a significant shift, particularly for Republicans close to the president who had helped design Reagan's initial tax and spending cuts and were principled opponents of the basic premise behind the EITC. During the OBRA fights, David Stockman announced that he and the administration did not share "the assumption that the Federal Government has a responsibility to supplement the incomes of the working poor."[88] Former Nixon aide Martin Anderson had attacked the EITC in a 1978 book as "a separate welfare program run through the Internal Revenue Service," one that "severely distort[s] the financial incentive effects of the federal income tax."[89] Anderson was now a senior adviser to Reagan for domestic and economic policy. It was no small matter, then, for the Reagan administration to agree to promote an expansion of the EITC. Equally important, Treasury officials made a case for the EITC based on distributional equity—not primarily on the need for welfare reduction, which had been Long's central aim in creating the program.[90] The Reagan administration was endorsing the underlying logic of a permanent and major income assistance program for all working-poor families.

Once Treasury had opened the door to using the EITC as a way to aid the working poor and restore fairness to the tax code, members of Congress from both parties rushed in with further proposed increases. As the tax reform bill began to take shape in 1985 and 1986, Republicans increasingly joined Democrats in turning to the EITC to retain a level of distributional equity in the bill. After adding various provisions to Treasury's proposal that would benefit upper- or middle-income taxpayers, lawmakers turned repeatedly to EITC increases as a way to balance the equation. Senior administration officials had expressed concerns about income supplements for the working poor, but faced now with a difficult political calculation, White House budget leaders did not object to proposed EITC expansions. In the end, the increases were even larger than what Treasury had proposed.[91]

Championed by Ronald Reagan as a way to make the tax system "fair for all," the 1986 Tax Reform Act gained widespread attention for simplifying the tax code and for cutting the top tax rate for wealthy individuals from 50 to 28 percent.[92] It also introduced a major change in policies toward the working poor, however. The act effectively removed the working poor from the income tax rolls, through simultaneously increasing the EITC, the standard deduction, and the personal exemption. Each was also indexed to the cost of living.[93] After the tax bill's passage, the poverty-line family of four described earlier received a tax credit equivalent to approximately 5 percent of the family's income. After paying its share of payroll taxes, the family paid 2.3 percent of its earnings in taxes, rather than the 10.5 percent it paid before the reform.[94]

Liberal welfarists supported the expanded EITC, though many emphasized its inadequacy as a solution to the larger problems of poor families. Some pointed out that the move merely helped these families make up ground they had lost over the previous two decades. Others recognized that the EITC increase and other adjustments in the 1986 tax reform did nothing to alter the underlying weaknesses in the low-wage labor market. The working poor, noted Representative Charles Rangel (D-N.Y.) with irony, might be forgiven for failing to say "thank you" for the measure: "They were too busy trying to make ends meet" in low-wage jobs.[95]

With broad bipartisan support, the EITC would become a centerpiece of the new workfare regime. Republicans had been pushed—by the political consequences of economic shifts and their own budget and tax-cutting policies—to seek a policy response to their political dilemma, and Long's tax credit for the working poor had served this function. Motivated in part by their own political interests in winning the allegiance of low-income voters, they had compromised on the principle of providing government assistance to working families, and they had accepted a rationale for expanding the EITC on broad tax equity grounds. Having conceded this much, they would soon learn that it would be difficult to block subsequent expansions supported by Democrats but opposed by most Republicans, and it would be politically costly to try to cut the program back once it had expanded.

In the cases of both JTPA and the increased EITC, most conservative Republicans would have preferred no new programs or expansions for the poor, had they not been forced to act. Yet in each case, conservatives won the larger battle over how to define the causes of and solutions to working poverty. The hardships facing poor families in the 1980s had many structural sources. But Democrats lacked the party unity, the votes, and the political will to confront Republicans effectively on these issues. Their relative weakness gave Republicans significant latitude in deciding not whether but *how* to respond to calls for "fairness" in the 1980s. And Republicans chose not to address the woeful levels of poor families' pre-tax income and economic security, but to seek greater post-tax equity through the EITC without fundamental labor market reforms. Both JTPA and the EITC increase marked expansions of social welfare assistance for poor families—but, in both cases, they expanded the emerging workfare state, not the liberal welfare state.

The Liberal Retreat on Welfare: The Family Support Act

By many measures, the Reagan team seemed to have reached the limits of their ability to dismantle the welfare system by the mid-1980s. Though they had made deep cuts in core programs and secured state AFDC waivers, they had been singularly unsuccessful in eliminating or reforming the basic structures of New Deal welfarism. All of the major programs remained in place, federal authority over them had not been replaced by block grants, and the entitlement to aid for all eligible families was intact.[96] Reagan opened up another front in the larger contest over work and welfare in 1986, however, taking renewed aim at welfare programs in his State of the Union address: "We must escape the spider's web of dependency. . . . I am talking about real and lasting emancipation, because the success of welfare should be judged by how many of its recipients become independent of welfare."[97] The administration elaborated an unsparing critique and tough reform agenda in a report called "Up From Dependency."

Although Reagan reopened the debate, it would be liberal welfarists themselves who would take the next steps from welfare to workfare. Democrats introduced legislation in 1987 that would eventually become the Family Support Act (FSA), the first major welfare reform since the 1960s. Conventional accounts describe a bipartisan compromise on work-based welfare reform, but the legislative history tells a different story.[98] The FSA was in large measure a product of *intraparty* compromise. It began as a largely liberal attempt to incorporate priorities from the party's competing wings, providing both an expanded safety net (including minimum benefit standards for states) and carefully crafted new work promotion measures. When conservatives in both parties voiced strong opposition to key provisions, liberals staged a protracted retreat from core welfarist commitments.[99] Most of the initial steps were not taken to win bipartisan support. They were taken to head off Democratic defections (particularly in the House) and to secure the support of party conservatives.

The strategic retreat began when House Democratic leaders agreed to slash the funding for their proposed reform by nearly half—from $11.8 billion to $6.2 billion over five years—and to drop the provision to create a national minimum benefit standard. Conservative Democrats remained opposed to what they saw as an expanded federal safety net, and they joined Republicans in rejecting the measure on key procedural votes. Of the forty-eight Democrats who defected, thirty-two were from the South. It took the intervention of Southern centrists who liked the workfarist tilt of the emerging legislation—including Governors Bill Clinton of Arkansas and Buddy Roemer of Louisiana—to break the stalemate. Sixteen Southerners (and six other Democrats) reversed their opposition, and the measure passed the House at the end of 1987 without a single Republican vote or the support of the Reagan administration.[100]

In the Senate, where Democrats had regained the majority in the 1986 election, the party's leaders on social policy had changed. With the retirement that year of Russell Long, Senator Lloyd Bentsen (D-Tex.) became chair of the Finance Committee, and Senator Daniel Patrick Moynihan (D-N.Y.) emerged as the party's preeminent leader on welfare issues. They put forward a bill even more conservative than the final House version, with the goal of winning bipartisan (and Reagan administration) backing. But Republican support did not come easy: the administration balked until the spring of 1988, when the bill was amended by Senator Robert Dole (R-Kans.) to include a federal work requirement for AFDC-UP recipients. Moynihan fought the amendment and lost, but Senate Democrats continued to move the bill to passage.[101] In the House, Southern Democrats then tipped the balance to produce a more conservative bill. When House and Senate negotiators met to produce final legislation, conservative Southern Democrats joined Republicans in pressing for a bill that was closer to the more conservative Senate version, with its lower funding levels and stronger work requirement.[102]

Despite major differences between the resulting bill and their initial reform proposals, Democratic leaders decided to support the legislation, rather than scrapping it and trying again with a new president and Congress after the 1988 elections. The Family Support Act was signed into law by Ronald Reagan in October 1988.[103]

Table 5.2 House Support for Conservative Version of the Family Support Act of 1988

	JULY 7, 1988	
	Yes	No
Southern Democrats	41 (54.7%)	34 (45.3%)
Northern Democrats	25 (16.1%)	130 (83.9%)
Republicans	162 (97.6%)	4 (2.4%)

Source: Author's calculations based on vote totals reported in *Congressional Roll Call, 100th Congress, 2nd Session* (Washington, D.C.: Congressional Quarterly, 1989), 14B.
Note: The division between Northern and Southern Democrats emerged again when House Republicans pressed for a vote requiring House negotiators to accept the (more conservative) Senate version of the FSA, rather than the (more liberal) House version, in conference committee. Southern Democrats provided Republicans with the margin of victory on a motion by Representative Brown (R-Colo.) backing the lower funding level and tougher work obligations in the Senate bill. The motion to instruct the House conferees passed 227–168 on July 7, 1988.

The FSA was widely hailed as a mix of liberal and conservative measures, a middle ground between Democratic and Republican proposals. But the outcome reflected a far deeper compromise on the liberal welfarist side. Liberals gave ground not just on funding levels but on core questions of policy direction, as described in a detailed account of the FSA by Robert Reischauer (at the time a Brookings fellow, and later head of the Congressional Budget Office).[104] On issue after issue, the FSA marked a retreat from New Deal welfarist principles embraced by party leaders through the mid-1980s. Three were particularly significant for the turn toward workfare.

The first was economic security. Since AFDC's inception, one of the goals of New Deal Democrats was to ensure that the program provided a guaranteed safety net for eligible poor families. AFDC had never provided enough support to lift families out of poverty, but welfarists had steadily increased overall assistance levels through the 1960s.[105] By 1986, however, after years of inflation and cutbacks, the benefit in the median state for a family of four receiving AFDC and food stamps was only 65 percent of the poverty line.[106] A top priority of liberal and moderate Democrats through the mid-1980s was to arrest this decline. But when conservatives pushed to strip benefit increases out of the FSA, Democratic leaders acquiesced, and the final measure contained virtually no provisions to address the steep drop in benefits.

Equity was a second core welfarist principle: liberals had long argued that a true federal guarantee of aid should extend broadly equitable benefits to eligible families in all parts of the country. Though assistance levels were still uneven and progress slow, the reform trend for over four decades had been toward nationalization and standardization to reduce interstate variation, and welfarists continued to push for a national minimum benefit for the program.[107] Reagan had begun to turn back the tide, seeking through his state waiver initiative and budget cutbacks to change the political equation on federal control and state discretion. The administration had advanced an assertive federalism, arguing that states should retain maximum control over their own eligibility and benefit levels, and that they should be allowed to "experiment" with alternatives to existing welfarist rules. In the FSA, liberals not only proposed a modest minimum federal benefit level for all states, but also offered states a higher federal match for increased benefits. But the minimum was rejected, and funding for the match was cut—and Democratic leaders continued to support the measure.[108] Though debates continued over the parameters of state waiver experiments, the final legislation was silent on the issue, allowing the state-level trend toward workfare to continue.[109]

A third issue in the FSA debate concerned welfare and work. Liberals and conservatives now largely agreed that those who could should move from welfare to work, but they disagreed on the role of federal policy and on whether work should be required as a condition of assistance, as earlier chapters have explained. Liberals argued for reducing the barriers to employment through work support services (such as adequate day care, transitional Medicaid benefits, and transportation assistance), and for education and training to facilitate greater income mobility and economic independence in the long run. Conservative workfarists countered that welfare reforms should move recipients quickly into the workforce, where they would develop the necessary skills for success and upward mobility in the labor market.[110]

In the struggles over work in the FSA, welfarists again made major concessions. Liberal Democrats did succeed in incorporating some of their priorities: the final legislation included several provisions to support the transition from welfare to work. Many of these supports were incorporated into the Job Opportunity and Basic Skills Training (JOBS) program established by the FSA to replace WIN.[111] But welfarists yielded more important ground to conservative Democrats and Republicans when they conceded that a successful welfare reform must reduce reliance on welfare through work obligations. This principle (first advanced in the WIN debates of the 1960s and 1970s) meant that the test of welfare-to-work programs would be a drop in welfare enrollments—rather than evidence that the program had improved the economic well-being of families. The law also imposed the first federal-level work requirement on individuals (rather than on states) as a condition for AFDC benefits, a requirement that would be broadened in the years ahead.[112]

More fundamentally, the FSA marked a retreat from the New Deal notion of a welfare entitlement owed to recipients by government, to the concept of a "reciprocal obligation" in which aid is offered in exchange for actions or behaviors by recipients. This would become a hallmark of the centrist workfare position in the early 1990s.[113] As the FSA moved through Capitol Hill in 1988, the idea caught on among moderate Democrats and some liberals. Senator Moynihan called for a new social contract; Representative Thomas Downey (D-N.Y.) urged a "contractual relationship" between recipients and public assistance programs.[114] Armed with the new language of reciprocity, Democrats became more vigorous champions of work as the solution to poverty and welfare reliance.[115]

Just as the 1986 Tax Reform Act represented a breakthrough to bipartisan support for an expanded EITC, the 1988 Family Support Act reflected a new agreement on a tougher social contract for the welfare poor. The FSA's main Senate sponsor, Daniel Patrick Moynihan, touted it as a product of consensus: "Conservatives have persuaded liberals that there is nothing wrong with obligating able-bodied adults to work. Liberals have persuaded conservatives that most adults want to work and need some help to do so."[116] But, in fact, the law reflected a compromise, not a consensus. Many liberal Democrats remained opposed to the principle of tough work requirements, and the language of the law reflected an uneasy and awkward agreement on the question of work: it stated that welfare recipients should be "encouraged, assisted, and required to fulfill their responsibilities to support their children by preparing for, accepting, and retaining such employment as they are capable of performing."[117]

In the end, the FSA "compromise" was an uneven one. On the key issues of benefit levels, the federal entitlement, and work requirements, almost all of the ground given was on the liberal welfarist side. This reflected a shift in the Democratic position on welfare over the course of the decade. The party's 1980 candidate, Jimmy Carter, had run on a party platform that called for an "income floor" for the working and nonworking poor, and fulfillment of the welfarist promise to "provide assistance in an integrated, humane, dignified and simple manner . . . for those persons who cannot work and who have no independent means of support." In 1984, despite continued liberal leadership in Congress, the platform discussion of public assistance was extremely limited, stressing the need to "preserve the self-respect of those who are unable to be completely self-sufficient . . . and to help them toward as much independence as possible." By 1988 the platform was almost entirely silent on welfare, with the exception of a brief statement calling for the creation of a "first-rate full employment economy," which, among other benefits, would "help people move from welfare to work."[118]

Acquiescence on the FSA also positioned liberals for further concessions to conservatives in the future. Once they had formally agreed that a central goal of reform must be to reduce welfare reliance, and that a primary means toward this end should be work obligations, liberal Democrats had locked themselves into a new policy debate. Welfare was no longer defined primarily in welfarist terms—as the policy response (however inadequate) to the social problem of poverty. It had become the problem itself. Ending welfare "dependency," rather than reducing poverty, had become the shared aim of reform, and liberals and conservatives would now argue over the best combination of carrots and sticks to reach this end. Debates over work requirements, meanwhile, would drift toward harsher measures as policymakers focused on the most effective way to achieve a drop in the rolls in the context of a deteriorating low-wage labor market.

One month after President Reagan signed the 1988 FSA, George H. W. Bush was elected president. Bush's administration devoted little attention to issues concerning welfare or the working poor, and the action shifted to the state level. States were struggling to absorb years of cuts in federal assistance as well as an economy-driven drop in state revenue growth. Faced with this fiscal picture, state officials were reluctant to allocate more of their own monies to match the federal funds available through the Family Support Act, even for promoting work, and the law was not fully implemented. In 1991, for example, only $600 million of the authorized $1 billion in federal FSA funds was used.[119]

Meanwhile, state experimentation with welfare reform continued, with the active support of President Bush. In his 1991 State of the Union address and again in 1992, Bush effectively invited states to opt out of the federal welfarist system, urging governors to seek exclusion from federal welfare regulations so as "to replace the assumptions of the welfare state and help reform the welfare system."[120] Much of this experimentation emphasized new cost-cutting measures. In 1991, states accounting for 96 percent of the AFDC caseload either cut benefits outright or simply froze them, allowing them to lose ground in real terms in the face of inflation at a rate of more than 5 percent that year alone.[121]

The Liberal Retreat on Work and Poverty

The debate on the working poor had also moved to the right over the course of a decade. The structural economic changes described in the previous chapter were eroding employment, precisely as the turn to workfare was tying the fates of more poor families to conditions in the labor market. In Washington, a growing number of policymakers saw work as the solution to the welfare problem. What, then, was the solution to the work problem, particularly for poor families?

The answer came incrementally in the 1980s, in policy decisions about job creation and training, tax credits for the working poor, work requirements for welfare recipients, and the minimum wage. Each rendered an implicit judgment on the larger question of what low-wage work should deliver and what government's responsibility was to those who sought work as a ticket out of poverty. By the end of the decade, the cumulative effect of these policy decisions was to locate both the sources of and solutions to economic insecurity in *individual workers* rather than structural weaknesses in the low-wage labor market.

From the earliest days of the Reagan presidency, the battle of ideas in the debate over the working poor was clear. The starting point for liberal welfarists was the New Deal–era vision that jobs and related social protections should permit workers and their families a basic minimum standard of living. The administration's position was that the market should determine opportunities and outcomes in the workforce, and that government efforts to assist low-income workers could inhibit private-sector job creation, in the end harming the very people government sought to help.

What triumphed by the end of the 1980s was a modified version of Reagan's pro-market position. It was a workfare stance acceptable to (if not preferred by) conservative Republicans and supported by conservative-to-moderate Democrats, including the large Southern contingent. Labor market outcomes should be accepted as is, workfarists agreed, and government's responsibility was to provide assistance to families with minimal intervention in the pricing, supply, or allocation of labor. This meant increasing the EITC (which did not interfere with the market price of labor) but rejecting increases in the minimum wage (which did). It meant offering job training (which did not interfere with private-sector job creation or allocation) but rejecting public-sector employment or guarantees (which did). And it meant supporting and requiring the transition to work by welfare recipients (which did not limit the supply of low-wage labor) but rejecting public assistance support for those unprepared or unwilling to make this transition (which did).[122]

The drift toward workfare solutions for the working poor in the 1980s reflected not only the unflagging persistence of conservatives, but also the failure of liberals to mount a viable defense of long-standing Democratic Party positions on work and economic security. By early in the decade, the implicit threat to these principles was unmistakable: the economy was generating deepening inequities in job opportunities and wages, and Reagan's policies were exacerbating rather than compensating for these problems. Yet the focus of the poverty debate quickly narrowed to the question of how to move the welfare poor into available jobs, and by 1988 both parties shared this agenda. Likewise, the economic "fairness" debate launched by the Democrats settled on a narrow range of policy solutions for the working poor by 1986, focusing less on the lack of fairness in the labor market than on the Reagan tax policies that worsened the effects of market outcomes. The discussion largely sidestepped the structural sources of income insecurity and instability, and concentrated instead on how to adjust the tax code to deal with the problem after the fact. Speaker O'Neill's closing speech in the House in favor of the 1986 tax reform was telling. Calling the legislation "the best anti-poverty bill in this House for at least half a dozen years," he lauded it for removing the tax burden on six million working-poor Americans—but he said little about the fact that although they would no longer pay taxes, most would remain poor.[123]

Throughout, liberals were constrained not only by Republicans but also by their own conservative Southern wing, which was perennially positioned to strike a compromise across the aisle and to back it up with votes if needed. The result was a gradual acquiescence to a new pro-market interpretation of the causes of and solutions to economic insecurity in the low-wage sector, and to policies promising workfare supports for the working poor rather than labor market reforms.

The policy shift unfolded in stages, from CETA's replacement by JTPA to the greater reliance on the EITC to passage of the FSA. But it was the minimum wage debate that would consolidate the workfarist response to the working poor. Every Democratic president since passage of federal minimum wage legislation in 1938 had pursued and won an increase, and even Republican presidents had signed increases passed by Congress—until Reagan.[124] Never generous, the minimum wage nonetheless remained at a level adequate to lift a full-time worker in a family of three out of poverty, from the late 1950s through the 1970s.[125] During most of this period, advocates successfully kept the minimum wage at approximately 50 percent of the average wage for nonsupervisory workers. Its value dropped precariously in the 1980s, falling to only 36 percent of the average wage by the middle of the decade. Full-time year-round work at the minimum wage left even a worker with one child below the poverty line in 1986.[126]

Yet liberal leaders chose not to pursue an increase until the end of the 1980s. They knew that the Republican White House was strongly against it. And they knew that the Democratic coalition was divided on the issue. With a few notable exceptions, Southern Democrats since the late 1930s had opposed boosting the federal minimum to address poverty among working families. Historically, Southerners broke with Roosevelt over the New Deal's Fair Labor Standards Act in 1938, and from the 1940s to the 1980s, attempts to block increases were spearheaded by the conservative coalition of Southern Democrats and Republicans, bolstered at critical points by major low-wage employers.[127]

Only after the Democrats regained control of the Senate in the 1986 midterm elections were party leaders prepared to act. They proposed raising the minimum from $3.35 to $4.65 an hour over three years, and more importantly, to index the wage to inflation. Liberal arguments reflected familiar New Deal notions of what work—even in the low-wage labor market—should provide, and where government responsibility lay. Senator Edward Kennedy said:

> A minimum wage that does not permit full-time workers to provide the bare necessities for their families is unacceptable. It permits unscrupulous firms with significant market power to exploit their lowest-paid workers. It violates the work ethic by condemning to lives of hardship and deprivation millions of citizens who are ready, willing, and able to work. A full-time job in the workplace should never mean a lifetime of poverty or welfare dependency. What we have today is a failed system in which the taxpayers are making up the difference.[128]

By the late 1980s, however, the public debate about the causes of economic hardship among low-wage workers had shifted, after a steady drumbeat of conservative opposition to New Deal policies and premises. Many conservatives flatly rejected the notion that government had an obligation to provide a basic wage floor. Indeed, the president asserted in 1981 that the minimum wage "has caused more misery and unemployment than anything since the Great Depression." He had twice tried to secure a subminimum wage for young entry-level workers.[129] Now, confronted with a proposed increase, the Reagan White House was unrepentant. "The last time I looked, we wanted the minimum wage lower, not higher," said a senior administration official.[130]

Labor Secretary William Brock set out the administration's interpretation of the trend toward declining wages. The conservative view on wages and worth in the low-wage sector pinned responsibility on workers—not the state of the labor market. "Gone are the days when functional illiteracy can be disguised by an unskilled—and high-paying—assembly line job. The one-way ticket out of poverty today and into the year 2000 is skills—basic literacy and skills," Brock testified in congressional hearings.[131] As in the battle over JTPA, leading congressional Republicans effectively argued that the solution to low wages was for workers to build their skills and market value.[132]

Even more significant was the fact that opponents now had a new tool to deflect proposed minimum wage increases, the EITC.[133] Taking a page out of the book of Russell Long—who had used the EITC to defeat FAP—congressional conservatives and moderates of both parties turned to the EITC to block liberal attempts to raise the wage floor.[134] Liberal Democrats opposed the tradeoff and argued for increasing both the minimum wage and the EITC. But they failed to make a persuasive case that the EITC alone could not address the structural problems of insecurity, instability, and lack of mobility in the expanding low-wage sector.[135]

Despite strong public support for an increase, conservative opponents blocked action on the minimum wage for two and a half years, even as the FSA wound its way through Congress.[136] When Democratic leaders finally won passage in the spring of 1989, the increase was vetoed by President George Bush. They were unable to muster the votes in the House to override the president when the conservative coalition reemerged to back Bush's veto. Twenty-eight Democrats (twenty-five from the South) joined 150 Republicans in supporting the White House.

It was not until November 1989 that a reduced increase (to $4.25 an hour) was finally signed into law. There was no indexation for inflation, and a provision was added for a subminimum "training wage" for young people.[137] As with welfare reform, the price of victory was a further retreat from a central Democratic commitment. Liberal Democrats' compromise on the legislation signaled a change in expectations. The new wage level was lower in real terms than it had been through most of the 1960s and 1970s, and it marked a step back from long-standing aspirations to keep the value of the minimum at roughly 50 percent of the average wage. By the end of the 1980s, a rising number of policymakers seemed to accept the notion that full-time work at the minimum wage may not provide a family with basic economic security.

Meanwhile, the EITC continued to benefit not only from the "tax fairness" debate, but also from its appeal as an alternative to traditional liberal initiatives (including childcare support and the minimum wage). In November 1990, the EITC was substantially increased as part of the budget reconciliation bill, with support from the Bush administration.[138] Politically, the quiet expansion of the EITC stood in sharp contrast to the modest but highly controversial boost in the minimum wage.

*　*　*

The minimum wage debate at the end of the 1980s confirmed the broader shift in ideas about the causes of and solutions to the economic insecurity confronting low-wage workers. Increasingly, the answer was that the problem lay with individuals, not the structure of the labor market, and the solution lay with markets, not government. Three related debates were converging on this formulation by the late 1980s—in policies toward poverty and welfare, toward the minimum wage, and toward job creation and training. "Just as much of the literature on poverty and welfare was moving away from structural concerns and focusing more on behavioral traits, so too was the debate about the minimum wage," wrote Oren Levin-Waldman in his historical account of the minimum wage. "The burden had been shifted from those industries paying substandard wages . . . to individuals."[139]

Gordon Lafer's study of job training strategies tracked a similar change in approach. Previous policies assumed that unemployment was in part a function of a lack of jobs providing adequate pay, and therefore envisioned the government as a player in job creation, including in some cases as employer of last resort. Particularly after the passage of JTPA, employment policies assumed that "the problem for poor people . . . was not a lack of jobs but a lack of skills."[140] JTPA's short-term job training model rested, above all, on "the conviction that poverty and unemployment must ultimately be blamed on shortcomings in American workers themselves, and that the hope of renewed prosperity lies primarily in self-improvement."[141]

That arguments in three areas of social policy (welfare, wages, and jobs) would shift rightward in a period of conservative ascendance is hardly surprising. But these were not unrelated policy developments. Together, they lengthened the causal chain of individual responsibility for economic insecurity. The welfare poor had long been faulted with refusing to earn their own support: an individual's will to work was presumed to be both necessary and sufficient to provide a ticket out of poverty. Now the unemployed poor were held responsible for lacking the skills to appeal to employers and thereby obtain a job, even in an economic downturn. The minimum wage debate at the end of the decade added still another link to the chain. Even those who had secured a job and were working—but still poor—were held responsible, this time for lacking the skills and abilities to fetch higher wages. The working poor could perhaps expect a wage subsidy from the EITC to help make ends meet, but neither the market nor government provided a bridge from the unstable jobs of the low-wage sector to the secure, middle-class jobs that came with floors, ladders, and nets.

Over time, federal policy had incrementally stepped back from previous commitments—first, to aid all eligible nonworking poor families on welfare; then, to assist the unemployed poor through limited job creation as well as training, and finally, to ensure that the employed poor received a minimum wage sufficient, at full-time work, to sustain a small family above the poverty line. In each case, the previous policies provided partial and patchwork assistance at best: assistance under job training and creation programs such as CETA was extremely restricted, welfare never reached all eligible families nor provided adequate aid, and the minimum wage had always been low. The real significance of the changes was in the retreat from core principles: that those willing and able to work should find a measure of economic security and mobility, that those who could not work should find a basic safety net, and that government had a responsibility to ensure that they did.

At the end of the 1980s, conservative advances and liberal retreats had left the basic structures and policies of New Deal welfarism standing. But the system had been hollowed out by a combination of budget cuts and policy changes, and its underlying principles had been severely tested and scaled back.

CHAPTER 6

The New South and the New Democrats

The welfare reforms of the 1990s have posed a puzzle for policy analysts: how and why did Bill Clinton, a moderate Democrat, rewrite the social contract for poor families on terms that would be the envy of Ronald Reagan? Accounts of the Clinton welfare reform focus on a number of proximate factors: the role of an activist Republican Congress, Clinton's 1996 reelection bid, political positioning by leaders of both parties, and deepening political opposition to the AFDC program.[1] All of these factors may have contributed. But none explains why the most conservative and far-reaching policy shift in sixty years would occur in the mid-1990s, on the watch of a Democratic president.

The 1980s, after all, closed with a stalemated debate over work and welfare. Liberals had given ground in the struggles over the Family Support Act, but they had held the line against efforts to dismantle the New Deal welfare system. Conservatives seemed spent after launching a forceful assault that hollowed out but did not restructure the welfare system under Reagan. Clinton's early campaign pledges to "end welfare as we know it" were bold but studiously ill defined, and they left the new administration plenty of room to build on the framework of the Family Support Act, which Clinton himself had helped construct as head of the National Governors Association. All indicators pointed to at most incremental policy change on work and welfare in the 1990s. Yet the reforms were sweeping.

Previous chapters have identified several historical and structural factors that make sense of this outcome; namely, the conflicts within the Democratic Party over the purposes of public assistance, the gradual rise of a workfare regime to replace a declining welfarist one, and the evolving role of Southern leaders in both processes. In the 1990s, Bill Clinton stood at the juncture of these political developments, unfolding simultaneously in his party, his region, and federal social policy.

Analyses of the policy conflicts of the mid-1990s highlight the bitter partisan struggles over welfare between the Democratic White House and an assertive new Republican leadership in Congress. But as this chapter and the next demonstrate, the decisive conflicts and compromises over antipoverty policy did not take place between the two parties. They took place between Democrats, and between Southerners of both parties. The reforms of the 1990s, moreover, were not solely about the fate of welfare, but about the rise of workfare for all poor families. Indeed, it was the consolidation of policies toward the working poor (including an expanded EITC) that led many policymakers to accept the demise of welfarism (including a dismantled AFDC). These developments were two sides of the same coin.

Clinton would serve as the final architect of a new social contract for poor families after a series of struggles with others in his party and from his region. The new workfare settlement was constructed on different premises and policies than those of the New Deal or the Great Society.[2] And its terms were closer to the position and legacy of Southern Democratic congressional leaders of the 1970s than to the positions of either party's leaders at the outset of the 1990s.

To understand the sources of the policy settlement demands attention to the larger and longer transformations in Southern politics and in the Democratic Party that shaped federal policy changes on work and welfare in the 1990s. In each case, the changes began well before but culminated in the Clinton years. This chapter opens with an analysis of the changing landscape in Southern politics and policy, then turns to developments within the Democratic Party that led to the rise of the Democratic Leadership Council (DLC) and Bill Clinton.

The South: New Politics and Old Policies

A new generation of Southern leaders took center stage in defining national welfare policy in the 1990s. Their purposes and positions were distinct from the last contingent from their region to seize the spotlight on these issues, leaders such as Russell Long, Herman Talmadge, and Wilbur Mills. Long had retired, Talmadge had been unceremoniously voted out of office, and Mills had left in the wake of personal scandals. The new group of Southern lawmakers included fewer Democrats and more Republicans. The roster of Democrats still featured some of the party's most stalwart conservatives, but it also had many more moderates and a larger sprinkling of liberals. This new cohort of Southerners—led by moderate Democrats and conservative Republicans—would determine the parameters of federal public assistance policies in the 1990s.[3]

The years between the election of Russell Long's cohort and the ascendance of the new Southern leadership had brought far-reaching changes to the region. The Southern economy grew rapidly, driven by manufacturing, tourism, and services, along with expanding defense and high-tech sectors.[4] Both population and income levels increased markedly from the mid-1960s to the mid-1980s, and the South became much more integrated into the national economy and society.[5] Even as growth slowed elsewhere, it continued in much of the South: the large-scale deindustrialization that devastated other regional economies in the 1970s, for example, benefited parts of the South, as companies searched for less-expensive business climates. Businesses on the move were drawn in particular to the region's low levels of taxation and unionization, and the low costs of both land and labor.[6]

These regional socioeconomic shifts had major effects on the political orientation of newly elected officials in both parties, from congressional leaders to governors and mayors. Most notably, they led to significant gains for the Republican Party. The initial surge in Southern Republicanism, of course, came when segregationists fled the Democratic Party over race and civil rights issues in the 1960s; it spiked again when Ronald Reagan proved widely popular among Southern voters. But the region's economic transformation also produced distinct new sources of Southern support for the Republican Party: it was the boom towns in Florida and Texas, in fact, that led the turn to Republicanism.[7] From outside the South, a steady stream of professionals, skilled workers, and business leaders arrived to take positions in relocating or expanding industries, including defense and research. By the end of the 1970s, the number of non-Southern whites had doubled in nine Southern states, and it had tripled in Georgia and the Carolinas. Many voted Republican. A new class of urban business professionals from within the South—some of whom moved from smaller towns to expanding urban or suburban centers—arose alongside these "Republican transplants."[8] Southerners were sending more Republicans to represent them in Congress, and the party's Southern contingent soon made its mark: "Southern Republicans tend to be more conservative, they tend to be more philosophically committed, and they tend to be more confrontational," observed Phil Gramm of Texas, who changed his party affiliation from Democratic to Republican in 1983.[9]

At the same time, the regional social and economic transformations ushered in a more diverse cohort of Southern Democrats. The party's Southern contingent included a solid corps of traditional conservatives: the Conservative Democratic Forum still claimed nearly fifty members and continued to meet weekly in 1990, and the Blue Dog Coalition of twenty-five House Democrats emerged in the mid-1990s as successors to the boll weevils.[10] Many of these conservatives saw their role as distinct and essential within American politics. Unlike the region's ascendant Republicans, they were not antigovernment, market fundamentalists. And among Democrats, they believed they represented a vital political position, particularly at a time when the party's base was shifting toward the more liberal Northeast and West Coast: "I think that it's important that the Democratic Party have a conservative influence in it to counterbalance the ultraliberal wing," said Marvin Leath (D-Tex.).[11]

At the other end of the spectrum was a small but visible contingent of Southern liberals. They were elected partly as a result of wide-scale black political mobilization in the two decades after the Voting Rights Act. "One thing about white Southerners is that they can count, and after the Voting Rights Act, they learned to count very well," John Lewis (D-Ga.) dryly observed of his fellow Southerners in the House.[12] Urbanization boosted the ranks of liberal lawmakers in the South, and redistricting increased the ranks of black and (particularly in Texas) Hispanic members, many of whom were liberal.[13]

But the dominant new cohort among Southern Democrats consisted of Southern centrists—pro-development leaders who embraced a robust form of business progressivism. Many were racial moderates, opposed to segregation and supportive of civil rights. The overarching priority of most of this cohort was to facilitate the region's continued economic development and expansion.[14] The rise of Southern centrists reflected not only broad popular support for extending the recent growth trends, but also a changing electorate: by 1980, the region's new middle class had eclipsed its working class in size. In their study of the Southern polity of the 1980s, Earl and Merle Black examined the political orientation of newly elected leaders from the area, including these Southern Democratic moderates:

> The reigning political philosophy of the new Southern middle class is . . . entrepreneurial [and] . . . individualistic . . . a blend of conservative and progressive themes. In its emphasis on low rates of taxation,

minimal regulation of business, and resolute opposition to unions and redistributive welfare programs of have-nots and have-littles, the current political ideology retains important continuities with the traditionalistic political culture. Its progressive element consists in its willingness to use governmental resources to construct the public infrastructure—highways, airports, harbors, colleges and universities, research parks, health complexes—that in turn stimulates and makes possible additional economic growth.[15]

In the more diverse political context of the "new" South, partisan competition was at times intense. Republicans battled for Democratic votes, as Democrats fought to hold onto their majorities. As chair of the Republican National Committee in the late 1980s, Lee Atwater, a South Carolinian who had worked for Senator Strom Thurmond (R-S.C.), was renowned for his political tactics: "Atwater's political skill," noted an aide to Bill Clinton, "was in updating an old-fashioned Southern antipopulism, using coded racial issues to prevent the white working class from allying with blacks on common economic interests, and to peel off enough white votes on that basis to defeat the New South Democrats."[16]

Even in this partisan environment, the pro-growth agenda would often unite Southern leaders of both parties where other issues, from race to abortion, would divide them.[17] The drive for economic development had broad implications for policies toward poor families. As Southern leaders championed the region's rapid growth, they confronted enduring problems of poverty and economic insecurity. Stories of Sunbelt prosperity were optimistic and ubiquitous, but the expansion was profoundly uneven in its impact. The point was not lost on many Southern observers. The 1986 report of the Southern Growth Policies Board, convened by twelve of the region's governors, observed, "During the 1970s, the fabled 'New South' seemed to become at long last really *new*, not just an Old South painted over." But the report concluded:

> The sunshine of the Sunbelt has proved to be a narrow beam of light, brightening futures along the Atlantic Seaboard, and in large cities, but skipping over many small towns and rural areas. The decade's widely publicized new jobs at higher pay have been largely claimed by educated, urban, middle-class Southerners.... Twenty years ago ... people with grade school educations could still find jobs. Today, the

will to work must be matched by the skill to work. For all their struggle to hold onto vanishing jobs, some of our citizens have settled into a quicksand of poverty at the very bottom of Southern society.[18]

Some of the patterns of economic hardship and inequity that the board and others described resulted from old structural disparities and hierarchies that even rapid growth could not erase. Others resulted from new forms of economic expansion. The rise of "footloose industries" in light manufacturing or services was a case in point. Unlike older manufacturing firms restricted to areas with access to rail, water, or raw materials, these industries could operate anywhere. They quickly sought out the most attractive business climates of the South, often settling outside of major urban centers. Many paid low wages and employed unskilled laborers. As a result, "poverty persisted in those areas outside the orbit of the wealthier cities," producing a "divided economy and a divided labor force," recounts historian Bruce Schulman. The division was exacerbated when high-tech employers, including many in the defense sector, imported much of their high-skilled and managerial labor force, and "hired locals for manual and custodial positions."[19]

The consequences of rapid, uneven development soon became clear: by the early 1980s, the economic progress of some Southerners had lifted the region's per capita income to 88 percent of the national average—but the number of Southerners still struggling in poverty had not changed since 1965, and the region was still marked by profound income inequality.[20] Deep and abiding racial disparities lay behind the numbers, and the structure of the Southern labor market was at their core. The poverty rate among black families in the South was 30 percent at the turn of the 1980s, four times the 7 percent rate of white families. Black Southerners "lagged far behind white Southerners in obtaining new middle-class employment."[21]

Meanwhile, Southern leaders watched in dismay as many businesses that had moved to the South moved on once again, often overseas, in the relentless search for lower-cost labor and less-regulated markets. "Some businesses which came South seeking cheap land and labor have now moved to other countries where production is much cheaper," noted the Southern Growth Policies Board. Left behind were Southerners "who did not leave their jobs but whose jobs left them—some moving to Taiwan and Bangladesh and Hong Kong and Mexico where wages are often less than a dollar an hour."[22]

Confronted with the dilemma of the region's continued economic and racial inequalities, the new Southern moderates might have been expected to embrace more liberal policy approaches than their conservative predecessors. But Southern leaders reached largely for policy solutions that were consistent with their focus on economic growth and expanding individual opportunity, and that did not depart sharply from the region's traditional response to social needs. There was increased and vocal support for expanding education, for example, but far less for expanding the basic safety net or reforming the structure of the low-wage labor market. Centrist Democrats shared with conservatives a reliance on limited welfare, state-level workfare and other pro-market responses to poverty, and a reluctance to intervene in the wage-setting or job-allocating functions of the market with measures such as minimum wage increases or job creation; these principles continued to guide Southern policies toward work and welfare.

In many cases, even liberal leaders "joined in the chorus, often tabling welfare and relief programs to court their cities' economic elites ... [seeking] investment and tout[ing] their cities like other Southern boosters."[23] The shared pro-growth agenda often sidelined issues of economic and racial inequality. The result, in certain cases, was "the subordination of racial conflict, and to some extent even racial justice, to economic growth," concludes Schulman.[24] By the mid-1980s, the political ascendance of the new Southern centrist Democrats and their distinct agenda was clear to observers of the region: "A judicious fusion of conservative and progressive themes expresses the essence of modern southern Democracy," wrote Merle and Earl Black in 1987, "and constitutes an operational definition of political 'moderation' in the South."[25]

The Democratic Party: Old Divisions and New Democrats

The trends in Southern politics in the 1980s and 1990s intersected with transformations in the Democratic Party—and in particular, the rise of the Democratic Leadership Council (DLC) and of Bill Clinton.

The DLC's triumph followed a protracted internal debate over the party's trajectory. Democrats had been troubled by signs of the party's political decline—and divided over what to do about it—since 1968. That presidential contest fractured the New Deal coalition that had enabled the Democrats to dominate Washington for most of the previous forty years. Beginning with Nixon's election, Republican control of the White House was interrupted only briefly by Jimmy Carter's presidency in the wake of Watergate. After Carter's failed reelection bid in 1980, the debate among Democrats took on a new urgency.²⁶

The struggle that ensued produced a two-phase confrontation with New Deal liberalism, including welfarist principles and policies. The first challenge came from neoliberal leaders within the party; the second, from the New Democrats within the DLC. By the early 1990s, the battle lines within the party over social policy were clear: they divided the New Deal liberals from the New Democrat centrists.²⁷

New Deal liberal stalwarts such as Tip O'Neill continued to control the party's political strategy and policy agenda through the early 1980s. In debates over the party's direction, liberal leaders argued that Democrats should return to first principles, to the ideas and constituencies at the heart of the New Deal coalition. The party's problems, in this analysis, stemmed from its departures from these commitments. Democrats should therefore redouble their efforts toward economic fairness, redistribution, and other liberal ideals. Strategically, Democrats should expand the party's base through registering new and underrepresented low-income voters, who were natural constituencies. This thinking led liberal leaders to tap Walter Mondale as the party's nominee for president in 1984. Mondale ran a campaign that hewed closely to long-standing Democratic principles and constituencies. He called for reversing Reagan's social and economic policies, directing federal aid to distressed workers, public-sector job creation, and policies of full employment.²⁸

Well before the election, House liberals confronted mounting opposition among party centrists. "Members of my own party," recalled O'Neill, said "that we needed new leadership, we needed new ideas. And I said that we shouldn't run away from the things we can be most proud of."²⁹ Mondale's crushing defeat further galvanized the centrist factions. They charged that both the policy vision and political strategy of New Deal Democrats were outdated. To build a new Democratic majority, the party needed to expand its reach by embracing the "center" in American politics.

The initial challenge to New Deal liberal dominance came from neoliberal reformers such as Senator Gary Hart (D-Colo.), Senator Paul Tsongas (D-Mass.), and Governor Michael Dukakis (D-Mass.). The neoliberals argued for a new economic policy, one that rejected the old politics of redistribution for the promise of economic growth. Strategies such as free trade, fiscal restraint, and strategic public investment in areas like research and education would bring sustained economic expansion that would benefit all Americans, they maintained, and would avoid the divisive and unpleasant debates over how to redistribute existing economic resources. On social issues and foreign policy, they generally shared the positions of the party's liberal wing. Politically, their focus was on broadening the party's support among college-educated voters in the nation's growing suburbs.[30]

The New Democrats associated with the Democratic Leadership Council shared the neoliberal economic vision, but they pressed further for fundamental change in the party's positions on social policy, cultural issues, and defense and foreign policy. DLC Democrats were tougher on crime as well as welfare, skeptical of affirmative action measures, and more pro-defense. They wanted not only to add new suburbanites to the party, but, more importantly, to win back the droves of white working- and middle-class voters who had abandoned the party by the 1980s.[31]

Several centrist Democrats faced off in the 1988 presidential primaries. Three prominent candidates—Gary Hart, Southern DLC member Al Gore, and Richard Gephardt (who was a founding member of the DLC but would later move to the liberal fold)—were out of the race by April. The Democratic choice came down to Jesse Jackson, who carried the liberal Democrats' banner, and Michael Dukakis. Dukakis supported the core neoliberal agenda—fiscal restraint, including no new taxes, a balanced budget, and an investment in entrepreneurialism to encourage growth. His choice of Texas senator Lloyd Bentsen as his running mate, a Southern conservative and DLC member, appealed to party centrists.[32]

When Dukakis lost to George H. W. Bush in 1988, Democrats were shell-shocked. Of the last six presidential elections, they had now lost five. Remarkably, George Bush had carried majorities at all income levels except those at the very bottom. If a pro-business Republican from a privileged background could win most white working-class votes, party strategists concluded, something was very, very wrong.[33] Leading New Democrats read the results in part as a verdict on the inadequacy of a neoliberal economic plan joined to a still-very-liberal agenda on social policy and other issues. They rolled up their sleeves and launched an aggressive campaign to redefine the party's trajectory and retake the White House in the next election. This time, they would succeed.

* * *

One of the party strategists watching closely as Michael Dukakis lost a commanding lead and went down to defeat was Al From, executive director of the Democratic Leadership Council. From had served as a top aide to Representative Gillis Long (D-La.), a cousin of Russell Long, from 1981 to 1985, and the two of them helped launch the DLC in 1984 and 1985.[34]

Conceived in part during a meeting held in Gillis Long's hotel suite during the 1984 Democratic convention, the DLC had deep Southern roots and remained an institutional haven for Southern Democrats. Attending the initial 1984 meeting were Virginia senator Charles Robb, Florida senator Lawton Chiles, Georgia senator Sam Nunn, and Arizona governor Bruce Babbitt, as well as Gephardt. The organization's first five chairs were all from Southern or border states; they included Gephardt, Robb, and Nunn, as well as Bill Clinton and Louisiana senator John Breaux.[35] Unlike the boll weevil conservatives who organized the Conservative Democratic Forum, the founding members of the DLC were centrist representatives of the changing region and "products of the 'New South,'" observed former Gore speechwriter and DLC chronicler Kenneth Baer.[36]

DLC members would eventually include elected Democratic officials at various levels of government from every state in the nation, totaling more than 750 by the early 1990s. Its leaders sought deliberately in the DLC's early years to reach beyond its bastions in the South and West to build a broader base. This initial "big tent" approach was in part an attempt to avoid being labeled conservative or, worse still, racist. The DLC nonetheless drew suspicion within the party, and many continued to refer to it as the "Southern white boys' caucus."[37] The DLC's aggressive law-and-order agenda, opposition to affirmative action, and support for welfare reform were viewed by many as thinly veiled appeals to white working-class voters uneasy with the gains of the civil rights movement.[38]

The group's ambitious plan to remake the party was as much a defensive as an offensive maneuver on the part of Southern Democratic elected officials. Regional leaders were watching, with growing concern, the steady drift of Southern voters to the Republican Party. In the 1984 election, the nation as a whole swung toward the Republican column, but the swing was three times as high in the Deep South, and twice as high in the outer Southern and border states. White Southerners threw their support behind Ronald Reagan by a margin of five to two.[39]

By the late 1980s, DLC leaders became convinced that the party's economically and culturally liberal image "could lead to its extinction" in the region.[40] To address these concerns, Southern Democrats had helped to reconfigure the electoral map and schedule for 1988 by creating the "Super Tuesday" primary contest. Holding coordinated primaries in a number of Southern states early in the season, they hoped, would end the dominance of Northeastern liberals within the party. When, despite Super Tuesday, none of the DLC candidates (including Southerner Al Gore) won clear victories even in the South, Al From concluded that a more decisive strategy was needed, and urgently.[41]

From fired off a memo in November 1989 to his board, made up of four prominent Southerners—Nunn, Robb, Breaux, and Bill Clinton. The Democrats, he said, were still in the grip of "liberal fundamentalists," and the DLC needed to wage nothing short of "a bloodless revolution in our party." His plan included capturing the public imagination with a bold statement of the DLC's philosophy at the group's upcoming New Orleans conference. It also included convincing Bill Clinton to assume the chairmanship of the DLC as a springboard to the presidency.[42]

From wanted to abandon the DLC's initial "big tent" effort to build a more demographically and ideologically varied base by avoiding rhetoric that might offend party liberals. Instead, the focus should be on developing a sharp critique of and alternative to the party's liberal issue agenda and failed electoral strategy.[43] This meant spotlighting rather than softening the distinctions between the New Deal liberalism of "old" Democrats and the "progressive centrism" of New Democrats. These differences spanned a range of issues. Among the most significant were social and economic policy—including the question of how to address the economic insecurity of poor families. Old Democrats stood on one side of the welfare/workfare divide, and New Democrats stood on the other.

The DLC's agenda was articulated in its New Orleans Declaration, a statement of principles endorsed by the group in March 1990 that described its political vision. In it, the DLC rejected three fundamental principles at the heart of New Deal liberalism: the goal of redistribution for economic security, the principle of entitlement, and the role of federal government authority in pursuing these ends. Rather than redistribution, the New Democrats advocated the neoliberal agenda of "growth." Rather than entitlement, they emphasized opportunity and urged "reciprocal responsibility." And rather than central government authority, they sought to rely on the "free market ... the best engine of general prosperity" where possible, and on partnerships with state and local governments.[44]

Broadly, this translated into an economic program advocating fiscal discipline and greater use of market mechanisms to achieve social ends. Growth—

in the post-industrial, information-age "new economy"—was to be encouraged through free trade and deficit reduction, along with educational opportunity and job training. "We believe the Democratic Party's fundamental mission is to expand opportunity, not government," asserted the New Orleans Declaration.[45] Not all of the New Democrats' themes were new, of course: "opportunity" had been a catchphrase of Lyndon Johnson's Great Society, and it was promoted then as a vital complement to the goals of fighting poverty and expanding the basic safety net.[46] But the DLC explicitly sought to use these themes as a counterpoint to the party's liberal past, and nowhere was this clearer than in social policy.

The DLC agenda recast a basic New Deal premise about the role of government: rather than protect citizens from market hazards or failures, or redistribute wealth and income to correct for market-produced inequities, government's function was to ensure an expanding private market and prepare individuals to succeed as best they could within it: "We believe that economic growth generated in the private sector is the prerequisite for opportunity, and that government's role is to promote growth and to equip Americans with the tools they need to prosper in the New Economy."[47] Accordingly, the DLC wanted to replace the "politics of entitlement with a new politics of reciprocal responsibility." This meant scaling back the notion that eligible poor Americans had specific claims to government benefits, in favor of the notion that individuals must take the responsibility to seize opportunities provided to them, and to meet societal obligations.[48]

The argument for forging a new Democratic agenda and analysis of the party's electoral failures was hotly debated in the late 1980s. It was distilled in a 1989 paper by William Galston and Elaine Kamarck titled "The Politics of Evasion" and subsequent pieces, which became, in Galston's words, "the template for the thematic and policy development" within the DLC between 1989 and 1992.[49] The authors leveled an indictment at the party's electoral strategy, which they claimed had pushed white middle- and working-class voters into the arms of the Republican Party. It was, they argued, a "mistake to believe that Democrats can construct majorities based on a swelling pool of poor and near-poor Americans waiting to be mobilized by an old-fashioned politics of redistribution."[50] The party's failure to win the presidency "proved that contemporary liberalism, an amalgam of New Deal, Great Society, and McGovernite propositions and programs, had lost credibility and was no longer politically viable," concluded Galston.[51] DLC analysts argued instead that the Democratic Party had to revamp its policies and programs in order to avoid being relegated to permanent minority status, and to "regain competitiveness among voters it has lost." These were not the liberal or black voters who had backed Mondale by more than 70 and 90 percent, respectively, but the "middle-income voters" who had abandoned Dukakis, and "working-class whites [who] were deserting the Democratic nominating process in droves."[52] The verdict was clear: the Democrats could not win unless the party defined a new public philosophy and issue agenda for middle-class, mainstream voters. This was the DLC's mission.

These conclusions dovetailed with the findings of Democratic political consultant Stanley Greenberg, who would become Bill Clinton's pollster in the 1992 campaign. In the mid-1980s, Greenberg had been asked by party leaders in Michigan to help assess a disturbing trend: why were voters in Democratic strongholds like Macomb County, Michigan, leaving the party and self-identifying as Reagan Democrats? To find out, Greenberg conducted a series of surveys and focus groups of white, working-class Democrats in the area. His conclusion was that "these traditional Democratic voters felt squeezed and neglected, pressed on one side by richer people who carried few burdens and paid no taxes and the other side by poorer black people who are the recipients of free programs and also paid no taxes."[53]

The political significance of Greenberg's conclusions was not that these voters felt squeezed by the rich, but that they felt squeezed by the poor as well—and for many, this meant the black poor. The implication was that government and especially the Democrats had done far too much for poor minorities, at the expense of the white middle and working classes. They saw themselves as struggling, Greenberg said, and they did not see the poor as sharing their struggle: "The 'upper class—they got all the tax breaks,' so they were privileged; but so too were 'the people that are on welfare.'"[54] Given this framework, the familiar liberal-Democratic call for "fairness" triggered hostility rather than support among these voters. "The word fairness (the touchstone of Mondale's 1984 campaign) had become a pejorative term for special pleading—as one Macomb housewife put it, 'some blacks kicking up a storm,'" Greenberg wrote.[55]

Greenberg's report "caused something of an uproar" among national party leaders, he later wrote, and a number of them "sought to cut the discussion short." Others were quite interested, however, including the DLC's Al From and Bill Clinton.[56] Greenberg's strategic conclusions converged with several DLC priorities—such as the effort to place the middle class front and center among the party's constituencies, and to cast social policies in ways that appealed to, rather than repelled, these voters through emphasizing themes such as work and responsibility.

The emerging DLC analysis was carefully cast in broadly inclusive language. But it implied an unmistakable zero-sum formulation. The logic was that assistance to one group (the poor, especially blacks) had come at the expense of another (the middle class, especially whites), and it was time for a measure of redress. This stance departed sharply from the long-standing liberal-Democratic position that the nation as a whole benefits from social programs to lift up the poor, because such programs not only reflect the federal government's obligation to aid the disadvantaged, but also strengthen the society and economy overall.

On social policy questions, the DLC crafted a strategy designed to appeal to the middle class by repudiating New Deal and Great Society liberalism with a moderate version of workfare. The DLC's organizing principle was not the defense of economic security FDR promoted, the combination of entitlement and opportunity advanced by LBJ, or the call to "fairness" voiced by liberal Democrats in the 1980s. It was the promotion of individual opportunity in an expanding private market. The approach was to identify policies that would support, enable, and require the poor to take responsibility for seizing opportunities to enter and advance in the job market, rather than relying on government aid. This meant moving away from welfarist social protections, from "constructing safety nets that protect people falling on hard times.... Safety nets, however fiscally appealing, represent bad politics and a moral trap that ultimately separates the poor, as well as the Democrats, from the majority."[57]

For the working poor, meanwhile, the DLC approach rejected liberal interventions such as job creation or minimum wage increases that sought to change the structure of opportunities within the labor market. The DLC strategy relied primarily on creating opportunities for individuals to compete for employment in the existing labor market, including job readiness and placement programs. In the words of one New Democrat, the difference was clear: "whereas a traditional Democrat would advocate guaranteeing a public-sector job to the unemployed, a New Democrat would support giving that person aid to enable him to acquire the training he needed to enter the workforce, if he so chose."[58]

The New Democrats' issue agenda was clearly informed by the strategic analysis and polling of experts such as Greenberg, Galston, and Kamarck.

But the agenda was also rooted in the experience and views of the DLC's members, including its dominant Southern contingent. DLC leaders at times downplayed this connection with assertions that the group's mission was to reinvigorate the party. In the words of Bruce Reed, an aide to Senator Gore who joined the DLC staff as policy director in 1990, "Despite the fact that it was first founded by Southern conservatives, its purpose was not to move the party to the right, although some in the DLC would like that to happen. The DLC exists to revitalize the Democratic party, and it will do whatever it takes to make that happen. We're not trying to move the party to the left or right, we're trying to move it forward."[59]

Although DLC leaders promoted their views as "new" ideas, "neither conservative nor liberal," and designed to attract middle-class voters, many of its positions on social welfare issues were tried and true ideas held by Southern leaders for decades. The DLC's opening salvo on the policy front was a case in point. It came from the new DLC think tank, the Progressive Policy Institute (PPI), headed by Will Marshall, a former speechwriter for Gillis Long. PPI's first policy paper in June 1989 was planned as "a controversial break from Democratic Party orthodoxy." It attacked proposals to increase the minimum wage, a policy that continued to draw overwhelming support among coveted middle-class voters and that Democrats had repeatedly used to their partisan advantage—but that drew little enthusiasm or unified support from Southern Democrats.[60]

The DLC's broader social and economic policy agenda closely tracked the core positions of many centrist Southern leaders. The dominant growth model in the New South, including low taxation, limited social services, and active state promotion of business expansion, aligned with the DLC's call for a shift from redistribution to growth, and from reliance on federal government authority to reliance on private-sector resources and market-oriented models.

Southern Democrats in Washington had argued over the years for a reduction in the size and scope of the federal government, and for fiscal discipline and deficit reduction. The DLC's push for opportunity rather than entitlement echoed Southern leaders' long-standing preference for maintaining a minimal social safety net for poor families and instead directing single parents on welfare into the workforce.[61] The organization's preference for relying on the EITC—rather than the minimum wage or labor market reform—to aid the working poor was likewise consistent with Southern leaders' inclination not to intervene in local labor markets. The DLC's strategy of evading race as an issue, urging instead expanded opportunity for all, also converged with the positions and priorities of many moderate New South Democrats. Macomb County was a long way from the poor rural and booming urban centers of the modern South, but both pointed moderate lawmakers in the same direction: toward avoiding thorny issues of persistent racial and economic inequality by subsuming them in a larger, color-blind agenda of growth and opportunity.[62] The DLC's strategic agenda thus reflected both the analysis of party strategists and the ideas and influence of the new cohort of Southern leaders who were its core members.

* * *

One of these leaders was Governor Bill Clinton, who proudly introduced himself as "a fifth-generation Arkansan, a Southerner born and bred."[63] Clinton had risen on the regional stage as the head of the Southern Growth Policies Board, and he moved onto the national stage as head of the National Governors Association. He was, in Al From's view, the ideal leader to deliver the DLC's message. In 1989, From traveled to Little Rock to make his pitch to the Arkansas governor. "I said to Clinton, 'Have I got a deal for you. If you take the DLC chairmanship, we will give you a national platform, and I think you will be President of the United States. And you will do a lot of good for us because it will make us a national organization.'"[64]

The DLC had something else to offer Clinton. Its message of budgetary restraint, nonintervention in the labor market, and financial and business deregulation had struck a chord among moderate Democrats in the private sector, and the organization was proving adept at raising money beyond the party's traditional sources of unions and liberal activists—including on Wall Street. The DLC introduced Clinton to New York–based financial industry donors, and his prolific fundraising was a significant advantage in his quest for the nomination. Many major donors backed his campaign, in the words of one reporter, because of his commitment to the "politics of free trade, free markets and fiscal discipline advocated by the DLC."[65]

From later explained what the DLC expected of Clinton in return, including loyalty to the New Democratic cause in reclaiming the party from the liberal fundamentalists. Although the DLC had in the past "side-stepped major fights" within the party, From emphasized, it would no longer do that—and he wanted Clinton to commit to a "willingness to play political hardball."[66] Although Clinton leaned left of the DLC on some issues, he would not disappoint on questions of work and welfare.

Clinton's priorities and policy agenda were defined in the context of a new economic downturn. The recession from July 1990 to March 1991 prompted another round of downsizing and other cost-cutting moves by business, leading to greater job losses among white-collar workers than in previous recessions and rising anxiety among middle-class Americans.[67] Equally worrisome but less prominent in the media were disturbing new poverty trends. The number of poor Americans rose for three years in a row beginning in 1990, reaching almost thirty-eight million and 14.8 percent in 1992, the highest number since 1962 and the highest percentage since 1966. The problem of working poverty was also growing: 18 percent of full-time workers in 1992 earned incomes that fell below the poverty line for a family of four, an increase of 50 percent since 1979.[68]

When Clinton announced his candidacy in Little Rock in the fall of 1991, he pledged that his campaign would be "for the forgotten, hardworking middle class."[69] His economic and social agenda reflected the DLC's emphasis on growth, markets, and fiscal discipline: "We believe in free enterprise and the power of market forces. . . . Economic growth will be the best jobs program we'll ever have." But Clinton's early proposals also advanced ideas about how to rebuild the economy's foundation to make it more fair, through government initiatives in national health insurance, expanded education, and job creation. Some of these ideas were also backed by the DLC; some reflected the influence of more liberal advisers in Clinton's circle, including his old friend (and future labor secretary) Robert Reich. His "public investment" strategy, Clinton promised, would devote "more than $50 billion each year over the next four years to put Americans back to work," in part by "creat[ing] millions of high-wage jobs."[70]

His initial plan on work and welfare, described in the campaign manifesto *Putting People First*, might be called "workfare-plus." The "plus" consisted of the liberal additions that Clinton supported—but would not, in the end, fight for or insist on in the face of opposition. For the working poor, the plan featured a proposed EITC expansion and a minimum wage increase. For the welfare poor, the commitment was to "scrap the current welfare system and make welfare a second chance, not a way of life." The full proposal pledged more:

> We will empower people on welfare with the education, training, and child care they need for up to two years, so they can break the cycle of dependency. After that, those who can work will have to go to work,

either by taking a job in the private sector or through community service.... [We will] provide placement assistance to help everyone find a job, and give people who can't find one a dignified and meaningful community service job.[71]

On the campaign trail, however, the message was less nuanced, reflecting his own priorities and experience with the issue in Arkansas and with the National Governors Association. As the campaign heated up, he promised simply to "end welfare as we know it," adding, for emphasis, "two years and you're off." This pledge would compose the heart of his welfare agenda.[72]

As on other issues, Clinton's positions on social welfare were also part of a political strategy to reach the middle class with a message that it was finally their turn. This was a difficult balancing act: he wanted to help poor families, but only through strategies that were acceptable to the white middle-class electorate. Clinton "proposed renegotiating the liberal ideal of the social contract, but not breaking it," in the words of two national political reporters who tracked and wrote a detailed account of Clinton's rise and first years in office.[73] Many liberal Democrats and core party constituencies viewed Clinton's agenda suspiciously. Labor leaders opposed his free-trade, pro-market positions. Civil rights advocates saw his pitch to the middle class and personal responsibility rhetoric as subtle attempts to tap into deep-seated racial antagonisms among lower-income whites.[74] There was reason for concern: liberals had just experienced twelve years of barely disguised racial appeals to working- and middle-class whites by Ronald Reagan and other conservative leaders. With stories of Cadillac-driving "welfare queens," conservatives had driven a race-laden wedge between the working and welfare poor by suggesting that the taxes and hard work of the former were supporting the idleness and profligacy of the latter. Clinton's (and the DLC's) more nuanced message ventured far too close to these divisive conservative claims, in the view of some liberals.

A weak field of candidates in the Democratic primary—and particularly the absence of a strong liberal candidate once New York governor Mario Cuomo decided against a presidential bid—left Clinton free to press his New Democratic positions.[75] After clinching the nomination, he drew even more heavily on moderate and conservative themes, emphasizing the distinctions between his agenda and that of New Deal liberals. His message was finely honed to appeal to voters among the "forgotten middle." A campaign commercial at the outset of the general election declared: "They are a new generation of Democrats, Bill Clinton and Al Gore. And they don't think the way the old Democratic Party did. They've called for an end to welfare as we know it, so welfare can be a second chance, not a way of life.... And they've rejected the old tax-and-spend politics."[76]

The "old Democratic Party," meanwhile, held its tongue and waited in the wings. Party leaders were desperate to capture the White House. They were elated on November 3: Democrats had won back the presidency and maintained control of both houses of Congress, despite losing nine seats to Republicans in the House. Now the question was what the election of a New Democrat would mean for policy priorities and outcomes.

Clinton's election was hardly a mandate for Democrats of any stripe. He won a strong electoral college showing with just 43 percent of the popular vote, slightly less than Dukakis's 45.6 percent. And despite the DLC's electoral strategy, his win was not attributable to an expanded Democratic coalition that included a reclaimed base of middle-class, moderate voters. It resulted from the pro-Clinton votes of traditional Democratic constituents—in a race in which Republicans lost votes to independent candidate Ross Perot. Clinton's level of support among the swing counties and demographic groups to which he targeted his appeals was in the end very similar to Dukakis's four years earlier.[77]

The divisions within the party, moreover, were by no means resolved by Clinton's election. The Southern wing of the party was revived by the victory, and DLC advocates were ready to press their agenda into action, yet Northern liberals held the main leadership positions in Congress. Politically, most congressional Democrats did not fully embrace the Clinton/DLC agenda. House Democrats, in particular, remained committed to the core issues and constituencies that defined the liberal New Deal vision, including labor and civil rights.[78] Democrats were nonetheless optimistic. The party had maintained strong, though not commanding, majorities in the House (258–176) and Senate (57–43). And after successive Reagan and Bush presidencies, Democrats controlled both Congress and the White House for the first time since the Carter years.

* * *

The election of Bill Clinton marked a milestone in the political development not only of the Democratic Party, but of the South. Transformations in both his party and his region had led to his nomination and presidency. Across the South, the Sunbelt boom and the rapid social and political changes that accompanied it had reconfigured the region's politics. Now Southerners—in both parties—were challenging the ideological direction of their party leaders and moving into positions of national political power. On the Republican side, Representative Newt Gingrich of Georgia led a growing caucus of Southern conservatives prepared to take on moderate party leaders and advance an assertive free-market and antistatist agenda. Among Democrats, the failure to block the Reagan policy agenda and to recapture the White House had generated internal challenges to the party's traditional liberal leadership. A new cohort of Southern centrist Democrats was now on the rise, and Bill Clinton represented its leading edge.

CHAPTER 7

Showdown and Settlement

Democratic Party liberals were cautiously optimistic as Bill Clinton prepared to enter the White House in 1993. Despite the New Democratic rhetoric, there were enough liberal proposals sprinkled through his stump speeches for liberals to hold out hope that Clinton shared their core commitments in social and economic policy. He had hit hard on issues of economic insecurity throughout the long campaign.[1] He pledged a change in course, and an economic program that would "put people first." Many liberals were encouraged by his promised public investment strategy and buoyed by key cabinet appointments, including Robert Reich at the Department of Labor and Donna Shalala at Health and Human Services.

Others were watching, warily, the appointments of a centrist economic team—headed by Lloyd Bentsen (Secretary of Treasury), Robert Rubin (director of the National Economic Council), and Leon Panetta and Alice Rivlin (Office of Management and Budget). Less visible was the political and policy team Clinton and Gore had built during the campaign and transition. Key players included Al From, Will Marshall, and Bruce Reed—prominent DLC activists who would shape the unfolding debates and decisions on work and welfare.[2]

The new president turned first to policies toward the working poor, then to the struggle over welfare reform that would define his social policy legacy. By the end of his first term, Clinton had struck what he called "a new social bargain with the poor."[3] The bargain meant abandoning need-based entitlement welfarism and adopting workfare policies to promote, reward, and require work.

This new policy settlement was forged through two rounds of conflict. The first took place within the Democratic Party, where the president's liberal allies fought to ensure that Clinton's plan preserved core welfarist principles.

Clinton initially embraced the liberal components of his welfare reform proposal, then backed away from these commitments as the legislative battles heated up. The second round of conflict and compromise unfolded between Southern moderate Democrats led by Clinton and Southern conservative Republicans in Congress. By early 1996, they had found common ground. The final welfare reform measure reflected a compromise acceptable to both sets of Southerners, leaving the president's liberal allies looking on from the sidelines.

The Working Poor: "Any Job Is a Good Job"

The centerpiece of Bill Clinton's early agenda for working families, unveiled during his presidential campaign, was an ambitious multi-year public investment plan. Though not fully developed, the plan had the potential to address a number of the structural sources of economic insecurity confronting low-income families, including the decline of stable, high-wage jobs.[4] As his advisers turned to the task of developing Clinton's economic program after the election, they weighed options for pursuing public investment in combination with other economic priorities. Liberals in Congress, led by Representative David Obey (D-Wisc.), pressed for immediate action on job creation, in part through increased government spending.[5]

One month after entering office, the president's team delivered a three-part economic program to Congress. It contained a short-term economic stimulus proposal to speed up a sluggish recovery from the 1990–91 recession, a long-term deficit-reduction scheme, and plans for an additional $100 billion in public investment over four years. The administration released a report that laid out a clear and bold case not only for spurring immediate economic growth, but also for public policies to address labor market conditions over the long term. Public investment "in the broadest sense" was required to "ensure more productive, higher-wage jobs and greater economic opportunities for ourselves and our children."[6] The investment strategy was highlighted as a central component of the Clinton economic program. The White House presented the stimulus package as a "down payment" on the president's larger plans for redirecting the economy and strengthening the labor market through new investment—in infrastructure, high-tech projects, and above all, in workers. Funds were to be devoted to unemployment insurance, worker retraining, and summer job creation programs for young people.[7] Even the deficit cuts in the plan were cast within this larger framework: "Deficit reduction at the expense of public investment has and will continue to be self-defeating.... One without the other will not work."[8]

To the dismay of party liberals, however, the commitment to broad public investment soon evaporated and even the short-term stimulus was scaled back radically, as deficit reduction emerged as the primary focus of the administration's economic agenda. Although the investment strategy had early and persistent advocates in the White House, most notably in Labor Secretary Reich, the administration was divided—and the balance of power in internal administration debates lay with fiscal discipline. "Deficit, deficit, deficit.... We have to cut it. By how much? That's all we talk about in the Roosevelt Room," fumed Reich in February 1993. "Day after day I clatter on about public investment, but I'm not heard by anyone around the table.... Bentsen, Panetta, and Rivlin want to cut the deficit by $500 billion over the next five years, mainly by cutting spending. If they have their way, the investment agenda is stone-dead."[9]

There were various forces driving the focus on deficits. The president's own priorities were one factor. Like many Southern leaders, Clinton was wary of deficits: he proudly advertised his record of eleven consecutive balanced budgets in twelve years as governor.[10] In Congress, meanwhile, members of both parties had grown alarmed by the sky-high deficits incurred in the 1980s. Confronted with the potential contradictions between spending increases for public investment and reducing the deficit, Clinton's economic team chose fiscal restraint.[11] Bentsen, Rubin, and Rivlin were concerned with maintaining the confidence of business leaders and the good will of Federal Reserve chair Alan Greenspan. They argued that bringing the deficit under control and reining in spending were the prerequisites for the new private-sector investment needed to spur the economy, and the key to persuading Greenspan to cut interest rates for faster growth. "It is repeatedly said that we must reduce the deficit because Wall Street needs to reassured, calmed, convinced of our wise intentions," noted Reich. "[Greenspan] wants the federal budget to be balanced. He doesn't want taxes to be raised. That means that spending must be cut, and the Street couldn't care less what the spending is for."[12]

The problem with this strategy, Clinton's liberal advisers countered, was that even if deficit reduction achieved its end—providing the private sector more and cheap capital to invest—there was no guarantee that the increased private investment would translate into the gains for working families Clinton had promised: "Companies intent on maximizing returns to their stockholders might invest the extra dollars in production abroad, or in labor-saving equipment intended to reduce wages and cut jobs, or in mergers, acquisitions and divestitures that result in mass layoffs," Reich pointed out.[13]

In the end, the administration split apart the components of the economic package, despite concerns from liberals in Congress that doing so would splinter support and imperil key elements of the plan, including the long-term spending and investment strategy. "If they let it get split up," said Senator Tom Harkin (D-Iowa), "that will be the end of it." The administration introduced two legislative initiatives: a short-term stimulus measure and a deficit reduction proposal; the plan for large-scale public investment was floated in Congress but went nowhere. Clinton's stimulus legislation sought $30 billion to jump-start the economy, with $16 billion in proposed new spending and $14 billion in tax cuts; the spending was presented as a small start on public investment.[14] Despite the fact that Democrats controlled both houses of Congress, even this scaled-back stimulus package soon ran aground politically. After passing the House, the proposal encountered serious opposition in the Senate. Republicans there argued that spending increases had to be matched by cuts in other programs. A vocal group of centrist and conservative Democrats led by John Breaux (La.), David Boren (Okla.), and Richard Bryan (Nev.) concurred. The stimulus was first trimmed, then delayed; ultimately, the only element that passed was a $4 billion increase in spending for extended unemployment benefits.[15]

The deficit reduction plan, meanwhile, was introduced through the Omnibus Budget Reconciliation Act (OBRA) of 1993 and passed in August. It proposed to slash the deficit through a combination of spending cuts (particularly in defense and entitlements such as Medicare) and tax increases (particularly for those in upper-income brackets).[16] The focus on deficits and the collapse of the public investment initiative sent an early signal not only of the new president's priorities, but also of the limits of the Democratic Party's consensus on an economic agenda to address the structural sources of income insecurity in the early 1990s.[17]

If the decision to back away from the public investment strategy was the first measure of the administration's policy commitments regarding the working poor, then the second was the retreat from Clinton's pledge to boost the minimum wage. Clinton had supported a wage increase in principle on the campaign trail, and liberal leaders wasted no time in calling for action on the minimum wage.

But "at the start of 1993, Democrats didn't want to talk about raising the minimum wage (and Bill Clinton didn't want to get near the issue) because it was seen as something that 'old' Democrats worried about," his labor secretary later explained.[18] Instead, Clinton delivered a major expansion in the EITC, favored by New Democrats as a market-friendly solution to working poverty, as part of the OBRA deficit reduction bill. Proposing a $28 billion increase over five years, Clinton pledged to use the EITC, in combination with food stamps, to ensure that "for the first time, people who work 40 hours a week with children in the home would be lifted above poverty." He also proposed extending EITC benefits to low-income workers with no children.[19]

Republican leaders balked at the EITC proposal, particularly at the size of the increase. House Republicans led by Bill Archer of Texas tried unsuccessfully to eliminate it from the bill, as part of a deal to reduce the new energy tax, but the EITC had won significant bipartisan support by the early 1990s, and Archer's attempt was foiled in the Ways and Means Committee. In the Senate, however, the Finance Committee cut the increase significantly, from $28 billion to $18 billion. The president used Russell Long's arguments to fight back—insisting that an increased EITC was needed to maintain incentives for poor families to choose work over welfare—while also pressing for expanded eligibility for the program.[20]

The House–Senate conference ultimately agreed to a $20 billion increase and to make childless adults eligible.[21] Clinton and the Congress had taken a further step toward turning the EITC into a broad-based program of assistance for the working poor. The credit for childless workers was very small, but it crossed an important line in the program's political development. Originally created as an alternative to welfare expansion, the EITC was gradually becoming the favored solution to the problem of low-wage work. Together with the 1990 increase, the 1993 expansion led to rapid growth in the number of recipients and the level of benefits; within two years, the EITC would be larger than AFDC.[22]

Party liberals were growing impatient about the minimum wage, however. They had assumed that with Democrats now controlling the White House and Congress, the wage floor would be restored to its former level and even indexed for inflation. Other Democrats—including Panetta, Rubin, and Bentsen—resisted the idea.[23] Clinton delayed taking action until January 1995. By then, Democrats had lost control of Congress to the Republicans.

Clinton's call for a higher minimum wage in the State of the Union speech was brief and subdued.[24] But it was enough to spark debate in Congress, and it lent new legitimacy and energy to liberal efforts. Senator Edward Kennedy (D-Mass.), joined in the House by Minority Leader Richard Gephardt (D-Mo.), launched a vigorous campaign for what he termed a long-overdue increase.[25] The hourly minimum, at $4.25, had fallen far below the minimum of the late 1960s in real terms; its purchasing power was near a forty-year low. Over four million Americans earned the minimum wage, most of whom were adults, and some 40 percent of whom were their family's only breadwinners. The president proposed a very modest increase of ninety cents an hour—which would bring the purchasing power of the minimum wage not quite to where it was in the early 1980s, providing little more than an adjustment to account for inflation.[26]

The terms of debate within the Democratic Party over this classic liberal-Democratic issue had changed in the intervening years, however. In a meeting of House Democrats, liberals pressed their case in familiar welfarist terms. Representative Rosa DeLauro (D-Conn.) insisted, "There's nothing more basic to the Democratic philosophy than the idea that people who work hard should get a fair day's pay." But others in the party argued that the Democrats' sweeping congressional losses in the 1994 midterm elections had changed the equation. "Take a good look around this room," one member said. "Why do you think there are so few of us left? Because this party couldn't let go of old Democratic ideas that are obsolete, like raising the minimum wage." A young Southern Democrat said, "I'll wager anyone in this room, if we come out for a minimum-wage increase . . . the voters in my district just aren't gonna elect a Democrat again."[27]

For their part, the DLC remained strongly opposed to the minimum wage increase and waged a visible campaign against it.[28] In hearings entitled "Evidence Against a Higher Minimum Wage," Republicans in Congress used the DLC's attacks on the proposal—and Clinton's own 1993 statement that it was "the wrong way to raise the incomes of low-wage workers"—to discredit the plan.[29] Prominent Republicans emphatically registered their own opposition. Representative Dick Armey (R-Tex.), a former economics professor, defended the market fundamentalist view that the minimum wage should be abolished.[30] Senator Robert Bennett (R-Utah) likewise advocated eliminating the wage altogether and allowing the market alone to determine the value of a person's labor. He stated flatly in a televised debate, "If someone isn't worth $4.25 an hour, he should be paid less."[31]

Within the Democratic coalition, liberal leaders had to work hard to keep the caucus united behind an increase. Southern and Western moderates and conservatives were hesitant. They faced pressure from small businesses and major national chains to oppose the increase.[32] The proposal also needed

Republican votes to pass. In the face of strong public support, Republicans finally backed the wage boost—after it was tied to a package of tax breaks for small businesses worth more than $20 billion over a decade.[33] Congress passed a modest increase in August 1996 that took effect just before the November election.

Once again, the limits of the minimum wage victory were clear. Between ten and eleven million workers received a pay raise, but it was a small one, at less than a dollar an hour, phased in over two years. At $5.15 an hour it did little more than restore lost purchasing power, and it would not be enough to lift a family of two or more with a full-time worker out of poverty.[34] The minimum wage would stay at that level, losing ground to inflation, for another decade. Led by Clinton, the Democrats had set their sights low, opting not to press for indexation or for a substantial increase.

The parameters and policies of the Clinton agenda for the working poor were thus set early in his first term, and they were was never seriously revisited. The bold plan to address weaknesses within the labor market through a public investment strategy had collapsed, and the EITC was the policy tool of choice to address the problems of poor workers. An untenable burden rested on the program. The EITC was a wage supplement, no less and no more. It would not alter the wage structure of the labor market, the way an indexed minimum wage would, exerting upward pressure on wages immediately above the minimum. More fundamentally, the EITC was unable to address the lack of security, stability, and social protections provided by low-wage jobs. Nor could it provide mobility for workers seeking stable middle-class employment; what was missing was a bridge from the low-wage sector to the more secure jobs of the middle class.[35]

The administration's approach to low-wage labor was summed up succinctly in a 1994 memo to the president from his domestic policy adviser, Bruce Reed: "The EITC turns a minimum wage, $4.25 an hour job into a $6 an hour job. With the EITC and health reform, any job is a good job."[36] With this as a guiding principle, the administration signaled that it would not reopen the debate over what work should provide: if "any job" the market produced, backed by limited government supports, was a "good job," then the struggle to ensure that the labor market provided good jobs was, for all intents and purposes, over. Fully aware of the diminished possibilities within the low-wage sector, centrist Democrats in the Clinton White House were settling for a different and much attenuated aim than that of liberal welfarists. They had scaled back the party's vision to one that accepted labor market conditions as a given (and jobs as they came) and compensated for poor wages after the fact.[37]

Showdown on Welfare Reform

As the policy debate over the working poor was unfolding, the political storm over the welfare poor was gathering strength. Although the Democratic Party's position on welfare had shifted rightward in the 1980s, the points of intraparty disagreement were neither few nor trivial in the early 1990s. Liberals were prepared to accept—and in some cases even embrace—the compromises over work and welfare embodied in the Family Support Act. But there was little evidence that they were willing to retreat further on the core principles of New Deal public assistance for poor families. Many liberals saw the next step in welfare reform as the full implementation of the FSA, combined with increased funding for transitional supports for families moving from welfare to work.[38] DLC centrists, on the other hand, saw ending dependence on AFDC as the primary goal and were not constrained by the welfarist commitments of "old" Democrats. Economic independence and opportunity for advancement—not economic security—were their watchwords, and work requirements were at the center of their proposals.

Stifled for the sake of party unity during the campaign, the policy differences between liberals and centrists arose immediately after Clinton took office in January 1993. The domestic policy advisers on Clinton's transition team—such as DLC leaders From and Reed—wanted him to take up welfare reform immediately. He could build confidence among middle-class voters, they believed, by delivering quickly on his campaign promise to get welfare recipients off the rolls and into jobs.[39] Liberal leaders in Congress disagreed, and urged delay. Taking on welfare reform, they argued, would "blow up" the Democratic caucus. House Speaker Tom Foley (D-Wash.) and House Majority Leader Richard Gephardt met privately with the president and his advisers. They knew that the issue was hotly contested within the party, and they voiced concern that it would split the caucus not only along policy and ideological lines—with welfarists opposing workfarists—but also on the issue of race, given the racially charged history of the welfare policy debate.[40]

The Clinton team ultimately decided to focus on health care as its initial domestic policy priority, and Clinton's first significant decision on welfare reform was thus to delay action: his administration did not take steps to define a reform plan or begin to mobilize support.[41] It would prove a costly decision. Neither camp in the intraparty struggle could have anticipated how quickly or dramatically the prospects for a liberal-moderate Democratic compromise would deteriorate.

The consequences of delay became evident both in the debate on Capitol Hill and in developments at the state level. The conversation among Democrats in Washington may have reached a stalemate over the welfare versus workfare question, but the strategic discussion among Republican lawmakers and conservative intellectuals was advancing rapidly. The conservative debate had drifted rightward in the late 1980s and then took a decisive turn in this direction in the early 1990s. An important catalyst was an October 1993 editorial by Charles Murray in the *Wall Street Journal*. Murray used the piece to take the argument he made in *Losing Ground* to its logical and stark conclusion, beyond workfare. It was no longer enough to require welfare recipients to work. The government, he stated, should simply cut off all public assistance to poor women who have children outside of marriage. Other conservative thinkers—including William Bennett, William Kristol, Robert Rector, and James Q. Wilson—added intellectual firepower to the revived assault on welfare.[42] Conservatives had long sought to join work obligations with other requirements for AFDC recipients, but their legislative focus had been on moving recipients from welfare to work. Social conservatives now wanted to mount a full-scale campaign to use federal welfare rules to reform the behaviors of poor single mothers that they concluded were at the root of poverty and welfare use: "Illegitimacy is the single most important social problem of our time," warned Murray.[43]

Republican lawmakers were divided. Some argued for an increased emphasis on out-of-wedlock births, returning to a theme that had been raised by conservatives (including Southern Democrats such as Mills and Long) in the 1960s but had not been central to Republican policy goals. It was not featured in the party's national platform until 1988—unlike work requirements, which emerged in the 1972 platform.[44] As the new wave of antiwelfare arguments now made workfare an unsatisfying middle ground for hardline conservatives, some sought to end assistance for children with unmarried mothers.[45] Other Republicans insisted that the focus should remain on strengthening welfare-to-work policies. Many adopted an increasingly forceful "work-first" approach that required immediate labor force attachment rather than allowing some education or training for welfare recipients.

With the president's pledge to "end welfare as we know it" as a spur to action, congressional Republicans got to work on legislation. They assumed, wrongly, that Clinton would move quickly on his campaign promise. The Republican bill took a strong position on work and aid to unmarried recipient mothers. Yet some in the Republican caucus—led by Asa Hutchinson of Arkansas and Jim Talent of Missouri—wanted to go further. In part, they wanted to stake out a position distinct from Clinton's pro-workfare stance by moving to the right. They developed an alternative that hewed closer to Murray's position—and then convinced fellow Southern Republicans Gingrich and Armey to incorporate these proposals in the party's campaign manifesto for the 1994 election, the Contract with America.[46]

Clinton's decision to throw down the gauntlet on welfare reform during the campaign and then delay action on his own plan once in office had thus helped lead hardline Republican conservatives to define an even tougher position in the debate on Capitol Hill.[47] At the state level, meanwhile, Clinton had unleashed another force for workfare. He had extended the Reagan–Bush policy of granting state waivers and, as the House Ways and Means Committee reported, "accelerated the waiver process" by making administrative changes in how waiver requests were evaluated.[48] Support for state-level action reflected Clinton's experience and perspective as a state executive and a Southerner. "He was a governor, and he always viewed welfare through a governor's eyes," observed David Ellwood of the Harvard Kennedy School, who co-chaired the administration's welfare reform task force as Health and Human Services (HHS) assistant secretary. "In general, he felt, why should a bunch of federal bureaucrats decide what a state can and can't try to do?"[49]

But in the political and fiscal context of the early 1990s, this was not a neutral act. The states were not simply "laboratories of democracy," experimenting with policies across the spectrum to see what worked. During the Reagan and Bush years, waivers had been used repeatedly—with White House support—to cut costs through work requirements and other restrictions. The Clinton administration offered no new guiding vision for its evaluations of waiver requests. In the words of Mary Jo Bane, assistant secretary of HHS for public assistance: "We are not in the business of turning down waiver requests. We are in the business of helping states do what they want to do." Sidestepping the question of the policy directions reflected in state programs, the administration portrayed pragmatic experimentation itself as progress on welfare reform. Clinton boasted that his administration had approved state welfare experiments in thirty-two states in its first two and a half years, affecting half the nation's fourteen million welfare recipients, more than all previous administrations combined.[50]

These state-level initiatives contributed directly to a larger national shift toward workfare. As the detailed case studies conducted by Robin Rogers-Dillon demonstrate, the waivers redefined what welfare meant in the public mind between 1992 and 1996—well before Congress and the president had reached agreement on federal policy changes. Through implementing workfare and other reforms on the ground, the waivers weakened welfarist policy legacies from below. They served, in Rogers-Dillon's term, as a "shadow policymaking institution," through which welfare was cast less as a safety net for poor families and more as a temporary measure meant to reform the behavior of the poor and move them into the workforce. Florida's 1994 program, for example, established the nation's first time limit on welfare receipt. Other states imposed conditions on recipients' behavior that would later be incorporated in federal law.[51] By 1996, the Council of Economic Advisers reported that the administration had approved waivers for forty-three states, and that, increasingly, waiver requests that included "sanctions imposed on workers who did not live up to their work or job search requirements are most common."[52]

It was not until his second year in office, in the midst of a lengthy and ultimately unsuccessful battle for health care reform, that Clinton outlined his own position on welfare, in his 1994 State of the Union address. He wanted to balance the twin goals of moving recipients from welfare to work—and providing the means and support for them to do so. Most importantly, Clinton's proposed reforms stipulated (in the details) that those who did what they could but were unable to find work would still receive help from the government; the entitlement to assistance would remain intact.[53]

Clinton's timing was inauspicious. Although the economy was growing after the 1990–91 recession, many families had been left behind, with less job security, lower average weekly earnings, lengthening unemployment spells, and a poverty rate that reached 14.5 percent in 1994. There was little discernible public support for addressing the rising rate of poverty, however. Middle-class workers were themselves facing economic uncertainty and stagnant incomes. And the New Democrats, led by Clinton, had made the case that the middle class should not be expected to provide more tax dollars to support the have-nots.[54]

As the administration considered its approach to welfare reform, intense debates unfolded over costs. Ellwood laid out the facts squarely. To do what Clinton wanted—to move people from welfare into long-term positions in the workforce—would cost *more*, not less, than the existing welfare program, a minimum of $2 billion a year more. The costs were tied to the instability and insecurity of low-wage work. Ellwood explained to the president that 70 percent of welfare parents found jobs within two years, but fell back onto welfare when they were unable to support their families on low-wage incomes, unable to afford child care or private health insurance, and unable to find or qualify for better-paying jobs. Spending would be needed for measures such as child care, training, and public jobs. This posed a political as well as a fiscal problem. No groundwork had been laid to prepare the public for the costs of compensating for the weaknesses of the low-wage labor market to ensure that welfare-to-work strategies could succeed. Now Clinton wondered, "How do we explain to the public that we're adding $2 billion of spending a year in order to limit welfare benefits to two years?"[55]

Clinton's welfare reform task force, co-chaired by Ellwood, Mary-Jo Bane, and Bruce Reed, honed the administration's proposed legislation in the summer of 1994.[56] The bill proposed to end the current welfare system and to replace it with two years of aid and a requirement that recipients begin to move from welfare to work in this period. While doing so, they would receive education, training, and child care assistance. After the two-year time limit, those unable to find jobs in the private sector would be provided with public (or publicly subsidized) employment. The plan offered one- to two-year extensions for those pursuing their high school equivalency diplomas or other educational goals. It also included numerous and liberal exemptions from the time limit for those who faced obstacles to employment or were unable to gain access to the relevant government programs, such as the JOBS program created under the Family Support Act.[57]

Several of Clinton's liberal advisers—including Reich and Peter Edelman, a leading policy expert who was serving as an assistant secretary at HHS—believed that this early plan reflected an acceptable balance between liberal welfare policies and the administration's vision of moderate workfare.[58] The plan reinforced the FSA compromise: it would more aggressively promote and require work, but also preserve the basic safety net.[59] But Clinton's liberal supporters may have overestimated his commitment to the liberal measures in his proposals—and underestimated his conviction to use workfare to end welfare reliance. For welfarists, the commitments to the federal entitlement and to providing adequate work supports were a necessary precondition for reform. For the president, these were desirable provisions, but expendable if necessary.[60]

Centrist Democrats in the DLC and Congress, meanwhile, lauded the aims of the Clinton plan but denounced the old-style, liberal welfare supports that had been added. These "expanded the existing welfare bureaucracy, pumping more money into education and training programs that have largely failed to connect welfare recipients to the world of work and responsibility," according to the DLC.[61] In Congress, moderate Democrats led by Representative David McCurdy of Oklahoma (a co-founder and national chairman of the DLC) had come together in a group they called the Mainstream Forum. The group included a number of prominent Southerners, and welfare reform was one of its aims. Working with DLC leaders From and Marshall, they pursued a legislative strategy to move the administration toward a more purely "centrist" workfare reform, unencumbered by liberal additions.[62]

The liberal-moderate compromise emerged too late to frame the welfare debate in any case. The administration's bill was introduced in June 1994, when Congress and the White House were consumed with battles over health care and crime legislation. The bill died in the 103rd Congress—and by November, the administration had run out of time to set the agenda on terms of its choosing.[63]

* * *

Democratic leaders had steeled themselves for Republican gains in the 1994 midterm elections, but few were ready for the tidal wave that arrived on November 8. The Republicans scored overwhelming victories nationally. Fifty-four seats shifted from the Democratic to the Republican column in the House, giving Republicans a majority in that chamber for the first time since 1954. In the Senate, Republicans picked up eight seats from Democrats, winning back the majority they had lost in 1986.[64]

The elections also marked a turning point in Southern politics. This was the year, as journalists Dan Balz and Ronald Brownstein observed, that "the Republican party captured the South and the South captured the Republican party."[65] For the first time in the modern era, the South elected more Republicans than Democrats in the House (74–63) and Senate (16–10). Across the South, white voters in every income group, except those earning less than $15,000, had fled the Democratic Party for the Republicans.[66]

Within the Republican Party, the ascendance of its conservative Southern wing was captured by the rise of Newt Gingrich of Georgia to Speaker of the House, following the retirement of moderate Minority Leader Robert Michel of Illinois. But the Republican leadership change went much deeper. Southern conservatives Richard Armey and Tom DeLay, both from Texas, were elected House Majority Leader and Whip. Bob Livingston of Louisiana was named to chair the Appropriations Committee, and Bill Archer, another Texan, was elevated to head Ways and Means; these two committees were the most powerful committees in the House. In the Senate, Southern conservatives soon occupied the leadership ranks directly below the more moderate Majority Leader Bob Dole—including Phil Gramm of Texas, Trent Lott and Thad Cochran of Mississippi, Don Nickles of Oklahoma, and Connie Mack of Florida.[67]

For social policy, the implications were clear. The new drive for conservative reform would be not only a Republican project, but also, in many respects, a Southern project. Through the party's Contract with America and other initiatives, Southerners such as Gingrich and Armey had been leaders in the effort to craft the Republican agenda on welfare and related issues for years. Now Southern Republicans dominated the leadership on Capitol Hill, and the power of liberal Democrats was radically reduced.

Many of the first-term Republican lawmakers came to Washington "committed to rolling back the New Deal and the War on Poverty."[68] Their agenda was expressed in their proposed budgets, which in many ways resembled Reagan's budgets. Along with a balanced-budget amendment to the Constitution—which they pressed hard for and lost—they sought to eliminate the core federal entitlements to AFDC, Medicaid, and food stamps, and to partially privatize Social Security and Medicare. They sought to transfer to the states significant responsibility for aiding the poor, and to end the guarantee that funding for key federal social programs would automatically increase with inflation or rising levels of need.[69]

The Republican budget bills also proposed deep cuts in spending, with nearly half coming from programs for the poor—including the EITC. Charging that the EITC had become riddled with fraud and abuse, Republicans prepared to launch a series of compliance hearings, and tried to slash what they saw as a burgeoning new welfare program disguised as a tax cut. Among other things, they sought to eliminate the benefit for all (four million) childless workers. Echoing Russell Long's argument that the EITC should be reserved for potential welfare families, Bill Archer stated bluntly, "We do not think single men should get the EITC."[70] The Clinton administration rejected the Republican budget plans (largely on the basis of their cuts to Medicare and Medicaid), and the standoff produced two partial government shutdowns at the end of 1995 and early in 1996. When Republicans drew criticism from the public and the press, they backed away from many of their most ambitious plans, including the proposed EITC cut.

Even as he faced down the most radical of the Republican budget proposals, the president's political response to the midterm election results was to move to the right. After two years of attempting to straddle liberal and New Democratic positions, Clinton renewed his commitment to the centrist agenda shared by the DLC. The clearest indication came in his June 1995 budget proposal. It provoked a firestorm of protest from liberals in the administration and on the Hill, particularly over its plan to balance the budget over ten years. In social policy, the president proposed a further shift in focus from guaranteeing economic security to promoting economic opportunity for individual workers.[71]

On issues of work and welfare, the differences separating Southern moderates like Clinton from the new Southern Republicans were often more a matter of degree than of kind. To be sure, many Southern Republicans were avid market fundamentalists or fierce social conservatives, and relatively few Southern Democrats were either in the 1990s. But this left plenty of common ground on policies toward the welfare poor and the working poor, and Southerners' approaches to social programs and the low-wage labor market were similar in important respects. Southerners of both parties were the staunchest advocates of state and local control over federal programs. In the 1990s, this translated into support for block grants.[72] And Southerners were generally more supportive of restricting AFDC for poor families, instead favoring the EITC (in the case of Democrats) or simple aid cutoffs (in the case of Republicans).

These positions were evident in the distinctive character of the Southern safety net in the 1990s. Southern leaders of both parties had continued to use their state discretion to set AFDC benefits at low levels, and their programs reflected lower-than-average expenditures. In 1995, the year Republicans took control of Congress, only seven states nationwide provided AFDC benefits of $200 per month or less, and all were in the South.[73]

Table 7.1 Southern States' AFDC Programs, 1995

State	Average Monthly Payment (dollars)	National Rank (of fifty states)
Oklahoma	282.96	35
Virginia	272.84	37
Florida	263.17	38
Georgia	248.28	41
North Carolina	243.46	42
Kentucky	210.15	43
Texas	188.42	44
Arkansas	184.91	45
Tennessee	184.10	46
South Carolina	180.14	47
Louisiana	161.39	48
Alabama	148.51	49
Mississippi	121.77	50
National average	**$377.65**	

Source: U.S. Department of Health and Human Services, Administration for Children and Families, Office of Family Assistance, "Characteristics and Financial Circumstances of AFDC Recipients FY 1995," Table 34.
Note: Through the mid-1990s, Southern states' AFDC benefits remained the lowest in the nation, far below the national average. The data here report average monthly AFDC benefits for families with two children in fiscal year 1995.

At the same time, Southern leaders drew disproportionately on federal funds for the elderly and disabled poor and the working poor. The Southern safety net included higher-than-average expenditures for federally funded SSI, and higher-than-average reliance on the EITC. Indeed, among the ten states in which 20 percent or more of tax filers claimed the EITC, nine were in the South. Mississippi and Louisiana had the highest EITC participation in the nation, at 32 and 27.1 percent. Twelve of thirteen Southern states were above the national average of 16.7 percent.[74]

Southerners of both parties also favored unregulated labor markets more than their counterparts from other regions. Twelve of thirteen Southern states had "right to work" laws that made it more difficult to unionize. And of the twelve states nationwide that had state minimum wages below the federal level (or no state minimum at all), ten were in the South.[75]

The shared record on work and welfare did not eliminate important distinctions in the policy positions of Southern Democrats and Republicans. It

Table 7.2 Southern States' EITC Programs, 1994

State	Percentage of Tax Returns with EITC	Rank	Average Credit per Return ($)	Percentage of Total U.S. EITC Expenditure	Percentage of Total U.S. Population
Mississippi	32.0	1	1,312	2.1	1.0
Louisiana	27.1	2	1,243	2.7	1.7
Alabama	24.9	3	1,251	2.6	1.6
Texas	23.7	6	1,221	10.6	7.0
South Carolina	22.9	7	1,183	2.0	1.4
Georgia	21.0	8	1,172	3.6	2.7
Oklahoma	20.7	9	1,108	1.4	1.2
Tennessee	20.4	10	1,123	2.5	2.0
North Carolina	19.8	11	1,152	3.4	2.7
Arkansas	24.0	12	1,195	1.4	0.9
Florida	19.3	14	1,096	6.3	5.4
Kentucky	19.2	15	1,078	1.5	1.5
Virginia	14.9	25	1,079	2.2	2.5
Southern States	**22.3**		**1,170**	**42.3**	**31.6**
United States	**16.7**		**1,101**	**100**	**100**

Source: Internal Revenue Service, *Statistics of Income Bulletin* 14, no. 4 (Spring 1996): 106–58. U.S. Census Bureau population figures.
Note: Southern states had the highest percentage of tax returns that include EITC credits in the mid-1990s (representing eight of the top ten states). Payments were in most cases (ten of the thirteen Southern states) above the national average. Combined, Southern states accounted for just over 30 percent of the U.S. population, and received more than 40 percent of all EITC benefits.

did, however, provide a basis for compromise between the two that would be exploited over the next two years.

* * *

With the Republicans now in control of Congress, a three-way standoff on welfare was imminent. Each camp had a stake in the outcome. The new Republican leadership had identified welfare reform as one of their top three legislative priorities for the session, along with tax cuts and a balanced budget agreement; reformers sought a combination of pro-market and social conservative measures.[76] Bill Clinton and the DLC had staked Clinton's credibility on his campaign promise to reform welfare. They also saw their agenda for replacing welfare with workfare as one of the most important issues distinguishing New Democrats from old Democrats. Leading liberal Democrats had drawn a line at the compromises reached over the Family Support Act. With the FSA yet to be fully implemented, they had little intention of giving new ground on welfarist principles and programs.

The debate boiled down to a few key issues. One was the question of whether welfare would remain a federal entitlement. A second was the issue of work requirements, and whether they would include job guarantees and transitional assistance for those leaving welfare for work. And a third was time limits, and whether families unable to meet requirements would face an absolute cutoff of assistance.

When Republican leaders began to craft a new bill soon after the midterm election, they were joined by a powerful new player on the Republican side: state officials. Republican governors held a majority of statehouses after the 1994 elections, and a top priority for them was to turn more social welfare programs into block grants to the states.[77] Many officials had on-the-ground experience with welfare reform, courtesy of Clinton's accelerated waiver process. The significance of block-granting and limiting AFDC funds went beyond the issue of state control: in one stroke, this move would eliminate the federal entitlement. It would end the New Deal–era guarantee of assistance to all eligible families, a guarantee that was inscribed in federal law. It would also end the guarantee to states that the federal government would provide funds on a matching basis to meet levels of need as they fluctuated with the economy. In addition, block-granting assistance would undercut the welfarist commitment to achieving national and standardized assistance to eligible poor families by giving states even more power to set their own eligibility criteria and benefit levels.

Newt Gingrich and other Republican leaders were enthusiastic about the governors' block-granting proposal. It advanced their interests in reducing deficits, curbing federal control, and cutting welfare spending. Social conservatives in the party complained, however, when the governors insisted that the block grants come with "no strings attached"—without, in other words, new federal regulations governing welfare recipients' behavior.[78]

For the Democrats, the block-grant issue proved to be something of a litmus test on the welfare versus workfare question. Liberal welfarists recognized at once what would be lost, and why it mattered. Workfarists in the Democratic Party, including many Southern Democrats, did not share their concerns. Indeed, Russell Long's position on block grants—set out clearly in legislation that he and Senator Dole had introduced in the late 1970s—was remarkably similar to the "new" Republican reform proposals now on the table. Long's proposed legislation sought to "replace the present program of federal matching of state costs for Aid to Families with Dependent Children (AFDC) with federal block grants that the states would administer."[79]

While the governors were pressing for block grants, conservative Republicans in Congress pushed their own version of strict time limits.[80] They combined the principle with the social conservative aim of discouraging childbearing by nonmarried mothers. These proposals had political as well as ideological purposes. With Clinton claiming workfare as his own, many Republicans wanted to define a more radically conservative reform agenda for the party.[81]

The House bill, introduced by Representative Clay Shaw (R-Fla.) in early 1995, ultimately reflected a compromise between Republican governors and Republican social conservatives in Congress—one that resulted in an even more conservative bill than either would likely have proposed alone. It ended the entitlement by converting welfare to a block grant, but also included new requirements for states favored by social conservatives.[82] Liberal Democrats characterized many of the measure's provisions as cruel; Ways and Means chairman Archer shrugged off the comments as "the dying throes of the federal welfare state."[83]

Urged on by their party leader in the White House, meanwhile, House Democrats rallied behind a proposal advanced by Representative Nathan Deal, a conservative Georgia Democrat. It included a work requirement and time limit, but it did not go as far as the Republican measure and did not formally end the entitlement to aid. Deal's proposal was defeated (only one Republican backed it), and the Republican measure passed 234–199 on a largely party-line vote in March 1995.[84]

In the Senate, the pace slowed. Exasperated by disagreements not only with Democrats but within his own caucus, Dole scrapped the House bill and started from scratch in August. The Republican Senate bill was tempered by amendments from moderates of both parties before coming to a final vote in September 1995. The overall spending cuts in the Senate bill were about half as deep as in the House, and the legislation allowed more exemptions from the time limit and work requirement. Yet the bill preserved all of the core conservative provisions that divided workfarists from welfarists. It included a tough work requirement, imposed a five-year time limit without a job guarantee, pledged to turn welfare into a block grant, and ended the entitlement.[85]

Behind the scenes in the Clinton administration, the debate between welfarists and workfarists had been heating up rapidly in a series of internal memos about how to respond to the emerging legislation. The debate pitted liberals at HHS against political and policy advisers in the White House, notably Bruce Reed and Rahm Emanuel. Days before the House vote in March, David Ellwood sent a memo to Reed, who had drafted Clinton's response to the Republican bill. It "seems too conciliatory for this stage in the debate," wrote Ellwood; the president "needs to express more concern and greater opposition."[86] Six weeks later, Ellwood's office weighed in on the administration's strategy in the Senate, urging the Clinton team not to appear "too 'hungry' for an agreement" and not to "preempt the entitlement-based alternatives to be announced by Senate Democrats."[87]

But Reed and Emanuel were focused primarily on building a workfare alternative, not on defending the welfarist entitlement. In late May they told Clinton, "You will come under increasing pressure to outline the specific conditions of what kind of welfare reform bill you would be willing to sign." They noted that "Moynihan is rallying liberals and editorial boards to press for a veto threat over the individual entitlement," and urged Clinton instead to "shift the debate back to our terms, by saying work is your bottom line: If Congress passes a bill that is serious about moving people from welfare to work, you'll sign it. If Congress passes a bill that is phony and fails to promote work, you won't."[88]

All eyes now turned to Clinton. The president's response would determine in part whether moderate Democrats—particularly those facing reelection—would swing to support the turn to workfare, or stand with the party's liberal leaders. Welfarists in the administration sought a clear signal from him that the Senate bill was unacceptable, because it violated basic principles of the New Deal safety net. Four days before the Senate vote, HHS secretary Donna Shalala handed the president a study commissioned by her staff suggesting that the measure was likely to push more than a million children into poverty; she had also provided a lengthy analysis of the negative impact of block-granting welfare.[89] Liberals in both the administration and Congress were convinced that they could mount a successful defense against the measures that undermined welfarism, but they needed to retain the support of moderate Democrats to do so. As one senior administration official argued: "Had [Clinton] signaled that he remained firm in opposing block grants and the arbitrary time limit, there is every reason to believe that all but a handful of Democratic senators would have stayed with him. The opposite signal left them with no political cover for a vote against the Senate bill. It invited them to vote for the bill."[90]

When Clinton indicated that he would support the Senate bill, liberals were furious. The bill, argued Senator Edward Kennedy, amounted to "legislative child abuse."[91] The Senate measure abandoned long-standing party principles. But the fact remained that the bill's core components were not fundamentally objectionable to the president. Senate Democrats offered amendments to soften the bill, but they were defeated. With Clinton saying he would support it, most Democrats reluctantly backed down. The bill cleared the Senate on September 19, 87–12.[92]

All that remained was for Republican leaders to reconcile the two bills and send the result to the president. With an eye on the upcoming 1996 presidential election, however, the Republicans had a different strategy in mind—one that offered the president a final opportunity to walk away from their proposed dismantlement of AFDC. Reasoning that their most promising electoral strategy was to campaign on the argument that Clinton had failed to deliver on his pledge to reform welfare, the Republicans sent Clinton only bills he would be sure to veto, by including unacceptably harsh provisions toward disabled children, foster care, and especially Medicaid reform. Clinton delivered the promised vetoes at the end of 1995, and by the spring of 1996, the debate seemed to have stalled.[93]

Just as welfarist advocates were beginning to believe that AFDC had dodged a bullet, however, the president's political advisers were concluding that he needed a victory on welfare for the 1996 election. They began to meet privately with Republicans to persuade them to cut a deal. Edelman recalls that behind the scenes, "White House political people—Rahm Emanuel and Bruce Reed, in particular—were telling Hill Republicans almost daily that if they separated the welfare and Medicaid bills, they could get a bill that the president would sign."[94]

As the election campaign heated up, the calculus of congressional Republicans also changed. The presidential prospects of the party's presumed nominee, Senator Dole, looked slim—and members of Congress facing re-election worried that their own record of accomplishments might appear a bit thin to voters. Welfare reform might be considered a Clinton victory, but it would also be seen as an achievement by congressional Republicans committed to enacting their Contract with America.[95]

In late spring of 1996, another channel opened up. Trent Lott, a stalwart conservative from Mississippi, became Senate Majority Leader after Dole resigned to campaign full-time for the White House. Lott's rise brought the Senate much closer ideologically to the House. "For the first time in history, the top Republican leaders in both houses of Congress were from the South," Lott noted, marking "the culmination of a political transformation" in the party.[96] The night after he assumed his new leadership position, Lott received a call from political consultant Dick Morris. Morris, who had worked for numerous Republicans over the years, including Lott, was now quietly advising Clinton on his reelection strategy. "What Morris proposed was a highly unusual alliance between the president of the United States and the majority leader of the opposing party," Lott observed, with the aim of breaking the logjam in Congress and enacting several pieces of major legislation—including welfare reform. Lott agreed, and the result was a "backstairs relationship with the Oval Office that relied on telephone calls with Dick . . . and eventually scores of direct conversations between President Clinton and me."[97]

On welfare reform, the two Southern leaders would be joined by a third, Speaker Newt Gingrich from the House. Cutting quiet deals on major legislation meant deceiving and defying party members on both sides of the aisle. Lott knew that he "was treading on dangerous territory" and might undermine Dole's campaign strategy. But he had concluded that "Dole wasn't providing as much coat-tail for other Republicans on the ticket as we had hoped," and that it was more important "to make sure the electorate got the message that the Republicans in Congress were the folks making things happen on behalf of the nation."[98]

Clinton circumvented liberals in Congress and in his own administration with his maneuvers. Word spread of the back-channel negotiations, and Lott recalled: "Faced with this new GOP–White House alliance, the Democrats proved envious and petulant. In the end, it didn't matter; with Morris's help, Clinton, Newt Gingrich, and I engineered all the changes. The Senate Democrats were like a fifth wheel. We didn't need them."[99]

Whether or how the three leaders' shared Southern roots shaped their negotiations cannot be surmised from the record. What is clear, however, is that their dealmaking rested on the fact that there was enough common ground between them on welfare reform to craft a compromise. Clinton was prepared to abandon core welfarist commitments—on issues such as the entitlement and time limits—that liberals in his party considered non-negotiable. Lott knew the stakes of such a reform, commenting proudly that "our proposals were bold and strong enough that even the protective walls of the old Democratic welfare establishment buckled before them." He also knew "from my conversations with Clinton" that the president agreed with the Republican leaders on the importance of time limits and work requirements; after some hesitation, Clinton also "told me that he was prepared to accept the revolutionary shift from entitlements to block grants."[100]

On Capitol Hill, the turning point came when Republican lawmakers agreed to separate welfare reform from Medicaid reform in mid-July. The proposed changes to Medicaid had been a deal breaker for both congressional Democrats and the White House.[101] The Republican leadership now began to steer a welfare bill quickly through both houses.

House Democrats again advanced an alternative offered by a Southerner, this time by Representative John Tanner (D-Tenn.), a member of the Mainstream Forum group. Rather than defending the entitlement, Tanner's bill called for replacing AFDC with a block grant to the states, work requirements, time limits on adult receipt of AFDC, and vouchers to assist children removed from the rolls when their families reached the time limit. The White House called on Democrats to accept a block grant "as long as it provides health care and child care to move people from welfare to work," and to support the Tanner alternative.

The Tanner amendment was defeated by Republicans on a party-line vote in the House—but in corralling party moderates and even liberals to vote in favor of block grants in the name of party unity, it moved the bar of acceptable Democratic compromises even further in the conservative direction.[102] Statements emanating from the White House, meanwhile, underscored the fact that the president's position was in many ways in line with that of Republicans. The president, suggested Vice President Gore on *Face the Nation*, had no objections to ending the entitlement to welfare, but he would prefer to include a provision promising vouchers for children, as in the Tanner bill; this would soften the impact of reform.[103]

This time the conference version of the bill was much closer to the Senate bill that Clinton had said he would support. The conference report went back to the House and Senate for final floor votes at the end of July and beginning of August. Once again, Democrats in Congress—still deeply divided between welfarists and workfarists—waited to see what Clinton would do before deciding their own course of action.

Bill Clinton had to make a choice, and it would determine whether the New Deal welfarist framework, battered by years of erosion and compromise, would be defended and strengthened or replaced with a workfare model. The president had signaled his approval of the Senate bill, but there was still room to reject the final measure based on new provisions that had been added (including a cap on spending for the block grant and deeper funding cuts)—and Republicans did not have the votes to override.

The president called Morris to discuss the issue late one evening at the end of July. As he had done repeatedly, Morris strongly advised him to approve the reform. He knew that Clinton fundamentally supported work requirements, time limits, and an end to the entitlement, but worried about the depth and breadth of various spending cuts in the Republican bill. Recognizing the degree to which Clinton's core reform agenda departed from liberal Democratic welfarism, Morris pointed out that Clinton could win passage of his desired reforms only with Republican support. He told Clinton: "You'll never get a bill with strict enough cut-off requirements out of a Democratic Congress to have any real credibility. You'll get this end of the equation—the 'responsibility' end—only from a Republican Congress. So take it while it's on your desk, then win the election. Once you win . . . you can get to stage two: fixing the bill."[104] Clinton had received similar advice from his domestic policy adviser Bruce Reed, he told Morris. Reed "says this is a good welfare-reform bill buried in a bad budget cut bill. After all, the welfare parts of it are okay. . . . It's got all the things I've been fighting for over the years." And the budget cuts could be corrected later.[105]

On July 31, the long-running intraparty debate over the purposes of public assistance moved into the White House Cabinet Room. The president called a morning meeting on the issue. His advisers were asked to make their final arguments on the bill, for or against. The atmosphere in the room, recalled political adviser George Stephanopoulos, was "statesmanlike . . . which was appropriate. The decision to end a cornerstone of the New Deal was historic, and lives hung in the balance."[106] The position of his top policy advisers, largely liberal Democrats, was an overwhelming "no." Most of his cabinet, along with his chief of staff, Leon Panetta, urged him to veto the bill. Those advocating "yes" included Vice President Gore, Bruce Reed, and Rahm Emanuel.[107]

The meeting was subdued; the positions were familiar to all. Clinton himself said little, mainly expressing his objections to the bill's provisions to cut food stamps and benefits for legal immigrants. After listening for two and a half hours, the president said, "Okay . . . I've worked on this for 16 years. I'm going to go into my office and make up my mind." He headed into the Oval

Office with Gore and Panetta—each representing a different side in the debate. Panetta emerged fifteen minutes later and instructed the speechwriters to complete the "yes" speech.[108] House leaders had been waiting for the president's announcement before beginning the vote. It came in a mid-afternoon presidential press conference, and the House began voting at 5:00 p.m. The bill passed 300–101; the Senate followed suit the next day, approving the measure 78–21.[109]

Clinton's decision produced a political settlement on the issue, but not a consensus within his party. Even with many following the president's lead in an election year, the vote split the Democrats down the middle. In the House, precisely half voted for the bill, half against it. In both chambers, a majority of Northern Democrats and the party's leaders were opposed; a majority of Southern Democrats supported the legislation. Both parties recognized the magnitude of the policy change and its departure from New Deal Democratic principles. Bill Clinton, the Dole campaign observed, had succeeded in "selling out his own party."[110]

The significance of Clinton's looming reelection bid in his decision was widely debated by analysts. Certainly Dick Morris and Clinton's political team saw the welfare bill as critical and felt that a veto could spell defeat.[111] But the evidence was hardly conclusive. Clinton was twenty points ahead in the polls when he decided to sign the bill. He had poll numbers that said a decision to veto the bill would be unlikely to change many votes in the election.[112] Beyond the electoral impact of the reform, Clinton's larger partisan agenda was to ensure that Republicans could not use the racially charged welfare issue against the Democrats. White House aide Sidney Blumenthal explained: "One publicly unstated factor in the president's decision was his belief that the welfare reform law would remove race as an issue from the upcoming presidential campaign and beyond. For decades, conservative politicians had exploited race by using the New Deal's and Great Society's welfare programs as a bludgeon against Democrats. . . . With welfare reform, this coded issue . . . was mostly erased."[113]

Many liberals close to Clinton were bitter about his decision to embrace a bill that so fully repudiated welfarist commitments. "The game was over," Edelman concluded. "Now no one could ever say again with any credibility that this President is an old liberal."[114] But of course, Clinton never had been an "old liberal" on issues of work and welfare. He was a centrist Southern Democrat who had long ago made clear his support for workfarist ideas over welfarist ones, in his policies as Arkansas governor, in his campaign prom-

Table 7.3 Congressional Support for 1996 Welfare Reform

	HOUSE, JULY 31, 1996	
	Yes	No
Southern Democrats	36 (*62.1%*)	22 (*37.9%*)
Northern Democrats	62 (*44.9%*)	76 (*55.1%*)
Republicans	230 (*99.1%*)	2 (*0.9%*)

	SENATE, AUGUST 1, 1996	
	Yes	No
Southern Democrats	8 (*88.9%*)	1 (*11.1%*)
Northern Democrats	17 (*45.9%*)	20 (*54.1%*)
Republicans	53 (*100%*)	0 (*0%*)

Source: Calculations based on vote totals reported in *Congressional Quarterly Almanac* 52 (1996): 6-3 to 6-24.

Note: In both the House and Senate, a majority of Northern Democrats opposed passage of the conference report on the Personal Responsibility and Work Opportunity Reconciliation Act (PRWORA), the 1996 welfare reform. A majority of Southern Democrats supported the measure in both chambers; Republicans voted almost unanimously in favor. By this point, of course, most Southern lawmakers were Republicans, and they voted with their party. The PRWORA was passed in the House 328–101 on July 31, 1996. It passed the Senate 78–21 on August 1, 1996.

ises, and in the initial policy decisions he made as president.[115] His agreements with liberals to protect the entitlement and add transitional supports for welfare recipients did not reflect core commitments for him. They could be (and were) negotiated away when necessary. On the central issues, his beliefs were much closer to the Southern Republican leadership than to the liberal Democrats.

Some liberal allies were well aware of where the president stood on the issues, even if they came to the realization slowly. Wendell Primus, a longtime senior congressional aide who worked on welfare reform at HHS, said, "I know he didn't have a problem with the block grants. I know he didn't have a problem with the loss of entitlement. . . . I don't think there were many things that disturbed him in this welfare bill."[116] Faced with Clinton's imminent decision to sign the 1996 legislation, George Stephanopoulos expressed his misgivings about the campaign strategy: "In 1992, I had been eager to put millions of dollars of television advertising behind the phrase 'end welfare as we know it,' even though I knew full well that it sent a message far more powerful than, and somewhat contradictory to, the fine print of our proposal in *Putting People First*, which had promised more assistance to welfare recipients looking for work, not less."[117] Soon after Clinton signed the reform, several of the administration's most prominent poverty policy experts—Edelman, Primus, and Bane—resigned in protest. Ellwood had left a year earlier.[118]

The new welfare law (P.L. 104-193, the Personal Responsibility and Work Opportunity Reconciliation Act of 1996) radically rewrote public assistance policy. It replaced AFDC's guaranteed safety net with a block grant to the states (Temporary Assistance to Needy Families, or TANF), with funding fixed at 1994 levels regardless of subsequent changes in levels of need. This funding "cap" broke the link between assistance and economic conditions. Under the previous law, if caseloads rose due to a recession, federal funding could rise to keep pace. States were also granted significant flexibility with federal block grant funds (and TANF-related state monies), as long as they were used to promote the law's broad objectives, related to caring for needy children, promoting work and marriage, and reducing unmarried pregnancies. States were permitted to cut funding dedicated to basic income support for families and to redirect resources to child care, welfare-to-work programs, and various services. They could deny eligibility to any poor family or category of families. The law also imposed strict work requirements for families receiving TANF funds and set a lifetime limit of five years to receive benefits.[119]

The welfare reform proposal that Clinton originally introduced in 1994 called for nearly $10 billion in additional spending over five years on programs to assist the poor in the transition to work. The new welfare law that he signed in 1996 instead cut federal funding for various public assistance programs (particularly food stamps and benefits to legal immigrants) by nearly $55 billion over five years.[120] In the budget agreement the following year, Clinton won a number of funding concessions to blunt the immediate impact of the 1996 welfare reform law, particularly on legal immigrants. But the budget agreement did not change the fundamental logic of the reform.[121] The core welfarist structure of the New Deal AFDC program had been replaced by a workfare model under TANF.

Workfare for All

As the new terms of public assistance made their way into policy and practice, programs for the working poor were changing as well. Welfare reform would be accompanied by a pro-market "work-first" approach to employment and job training for both the welfare and the working poor. The work-first model marked a departure from long-standing job training strategies stressing the development of education and skills ("human capital") in order to position workers for better employment opportunities. Though they had little track record of success under the adverse conditions of the low-wage labor market, human capital strategies were widely supported by Democrats and many Republicans through the 1980s. Work-first approaches, in contrast, emphasized rapid entry into the workforce. Participants were urged to take the first available job, and programs assisted with job readiness and immediate job placement.[122] By the end of the 1990s, state-level welfare-to-work programs across the country followed the work-first model. It was also incorporated in the federal Workforce Investment Act of 1998, which superseded JTPA.[123]

The policy rationale for abandoning the human capital model was supplied in part by DLC analysts. The case was made succinctly in a 1994 DLC policy brief by Will Marshall: "Job placement ... should be the primary mission of a redesigned welfare policy. The current system's emphasis on education and training may occasionally lead to marginal increases in earnings, but such gains are rarely enough to lift families out of poverty. . . . For most people on welfare, the surest and most direct route to independence is a job."[124]

Lawrence Mead pressed the argument in testimony before the Senate Finance Committee in the spring of 1995. Mead criticized the initial welfare reform plan developed by the Clinton administration in 1994 for proposing to spend "unnecessary sums on public jobs, training, [and] childcare" and encourage "vast numbers to pursue higher credentials, usually to little good, in place of working."[125] Education and training, he concluded, would fail the poor if they could rely on public assistance, because assistance "shields them from the need to accept available jobs." The promise of education would lead recipients to undertake "training for positions that were, practically speaking, beyond their reach, and this made them more reluctant to do the more menial jobs actually available to them."[126]

The logic behind the work-first strategy was not new. The 1971 WIN amendments spearheaded by Georgia senator Herman Talmadge (D-Ga.) had urged a similar shift toward more immediate job placement for AFDC recipients. What had changed, however, was the economic and social policy context. For years, the low-wage labor market had offered diminished access to stable and secure jobs, and the safety net that had been AFDC was no longer there to catch families that fell through the cracks.

In this changed context, the embrace of work-first strategies by a Democratic administration had important implications. It helped redefine the function and focus of job training. Traditionally, the core purpose of training programs was to lift the wages and job prospects of participants *beyond* what they could otherwise be expected to achieve in the labor market, thereby advancing their chances for economic security and mobility. Work-first programs, in contrast, sought to facilitate immediate entry into the first available job for which the participant was currently qualified.

Implicit was a shift in focus from the needs of workers to those of employers in the current market. The DLC policy brief observed: "Almost by definition, welfare recipients would benefit from more education and training.... However, employers value formal training less than the informal skills and habits that make for a dependable worker, such as showing up for work on time, doing a conscientious job, notifying employers of absences, and communicating well with co-workers."[127] Many employers—particularly in the low-wage sector—needed workers with little more than a good work ethic. Workers, on the other hand, needed much more than a good work ethic to exit the world of low-wage work for solid, middle-class jobs. The work-first model, critics charged, represented "the large-scale abandonment of job training as a strategy for upward mobility."[128]

More fundamentally, a strategy for economic security that relied on work-first training without public job creation or labor market reform had proven flawed, particularly in the context of the post-1970s job market. It assumed that securing a job immediately would provide a worker a position on the employment ladder, and allow that worker to move toward jobs with better earnings and security over time. Yet by the 1980s, this was not a reliable assumption, and even as labor markets tightened in the late 1990s, many low earners found that the rungs on the ladder to the middle class were simply missing.[129] Labor market shortcomings such as these explain the disappointing results of most job training efforts over time, according to Gordon Lafer's study: "Four decades of experimentation show that poverty and unemployment cannot be solved on the supply side, that is, by changing something about workers; instead, we must focus on the demand side of the labor market by working to improve the quality of jobs available to working-class Americans."[130]

It was welfare reform that seized the headlines in Bill Clinton's first term and defined his domestic legacy. But these years also saw the quiet consolidation of policy trends toward low-wage workers. The dividing line between the welfare and the working poor had been blurred—with most welfare recipients now required to work (under TANF), and working families receiving income assistance (under the EITC). The social contract for poor families rested on a workfarist, not welfarist, foundation. By the end of Clinton's first term, the welfare and the working poor, together, confronted the new world of workfare.

CHAPTER 8

The New World of Workfare

Major questions remained in the wake of the Clinton reforms. Would the policy settlement on workfare hold? What impact would the new policy framework have, given conditions in the job market? Would workfare create new opportunities or new sources of insecurity for poor families?

The next decade and a half provided an unprecedented opportunity to answer these questions under varied political and economic conditions. Changes in party control of the White House and Congress tested the political durability of the workfare settlement under every imaginable arrangement. From 1996 to 2014, the White House was controlled by Democrats (Clinton and Obama) for eleven years, and a Republican (Bush) for eight years. In Congress, Republicans controlled both the House and the Senate for nine years, Democrats did for four, and the remaining six years saw divided party control. For six of these years, the party in the White House also held majorities in Congress; for the other thirteen, party control of the executive and legislative branches was divided.

These years also provided an extraordinary test of the effectiveness of the work-conditioned safety net. By many economic measures, this period included the best of times and the worst of times of the postwar era. The late 1990s brought the strongest economy and labor market in a generation, with growth rates reaching 4.8 percent in 1999 and unemployment falling to 4 percent the following year, the lowest annual level since 1969. Ten years later, the economy saw the most severe downturn since the Great Depression, followed by a painfully slow recovery. In the depths of the Great Recession in 2009, the economy contracted by 3.1 percent, and unemployment topped 10 percent in October.[1]

Despite evidence of the new system's shortcomings in meeting the needs of poor families, the workfare state was consolidated in this period by Democrats as well as Republicans. These years also saw a rightward shift in the larger domestic policy agenda of the Democratic Party, as this chapter demonstrates, evident in Bill Clinton's second term and continuing under Barack Obama. The chapter's first section argues that on social and economic policy, Clinton did much more than reform welfare in his two terms in office. His policy decisions recast the Democratic Party's agenda in enduring ways. Clinton would leave in place a distinct—and more conservative—domestic policy paradigm, one that departed in several respects from New Deal principles and approaches, and would later be taken up by Obama.

It embodied a preference for deficit reduction and budget balancing over job creation, for policies that focused on expanding the economic pie rather than redistributing the slices, and for programs that emphasized the government's role in providing incentives and opportunities for self-advancement, rather than job guarantees or economic security. Both the rhetorical and the policy focus of the revamped Democratic social policy agenda were redirected at the "middle class," the boundaries of which were stretched to encompass those earning near-poverty incomes as well as those earning almost $100,000, without regard for the harsh conditions that distinguish a low-income existence from a middle-income one.[2] For the working poor, the policy model opted for tax credits to subsidize existing wages and "work-first" job training, rather than labor market reforms. And for the welfare poor, there was a continuing commitment to temporary, work-conditioned assistance administered by states, rather than need-based aid delivered according to robust national standards. Clinton aides were confident they were forging a significant and durable new social policy model. Domestic policy adviser Bruce Reed assured Clinton that this "new synthesis has provided a solid philosophical basis for activist government—to help those willing to help themselves—that may have greater staying power than either the New Deal or the Great Society."[3] At the heart of the "new synthesis" were old Southern Democratic priorities, revisited and modified over the years by successive cohorts of centrist leaders. Though most conservative Southerners had left the party by the mid-1990s, their legacy on work and welfare remained.

The nation's next Democratic president, Barack Obama, arrived amid a devastating economic crisis and high expectations of progressive policy change. The economic downturn had cast a bright spotlight on the faltering labor market and rising income inequality.[4] The newly elected president had high approval ratings, a bold agenda, and Democratic majorities in both houses of Congress. Within weeks, he had secured congressional support for a massive stimulus program that might have reconfigured the government's role in responding to economic insecurity. As the second section of this chapter demonstrates, Obama's presidency would ultimately consolidate the Clinton-era turn toward workfare, however. With the country mired in a slow recovery well into Obama's second term, the workfare system's performance as a safety net for poor families proved dubious at best, as assessed in the concluding section of the chapter.

Consolidating the Workfare State: From Clinton to Bush

Days after signing the welfare bill, Bill Clinton stood before the party faithful at the Democratic Convention in Chicago. "The welfare reform law I signed last week is a chance for America to have a new beginning—to strike a new social bargain with the poor," he said, adding, "Now we have a responsibility—a moral obligation—to make sure the people we are requiring to work have the opportunity to work."[5] Would Clinton, unburdened by reelection pressures, revisit his position on labor market policies? Would he return to his 1993 public investment strategy to ensure the creation of stable jobs, or, less ambitiously, revive the commitment in his first campaign to a "dignified and meaningful community service job" for welfare recipients who could not find private employment?[6]

As he began his second term, Clinton showed no inclination to do so. The president announced to his economic team that his highest priority was a conservative one: he wanted to secure a balanced budget agreement. This move was not simply a defensive maneuver in the face of a reelected Republican majority in Congress. Balancing the budget was for him a matter of principle and an act of political courage. "It wasn't Republican pressure that was forcing his hand," observed Gene Sperling, who was tapped to head Clinton's National Economic Council in the second term.[7] Clinton knew that the decision would not be popular with many in his party. And his liberal advisers understood that it would radically limit any increased spending for public investment or policy initiatives to address weaknesses in the labor market or social safety net.[8]

Cabinet and staff changes confirmed the administration's rightward shift, as liberals departed and New Democrats rose in the ranks. "The bracing liberal-centrist quarrels of earlier years were over," noted Michael Waldman, Clinton's chief speechwriter.[9] Perhaps the most important change was the arrival of Erskine Bowles, to replace Leon Panetta as White House chief of staff. Clinton passed over deputy chief of staff Harold Ickes, a New York liberal and longtime ally.[10] An investment banker from North Carolina and a Clinton confidant, Bowles was a "New South Democrat" with close connections to Republicans from the region.[11]

Bowles would be pivotal in the drive to achieve a budget deal, through a strategy that once again relied on back-channel communications and deal-making between the Clinton White House and Southern congressional Republicans. This time, the central figure was Speaker Newt Gingrich, with supporting roles played by House Ways and Means chair Bill Archer of Texas and Senate Majority Leader Trent Lott of Mississippi. Bowles shared with Clinton a personal commitment to the balanced budget concept, and as a straight-talking Southern businessman, he quickly won the trust of the Speaker. The key, Bowles believed, was to set up direct negotiations between Clinton and Gingrich. The process excluded other congressional leaders of both parties and infuriated House Democratic leaders.[12]

Minority Leader Richard Gephardt and other liberal Democrats had by then begun to conclude that they had to adopt a more moderate agenda, one that could win the backing of the entire caucus—including the more conservative Blue Dogs, most of whom represented Southern and rural districts. "The congressional Democrats were reading the same polling data as the White House," reported Elizabeth Drew. "Though numerous House Democrats were suspicious and even contemptuous of Clinton's march to the center, they, too, didn't want to be vulnerable to the Republican charge that they were 'big-government, tax-and-spend liberals.'"[13] But a budget-balancing deal with Newt Gingrich was too much. "From Gephardt's perspective," explained Clinton adviser and former Gephardt speechwriter Paul Begala, "Newt was undermining everything that he got into public life for: Social Security, Medicare, caring for the poor, a decent society. And my party's president, my leader, is sitting down and cutting deals that disadvantage me and my party." Bowles later commented that he had "more contentious meetings with House Democrats than with Republicans."[14]

After months of tense negotiations, "we tugged and shoved [the] bill through Congress," Lott said, and the president signed the Balanced Budget Act in August 1997.[15] It imposed caps on discretionary spending at "near-freeze levels," cut spending by $160 billion over a five-year period ($112 billion from Medicare alone), and was projected to produce a balanced budget by 2002. The deal included a mix of tax cuts and credits favored by each side totaling more than $150 billion over five years, including Republican-backed provisions to reduce the capital gains and inheritance taxes, and to provide a $500 child tax credit to middle-income families. In addition, Clinton secured $20 billion to create a new Children's Health Insurance Program (CHIP) and funding for new education initiatives, most in the form of tax credits.[16] The president also used the opportunity to revisit—but not reform—the 1996 welfare law. As part of the balanced budget deal, he restored $13 billion of the $55 billion that was cut from public assistance programs in 1996.[17]

As the balanced budget bill reached the floor, congressional Democrats pushed back against their party leader, voting more than three to one against the spending cuts and more than six to one against the tax cuts.[18] Clinton relied on broad Republican backing to win passage. Among Democrats, he had the support of some moderates and conservatives; DLC leaders had long urged fiscal discipline as a way to break the party's tradition of "tax and spend" liberalism.[19]

By the fall of 1997, "congressional Democrats were getting and staying mad," noted Waldman. After "welfare reform, the 1996 elections, and the balanced budget agreement, the rank and file of Democratic members were fed up."[20] Intraparty tensions rose when Gephardt gave a major speech in December advancing a competing vision for the Democratic Party rooted in liberal principles. Without mentioning Clinton or Gore, he condemned the approach of "some who now call themselves New Democrats but who set their compass only off the direction of others . . . who talk about the political center, but fail to understand that if it's only defined by others it lacks core values." Gephardt called for a renewed commitment to reduce inequality, increase the minimum wage, expand health coverage, and repudiate efforts to privatize Social Security or Medicare.[21]

As party liberals soon learned, however, the Balanced Budget Act would in many ways epitomize Clinton's second-term legislative strategy. It relied on negotiations with and votes from Republicans on key priorities and isolated liberal Democrats. And any serious attempts to address the needs of poor families, including "[making] sure the people we are requiring to work have the opportunity to work"—as he had pledged at the Democratic Convention—were now constrained by the multi-year spending limits of the act.

Despite the divisions within his party, Clinton remained confident in his direction. He had achieved a deal to cut the deficit and balance the budget. Congress was debating new job training legislation (the 1998 Workforce Investment Act) that would codify work-first strategies. And his welfare reform policies—buoyed by a rapidly expanding economy—seemed to be successfully moving many recipients from welfare to work. Economic growth had picked up, averaging more than 4 percent a year in the second half of the decade, and unemployment dropped below 5 percent in mid-1997 for the first time since 1973. An extremely tight labor market, together with the 1996 minimum wage increase, was slowly driving wages up.[22] At the same time, low-wage workers were benefiting from new EITC expansions legislated in the early 1990s. The combination of favorable labor market conditions and recent increases in both the minimum wage and the EITC was encouraging single mothers (including welfare recipients) to enter the workforce at historically high rates.[23]

On the first anniversary of the 1996 welfare law, Clinton gave a self-congratulatory speech underscoring its accomplishments. The welfare rolls had seen "the biggest decline in history," he pointed out. "We now have the smallest percentage of Americans living on public assistance we have had since 1970." The conclusion was clear: "A lot of people said that welfare reform would never work because the private economy wouldn't do its part or the government wouldn't do its part or we couldn't figure out how to get people from welfare to work. . . . But a year later, I think it's fair to say the debate is over. We know that welfare reform works."[24]

With workfare initiatives expanding, new budget caps in place, and liberal congressional leaders hamstrung by the Republican majority, the policy environment in late 1997 suggested little opening for change in policies toward the poor—absent a major shift in the political or economic winds. That shift arrived unexpectedly in the fall.

Reports from the Office of Management and Budget brought the welcome news that the federal deficit was dropping much more quickly than anticipated due to rapid economic growth and increasing federal revenues. The Balanced Budget Act had projected that the budget would move out of deficit in 2002; now analysts concluded that the government could expect a surplus (including both operating budget and Social Security surpluses) in 1998.

The implications for social and economic policy were significant. Since the 1980s, conservatives and moderates from both parties had argued time and again that desirable initiatives were simply infeasible because of "deficit politics," and this position had prevailed in the debates over budget-cutting versus investment in Clinton's first term. Now the deficit constraint was evaporating. Charged with crafting Clinton's State of the Union address for early 1998, Michael Waldman said that for Clinton, "it was another chance for a new beginning. After three years of treading lightly, seeking to rebuild confidence in government, he could propose a more ambitious program." The speech would be "a far-reaching attempt to persuade the public that government could do big things again."[25]

The question was just what those "big things" would be. But before the options could be fully aired, the discussion veered in another direction to counter a new Republican offensive. Party leaders planned to welcome the surplus by eliminating it with a huge tax cut, and the idea had "Mack truck momentum on Capitol Hill," said Waldman.[26] The Clinton team devised a counterstrategy: reserve all of the budget surplus until a plan for Social Security reform was adopted by Congress. The slogan was "Save Social Security First." Clinton advisers saw it as a brilliant political maneuver, cutting off the Republicans at the pass while preserving options for Democratic priorities later. There would be consequences to limiting future spending by dedicating surpluses to Social Security, but Clinton and his advisers believed the strategy would pay off over time. Al Gore underscored the stakes at a January 1998 meeting: "The decisions we make are going to affect the future of progressive government for decades."[27] He and the rest of the Clinton team decided to go ahead with the plan.

In all these discussions, one option that was not on the table for serious deliberation was revisiting the "new social bargain with the poor." The administration would not return to its high-priority goals of 1992 and 1993, when Clinton had made the case for public investments of $25 to $50 billion a year to boost productivity, sustain the creation of high-wage jobs, and strengthen opportunities and protections for low-wage and middle-income workers.[28] Nor would Clinton and his advisers reconsider launching a "massive program of inner-city jobs for people getting off welfare"—a plan they had described as "stage three" of welfare reform, to follow "stage one" (signing the legislation) and "stage two" (restoring some of the budget cuts in the Republican bill).[29] Despite the opportunities presented by a major budget surplus, the prospects for creating new jobs or strengthening the safety net faded quickly.

What Clinton meant by "saving" Social Security, meanwhile, would prove contentious. He was not simply aiming to extend the solvency of the Social Security Trust Fund. Working with Bowles, he wanted to craft another deal with Gingrich that would include the introduction of privately managed retirement accounts in some form while preserving the core elements of the existing program. In exchange for a Social Security reform that incorporated private investment, Gingrich would give up the push for another large tax cut. Both men saw the prospects for future collaborations, to reform Medicare and more. "The balanced budget bill was act I," Gingrich later commented. "This was act II."[30] Clinton knew he would face opposition from congressional leaders in his own party. He hoped to marshal enough Blue Dog conservatives and New Democrat centrists to join with Republicans in passing entitlement reform, as he had done with the balanced budget initiative.[31] His plans included dedicating most of the Social Security surpluses to shore up the trust fund, investing a portion (up to 20 percent) in the stock market, and launching a new individual retirement savings program to augment Social Security benefits.[32]

Had Clinton succeeded in reformulating basic entitlement programs like Social Security and Medicare through partial privatization and market-oriented initiatives, he would have challenged another pillar of the New Deal social contract. But the plan lost momentum, in part because Clinton's political capital plummeted when the Monica Lewinsky scandal broke two weeks before the State of the Union. Even Bowles realized "it was game over" for the bipartisan Clinton–Gingrich alliance.[33] The political environment was transformed overnight as Democrats—including most of the liberals he had alienated—closed ranks behind the beleaguered president, and Republicans united in condemnation.

Although his plan for reforming Social Security failed, Clinton did use the surplus to pay down the debt, and this decision set serious limits on Democrats' ability to define a progressive policy agenda for the coming decade. Taking projected surpluses (including those generated by Social Security) off the agenda—not only for tax cuts but also for spending—was a major departure from decades of past practice, and removed $160 billion in 1999 alone that ordinarily would have been available.[34] Projections for the surplus ballooned by the end of Clinton's tenure, yet he stayed the course on fiscal restraint: in fiscal years 1998–2000, the federal government used the surplus to pay down $363 billion in debt.[35]

In Congress, many liberals wanted to see a more progressive approach to spending and social policy. More than a third of House Democrats, for example, supported the Congressional Black Caucus's call for a massive increase "in domestic spending on education, housing and economic development."[36] But liberals stood alone in their push to use surplus funds to make up for years of shortfalls in public investment and cuts in social spending.[37] Their moderate and conservative Democratic colleagues joined Republicans in championing the turn to fiscal restraint, and many Republican leaders welcomed what they saw as a conservative shift in the terms of debate. Reagan economist Martin Feldstein argued that despite the failure to reform Social Security, "Bill Clinton had turned off the power on the 'third rail of politics,'" creating the political space for Republicans to pursue entitlement reform through privatization in the future.[38]

The Clinton administration's second-term strategy of setting tight limits on discretionary spending while negotiating with Republicans over priority programs and walling off the surplus left little room for substantive dialogue within the Democratic Party about social welfare and labor market policy, even in the context of robust growth and surpluses. The public investments and other spending that administration officials envisioned after saving Social Security, meanwhile, were never made.

* * *

By the time George W. Bush entered the White House in January 2001, the strong economic growth and tight labor markets of the late 1990s had come to an end. The high-tech bubble had burst in early 2000, and by late 2001 the economy entered its first recession in nearly a decade, followed by a historically long period of jobless growth. Unemployment topped 6 percent from April to October of 2003, and the average length of unemployment spells hit new highs.[39] The post-1970s pattern of stagnant wages returned for most workers, and poverty began to rise, reaching 12.5 percent in 2003.[40] In Washington, the Republicans under Bush passed large tax cuts, disproportionately benefiting high-end earners, in 2001 and 2003. The tax cuts not only led to a spike in deficits for a decade, but also accelerated the trend toward wealth and income inequality, which reached levels not seen since the 1920s.

The downturn was especially hard on low-wage workers and on families trying to leave welfare for work. The child poverty rate had fallen from 19.8 percent to 15.8 percent between 1996 and 2000. This trend, often cited as evidence of welfare reform success, was now reversed. The rate rose after 2000 and stood at 17.6 percent in 2007.[41] For many poor single mothers, the situation was particularly dire: in 2001, after four years of increases, income from three critical sources dropped. Their average wages fell by $343, EITC payments fell by $75, and child support fell by $61. The TANF safety net not only failed to catch their fall, but contributed to it, providing $137 less on average than the year before.[42]

Evidence of rising need—among those unable to find work after welfare, or unable to escape poverty despite finding work—drew little political attention during the Bush years.[43] On work and welfare, Republicans had declared victory on the central question of concern to conservatives, announcing that the "battle against welfare dependency is essentially over," *Congressional Quarterly* concluded in 2001. And congressional Democrats had retreated from their earlier position; for them, "the goal is no longer to fight time limits or work requirements, but to make sure poor families are being treated fairly within the boundaries of the new system."[44]

When it was time to reauthorize funding for the 1996 welfare law five years after its passage, there was no serious attempt to restructure the terms and conditions of public assistance. Democratic leaders sought to increase TANF funding and give states new incentives to reduce family poverty.[45] But the larger questions—about entitlements and time limits—were off the table: "This time around," observed *Congressional Quarterly*, "no one is questioning the new paradigm as temporary assistance only."[46] The reauthorization law, finally signed in 2006, in fact took a tougher stance on work obligations by increasing the percentage of families that states had to enroll in work-related activities (50 percent) to avoid a cut in their TANF block grants; it also restricted the types of individuals who could be exempted from the requirement. The reauthorization added new incentives to shape recipients' behavior, by promoting, for example, abstinence education, "healthy marriages," and "responsible fatherhood."[47] The requirements spurred administrative maneuvers by states, with the overall effect of refueling the momentum toward caseload restrictions and work incentives rather than meeting needs.[48]

Overall, the Bush years brought few initiatives on poverty and social welfare. The president backed tougher work requirements for welfare recipients, market-oriented job-training measures, and a prescription drug benefit for Medicare recipients.[49] Confronted with a minimum wage increase (from $5.15 to $7.25 an hour) after the Democrats won control of Congress in 2006, he signed the legislation.[50] Bush's high-priority campaign for a more far-reaching privatization of Social Security than Clinton had envisioned was thwarted by an unusually united Democratic caucus.[51]

Among Democrats, the policy model of the 1990s went largely unchallenged during the Bush years, as the party continued to reach out to centrists as well as liberals. The platform adopted at the 2000 Democratic convention "was the third Democratic platform in a row in which the party turned away from its liberal New Deal roots to a more centrist philosophy that called for economic growth, personal responsibility, family vitality, law and order, and military readiness," reported *Congressional Quarterly*.[52] Under the leadership of Speaker Nancy Pelosi, House Democratic leaders set new records for party discipline in a bid to reclaim the majority, as Republicans had done before them.[53]

Behind the display of unity, however, were new sources of tension and flux. In a trend that stretched from the 1990s through the 2000s, the Democratic Party's demographic base was changing. The number of Southern Democrats in Congress had never recovered after the losses of 1994, and Southerners continued to leave in large numbers. Increasingly, congressional Democrats were coming from the more liberal Northeast and West Coast.[54] Some were traditional liberals. Others were liberal on social issues but conservative or moderate on fiscal and labor policy questions. Many in the latter group strengthened the ranks of the reconstructed New Democrat caucus as its original Southern core diminished.

Liberal leaders like Pelosi may have been the most visible face of the Democratic Party, but conservatives and moderates in the Blue Dog and New Democrat factions remained powerful institutional forces in the caucus. The evolving New Democrat coalition reflected the shifting focus of DLC and other strategists away from the South and white working-class "Reagan Democrats," toward the West Coast, Northeast, and prosperous "new economy" workers. Through an expanding fundraising network, the New Democrats sought to create a counterweight to the party's traditional reliance on union backing, forging ties between centrist Democratic legislators and individual and corporate donors in Silicon Valley, Wall Street, and Washington's K Street lobbying corridor.[55] Party centrists continued to flex their muscles in presidential contests in the 2000s, winning nominations but not elections for prominent New Democrats in 2000 (Gore and Lieberman) and 2004 (Kerry and Edwards). Two years later, Rahm Emanuel (now a representative from Illinois and rising in the ranks of House Democrats) spearheaded a strategy to recruit a roster of centrist and conservative Democrats to challenge weak incumbents in Republican districts in 2006, taking advantage of growing popular disapproval of President Bush. Democrats won the House back that year, and their majority included a new influx of moderate members.[56]

Liberals were frustrated when the party's policy trajectory on many issues remained centrist, even as its congressional leadership—and much of its base—were more liberal. The DLC had "helped to paralyze the mainstream of the Democratic Party," charged economist Jeff Faux, by creating an environment in which Democrats were perpetually fearful of accusations that they support "Big Government."[57] Former DLC policy director Ed Kilgore, on the other hand, noted with satisfaction that over the course of the decade, "A lot of the political perspectives that 'New Democrats' . . . offered have been fully internalized by Democrats of every stripe."[58]

Economic Crisis and Obama's Opportunity

By 2008, the workfare settlement had been in place for more than a decade, and it seemed secure as long as Democratic centrists or Republicans controlled the White House. But the election of Barack Obama that year brought to office a Democrat with a record of liberal positions on poverty, work, and welfare, in the midst of the most severe recession since the 1930s. The Great Recession handed the Obama administration a crisis and an opportunity. The downturn threw millions out of work and many into economic distress, as incomes declined and poverty rose. The work-based safety net for the poor, limited even in the best of times, was not designed to perform when work itself was lacking. Although Obama did not have Clinton's budget surpluses, he would soon have nearly $800 billion in economic stimulus funds—aimed in part at easing the hardships created by both the failing labor market and the fraying social safety net—and Democratic majorities in the House and Senate. The question was how the president would use this opportunity, and whether he would take social and economic policies in a different direction.

Obama's background and early public positions provided some evidence of a leader committed to reinvigorating the Democratic Party's liberal tradition. He had not risen through the familiar ranks of recent Democratic presidential nominees, carefully groomed to cut a centrist profile. His voting record in the Illinois legislature and as a U.S. senator was solidly liberal, and he had voiced strong support for core New Deal principles.[59] Describing the postwar order, he wrote in 2006,

> For the average American worker . . . security rested on three pillars: the ability to find a job that paid enough to support a family and save

for emergencies; a package of health and retirement benefits from his employer; and a government safety net . . . that could cushion the fall of those who suffered setbacks in their lives. . . . Today the social compact FDR helped construct is beginning to crumble."[60]

He rejected what he considered the extreme individualism and antigovernment sentiments of conservatives, including the "belief that government entitlement programs are inherently inefficient, breed dependency, and reduce individual responsibility, initiative and choice."[61] Many of his campaign statements challenged free-market orthodoxies and pledged to pursue public investment and progressive tax and spending policies.[62]

Obama's views on poverty and social welfare were shaped by a range of experiences, including his mother's reliance on food stamps early in her life, his own reliance on college loans, and his work as a community organizer. "I moved to Chicago more than two decades ago to lift up neighborhoods that were devastated by joblessness and poverty," he said on the campaign trail. "I can tell you that the fight I waged then . . . will be a fight I carry into the White House for the next four years. . . . We need to lift up every American out of poverty. That is one of the goals of the Democratic Party."[63]

To many observers, Obama appeared ready to lead a Democratic administration that would embrace the party's New Deal accomplishments and update them for a new era. Public expectations ran high, with large majorities believing he would not only "promote a good economy" (64 percent) and lower unemployment (67 percent), but also "improve conditions for minorities and the poor" (80 percent).[64] "The social contract between the government and its citizens—particularly its workers—is about to be renegotiated," predicted *Congressional Quarterly*. "Not since the Great Depression have the stars so aligned to initiate a broad expansion of the government's place as society's protector."[65]

But Obama faced serious obstacles. The most obvious constraint was the intense partisanship that he encountered within days of taking office. He confronted not only the ordinary challenges in working with the minority party, but a strategy of extreme obstructionism by congressional Republicans, including unprecedented use of filibuster threats and other institutional roadblocks.[66] On issues of poverty, work, and social welfare, moreover, Obama inherited the policy legacies of the Clinton Democrats. Largely unchallenged since the 1990s, they favored a focus on the middle class, and on controlling deficits and expanding individual opportunity rather than ensuring economic security. Obama recognized that antipoverty initiatives were not popular in the political climate of the 2000s, and that as a black president, he risked a race-based political backlash in promoting them.[67]

Obama's progressive leanings were also tempered by his own centrist streak, and his strong preference for pragmatic, compromise-driven, "postpartisan" politics. Asked in an interview to define himself as a liberal, progressive, or centrist, he resisted: "I don't like how the categories are set up."[68] He emphasized his desire to transcend ideological differences with an appeal to pragmatism, arguing, "Both sides of the political spectrum have tended to cling to outdated politics and tired ideologies instead of coalescing around what actually works."[69]

Obama shared many DLC critiques of "old" Democratic policies. He embraced the need to "return to fiscal responsibility," pledging in his 2008 campaign manifesto "Change We Can Believe In" to "pay for all new proposals, return to conservative budget practices, and put forward tangible plans for immediate deficit reduction."[70] He questioned liberal policies of redistribution, chiding "Democratic policymakers more obsessed with slicing the economic pie than with growing the pie."[71] His campaign called for "economic security and opportunity," but the clear emphasis was on creating opportunity, particularly for the middle class. For the working poor, he supported an increase in the EITC as well as the minimum wage.[72] The Obama plan did not address welfare directly. Obama had been skeptical of Clinton's reform as an Illinois state senator, but he later wrote approvingly of Clinton's record. In his assessment, Clinton left office having restored "some equilibrium—a smaller government, but one that retained the social safety net FDR had first put into place."[73]

Obama, in short, was neither a New Deal liberal nor a typical DLC Democrat. Though he criticized conservative and centrist positions on poverty, work, and welfare for failing to grasp the complex character of these social problems, he would also adopt positions that reflected and reinforced the centrist orientation of the Democratic Party's social policies—and he would do so in a new and more precarious economic environment. Obama's legacy on social policy would be defined above all by the passage of his landmark health care initiative in 2010, the Affordable Care Act (ACA), which promised to expand health insurance coverage on a scale not seen since the creation of Medicare and Medicaid in 1965.[74] Yet the story of Obama's presidency is also a story of missed opportunities to enact social policies that might have modernized and reinvigorated core New Deal commitments in hard economic times.[75]

* * *

The die was cast early, in Obama's economic appointments. Obama asked former Clinton aide and DLC centrist Representative Rahm Emanuel (D-Ill.) to serve as his chief of staff, and he appointed a full roster of Clinton veterans to serve on his economic team, including Timothy Geithner (Treasury), Larry Summers (National Economic Council), Peter Orszag (Office of Management and Budget), Gene Sperling (Treasury), Jack Lew (State Department), and Jason Furman (National Economic Council). The two major exceptions were Berkeley economist Christina Romer, chosen to chair the Council of Economic Advisers, and liberal economist Jared Bernstein, who became Vice President Joseph Biden's head economist. To some Obama supporters, "the new team looked disappointingly like a third Clinton administration."[76]

The economic team's first major task was to craft an emergency stimulus measure to address the deepening recession. Signed into law on February 17, 2009, the American Recovery and Reinvestment Act was the largest economic recovery initiative in the country's history, at $787 billion in spending and tax cut measures. Its central purpose was to stem the downturn by stimulating economic growth, and it did so.[77] The stimulus was also considered by some to be "Obama's most ambitious and least understood piece of legislation, the purest distillation of what he meant by change." In his detailed account, Michael Grunwald describes the legislation as an attempt "to repair a broken economy while reforming our approach to energy, health care, education, taxation, transportation and more."[78]

A one-time expenditure of this scale also had the potential to transform aspects of social policy. Yet as designed and implemented, the stimulus ultimately reinforced the character and trajectory of existing social welfare and labor market policies. The final package reflected two missed opportunities. It failed (with a few modest exceptions) to take steps to repair and modernize the safety net. And it failed to adequately respond to the problem of insufficient and low-wage employment through creating enough jobs in—or pathways to—the middle class.

The political maneuvering over the stimulus package began months before the new president entered the White House. Decisions about its content had implications for the short-term economic and political success of the stimulus, and also for its longer-term impact on social welfare and employment. Obama badly wanted to win bipartisan approval of the package. He and his advisers also wanted to avoid being seen as traditional "tax-and-spend" liberal Democrats. "There was the concern that we would look wacko lefty," explained Peter Orszag.[79]

Early internal debates focused on how big the stimulus should be. Clinton's 1993 proposal for a $16 billion stimulus had proved too much for Congress to swallow. In 2008, the proposals circulating on Capitol Hill quickly reached $500 billion. The sheer magnitude stunned many of the planners, though prominent liberal economists were arguing for a package big enough to fill a recession-generated shortfall totaling $2 trillion in economic output.[80] Larry Summers and Obama's political advisers drew the line at under a trillion dollars, convinced that Congress would not accept anything larger. By mid-December, they had settled on $700 to $800 billion, reasoning (wrongly, as it turned out) that they could return to Congress for more if needed to spur additional job growth.[81]

A second major issue was composition: tax cuts or spending? The team knew that tax cuts would be far less effective in stimulating demand but would be more politically palatable, particularly for Republicans.[82] Obama extended an early olive branch to Republicans, offering $300 billion in tax cuts, to win their support. This move would yield virtually no Republican votes (zero in the House; three in the Senate).[83] It meant, however, that the final stimulus legislation included the promised $286.9 billion in tax cuts and credits, a full 36 percent of the total package; the remainder was devoted to spending initiatives.[84]

When the Obama transition team turned to how the money should be spent, proposals were weighed according to their likely stimulus effect, their potential to achieve a broader and lasting purpose, and their projected timeframe (anything that might cause delays due to the need for reviews or hearings was avoided).[85] There were tensions between these objectives. On the one hand, Obama's campaign had emphasized that "the goal should be to lessen the pain that would occur from an economy-wide slowdown, not to use economic hardship as a rationale for enacting an ideologically-driven agenda."[86] On the other hand, the Obama team wanted to seize the opportunity to direct spending toward important ends. The stimulus was to be a "downpayment on long-term goals."[87] The argument for speed, meanwhile, created pressure to build on existing programs rather than generating new initiatives.[88] It also set limits on any long-term public investments that required advance planning. The spending was to be temporary, in order to win political support and to demonstrate fiscal restraint.[89]

Even with these limitations, Obama and his advisers recognized the potential for policy change presented by a spending package of this size. Their initial plan contained six primary spending areas. "Protecting the vulnerable" was one, along with energy, education, health care, infrastructure, and "other." Although relief for those hard-hit by the recession remained a prominent focus, internal discussions about the agenda for longer-term public investment and policy reform soon narrowed to energy, health care, education, and broadly defined economic reform.[90] There would be no major reform initiatives in employment or social welfare policy.[91]

Obama's advisers held conflicting views about what the federal government could and should do to create jobs. An expert on the Depression, CEA chair Christina Romer pointed out more than once that the Roosevelt administration had quickly put four million people to work through emergency jobs programs.[92] But the Obama team decided against a major public employment program; the Recovery Act relied instead on the private sector to create jobs.[93] The consequences of this strategy would prove significant. Although the stimulus saved or created two to three million jobs through aid to the states and measures that boosted economic demand, the recession's end in June 2009 did not bring the expected rise in employment.[94] For years, the country remained mired in historically high unemployment. This failure to generate rapid job creation was arguably the greatest shortcoming of the stimulus, both economically and politically. It fueled the public's sense that the stimulus (and government spending more generally) had failed, and that the administration had stabilized the economy for businesses and banks but ignored the decline in employment and income faced by American families.[95]

The Recovery Act also failed to include policy initiatives to restore or modernize the safety net. Not surprisingly, the majority of stimulus funds providing economic relief targeted middle-class Americans. In some cases, these had a real, if limited, antipoverty effect. The Making Work Pay tax credit, for example, was the largest single measure in the stimulus bill (funded at $116.2 billion). Though most of this temporary refundable tax credit went to middle-income earners, it kept 1.5 million Americans out of poverty in 2010.[96] But what of the more than $95 billion spent more directly on antipoverty measures?[97]

The main stimulus provisions targeting low-income Americans were an increase in unemployment benefits and benefit extensions for the longer-term unemployed (totaling $39.2 billion), and a temporary increase in food stamp

Table 8.1 Spending on Select Poverty-Reduction Programs in the American Recovery and Reinvestment Act of 2009

Program	Dollars (billions)
Expanded Unemployment Compensation (UC)	39.2
Supplemental Nutrition Assistance Program (SNAP)	19.9
Child Tax Credit (CTC)	14.8
Public Housing	8.0
Temporary Assistance for Needy Families (TANF)	5.0
Earned Income Tax Credit	4.7
Child Care for Low-Income Families	2.0
Head Start	2.1
Total	**95.7**

Source: "Tax Cuts and Spending Increases in the Conference Agreement," *Congressional Quarterly Weekly Report,* February 16, 2009, pp. 354–55.
Note: Many of these provisions involved temporary spending increases (for UC, TANF, and SNAP) or eligibility expansions (UC, CTC, and EITC). Unemployment Compensation benefits are not targeted to aid the poor, but are available to workers in all income groups; the UC expansions in the Recovery Act nonetheless kept 3.4 million people out of poverty in 2010.

benefits ($19.6 billion for the Supplemental Nutrition Assistance Program, or SNAP). The act also created a temporary TANF Emergency Contingency Fund, providing up to $5 billion for states to cover the costs of rising caseloads.[98] Two temporary tax provisions targeted low-income families—an increase in EITC benefits for families with three or more children ($4.7 billion), and an expansion of the Child Tax Credit for working families with lower incomes ($14.8 billion). Provisions to make these two increases permanent were included in Obama's first budget, but they were not enacted.[99] In addition, the stimulus included increases in spending for child care for low-income families ($2 billion), Head Start ($2.1 billion), and public housing ($8 billion).[100] At the height of the recession and slow recovery, these measures provided much-needed relief: the unemployment extension and increase, SNAP benefit boost, and EITC and Child Tax Credit expansions, for example, kept an estimated six million people out of poverty in 2010 alone.[101] But the impact was short-lived, as few initiatives were introduced to reform the social safety net.

The exceptions to this pattern highlighted the missed opportunities. The clearest case was unemployment insurance, where the Obama team seized the chance not only to increase payments temporarily, but also to reform an outdated system. The Recovery Act provided up to $7 billion in "incentive funds" to states that took specific steps to modernize their unemployment insurance laws, primarily by making the system more widely accessible and effective for workers in low-wage and nonstandard jobs, as well as those who faced difficult family circumstances. By the program's August 2011 deadline, thirty-nine states had claimed $4.4 billion in funds and enacted approximately one hundred reforms. The changes were expected to provide coverage to more than 200,000 additional people each year.[102]

Two smaller initiatives also illustrated the opportunities for change. The Recovery Act reauthorized and introduced a modest reform to the Trade Adjustment Assistance (TAA) program, which provides workers displaced by offshoring and trade-induced job losses with income support and assistance in training for and finding new jobs. Traditionally, the program aided only manufacturing workers. The stimulus program built in a reform that extended eligibility to service-sector and public-sector workers for the first time, signaling a role for government assistance in addressing job displacements across the labor market, including in lower-wage sectors.[103] Though limited in reach (and in the case of public-sector workers, temporary), the expansion was a response to changed work conditions of the post-1970s economy.[104]

In another small-scale initiative, the Recovery Act provided a one-time increase of $4 billion for job training programs, including grants to states. The increase nearly doubled existing spending on the programs under the Workforce Investment Act (WIA) and allowed greater program flexibility in how training was provided.[105] It also created an opportunity for states to challenge the dominance of the work-first approach. Targeting low-income adults and public assistance recipients, it provided explicit policy guidance to focus on education and skills training, rather than just job placement services. In some states, the funding increases and policy changes led to an increased investment in meaningful training, a greater focus on career development for low-income adults, and efforts to link training to high-growth occupations, including those paying a family-supporting wage. Advocates argued for using the Recovery Act's model as the basis for revising the WIA in the future.[106]

These modest reforms illustrate how more of the poverty-related stimulus funds might have been directed toward durable structural reforms in social and employment policies—through measures to make work more stable or secure, to advance workers up an earnings or career ladder, or to assist those without earnings over time, for example. Instead, the funds largely reinforced the existing workfarist safety net, providing temporary support for both the welfare and the working poor.

Beyond the substance of the stimulus, the administration's strategies for developing and defending the plan had far-reaching political consequences. The legislation—which combined several major initiatives into one package—was designed in ways that made its impact less transparent and comprehensible to the public. Obama chose, for example, to provide aid to low- and middle-income Americans primarily in the form of tax credits (such as Making Work Pay) rather than direct payments or services. In doing so, he adopted an approach that Suzanne Mettler has called "submerged policymaking." It has been used strategically by Democrats in recent decades to win support for expanded social welfare benefits from conservatives opposed to conventional social programs.[107] Tax credits are less visible to the public, less objectionable to conservatives, and often favored by centrists. Unlike more direct government action or spending, they often provide incentives for individuals or businesses to take desired actions in the market.[108]

Obama did little to publicly champion his stimulus legislation, either before or after its passage. When he did, he lowered the visibility of certain elements of the package, notably those focused on poor rather than middle-class Americans.[109] When a member of Congress commented to the First Lady at a reception that the stimulus was the most significant antipoverty legislation in a generation, "her reaction was 'Shhhh!'" according to Jonathan Alter. "The White House didn't want the public thinking that Obama had achieved long-sought public policy objectives under the guise of merely stimulating the economy."[110]

Obama cast his strategy as a prudent way to pass a large and controversial legislative initiative quickly.[111] There was arguably a price to pay, however. As Romer later explained, one of the economic benefits of FDR's highly public use of government action during the Depression was that it raised public confidence, which helped boost economic activity. The subterranean approach of the Obama program muted this potential economic benefit.[112] There was also a political impact. Many Americans never recognized that the stimulus was improving their financial circumstances. A year later, barely one in ten said (correctly) that their taxes had decreased; most thought they had stayed the same, and nearly a quarter thought they had increased.[113] Mettler noted that "hidden achievements" such as these stimulus provisions often fail to generate the public support needed to make them sustainable; more broadly, they "permit Americans to overlook or at least underestimate the role of government in their social provision and to exaggerate that of markets."[114]

Within months of its passage, the stimulus legislation, together with other emergency economic measures, began to show modest results. After plunging for months, state and local government spending ticked upward with the infusion of federal resources, and the rate of contraction in the economy slowed to 1 percent from a staggering 6.4 percent in the first quarter of the year. The recession formally ended in June 2009.[115]

The downturn was not over for millions still out of work and low on income, however; they faced a jobless recovery that stretched for years. In October 2009, unemployment reached 10 percent for the first time since the 1982–83 recession, and only the second time in the postwar period.[116] Many economists concluded that more stimulus was needed to spur job creation. But the Republican opposition had quickly and loudly condemned the stimulus as a "failed" initiative that had spiked the deficit and done nothing to stem unemployment. And Obama had done little to explain or defend it.

* * *

Soon after securing passage of the stimulus, the president made two critical strategic decisions. He chose to take on health care reform as a major policy initiative, reasoning that if he did not act immediately, the window for reform would close.[117] On the economy, meanwhile, Obama pivoted to deficit reduction rather than doubling down on the recovery, job creation, and economic security. In the context of an increasingly conservative and obstructionist Republican caucus, the result was a distinct rightward shift in the political debate over the social contract. The logic of cutting deficits to restore business confidence soon replaced the resurgent Keynesian logic of job creation, public investment, and social welfare spending.

Polls indicated growing public concern about deficit reduction, fueled in part by the Tea Party movement.[118] In the White House, Peter Orszag and Tim Geithner had emphasized the need for deficit reduction since the start of the administration. Summers wanted more stimulus in the short term, but he shared the view that fiscal restraint was vital. The former Clinton officials wanted to send a clear signal—to the public and to the bond markets—that this was not a "tax-and-spend" administration. But the liberals on Obama's team pushed hard for more stimulus. Romer drove home the high social cost of unemployment and pressed for a more serious jobs program, arguing that fiscal austerity was a mistake with unemployment climbing toward double digits. Noting the rapid loss of public-sector jobs, a mainstay of middle-class employment, Jared Bernstein urged more aid to the states to save government jobs and create new ones.[119]

Within the administration, the deficit-reduction camp won the argument, in no small part because Obama shared their perspective. Obama had always anticipated turning to fiscal discipline as soon as possible: "He seemed defensive about the stimulus, often noting that he never planned to start his presidency with a spending spree, complaining it reinforced the Republican narrative that he was a typical liberal Democrat," noted Grunwald. "Deficit reduction better suited his self-image as a centrist, a maker of hard choices, a cleaner of Bush-era messes; he joked about his 'inner Blue Dog.'"[120]

When liberal Democrats led by Pelosi mobilized in late 2009 for a second stimulus bill—one that would include new spending for job creation—Obama discouraged it.[121] He then used his 2010 State of the Union address to make the case for fiscal discipline. "Families across the country are tightening their belts and making tough decisions. The federal government should do the same," he said, in a direct repudiation of the Keynesian logic that guided the stimulus. "So tonight, I'm proposing specific steps to pay for the trillion dollars that it took to rescue the economy last year." The president announced that he would freeze discretionary spending for three years, and he launched a bipartisan National Commission on Fiscal Responsibility and Reform, to be co-chaired by Clinton adviser Erskine Bowles and former senator Alan Simpson (R-Wyo.).[122]

The president's pivot yielded no clear political gains for his party as the midterm elections approached. As voters went to the polls two years into the Obama presidency with unemployment still topping 9 percent, Democrats braced for the onslaught. Republicans reclaimed control of the House, gaining an astounding sixty-three seats, and cut deeply into the Democratic majority in the Senate, gaining six seats.[123] At the state level, Republicans won twenty-three of thirty-seven governor's races, and now controlled thirty of the nation's statehouses.[124]

Obama did not make a serious case for job creation to bring down the stubbornly high unemployment levels until the fall of 2011, when he submitted legislation to Congress and then stumped for it. His proposed American Jobs Act was a $447 billion plan to spur economic output and employment. It would have extended long-term unemployment benefits; committed $125 billion in new spending for infrastructure, modernizing schools, and rehiring state and local employees; and extended a temporary payroll tax holiday enacted in late 2010.¹²⁵ Analysts calculated it would create two to three million jobs and save over a million more.¹²⁶ Liberals welcomed the jobs bill, and expressed frustration when Obama did not make the plan a centerpiece of his 2012 reelection campaign.

Obama's focus remained on the deficit. He was convinced that reaching a long-term deficit deal with Republicans was not only good policy, but also vital to his reelection and an effective second term.¹²⁷ The president repeatedly signaled his willingness to accept deep spending cuts as well as major changes to Social Security to reach a bipartisan deal on deficit reduction, calling for a "grand bargain" with Republican leaders on spending cuts, a tax code overhaul, and entitlement reform.¹²⁸ The Republicans, however, steadfastly refused to consider any compromise that would raise taxes by any amount to boost revenues, scuttling prospects for a deal. In the course of these efforts, Obama and congressional leaders constructed a legislative straitjacket for themselves, mandating that if they did not agree on more than a trillion dollars in deficit reduction measures (to be crafted by a congressional "super committee"), then painful across-the-board "sequestration" cuts to both defense and domestic spending would automatically take effect in early 2013.¹²⁹

With his proposals for both job creation and deficit reduction blocked by Republicans, one of Obama's few sources of influence was the presidential bully pulpit.¹³⁰ Yet he was reluctant to use it forcefully to shape the debate on job creation, economic security, and the social contract, instead emphasizing the deficit and deflecting attention from poverty and social welfare issues.¹³¹ Republicans seized the opportunity to craft their own narrative of the president's social and economic agenda as the 2012 election approached. When House Budget Committee chair Paul Ryan (R-Wis.) presented the Republican response to the State of the Union in January 2011, he accused Obama of leading the country into a "future in which we will transform our social safety net into a hammock, which lulls able-bodied people into lives of complacency and dependency."¹³² Congressional Republicans attacked administration initiatives ranging from unemployment benefit extensions and food stamp increases to health care reform.¹³³ The April 2011 budget released by Ryan, which sailed through the Republican-led House, embodied a truly radical alternative conception of social policy. It proposed turning Medicaid and food stamps into block grants to the states, imposing massive cuts in federal spending of $5.8 trillion over a decade (including more than $1 trillion in health care for the poor through Medicaid), and transforming Medicare into a government-subsidized private insurance program.[134]

On the campaign trail, several Republican presidential candidates made it clear that Obama's attempt to sidestep issues of poverty and welfare would not shield him or the safety net from political attacks. Nor had Democratic support of welfare reform in 1996 ended the use of coded racial appeals in social policy debates, as the Clinton team had projected. Newt Gingrich repeatedly called President Obama "the greatest food-stamp president in American history" in a campaign for the Republican nomination that, in the words of the *New York Times* editorial board, "made racial resentment an integral part of his platform."[135] Senator Rick Santorum's (R-Pa.) critique of the Democrats' social welfare agenda was equally direct: "I don't want to make black people's lives better by giving them somebody else's money; I want to give them the opportunity to earn the money."[136]

If Republicans seemed to understand that, as Ryan put it, "the debate revolves around the fundamental nature of American democracy and the social contract," Obama and the Democrats did not.[137] Obama continued to steer carefully around these issues, referring generically to the "basic bargain at the heart of America's story," but avoiding direct references to poverty and the welfare state.[138] As his political team prepped him for the 2012 presidential debates, they counseled him to steer away from a strong defense of programs such as food stamps, because it would undermine the strategy of winning middle-class votes.[139]

While Obama tread cautiously, Republican candidate Mitt Romney was famously caught on tape at a private fundraiser in September 2012. His comments captured his views on social welfare programs and their recipients:

> There are 47 percent of the people who will vote for the president no matter what . . . who are with him, who are dependent on government, who believe that they are victims, who believe the government has a responsibility to care for them, who believe that they are entitled to health care, to food, to housing, to you-name-it. That that's an entitlement. And the government should give it to them. . . . My job is not to worry about those people—I'll never convince them they should take personal responsibility and care for their lives.[140]

Although Romney backed away from the comment as public outrage mounted, it was not a new idea among Republican leaders. Ryan had made a bolder claim in 2011, asserting, "Between 60 and 70 percent of Americans get more benefits from the government than they pay back in taxes. So, we're getting toward a society where we have a net majority of takers versus makers."[141]

The policy debate was shifting. By the end of the election season, the Republicans had offered a new definition of dependency (the "takers") and a new definition of whose work counts (the "makers"). In this retelling, the category of "takers" was much larger than most Americans understood. To reach his sweeping 60 percent figure, analysts noted, Ryan would have had to count all Social Security recipients as "takers" rather than (retired) "makers."[142] Likewise, the category of "makers" was much smaller: it did not include all who contribute to society through work in the labor force (or in the home), but only those who receive no support from certain government programs. The conflicts over work and welfare had turned on these questions. The new expansive definition now laid the groundwork for a broader battle to be waged—against programs like Social Security and the EITC as well as more traditional public assistance programs. Most importantly, the very legitimacy of mobilizing government to meet social needs in hard times was called into question, and Democrats had failed to stake out a clear position.

On November 6, Obama won a decisive victory and Democrats added two seats to their slim majority in the Senate, but Republicans held onto their majority in the House. Republicans were particularly effective in the South, gaining twenty-eight House seats from the region in 2010 and 2012. Among Democrats, conservatives faced the highest losses. The Blue Dogs' ranks were cut from fifty-four to fourteen in these two election cycles. The New Democrats held their own, with just over fifty members in their caucus after the 2012 election. They led the party's centrists, but still claimed fewer members than the seventy- to eighty-member Congressional Progressive Caucus.[143]

The election may have been a vindication for the president, but it did not alter the trajectory in Washington on social and economic policy. The sequester cuts went into effect in early 2013. Ryan again led Republicans in passing budgets in 2013 and 2014 that were as draconian as in previous years, seeking deep cuts in spending to aid lower-income Americans. He also unveiled plans to convert food stamps and other safety net programs into block grants to the states, citing the 1996 welfare reform as a model. The budget Obama presented in 2013, meanwhile, drew sharp objections from party liberals by proposing to rein in the costs of Social Security spending through changing the way benefits are calculated. Obama's advisers defended his actions, saying it would affect only wealthy seniors. But his critics cast it as the newest encroachment on one of the remaining bulwarks of the New Deal social contract. The president renewed his rhetorical commitment to a larger social and economic agenda after the election. He spoke eloquently of the vital role of government at his second inauguration, and presented a fuller analysis of the sources of long-term weaknesses in the economy in a series of addresses across the nation early in his second term. Rising inequality and declining mobility, he announced, posed "the defining challenge of our time." In his 2014 State of the Union address, Obama pledged to "build new ladders of opportunity into the middle class."[144]

The political constraints of his first term—some self-imposed, others imposed by congressional Republicans—remained firmly in place, however, and policy initiatives to address these challenges made little headway in Washington. Frustrated with federal inaction on the minimum wage, activists and elected officials won state-level minimum wage increases in more than half a dozen states in 2013 and 2014, and launched legislative debates in over thirty more. But Obama faced solid Republican opposition to his bid for a federal minimum wage increase, and to the new proposals for public investment in energy research, manufacturing, and universal preschool presented in his budget for 2015. The president found more support, not surprisingly, for his calls to expand the EITC in response to problems of economic insecurity: workfare's staying power was evident.[145]

Assessing the Workfare State: Lessons from the Great Recession

As political debates over the social contract continued, the new workfare system was being tested. A decade and a half of partisan shifts and electoral changes had left intact the work-conditioned safety net crafted by Clinton and congressional Republicans. How had it performed as a system of social protections for vulnerable families under good economic conditions (late 1990s) and bad (late 2000s)? What conclusions could be drawn about the strengths and weaknesses of the workfare state in these years?

Perhaps the most striking finding was the sharp contrast in its performance in the 1990s and in the 2000s. In the late 1990s—workfare in the best of times—the system provided fairly effective support to a wide range of poor families. Labor markets tightened as economic growth accelerated in the mid-1990s. Unemployment dropped to historically low levels for the postwar period, as did the length of unemployment spells and the percentage of long-term unemployed workers. Strong labor markets brought wage increases, including solid gains for those at the bottom of the wage distribution, and the trend extended to women, minorities, and less-educated workers who were confronting the new workfare system.[146]

Federal social policy for low-wage workers compounded these positive labor market effects in the late 1990s. The modest minimum wage increase (to $5.15 an hour) passed in 1996 went into effect in 1997. At the same time, the 1990 and 1993 EITC expansions had kicked in fully by the end of the decade. They drove a 54 percent increase in the number of program recipients and a 330 percent increase in the total value of EITC benefits, as the average family EITC credit climbed from $601 in 1990 to $1,675 in 2000.[147] Low-income families with a working adult also benefited from expansions in the Medicaid program (mostly for coverage of their children), and some were eligible for the new Child Tax Credit. Notably, these social policy supports were federally mandated, with standardized eligibility and benefit rules allowing little if any discretion for states.[148]

The combined effect of rising wages and new policy supports was to boost family resources just as the new workfare policies were increasing poor families' reliance on earnings and the EITC. Although structural obstacles facing low-wage workers remained in place, the increased family resources helped lower the national poverty rate, which dropped from 13.7 percent in 1996 to a low of 11.7 percent in 2001. These indicators in the first few years of workfare were encouraging to many observers.

The evidence from workfare in the worst of times—the years of recession and recovery in the late 2000s—was troubling, however. More than ever, Americans needed a system of social protections to shield them from the dramatic swings and long-term weaknesses of the labor market. Yet the work-based safety net frayed as work disappeared. In 2009, more than seventy million Americans—nearly one-quarter of the population—experienced poverty for at least two months during the year.[149] By 2010, the poverty rate climbed back up to 15.1 percent, and the number of people in deep poverty reached twenty million.[150] Many more faced serious economic insecurity, hovering just above the poverty line.[151]

Unemployment shot up from an annual rate of 4.6 percent in 2007 to 9.3 percent in 2009, then remained elevated for more than half a decade. The pattern of job creation was equally worrisome. Lower-wage occupations accounted for 21 percent of the jobs lost in the recession, but represented 58 percent of those added in the first three years of the recovery (from 2009 to early 2012). Mid-wage occupations saw 60 percent of the losses in the recession, but only 22 percent of the gains in the recovery.[152] Part-time work also rose rapidly in the recession, most of it among people who wanted full-time employment.[153]

Wages and family incomes declined across the board in these years, and the downturn erased twenty years' worth of wealth accumulation for the median American family.[154] The wage and income drops were steepest for the bottom two-fifths of families, with incomes falling 11.3 percent for the bottom fifth of families between 2007 and 2010.[155] Use of soup kitchens, food pantries, and homeless shelters rose, with unemployment and poverty hitting hardest in the South and West.[156]

How well did the new safety net protect vulnerable families during this severe downturn? Existing social programs, together with the measures enacted by the Obama administration, helped blunt its effects early on. The poverty rate in 2010 would have been nearly twice as high as it was (28.6 percent rather than 15.1 percent), and more than one in four Americans would have been living below the poverty line. Of the millions of Americans kept out of poverty by government assistance, most were seniors relying on Social Security benefits. Another 13.3 million were lifted above the poverty line by unemployment insurance, the EITC, food stamps, and other programs. And 7.5 million were kept out of poverty by temporary program expansions and the Making Work Pay tax credit under the 2009 stimulus and subsequent measures.[157] But the social policy supports enacted were largely temporary, and they were not enough to reverse the negative impact.[158] The safety net proved seriously inadequate for many of those who lost work (15 million between 2007 and 2009) or whose incomes fell close to or below the poverty line.[159]

On balance, programs appeared to be better able to respond to the effects of the recession when their eligibility criteria were federally standardized (rather than discretionary for states), and when their financing was largely federal (rather than dependent on state funds vulnerable to budget crises).[160] Another critical factor was the link to work: in a time of high and sustained unemployment and declining wages, programs in which the tie to work was less proximate or direct (such as Social Security and food stamps) were more effective in meeting needs.

Social Security was an essential bulwark during the downturn. The program bases benefits on a long record of past employment and is not targeted to aid the poor, yet its impact on poverty was dramatic. Some twenty million

Americans were kept out of poverty by Social Security benefits in 2010.[161] The contrast with nonseniors is revealing: in 2009, as the recession ended and the recovery began, the poverty rate for working-age Americans (ages eighteen to sixty-four) was 12.9 percent, a record high for this cohort. The same year, after increases in Social Security payments, poverty among those over sixty-five was 8.9 percent—also a record, but in this case a record low.[162] Reports also suggested, however, that hundreds of thousands of Americans who could not find work started to draw on their Social Security benefits early (at age sixty-two rather than at full retirement age), faced with long-term joblessness and inadequate income. The price they paid for using Social Security as wage replacement in a weak economy was severe—an estimated loss of 20 to 30 percent of the value of benefits every month for the remainder of their lives.[163]

The federal food assistance program, SNAP, was one of the most effective public assistance programs in the downturn. From 2007 to 2011, the average number of Americans using food stamps monthly climbed from about twenty-six million to more than forty-four million, or roughly one in every eight Americans.[164] The program kept 4.4 million out of poverty in 2010 and was the sole source of support for a growing number of poor Americans in January of that year.[165] SNAP benefit levels and eligibility requirements are largely set by the federal government. In part because SNAP benefits come from federal rather than state coffers, officials in many states worked to enroll more eligible participants and enacted state-level administrative changes to make qualifying for benefits less burdensome; this stood in contrast to their approach to TANF.[166]

Safety net programs that were directly conditioned on current employment, that required state-level funding, or that permitted significant state discretion in setting eligibility rules were less effective in responding to the recession and its aftermath. Unemployment insurance, for example, had a mixed record. Federal and state spending on the program grew from $33 billion in 2007 to a peak of $159 billion in fiscal 2010, when the program and its temporary expansions kept 4.6 million workers out of poverty (3.4 million due to the stimulus expansions alone).[167] But since most state laws had not been modernized to reflect the changing character of the job market, only 45 percent of the unemployed were receiving benefits by the end of 2008, one year into the recession. Emergency benefit extensions—and short-term benefit increases included in the 2009 stimulus—temporarily boosted the reach and effectiveness of the program as the recession wore on and recovery began. After the emergency extensions expired, the share of unemployed receiving jobless benefits plummeted—dropping below 30 percent by mid-2014—despite continued signs of weakness in the overall employment picture. The unemployment rate finally fell below 6 percent that fall—for the first time since 2008—but the labor participation rate remained disturbingly low. Discouraged by their job prospects, nearly five million people had dropped out of the labor force: they were neither employed nor actively looking for work, and often ineligible for unemployment insurance.[168]

The Earned Income Tax Credit is a core component of the work-conditioned safety net, but it has serious shortcomings as an antipoverty program, particularly during recessions. The EITC was of limited help to those most in need during the Great Recession, and the help came slowly. By design, the EITC assists low-income workers, not poor families without income. But even among those who work, the program concentrates benefits on those families near the poverty line, rather than those significantly below it.[169] Equally important, and in keeping with a thirty-year pattern, the EITC was slow to respond to the need created by the downturn.[170] In the first year of the recession, the number of Americans in poverty jumped by more than 2.5 million, yet the number of EITC recipients rose by just over 170,000. After the recession, the program grew at a more rapid clip, and in 2010 it lifted over six million Americans out of poverty—but its slow response limited its impact.[171]

One of the least effective programs in responding to the Great Recession was TANF, which replaced AFDC after 1996. Under AFDC, federal funding to the states had expanded to meet need during recessions—but TANF was established as a block grant program with a funding cap. Many families therefore went unassisted. TANF caseloads hit a historic low in mid-2008, and they did not begin to rise until more than six months into the recession. Even then, the increase in caseloads was modest.[172] TANF's poor response was a reflection of longer-term trends that pre-dated the recession and continued after it ended. Caseloads began declining in the mid-1990s, dropping from 4.7 million in 1995 to only 1.7 million in 2013. The decrease was not explained by an overall reduction in need: the number of families in poverty increased from 6.2 to 7.3 million in these years. Instead, fewer eligible families were receiving assistance, due in part to state-level policies discouraging or restricting enrollment.[173] At the same time, the value of TANF benefits declined in real terms, leaving recipient families in all but two states further below the poverty line in 2013 than they had been in 1996. Even a family that combined its TANF benefits with food stamps (as 80 percent of TANF recipients do) was still left under 75 percent of the poverty line in forty-nine states.[174]

In a reverse image of the late-1990s experience, the combined effect of a collapsing labor market and reconfigured social policies proved particularly damaging for those in the low-wage labor market. Households in the bottom 20 percent of earners experienced steep losses in wage income over the entire 2007 to 2010 period.[175] At the same time, the value of EITC benefits they received fell by more than 10 percent in the first two years of the downturn, compounding their wage losses, and the value of TANF benefits was effectively flat.[176]

The Great Recession also exposed a deeper structural consequence of the ever-tighter link between employment and social protections in the post-1970s labor market. The reach and significance of means-tested assistance has shifted in the modern workfare state: this aid has increasingly served a new purpose as a stopgap safety net for working families that lack basic income security in the current labor market, rather than serving primarily as a last-resort lifeline for a largely nonworking population of very poor families. The shift has provided a source of immediate support for many families facing economic hardship—but it has also created new dilemmas.

Working families who are above the poverty line but not securely in the middle class have turned in growing numbers to means-tested aid when work and social insurance fail to meet basic needs. They have sought not only wage supplements such as the EITC, but also in-kind assistance such as food stamps and Medicaid. In 2009, more than forty-five million Americans with incomes above the poverty line drew support from at least one of the major public assistance programs (not including the EITC).[177]

Though magnified by the recession, the pattern is not limited to economic downturns. An unreliable labor market and an outdated system of social provision have quietly transformed these programs into a vital line of defense for many working Americans, including those living in the precarious region just above the poverty line. Their numbers are disturbingly high. All told, 101.8 million Americans (about one in three) were poor or near-poor in 2013, according to new measures developed by the Census Bureau. This included fifty-two million Americans with incomes above the poverty line, but by less than 50 percent, according to the Bureau. One lost job or health emergency could move these families into poverty.[178]

As more families have come to rely on this stopgap assistance, they confront new vulnerabilities when the aid is conditioned on holding a job and earning a stable wage. For EITC recipients, for example, a decline in income (due to reductions in working hours or hourly wages) will bring a corresponding decline in the total resources received from wages and EITC benefits. The situation is even more dire for EITC recipients who lose their jobs, as millions do in recessions. At the point when they are most in need of assistance, their EITC benefits are eliminated entirely.[179] The Great Recession, in short, confirmed that the modern workfare state has not only left many nonworking poor families behind. In the post-1970s economy, it also poses new risks for working families who rely on the safety net when work fails.

* * *

The years stretching from Clinton's presidency to Obama's brought the consolidation of the American workfare state, even in the context of a severe economic downturn that laid bare its shortcomings. Congressional Democrats and the Obama administration inherited and ultimately reinforced the policy framework crafted by Southern Democrats and institutionalized by Bill Clinton. Old debates over welfarist aims faded as liberal Democrats focused on improving conditions for poor families within the workfare system.

As Southerners moved to the Republican Party, meanwhile, they assumed prominent new roles. Southern Republicans in Congress led the push for bolder departures—beyond workfare—seeking to roll back the New Deal welfare state by cutting and block-granting programs, such as Medicaid and food stamps, and privatizing middle-class entitlements. Imposing their own brand of social policy at the state level, Southern Republican governors in states including Alabama, Georgia, Louisiana, Mississippi, Texas, and South Carolina refused federal dollars for unemployment extensions, temporary TANF increases, or Medicaid expansions during and after the Great Recession, even as poverty and joblessness in their states soared.[180]

Nationwide, as the impact of the recession hit low- and middle-income families, the work-conditioned safety net enabled some working families to secure new sources of aid. But when work disappeared or declined, the weaknesses of the workfare system emerged in sharp relief. The experiences of the late 1990s, the slow-growth 2000s, and the Great Recession demonstrate that workfare functions best in times of economic prosperity and growth, with higher levels of job stability and mobility. The system is at its weakest when labor markets bring greater job shifting, stagnant wages, diminished mobility, or economic downturns—precisely when families experience the most profound and widespread social need.

Conclusion

There was much bold talk at the turn of the twenty-first century about leaving behind the old for the new. In social and economic policy, references to the changes wrought by the "New Democrats," the "New South," and the "New Economy" were ubiquitous. These were overlapping and mutually reinforcing categories in the battles over work and welfare in the 1990s. Many prominent New Democrats came from the New South; both New Democrats and proponents of Southern economic development lauded the arrival of the New Economy.

In each case, the implication was that there had been a break with the previous order—not simply movement along some preexisting continuum, but a fundamental rejection of the continuum itself. New Democrats argued that they were neither more liberal nor more conservative than old Democrats; they had charted a "third way."[1] The New South purportedly reflected not simply a transition from an agrarian to an advanced industrial economy, nor from a racially divided and stratified society to one less so: it was "post-industrial" and "post-racial."[2] And the New Economy embodied not a move along the old continuum stretching between the interests of capital and the interests of labor; instead, it was lauded as a "new deal" for both business and workers, extending opportunities for all.[3]

The labels are misleading, however. They suggest not simply the rejection of past politics—but that in each case the "new" order transcended politics altogether, with its array of conflicts, choices, winners, and losers. Proponents of the New Democrats, the New South, and the New Economy often obscured the salience of old divisions and hierarchies—not by settling them, but by presuming to escape them. Advocates held out the alluring proposition that in the "new" Democratic/Southern/economic order, everyone was or could become a winner. The New Democrats asserted that the party could embrace their policies for the white middle class without compromising its existing commitment to improving the economic prospects of poor minorities. Ardent boosters of the New South suggested that its rapidly rising economic tides and new political opportunities would lift all boats. And champions of the New Economy imagined the nation transcending not only industrialism but its many thorny and divisive distributive conflicts.

These proved false promises in the case of work and welfare policy. The account provided here is above all a tale of political struggles and choices that have yielded losers as well as winners in the search for economic security. Conflict and change in the Democratic Party, the South, and the economy are central to the three storylines that weave through this account of social policy transformation. Together, the storylines provide an explanation of who rewrote the social contract for poor families in recent decades—and how, when, and why they did so. And together, they begin to shed light on the consequences of the turn to workfare, for politics, policy, and the families at the center of the debate.

A Democratic Political Settlement

The first storyline follows the long-running struggle within the Democratic Party over poverty, work, and the purposes of public assistance. FDR's New Deal had defined the prevailing Democratic response to these issues in the 1930s. New Deal welfarism was always limited and never fully coherent, constrained by the patchwork character of the Social Security Act. The means-tested public assistance programs for discrete categories of poor Americans were the weakest part of the new system of social protections, both institutionally and politically; New Dealers themselves disagreed on their functions and future trajectory. Despite these limitations, New Deal public assistance reflected a need-based entitlement ideal: the aim was to ease the effects of poverty through extending a federal guarantee of assistance to eligible needy populations considered unable to support themselves adequately through work. A product of political compromise, it was a thin entitlement—never adequate to meet need, and routinely undercut by the discretion preserved for administrators in each state. But it was a welfarist framework nonetheless; it marked a departure from the pre–New Deal hodgepodge of state-level programs and private charity by staking out a role for the federal government in public assistance. And it provided a foundation on which leading New Deal liberals sought to build a more robust, need-based safety net.

The irony is that within a few short decades, Democrats instead began to construct a workfare regime alongside their welfarist system. It took root in the 1960s and was intended by liberals in the Kennedy and Johnson administrations as an adjunct to welfare. From the outset, however, the rise of workfare would be linked politically to the demise of welfarism, as Southern party conservatives seized the opportunity to advance it as a preferred alternative to the existing system. Over the decades, both the policy models for workfare at the federal level and the major political decisions to implement them were crafted largely by Democrats. In the end, every postwar Democratic administration from Kennedy to Obama would contribute to the gradual construction and consolidation of the modern workfare state for poor families.

The signal changes came in two distinct moments of reform. The first ran from the mid-1960s through the mid-1970s and included the passage of WIN, WIN II, SSI, and the EITC; it was led by Southern conservative Democrats in Congress. The second wave of reform came in the 1990s. It was led by Southern centrists in the White House and Congress, and it resulted in the dismantlement of AFDC and a major expansion of the EITC and other market-friendly policies toward low-wage labor. In each case, workfarists confronted welfarists within the Democratic Party, winning their acquiescence if not their approval. And by the mid-1990s, conservative and moderate Southern Democrats had replaced the New Deal system for poor families with a workfare regime.

Republicans were important allies at key junctures—but they were not the main architects of change. Indeed, Richard Nixon had proposed a major welfarist expansion through his Family Assistance Plan, Ronald Reagan had tried but failed to impose his own structural reforms, and the issue was largely ignored under both George H. W. Bush and George W. Bush. Even congressional Republicans in the 1990s found that their influence depended largely on the opportunities for compromise created by the Clinton administration. Workfare was, in short, a Democratic project.

The new workfare regime was a compromise—not a consensus—between the party's liberal and moderate-to-conservative wings. Organized under the banner of the centrist Democratic Leadership Council in the 1980s, the New Democrats helped define and produce the final compromise in the 1990s and consolidate it in the 2000s. Southerners left the party, Clinton left the White House, and the DLC closed its doors in 2011, but they left a policy legacy, and leading New Democrats from the Clinton administration played a role in consolidating workfare during the Obama years.

The workfare settlement proved a durable one, with no serious political challenges to its basic terms in its first two decades. The settlement combines policies to move poor families into the labor market with programs to provide basic income support for those who are working but still poor. It rests on a decision to replace a federal need-based entitlement for eligible poor families with a work-conditioned safety net. Despite intraparty conflict over its creation and periodic evidence of its shortcomings in the years that followed, no one on Capitol Hill made headway with a proposal to reintroduce a federal entitlement to aid, or to remove federal time limits and spending caps, either on the earlier U.S. model of need-based AFDC or on the European model of a universal family assistance grant. Instead, most liberal reform proposals sought primarily to build on and make more generous the programs of the new workfare regime, through increased work supports (such as childcare or medical assistance) and further expansions of the EITC and related programs.[4] Meanwhile, new cohorts of centrist Democrats rooted workfare policies in a broader centrist agenda on social and economic policy. In his second term, Clinton elevated deficit reduction and fiscal restraint over labor market reform and economic security. Eight years later, faced with an economic crisis and unprecedented partisan constraints on his agenda, Barack Obama carved a policy path that largely reinforced these priorities over the course of his own two-term administration.

Southern Leaders and Legacies

The second storyline in this account tracks the role of Southern leaders in rewriting the social contract for America's poor families. Southerners were present at every major turning point in the construction of the modern workfare state, although their institutional roles and agendas varied over time. In the late 1960s and 1970s, leading Southern Democrats exercised their authority as senior committee members in Congress to craft the basic template for the new policy settlement on workfare, including the first federal welfare-to-work requirements (under WIN) and the EITC. In the 1980s, conservative Southern Democrats used their vote margin to wield influence with both parties simultaneously. They provided Republicans with the extra votes needed to "hollow out" the welfare system through Reagan's budget-cutting initiatives. And they forced liberal leaders in their own party to abandon or scale back welfarist initiatives to avoid Southern defections on key votes. In the 1990s and 2000s, finally, centrist Southerners used the DLC as an institutional and political platform to promote and consolidate workfare reforms, in part through compromises crafted with Southern Republicans.

Even as the region's Democratic contingent shifted from a largely conservative cohort to a more diverse one dominated by centrists, workfare continued to figure prominently on many Southerners' agendas. Southern conservatives' initial drive to construct workfare in the 1960s and 1970s was fueled in part by the desire to defend local control over the South's large and heavily black low-wage labor force, in the face of Nixon's Family Assistance Plan and its perceived threat to the Southern social, economic, and racial order. By the 1990s, a new cohort of moderate Southern Democrats sought to preserve and extend a regional economic boom and to widen the opportunities it created. The Southern development strategy in these years did not advocate preserving or expanding the low-skilled, low-wage workforce—but nor did it seek to reform it; rather, its effect was to graft a growing new sector of high-end jobs onto the region's existing labor market. Workfarist social policies served these ends as well. Long, Mills, and Talmadge would have disagreed with successors such as Clinton, Gore, and Breaux on a number of issues, including race and civil rights. But they would have agreed on the broad outlines of a workfare alternative to New Deal public assistance.

The South also led the way in modeling both the possibilities and the limits of workfare. The Southern version of a safety net for poor families prefigured the transformed safety net under the new national workfare regime—not simply because of its work-based policies, but because it pursued these policies in the context of a divided economy with a large low-wage sector that promised few opportunities for economic security, job stability, or income mobility.

Southern states had consistently pursued pro-work and pro-market policies toward poor families for decades. In the immediate postwar years, the priority placed on labor control and regulation was overt and its racial impact undisguised—when, for example, local welfare officials simply cut off welfare payments to families during harvest season to ensure that all family members were available for field work.[5] Fifty years later, local welfare rules had changed, but the focus on requiring poor family heads to enter the workforce remained, reflected in "welfare-to-work" policies. Southern welfare strategies varied across states as well as over time, but typically shared several features. Most allowed state and local officials the latitude to determine who received aid and how much, imposed little or no fiscal burden on state budgets, and limited nonwage sources of income or in-kind assistance to potential workers.

Many Southern leaders viewed defending the discretion of local employers as an important role for elected officials, one that served Southerners' shared interest in growth. Southerners of both parties generally supported limited intervention in the region's labor market, whether through minimum wages, workplace regulations, or unionization. In part as a result, jobs in the South had long come with fewer protections (such as health and retirement plans) and lower wages; this kept labor costs low for employers.[6] In developing workfare policies, Southern leaders since Russell Long had sought ways to sustain low-wage workers without undermining private employers' ability to ensure entry and set wages through the market. Southerners in Congress were prepared to accept federal aid that met these criteria, but resisted imposing fiscal burdens on the region's states or businesses. Over time, this translated into a strategy of supporting subsidies of existing wages (through the EITC) but opposing or limiting aid that might replace wages (such as AFDC, FAP, and even extended unemployment benefits).

By the 1980s, the combined effect of the region's limited work-conditioned safety net and its labor market trajectory began to concern some Southern leaders. The chair of the Southern Growth Policies Board in 1986 was none other than Bill Clinton, and he posed a tough challenge to the board's Commission on the Future of the South: "Can the South at long last achieve a standard of living that is equal to or beyond that enjoyed by the rest of the country?" he asked, adding, "One thing is paramount. None of our states can ever be what we hope they will be if we have an increasing percentage of people living below the poverty line and no constructive response to it."[7] Commission chair and former Mississippi governor William Winter (D-Miss.) observed: "The heart of the problem has been to find a solution to the dilemma of the two Souths which are rapidly growing farther apart. One is represented by the popular image of the modern Sunbelt. But there remains that other South, largely rural, undereducated, underproductive, and underpaid that threatens to become a permanent shadow of distress."[8]

Noting the false promises of "other self-proclaimed 'New Souths,'" the report warned that in the wake of the region's most recent boom, a dual and divided economy was growing.[9] An expanding sector of stable and high-wage jobs in industries such as defense and technology had boosted the region's economy. But it existed alongside a still-large sector of low-wage and unstable jobs, and for too many Southerners, there was no reliable route from the latter to the former. The commission urged increased investment in education and workforce development and a more "hands-on" role for state governments in developing Southern industry. To address the region's poverty, one recommendation was that the South adopt classic welfarist strategies.[10] These were not pursued by most Southern leaders, nor by Clinton when he became president. Instead, during the 1980s and 1990s, Southern states continued to enact policies for the welfare poor that relied on limited benefits and increasing work requirements. For the working poor, the dominant pro-market approach translated into a strong preference for subsidizing existing wages rather than increasing the minimum wage. Not surprisingly, the region's main program for supporting working-poor families quickly became the federal EITC program.[11]

A decade after the commission's warnings, meanwhile, the South's economic structure did look more like that of the rest of the country—but not solely due to changes in the region. The transformation also reflected the fact that the nation as a whole had come to look more like the South, in the character of its low-wage labor market and social welfare policies.[12] For years, many parts of the country had seen stagnant wages, an expanding low-wage sector and a growing gap between the highest and lowest earners in the workforce. Even in periods of growth and rising high-end employment in technology and other sectors in the 1990s, the U.S. workforce was marked by deep inequality and diminished economic mobility. The early 2000s saw levels of economic inequality climb higher still. In the wake of the Great Recession, incomes for families with working-age adults were lower than a decade earlier, and the economy was rapidly replacing vanishing middle-class jobs with new low-wage jobs.

Comparisons between the diverse and complex national labor market and the Southern one should not be overdrawn. But in both cases, the trajectory was toward a divided labor market with limited upward mobility for low earners, not only in downturns, but even in the context of economic expansions.[13] By the mid-1990s, federal work and welfare policies also reflected the pro-market approach favored in the South. Today the nation, like the South, relies largely on market-friendly wage subsidies (the EITC) rather than non-wage cash assistance (such as AFDC/TANF) to provide income support to poor families, along with increased assistance to the disabled poor through SSI. This model had long characterized public assistance in Southern states: in the late 1970s, these states had the lowest rates of participation in AFDC and the highest rates of participation in the EITC, along with SSI. By the late 1990s, state programs in every region in the country had moved toward this policy model, cutting cash assistance and increasing reliance on the EITC as well as SSI.[14] In the aftermath of the Great Recession, barely a quarter of poor families with children received TANF nationally. The South continued to lead the way in cutting back this safety net: ten of thirteen Southern states fell below the national average in the percentage of these families assisted.[15]

There is a deep irony in the South's role in this story, one noted in scholarly debates on the region. In the mid-1970s, historians of the South such as George Tindall observed the region's gains since the 1930s, as local and national leaders sought to help the South "catch up" to the rest of the nation. By the 1990s, historian Bruce Schulman countered, "Where Tindall erred . . . was in his view of the South as mere follower. . . . In recent times . . . the tables have turned. The South, for good or ill, has been bidding the nation to follow its lead. The South has passed on much to other regions—a fondness for high technology, a craving for defense industry, a suspicion of unions, a divided economy, an antipathy to welfare, an uneasy accommodation between black urban leaders and white business conservatives."[16]

On work and welfare, the irony was captured, fittingly, by Russell Long. Long told his biographer that in 1972 he fought Nixon's Family Assistance Plan in order to stop "something that was going to make the whole nation into a welfare state."[17] Thirty years later, he and his fellow Southern Democrats had helped to turn the whole country into a workfare state. It was a system much more like that of the South, with its mix of a work-conditioned safety net and a minimally regulated labor market offering few exits or opportunities for low-wage workers.

A New Social Contract

The third storyline, finally, details the rise of the modern workfare state and parallel demise of the New Deal welfare system in the context of a changing national economy. The shift was gradual but marked.

For more than three decades after the New Deal, federal policy provided income assistance on the basis of need to certain categories of eligible families considered unable to earn their support. Many poor families combined work and welfare, of course; public assistance alone was never enough to lift a family out of poverty. But the system's underlying principle was welfarist entitlement, and the policy trajectory, though slow and uneven, was toward expanding coverage and standardizing and increasing benefits: both participation rates and benefit values for AFDC climbed for thirty-five years, then began a decline that was never reversed.[18]

With the turn to workfare in the 1960s, a formal link was forged between work and public assistance in federal policy—first through requirements that states create work and training programs in the late 1960s and early 1970s, and then through federal policies that explicitly conditioned aid on individual employment beginning in the mid-1980s and culminating in the mid-1990s. Higher levels of aid began to flow to the working poor from a wider range of federal programs in these years, and sources of aid for poor families outside of the labor market diminished markedly. By the end of the 1990s, a quiet transformation had taken place in the purposes and target populations of income assistance for the poor. The need-based entitlement had been eclipsed by workfare: the majority of the nation's income assistance was now conditioned on employment, and a central aim was to promote, require, and reward work among poor families in the low-wage labor market.[19]

What made this shift so consequential was that it took place in the context of sweeping changes in the labor market—and in policy assumptions about what work should provide and what government's obligation is when it fails. Work has always held a privileged role in American political culture: for centuries, social standing has been based in part on an individual's will and capacity to earn his or her way.[20] Since the New Deal, however, federal policies—from the Fair Labor Standards Act to the social insurance programs of the Social Security Act—have affirmed a broader principle. They inscribed the notion that work was not only an important social and moral obligation in and of itself, but that it should deliver a basic livelihood. Through regulations (such as minimum wage and workplace health and safety laws) and social protections (such as unemployment insurance and tax incentives for employer-provided health and pension plans), government sought to ensure that workers received a bare measure of security in an uncertain market. Though contested in its scope and reach, the principle that government has a role in defining and enforcing minimal standards and protections—that public policy can and should pave the path from bad jobs to good jobs—was rooted over time in multiple state and federal policies.[21]

Beginning in the late 1970s, however, many jobs fell short of these expectations, particularly in the low-wage sector. This, of course, was the underside of the "New Economy." The shift from a manufacturing-led to a service-based economy indeed produced a wave of new post-industrial, information-age employment for some. But the service economy also generated a flood of lower-paid, less stable jobs. Job growth expanded most in areas such as food service, customer service, retail sales, and clerical work.[22] It soon became clear that there were few career ladders within these occupations, and even fewer long enough to reach the high-paid jobs at the other side of the new economy.[23]

New patterns of job creation were generating new employment arrangements, and in the low-wage sector, standards needed to be modernized to ensure minimal job quality. The trend was clearest in the case of the minimum wage standard, which had dropped so low in the absence of legislative action that full-time work no longer guaranteed a basic livelihood for many families.[24] But it was also evident in the spread of subcontracting and outsourcing. These practices raised the question of who a worker's "employer" was—and enabled some firms (particularly in the low-wage sector) to misclassify workers as independent contractors to dodge liability under the Fair Labor Standards Act and other New Deal work laws. New standards and enforcement efforts were also needed to govern the quality of burgeoning temporary and part-time employment, much of which was underpaid.[25]

The challenge for government was not insurmountable: New Dealers had confronted similar puzzles, and European nations provided various models for governing contemporary part-time, temporary, and low-wage work.[26] The U.S. response came in piecemeal policies beginning in the 1980s toward job creation and training, tax credits and wage floors, and work requirements for welfare recipients. Confronted with the issue of what low-wage work should deliver and what government's responsibility was to those who sought work in order to escape poverty, policymakers responded by locating both the sources of and solutions to economic insecurity in individual workers rather than in the labor market. In a series of work and welfare policies, the problem was defined as one of individual will to work or skill to earn. By the 1990s, Democrats and Republicans alike had largely settled on a strategy to "let the economy generate whatever quality of jobs that firms choose and then, if necessary, compensate by enabling people to avoid the bad ones or by shoring up people who are stuck," explained economist Paul Osterman.[27] This pro-market approach had its own deep roots in American economic policy—but it ran against a policy current that had imposed basic national standards to shape the quality of jobs in the market beginning in the New Deal.[28]

By the 2000s, the pattern was clear. Rather than reforming the labor market to bring work closer in line with expectations, or reforming New Deal–era social insurance programs (such as unemployment insurance) to fit the new labor market, federal policies implicitly scaled back the expectation of what work should provide. The notion that jobs should ensure a reliable livelihood and a ticket out of poverty had been fading fast since the late 1970s, with fewer advocates for government action to strengthen and sustain job quality. In debates over work and welfare, work was increasingly viewed as an end in itself, even when its wages failed to provide a living. Government's role shifted accordingly, to require and to supplement the returns from low-wage labor, but not reform its terms or conditions. When the Great Recession hit, the spotlight fell first on the staggering number of jobs lost. But in the long run, the crisis was as much about quality as quantity: more than three-quarters of the jobs lost in the recession were in mid- or high-wage occupations, yet in the recovery, newly created low-wage jobs outpaced mid- and high-wage jobs by nearly three to one.[29]

The turn to work thus emerged as a cruel irony—rather than an opportunity—for many poor families. It was not the move to encourage employment that was at issue, but the fact that workfare policies were imposed—often unsparingly—in the context of a low-wage labor market that failed to offer a reliable path out of poverty.

Nearly two decades after passage of welfare reform, the impact of the reconfigured social contract for poor families in the current economy had become clearer. The modern workfare state has created new hierarchies in social policy, in the labor market, and among the poor. The United States now has a two-tier system of government social protections for workers. Those in middle-class jobs are the main beneficiaries of the more generous and reliable social insurance benefits of the New Deal welfare state, including unemployment insurance as well as government-subsidized, employer-provided health and pension benefits. Those in low-wage jobs are protected by a second-class safety net, relying on the EITC and Medicaid rather than stable and adequate earnings and job-based social benefits. They fail to qualify for many social insurance benefits (other than Social Security). Although they are more than twice as likely to face unemployment as those in higher-income positions, for example, low-wage workers are only one-third as likely to receive unemployment benefits. Likewise, only 24 percent of low-wage workers receive employer-provided health care benefits and 14 percent receive pension benefits, compared with 76 percent and 68 percent, respectively, in the top fifth of wage earners.[30] Despite their hardships, little public attention has been focused on the working poor, particularly since the Democrats strategically shifted their policy focus to the broad middle class in the 1990s. Policymakers have failed to confront the new labor market reality that growing numbers of workers rely on basic income supports not just between jobs and after retirement, but while working.

Workfare has also widened the gap in status between working and nonworking poor families. Although the former are not afforded traditional benefits of middle-class employment, many are better positioned than they were before. They have benefited most directly from the major expansions in the EITC, but also from other policy changes in health care and new tax credits for families with children.[31] At the bottom of the hierarchy are poor families who are outside of the labor market. These families are often the neediest and most desperate. Many have been unable to find or hold jobs due to health problems or family obligations.[32] Like the working poor, they may receive some Medicaid and food stamp benefits. But there is very little cash assistance available for them, given the shift from need-based to work-conditioned aid. Indeed, large numbers of families have simply slipped off the radar screen: they are not eligible for TANF (because they have reached time limits or have not met the program's requirements), nor eligible for the EITC. By a number of estimates, in the decade after the 1996 welfare reform, there were approximately one million poor mothers with two million children who were neither working nor on welfare. They no longer show up in public assistance statistics, but they are visible in the very large numbers of the poor (some 44 percent) whose incomes were below half the poverty line in 2013.[33] There is a troubling sense in which the federal government has washed its hands of responsibility for these families.[34]

The turn to workfare has thus created new hierarchies in work and welfare. It has also produced a profoundly problematic safety net, one that generates new and complex vulnerabilities for all groups of poor Americans. Because the logic of preserving work incentives trumps the logic of meeting needs for many core programs, workfare provides an inadequate system of social protection. The new rules of the game have changed the terms of both low-wage work and government assistance. Under the old system, safety nets for the poor were spread beneath families and would remain in place as long as those families demonstrated need and eligibility. Families could and did rely on public assistance when they were unable to work, including when they were between jobs or were seeking more stable employment. Under workfare, the densest safety nets for the poor are attached to jobs, not families. This makes the cost of losing or leaving a job much higher: when a low-wage worker loses a job, he or she may also lose the safety net provided by TANF or the EITC. To boost the incentive to increase work hours, moreover, higher EITC benefits are provided to those who earn more (to a specified ceiling). In 2013, the highest benefits ($6,044 for a family with three or more children) went to those earning at least $13,400; those earning half this amount received a credit of $3,026.[35]

From a workfare standpoint, the logic of such a system is compelling: all poor families must enter the workforce to gain assistance, and federal policy rewards and reinforces their work effort. From an antipoverty perspective, however, the system generates a perverse logic. In too many cases, the system is structured to work best when and where it is needed least. It is not just that those families with the lowest earnings and the deepest need often receive the least help from programs such as the EITC, for the reasons described above. Equally troubling, a workfare system is most effective when jobs are plentiful and the economy is strong (as in the late 1990s). When work is scarce (as in the Great Recession), the EITC can be of little help to families in need. And when hours are cut, so too are earnings (and the combination of earnings and EITC credits) for many of the poorest families in the program. Those required to work or face losing their TANF benefits, likewise, confront the most serious risks and the least promising prospects during economic downturns. At the individual level, the result is greater suffering and uncertainty in hard times. At the aggregate level, the result is a safety net that fails precisely when it is most needed. Indeed, in the first year of the Great Recession, TANF and EITC expenditures failed to rise, and their combined support for the poorest families actually fell as these families lost both jobs and job-based benefits. For them, the dual loss amplified rather than ameliorated the effects of the downturn.[36]

The failings of workfare have produced a deeply flawed system. A strategy that promotes and enforces work for poor families while neglecting structural weaknesses in the low-wage labor market is constrained by its own contradictions, with grave consequences for the working poor. And an antipoverty strategy that provides income assistance only to those willing and able to hold a job is abandoning a sizable number of the neediest families, as there will always be many who are unable to enter the workforce to escape poverty.

Unless low-wage labor conditions are addressed, the United States may find itself with a system of social protections that in the worst of times intensifies rather than alleviates the effects of recessions for many families, and in the best of times compels the poor to enter low-paying jobs, then subsidizes and stabilizes the low-wage sector without building bridges to secure, middle-class employment—while neglecting those who cannot or do not work. Current job training policies encourage rapid entry into the workforce, but they cannot ensure a supply of solid jobs or create a reliable path from low-wage work to more stable and remunerative employment. Nor do existing labor market regulations impose conditions or create incentives to discourage employers from generating more low-wage, low-benefit jobs.

For decades, conservative and centrist policymakers worried about a welfare system that was structured in a way that kept poor families economically dependent on government aid and "trapped" on welfare. They were concerned about the "churning" of recipients who cycled on and off of welfare, but never seemed able to leave permanently. It would be a hollow victory if the workfare system built to replace it produced not the promised route to economic independence for poor families, but instead a new trap for millions of the working poor—a government-subsidized low-wage sector with few exits—and a trapdoor for millions more who remain outside the labor market altogether.

NOTES

Introduction

1. See "Family Net Worth Drops to Level of Early '90s, Fed Says," *New York Times,* June 11, 2012; and U.S. Census Bureau, "Historical Poverty Tables—People," Table 2, https://www.census.gov/hhes/www/poverty/data/historical/people.html. There were 46.3 million poor Americans in 2010, 6.5 million more than in 1960, when the poverty rate was 22.2 percent. See also Lawrence Mishel, Josh Bivens, Elise Gould, and Heidi Shierholz, *The State of Working America,* 12th ed. (Ithaca, N.Y.: Cornell University Press, 2012); and *Wall Street Journal*/NBC News Poll, July 30–August 3, 2014, http://online.wsj.com/articles/the-wall-street-journalnbc-news-poll-1378786510?tesla=y.

2. The three main cash support programs are Supplemental Security Income (SSI) for the elderly and disabled poor, Aid to Families with Dependent Children/Temporary Assistance for Needy Families (AFDC/TANF) primarily for single-parent families, and the Earned Income Tax Credit (EITC) for the working poor. At the end of the 1970s, nearly 95 percent of aid across the three largest income-support programs was provided as a need-based entitlement. By 2008, most of this aid (60 percent) was conditioned on individual success in the labor market, with no government-guaranteed safety net if that market fails. IRS *Statistics of Income,* annual reports, 1976 to 1999, http://www.irs.gov/uac/SOI-Tax-Stats-SOI-Bulletins; Susan B. Carter, Scott Sigmund Gartner, Michael R. Haines, Alan L. Olmstead, Richard Sutch, and Gavin Wright, eds., *Historical Statistics of the United States,* vol. 2, part B: *Work and Welfare* (New York: Cambridge University Press, 2006); and *Budget of the United States Government, Fiscal Year 2009* (Washington, D.C.: Office of Management and Budget, 2008).

3. "Older, Suburban and Struggling, 'Near Poor' Startle the Census," *New York Times,* November 19, 2011. The 2010 figures are from U.S. Census Bureau, "Special Tabulation of Supplemental Poverty Measure Estimates," November 21, 2011, 4, http://www.census.gov/hhes/povmeas/methodology/supplemental/research/SpecialTabulation.pdf; and Kathleen Short, "The Supplemental Poverty Measure: 2013," U.S. Census Bureau, Current Population Reports, P60-251, October 2014.

4. See Lawrence Mishel and Heidi Shierholz, "Highest Unemployment Rate Since 1983," Economic Policy Institute, June 16, 2009, Table 5, http://www.epi.org/publication/jobspict_2009_july_preview.

5. At the end of 2008, as job losses soared, fewer than 50 percent of the unemployed were receiving benefits. Peter Katel, "Straining the Safety Net," *Congressional Quarterly Researcher,* July 2009, 649.

6. See, for example, Sheryl Gay Stolberg, "On the Edge of Poverty, at the Center of a Debate," *New York Times,* September 5, 2013; and "Thrifty Shoppers 'Sold!' on Grocery Auctions," *Associated Press,* March 25, 2009.

7. Kevin Slack, "Slump Pushing Cost of Drugs out of Reach," *New York Times,* June 4, 2009. See also Barbara Ehrenreich, "Too Poor to Make the News," *New York Times,* June 13, 2009.

8. Paul Osterman and Beth Shulman, *Good Jobs America: Making Work Better for Everyone* (New York: Russell Sage, 2011), 12.

9. Jason DeParle, "Welfare Limits Left Poor Adrift as Recession Hit," *New York Times*, April 7, 2012.

10. This account is drawn from Barbara Ehrenreich, "A Homespun Safety Net," *New York Times*, Week in Review section, July 12, 2009.

11. For a brief overview of state laws impeding participation in unemployment insurance, see "State Policies Affecting UI Access for Low-Wage Workers," National Employment Law Project, August 19, 2013, http://www.nelp.org/page/-/UI/2013/PowerPoint-Unemployment-Insurance-Access-State-Policies.pdf?nocdn=1.

12. See, for example, the data on AFDC participation and benefits in Steven Ruggles, "The Effects of AFDC on American Family Structure, 1940–1990," *Journal of Family History* 22, no. 3 (July 1997): 309, 312.

13. For a study examining the continuing importance of antipoverty programs and their increased ties to employment, see Arloc Sherman, Danilo Trisi, and Sharon Parrott, "Various Supports for Low-Income Families Reduce Poverty and Have Long-Term Positive Effects on Families and Children," Center for Budget and Policy Priorities, June 20, 2013, http://www.cbpp.org/cms/?fa=view&id=3997.

14. Grace Abbott, an architect of Title IV of the Social Security Act, wrote, for example, "This Act should not be considered as insuring 'security,' the quest for which must necessarily continue through the years, but as making progress 'toward security.'" Grace Abbott, *From Relief to Social Security* (Chicago: University of Chicago Press, 1941), 261. Later, as proposals were circulated for the 1950 Social Security Amendments, welfarists within the administration (backed by social service advocates) unsuccessfully sought a bold expansion that would create a new general assistance program for "all needy persons," addressing the gaps in the existing system and providing a federal safety net for those who did not meet state-imposed rules. Blanche D. Coll, *Safety Net: Welfare and Social Security, 1929–1979* (New Brunswick, N.J.: Rutgers University Press, 1995), 159–60.

15. In defining the South, this study uses the thirteen-state standard employed by *Congressional Quarterly Almanac* and most congressional studies of the region: the eleven ex-Confederate states (Alabama, Arkansas, Florida, Georgia, Louisiana, Mississippi, North Carolina, South Carolina, Tennessee, Texas, and Virginia) plus Kentucky and Oklahoma.

16. Accounts addressing Southern legislators' actions in the 1930s and 1940s include Ira Katznelson, *Fear Itself: The New Deal and the Origins of Our Times* (New York: W. W. Norton, 2013); Ira Katznelson, Kim Geiger, and Daniel Kryder, "Limiting Liberalism: The Southern Veto in Congress, 1933–1950," *Political Science Quarterly* 108 (1993): 283–306; Michael K. Brown, *Race, Money, and the American Welfare State* (Ithaca, N.Y.: Cornell University Press, 1999); Robert Lieberman, *Shifting the Color Line: Race and the American Welfare State* (Cambridge, Mass.: Harvard University Press, 1998); Jill Quadagno, *The Color of Welfare: How Racism Undermined the War on Poverty* (New York: Oxford University Press, 1994).

17. As discussed in Chapters 1 and 3, Southern Democratic congressional leaders who led the drive for workfare at the federal level in the 1960s and early 1970s acted from a position of institutional strength. The American South had a long history of electing only Democrats, enabling incumbents to accrue significant seniority in Congress. Congressional rules at the time afforded significant powers to committee chairs, including leading Southern workfare advocates.

18. This was particularly true from the mid-1960s on, when growing caseloads and a changing recipient demographic profile (more women of color and more never-married mothers) increasingly made welfare a target for racial and cultural resentments. See, for example, Martin Gilens, *Why Americans Hate Welfare* (Chicago: University of Chicago Press, 1999).

19. National business associations and local business leaders actively weighed in on the debates in workfare's formative years, as discussed in Chapters 2 and 3. For a general discussion of the role of business interests in work-oriented welfare reform, see Ellen Reese, *Backlash Against Welfare Mothers: Past and Present* (Berkeley: University of California Press, 2005).

20. On the role of work in American political culture, see, for example, Judith N. Shklar, *American Citizenship* (Cambridge, Mass.: Harvard University Press, 1991). On long-term paid employment as a condition for incorporation into the most generous programs of the U.S. welfare state, see Suzanne Mettler, *Dividing Citizens* (Ithaca, N.Y.: Cornell University Press, 1998), particularly 23–27; and Chad Alan Goldberg, *Citizens and Paupers* (Chicago: University of Chicago Press, 2007), 8–9. On the role of work in welfare historically, see, for example, Joel F. Handler and Yeheskel Hasenfeld, *We the Poor People* (New Haven, Conn.: Yale University Press, 1997), particularly chapters 2 to 4.

21. See Osterman and Shulman, *Good Jobs*, particularly chapters 2 and 5.

22. See, for example, Bruce Jansson, *The Reluctant Welfare State* (Belmont, Calif.: Wadsworth, 1998); and James T. Patterson, *America's Struggle Against Poverty in the Twentieth Century* (Cambridge, Mass.: Harvard University Press, 2000).

23. Revisionist accounts have challenged the conventional story of welfare-state expansion by probing the political and institutional choices made in the passage and first three decades of the Social Security Act, including the role of Southern lawmakers (see, in particular, Lieberman, *Shifting the Color Line;* Brown, *Race, Money;* and Quadagno, *Color of Welfare*); this study takes the inquiry to the turning points in the labor market and in antipoverty policy in the 1970s and after.

24. Exemplary works emphasizing the role of political and institutional factors in welfare reform and other social policy change include R. Kent Weaver, *Ending Welfare as We Know It* (Washington, D.C.: Brookings Institution Press, 2000); Christopher Howard, *The Hidden Welfare State* (Princeton, N.J.: Princeton University Press, 1997); Jacob S. Hacker, *The Divided Welfare State* (New York: Cambridge University Press, 2002); Marie Gottschalk, *The Shadow Welfare State* (Ithaca, N.Y.: Cornell University Press, 2000); Steven M. Teles, *Whose Welfare* (Lawrence: University Press of Kansas, 1998); and Theda Skocpol, *Social Policy in the United States* (Princeton, N.J.: Princeton University Press, 1995). Studies of the post-1970s labor market and economic changes include Osterman and Shulman, *Good Jobs;* and Mishel et al., *State of Working America* (Ithaca, N.Y.: Cornell University Press, various editions). See also note 27 in chapter 4.

25. For examples of works that explore the relationship between social policy and labor markets, see Frances Fox Piven, "Welfare Reform and the Economic and Cultural Construction of Low Wage Labor Markets," in Judith Goode and Jeff Maskovsky, eds., *The New Poverty Studies* (New York: New York University Press, 2001), 134–51; and Joel F. Handler and Yeheskel Hasenfeld, *Blame Welfare, Ignore Poverty and Inequality* (New York: Cambridge University Press, 2007).

26. See, for example, Jamie Peck, *Workfare States* (New York: Guilford Press, 2001); Jamie Peck, *Work-Place* (New York: Guilford Press, 1996); Bob Jessop, "Post-Fordism and the State," in Ash Amin, ed., *Post-Fordism: A Reader* (Oxford: Blackwell, 1994); Neil Gilbert and Rebecca A. Van Voorhis, eds., *Activating the Unemployed* (New Brunswick, N.J.: Transaction, 2001); and Joel F. Handler, *Social Citizenship and Workfare in the United States and Western Europe* (Cambridge: Cambridge University Press, 2004). For a classic statement on the political economy of workfare, see Frances Fox Piven and Richard A. Cloward, *Regulating the Poor: The Functions of Public Assistance*, updated ed. (New York: Vintage Books, 1993).

27. See, for example, Paul Pierson, *Dismantling the Welfare State?* (Cambridge: Cambridge University Press, 1994), which focuses on the 1980s; Michael B. Katz, *The Price of Citizenship* (New York: Metropolitan Books, 2001), and Paul Pierson, ed., *The New Politics of the Welfare State* (Oxford: Oxford University Press, 2001), which examine the 1980s and 1990s.

28. See Christopher Howard, "Is the American Welfare State Unusually Small?" *PS* 36, no. 3 (2003): 411–16; Christopher Howard, *The Welfare State Nobody Knows* (Princeton, N.J.: Princeton University Press, 2007); John Myles and Jill Quadagno, "Envisioning a Third Way: The Welfare State in the Twenty-First Century," *Contemporary Sociology* 29 (2000): 156–67; and Jill Quadagno and Deborah Street, "Recent Trends in U.S. Social Welfare Policy: Minor Retrenchment or Major Transformation?" *Research on Aging* 28 (2006): 303–16. See also Jacob S. Hacker, *The Great Risk Shift* (New York: Oxford University Press, 2006); and Jacob S. Hacker, "Privatizing Risk without Privatizing the Welfare State," *American Political Science Review* 98, no. 2 (May 2004): 243–60.

29. See Weaver, *Ending Welfare as We Know It*, chapter 4; and Pierson, *Dismantling the Welfare State?*, 125–26.

30. See Larry M. Bartels, *Unequal Democracy* (New York: Russell Sage, 2008).

31. See Jacob S. Hacker and Paul Pierson, "Winner-Take-All Politics," *Politics and Society* 38 (June 2010): 152–204, and *Winner-Take-All Politics* (New York: Simon and Schuster, 2010). For other perspectives on the politics of inequality, see Paul Krugman, *The Return of Depression Economics and the Crisis of 2008* (New York: W. W. Norton, 2009), and David B. Grusky and Tamar Kricheli-Katz, eds., *The New Gilded Age: The Critical Inequality Debates of Our Time* (Stanford, Calif.: Stanford University Press, 2012).

32. See, for example, Paul Pierson, "Not Just What, but *When*," *Studies in American Political Development* 14 (2000): 72–92.

33. This provides evidence, for example, for the claims advanced by Suzanne Mettler, *The Submerged State* (Chicago: University of Chicago Press, 2011). See also Kimberly J. Morgan and Andrea Louise Campbell, *The Delegated Welfare State* (New York: Oxford University Press, 2011); Howard, *Hidden Welfare State*; and Gottschalk, *Shadow Welfare State*. Howard, in particular, explores the persistent role of conservative Southern Democrats in supporting or promoting tax expenditures for social policy purposes.

34. On the role of welfare recipients and their allies, see, for example, Premilla Nadasen, *Rethinking the Welfare Rights Movement* (New York: Routledge, 2012); and Ellen Reese, *They Say Cut Back, We Say Fight Back!* (New York: Russell Sage, 2011).

35. Studies emphasizing the role of gender in welfare politics and social policy include Anna Marie Smith, *Welfare Reform and Sexual Regulation* (New York: Cambridge University Press, 2007); Marisa Chappell, *The War on Welfare* (Philadelphia: University of Pennsylvania Press, 2010); Linda Gordon, *Pitied but Not Entitled* (Cambridge, Mass.: Harvard University Press, 1994); Mettler, *Dividing Citizens*; and Gwendolyn Mink, *Welfare's End* (Ithaca, N.Y.: Cornell University Press, 1998). Studies of the role of race include Ira Katznelson, *When Affirmative Action Was White* (New York: W. W. Norton, 2005); Sanford F. Schram, Joe Soss, and Richard K. Fording, eds., *Race and the Politics of Welfare Reform* (Ann Arbor: University of Michigan Press, 2003); Lieberman, *Shifting the Color Line*; and Gilens, *Why Americans Hate Welfare*. For studies examining both race and political economy factors, see, for example, Brown, *Race, Money*; and Joe Soss, Richard C. Fording, and Sanford F. Schram, *Disciplining the Poor: Neoliberal Paternalism and the Persistent Power of Race* (Chicago: University of Chicago Press, 2011).

36. Other policy options under consideration in these years—from basic income guarantees to federal jobs programs to an increased and indexed minimum wage—had the potential to reform rather than stabilize the nation's low-wage labor market.

37. In the 2008 presidential campaign, both Barack Obama and John McCain pointed to the drop in welfare rolls as evidence of the success of federal antipoverty policies. In 2012, Obama and Mitt Romney sparred over whose welfare-to-work approach was most effective. See, for example, Trip Gabriel, "Romney Presses Obama on Work in Welfare Law," *New York Times*, August 7, 2012.

38. See Elise Gould and Hilary Wething, "U.S. Poverty Rates Higher, Safety Net Weaker Than in Peer Countries," Economic Policy Institute, July 24, 2012; see also Timothy S. Smeeding, "Poorer

by Comparison," *Pathways Magazine*, Stanford Center on Poverty and Inequality, Winter 2008, 3–5.

39. The EITC's poverty-reduction effect varies by year. For 2012, estimates are that the program lifted 6.5 million Americans out of poverty. (See "Policy Basics: The Earned Income Tax Credit," Center on Budget and Policy Priorities, updated January 31, 2014, http://www.cbpp.org/cms/?fa=view&id=2505.) On the increase in single-parent families receiving neither wages nor cash assistance, see Pamela J. Loprest, "Disconnected Families and TANF," OPRE Brief #2, Urban Institute and U.S. Department of Health and Human Services, Administration for Children and Families, Office of Planning, Research, and Evaluation (OPRE), November 2011. For data on the racial and gender distribution of workers with poverty-level wages ($11.06/hour in 2011), see Mishel et al., *State of Working America*, 192–93.

40. Historic trends in poverty rates confirm concerns about workfare. Poverty rates were cut in half from the end of the 1950s to the early 1970s (from 22.4 percent in 1959 to 11.1 percent in 1973). They stayed under 12 percent through the decade of the 1970s (except for 1975, which saw 12.3 percent). Poverty jumped to 13 percent in 1980, then climbed to 15.2 percent by 1982, and stayed in the 13–15 percent range until 1997 (except for 1989, at 12.8 percent). From another peak of 15.1 percent in 1993, poverty fell through the 1990s, slowly but steadily to 11.3 percent in 2000. It then climbed again, over 12 percent by 2002, and hovered in the 12–13 percent range before reaching 15.1 percent in the wake of the Great Recession, and remaining at 15.0 percent in 2011 and 2012, before dropping to 14.5 percent in 2013. U.S. Census Bureau, "Historical Poverty Tables—People," Table 2, https://www.census.gov/hhes/www/poverty/data/historical/people.html.

41. In 2007, before the Great Recession began, the official poverty rate was 12.5 percent (37.3 million people); it had been at the 11–13 percent level over the previous decade—about where poverty rates were four decades earlier (12.8 percent in 1968). In 2011, nearly three million poor adults worked year-round, full-time. U.S. Census Bureau, "Historical Poverty Tables—People," Tables 2 and 25, https://www.census.gov/hhes/www/poverty/data/historical/people.html. Between 1999 and 2011, expenditures for the EITC program alone were more than $580 billion. See Internal Revenue Service, *Statistics of Income Bulletin*, for tax years 1999–2011, http://www.irs.gov/uac/SOI-Tax-Stats-SOI-Bulletins.

Chapter 1. Democratic Divisions on Work and Welfare

1. See U.S. Committee on Economic Security (CES), *Report to the President of the Committee on Economic Security* (Washington, D.C.: U.S. Government Printing Office, 1935), Table 6.

2. Blanche Coll, *Safety Net: Welfare and Social Security, 1929–1979* (New Brunswick, N.J.: Rutgers University Press, 1995), 32. See also Harry Hopkins, "The Developing National Program of Relief," *Proceedings of the National Conference of Social Work at the Sixtieth Annual Session Held in Detroit, Michigan, June 11–17, 1933* (Chicago: University of Chicago Press, 1933), 65–71.

3. Josephine Chapin Brown, *Public Relief, 1929–1939* (New York: Henry Holt, 1940), 150.

4. CES, *Report to the President*, Table 2. Table 3 indicates that at the beginning of 1934, approximately twice as many people were receiving direct relief as work relief; by the end of the year, work relief cases had increased and the numbers were roughly equal. See also Brown, *Public Relief*, 160.

5. Franklin D. Roosevelt, "Message to Congress Reviewing the Broad Objectives and Accomplishments of the Administration," June 8, 1934, http://www.ssa.gov/history/fdrstmts.html.

6. Cited in Edwin E. Witte, *The Development of the Social Security Act* (Madison: University of Wisconsin Press, 1963), vii.

7. See U.S. Committee on Economic Security, *What Is Social Insurance?* (Washington, D.C.: U.S. Government Printing Office, 1935).

8. Arthur Altmeyer, *The Formative Years of Social Security* (Madison: University of Wisconsin Press, 1966), 5.

9. M. J. Miller, FERA Field Representative, memorandum to state administrators, December 14, 1934, cited in Brown, *Public Relief,* 443.

10. The CES cautioned, however, that states "should replace uncentralized poor law administrations with unified, efficient State and local public-welfare departments such as already exist in some States and for which all States have a nucleus in their State Emergency Relief Administrations." CES, *Report to the President,* 45.

11. This discussion of competing New Deal visions draws in part on Linda Gordon's detailed analysis of the legislative history of ADC. Linda Gordon, *Pitied but Not Entitled* (Cambridge, Mass.: Harvard University Press, 1994), particularly pages 255–65.

12. Brown, *Public Relief,* 304.

13. The Advisory Committee included "representative social workers and leaders in the field of public welfare." Brown, *Public Relief,* 304–5. It was distinct from the CES Advisory Council, which consisted of civic leaders appointed by the president to assist the CES.

14. For the views and roles of Children's Bureau leaders, see, for example, Gordon, *Pitied but Not Entitled* particularly chapters 3, 7, and 9. See also the section introductions by Grace Abbott (head of the Children's Bureau from 1921 to 1934) in Grace Abbott, ed., *The Child and the State,* vol. 2 (Chicago: University of Chicago Press, 1938).

15. Gordon, *Pitied but Not Entitled,* 267–68. Advocates repeatedly drew a contrast between the new social insurance programs for workers and the "dole." FDR himself articulated this position in his January 1935 pledge that the federal government "must and shall quit this business of relief." Franklin D. Roosevelt, "Annual Message to Congress," January 4, 1935, http://www.ssa.gov/history/fdrstmts.html.

16. New Deal welfarism, as I use the term here, embodied a commitment to provide a measure of economic security to eligible needy populations, as a matter of right and on the basis of need rather than of labor market participation. The workfarist approach, in contrast, is to encourage, promote, and reward work, and to maintain work incentives, exempting from the obligation to work only those physically unable to do so. For one discussion of the contrasting strategies, see Jamie Peck, *Workfare States* (New York: Guilford Press, 2001).

17. CES, *Report to the President,* 7.

18. CES, *Report to the President,* 5, 35.

19. CES, *Report to the President,* 36.

20. Grace Abbott, *From Relief to Social Security* (Chicago: University of Chicago Press, 1941), 211.

21. See, for example, Gordon, *Pitied but Not Entitled,* chapter 9; and Robert Lieberman, *Shifting the Color Line* (Cambridge, Mass.: Harvard University Press, 1998), particularly 48–56.

22. See Gordon, *Pitied but Not Entitled,* 275, 277.

23. Cited in Brown, *Public Relief,* 307–8.

24. Abbott, *From Relief to Social Security,* 279; see also Gordon, *Pitied but Not Entitled,* 267–71.

25. Title IV of the Social Security Act of 1935, Section 401, Chapter 531, *U.S. Statutes at Large* XLIX, Part I, 627–29.

26. Witte, *Development of the Social Security Act,* 162–65.

27. This broad definition would have allowed for aiding working-poor families and those unemployed but unable to find public employment. Brown, *Public Relief,* 309–10.

28. Gordon, *Pitied but Not Entitled,* 277.

29. See Gordon, *Pitied but Not Entitled,* 278. For discussion of the possibility of removing the link between federal funding and federal standards entirely, see the exchange between Katherine Lenroot, head of the Children's Bureau, and Finance Committee chairman Pat Harrison

in U.S. Congress, Senate, Committee on Finance, *Hearings, Economic Security Act, Before the Senate Comm. on Finance,* 74th Cong., 1st sess., January 22–February 20, 1935, pp. 342–44.

30. Social Security Board, Bureau of Public Assistance, quoted in *Aid to Dependent Children: A Study in Six States,* Public Assistance Report No. 2 (Washington, D.C.: Federal Security Agency, 1941), 2.

31. Jane M. Hoey, "Aid to Families with Dependent Children," *Annals of the American Academy of Political and Social Sciences* 202 (March 1939): 76.

32. See, for example, Ellen J. Perkins, "State and Local Financing of Public Assistance, 1935–1955," *Social Security Bulletin* 19, no. 7 (July 1956): 3–13. See also Suzanne Mettler, *Dividing Citizens* (Ithaca, N.Y.: Cornell University Press, 1998), 158–75.

33. See, for example, Lee J. Alston and Joseph P. Ferrie, *Southern Paternalism and the American Welfare State* (New York: Cambridge University Press, 1999), particularly chapter 2.

34. See Jill Quadagno, "From Old-Age Assistance to Supplemental Security Income: The Political Economy of Relief in the South, 1935–1972," in Margaret Weir, Ann Shola Orloff, and Theda Skocpol, eds., *The Politics of Social Policy in the United States* (Princeton, N.J.: Princeton University Press, 1988), 244.

35. Southern states also claimed four of the ten largest Aid to the Permanently and Totally Disabled (APTD) and Aid to the Blind (AB) programs by number of recipients, and three of the ten largest by cost. *Social Security Bulletin,* 25, no. 3, March 1962, 31–35. For explanations of the size and character of Southern public assistance programs, see Quadagno, "From Old-Age Assistance," and Edward Berkowitz, *America's Welfare State* (Baltimore: Johns Hopkins University Press, 1991), 56. Creating large Old Age Assistance programs with low individual payments also increased the percentage of payments that were covered by the federal government. See Michael K. Brown, *Race, Money, and the American Welfare State* (Ithaca, N.Y.: Cornell University Press, 1999), 124–25, 199.

36. *Social Security Bulletin,* 25, no. 3, March 1962, 31–35. The small size and low benefits in Southern aid programs clearly did not reflect a lack of need. All thirteen ranked among the bottom twenty states by per capita income in 1961 (including the eight lowest) and among the top twenty by percentage of families with incomes under $2,000 (including the top nine). *Statistical Abstract of the United States, 1962,* 83rd ed. (Washington, D.C.: U.S. Bureau of the Census, 1962), 319, 333.

37. Bureau of Public Assistance, *Aid to Dependent Children,* 1.

38. Florida's list of conditions for determining that a home was unsuitable, for example, included: "Failure of the parent or relative to provide a stable moral environment for the child, by engaging in promiscuous conduct." Coll, *Safety Net,* 188.

39. Winifred Bell, *Aid to Dependent Children* (New York: Columbia University Press, 1965), 40–59.

40. See, for example, Gwendolyn Mink, *The Wages of Motherhood* (Ithaca, N.Y.: Cornell University Press, 1995), and Mimi Abramovitz, *Regulating the Lives of Women* (Boston: South End Press, 1996).

41. For works that address employment restrictions, see, for example, Ellen Reese, *Backlash Against Welfare Mothers* (Berkeley: University of California Press, 2005); Jennifer Mittelstadt, *From Welfare to Workfare* (Chapel Hill: University of North Carolina Press, 2005); Nancy E. Rose, *Workfare or Fair Work* (New Brunswick, N.J.: Rutgers University Press, 1995); and Joanne Goodwin, *Gender and the Politics of Welfare Reform* (Chicago: University of Chicago Press, 1997).

42. Georgia, Alabama, and Louisiana had "farm policies" making able-bodied mothers ineligible for ADC when field work was available. In many cases, employment rules worked hand in glove with policies designed to maintain suitable homes. Bell, *Aid to Dependent Children,* 82, 107.

43. "If the mother is young, able to work, or has had work experience, she may be discouraged from applying [for ADC] in one agency, denied the opportunity in another, and referred to

private employment or Works Projects Administration in a third." Bureau of Public Assistance, *Aid to Dependent Children*, 46.

44. Coll, *Safety Net*, 190. See also Robert H. Mugge, "Aid to Families with Dependent Children: Initial Findings of the 1961 Report on Characteristics of Recipients," *Social Security Bulletin* 26, no. 3 (March 1963): 12.

45. Cited in Bell, *Aid to Dependent Children*, 34–35.

46. Cited in Bell, *Aid to Dependent Children*, 64–65.

47. Bell, *Aid to Dependent Children*, 53. For an example of the Bureau's attempt to monitor administrative practices, see Bureau of Public Assistance, *The Application Process in Public Assistance Administration*, Public Assistance Report No. 14 (Washington, D.C.: Federal Assistance Agency, 1948).

48. Patterson, *America's Struggle*, 85.

49. Cited in Coll, *Safety Net*, 190.

50. Jane Hoey, "The Impact of the War on the Public Assistance Programs," *Social Service Review* 17, no. 4 (December 1943): 474–75.

51. Bell, *Aid to Dependent Children*, 53–54. See also Daniel S. Gerig, Jr., "The Financial Participation of the Federal Government in State Welfare Programs," *Social Security Bulletin* 3, no. 1 (January 1940); and Bureau of Public Assistance, *Sources of Revenue for the State Share of Public Assistance, 1939–1947*, Public Assistance Report No. 15 (Washington, D.C.: Federal Assistance Agency, 1948).

52. If a state's monthly cost standard for basic living requirements was $90 for a family, then any family with monthly income of $90 or more would not be eligible. If the state raised the cost standard to $95, a new group of poor families (those with income between $90 and $95) would become eligible. Example provided in Ellen J. Perkins, "AFDC in Review, 1936–1962," *Welfare in Review* (November 1963), 2–5, excerpted in Robert H. Bremner, ed., *Children and Youth in America: A Documentary History*, vol. 3: *1933–1973* (Cambridge, Mass.: Harvard University Press, 1974), 550–51.

53. Bell, *Aid to Dependent Children*, 34, 55; see also Samuel M. Meyers and Jennie McIntyre, for the Social and Rehabilitation Service, U.S. Department of Health, Education, and Welfare, *Welfare Policy and Its Consequences for the Recipient Population: A Study of the AFDC Program* (Washington, D.C.: U.S. Government Printing Office, 1969).

54. See, for example, the debate within the administration over the 1950 Social Security amendments in Coll, *Safety Net*, 159–60.

55. Coll, *Safety Net*, 168.

56. On the role of Southern lawmakers in shaping the Social Security Act, see, for example, Jill Quadagno, *The Color of Welfare* (New York: Oxford University Press, 1994); Brown, *Race, Money*; and Lieberman, *Shifting the Color Line*.

57. *Congressional Directory* (Washington, D.C.: U.S. Government Printing Office, 1935–1977); *History of the Committee on Finance, United States Senate* (Washington, D.C.: U.S. Government Printing Office, 1981), 141–53. For discussion of the congressional reforms of the 1970s, see, for example, David W. Rohde, *Parties and Leaders in the Postreform House* (Chicago: University of Chicago Press, 1991).

58. For the argument that Southern lawmakers were eager to win more federal funds for the South as long as they determined who received aid and under what conditions, see Brown, *Race, Money*, 126.

59. On the Eisenhower administration's opposition to increasing the federal share of public assistance, see Gilbert Steiner, *Social Insecurity* (Chicago: Rand McNally & Company, 1966), 50–54.

60. See, for example, the statement by Representative Mills, U.S. Congress, *Congressional Record—House*, August 17, 1967, pp. 23052–53.

61. See, for example, Robert Haveman, ed., *A Decade of Federal Antipoverty Programs* (New York: Academic Press, 1977).

62. Patterson, *America's Struggle*, 125.

63. See, for example, Edward D. Berkowitz, *Mr. Social Security: The Life of Wilbur J. Cohen* (Lawrence: University of Kansas Press, 1995), particularly chapter 2.

64. Bell, *Aid to Dependent Children*, 58, finds that between 1950 and 1960 only one state (Colorado) removed suitable home restrictions and nine states added or increased them; eight of these were in the South. See also Reese, *Backlash Against Welfare Mothers*, particularly chapters 3–5.

65. Abramovitz, *Regulating the Lives of Women*, 326. ← Louisiana

66. See Mittelstadt, *From Welfare to Workfare*, particularly chapters 4 and 5, for an extensive discussion of the ways in which the first two Kennedy reforms challenged the "unemployable" status of ADC recipients, and the consequences of this.

67. John F. Kennedy, "Special Message to the Congress: Program for Economic Recovery and Growth, February 2, 1961," *Public Papers of the Presidents of the United States, John F. Kennedy, 1961* (Washington, D.C.: U.S. Government Printing Office, 1962), 46–47.

68. Wilbur Cohen had first brought the idea to Kennedy's attention in 1958. See Berkowitz, *Mr. Social Security*, 118–21; and Coll, *Safety Net*, 207.

69. A similar case was made in congressional hearings by liberal representatives of the American Public Welfare Association and Americans for Democratic Action. See U.S. Congress, House, *Hearings, Public Welfare Amendments of 1962: H.R. 10032*, 87th Cong., 2nd sess., February 7, 9, and 13, 1962, pp. 439–52.

70. *Congressional Quarterly Almanac* 18 (1962): 212–18.

71. For additional restrictions on ADC-UP added by the House Ways and Means and Senate Finance Committees, see *Congressional Quarterly Almanac* 17 (1961): 280–82.

72. See Coll, *Safety Net*, 210. See also, for example, the statement by Senator Eugene McCarthy (D-Minn.) cited in *Congressional Quarterly Almanac* 17 (1961): 282.

73. U.S. Congress, Senate, Committee on Finance, *Social Security Amendments of 1967*, pt. 1, 90th Cong., 1st sess., August 22, 23, and 24, 1967, p. 298. See note 15 in the Introduction for the definition of the South used in this account.

74. Wilbur J. Cohen and Robert M. Ball, "Public Welfare Amendments of 1962 and Proposals for Health Insurance for the Aged," *Social Security Bulletin* 25, no. 10 (1962): 4.

75. Cited in *Congressional Quarterly Almanac* 17 (1961): 282. Thurmond later switched to the Republican Party.

76. See Gilbert Y. Steiner, *The State of Welfare* (Washington, D.C.: Brookings Institution, 1971), 37.

77. See Mittelstadt, *From Welfare to Workfare*, particularly chapters 2 and 3.

78. See Martha Derthick, *Uncontrollable Spending for Social Services Grants* (Washington, D.C.: Brookings Institution, 1975), particularly chapters 1 and 2.

79. See Patterson, *America's Struggle*, 131–32.

80. Cited in Coll, *Safety Net*, 221. See also Mittelstadt, *From Welfare to Workfare*, chapter 4.

81. See Coll, *Safety Net*, 221–22.

82. See Coll, *Safety Net*, 224–25; and Patterson, *America's Struggle*, 128.

83. House Republicans attempted to eliminate the new spending but failed, and the Senate approved the measure. *Congressional Quarterly Almanac* 18 (1962): 213, 216.

84. See, for example, the liberal interpretation of Senate Majority Leader Mike Mansfield (D-Mont.), U.S. Congress, *Congressional Record—Senate*, July 17, 1962, p. 13878.

85. John F. Kennedy, "Special Message to the Congress on Public Welfare Programs, February 1, 1962," *Public Papers of the Presidents, John F. Kennedy, 1962* (Washington, D.C.: U.S. Government Printing Office, 1963), 98–100.

86. Cited in Patterson, *America's Struggle*, 127–28. Mills also highlighted the change in law allowing federal matching funds for local work programs, which he characterized as a direct consequence of the inclusion of "employable" adults through ADC-UP. U.S. Congress, *Congressional Record—House*, March 15, 1962, p. 4268.

87. House, Committee on Ways and Means, *Public Welfare Amendments*, 44.

88. Rose, *Workfare or Fair Work*, 89–90; see also Coll, *Safety Net*, 224.

89. Department of Health, Education, and Welfare (HEW), *Report to Congress on Community Work and Training Under Title IV of the Social Security Act as Amended by Section 409*, House Document 76, 90–91 (January 1967), p. 1.

90. Steiner, *Social Insecurity*, 258.

91. Cited in Meyers and McIntyre, *Welfare Policy and Its Consequences*, 4.

92. For the relationship between WET and CWT, which operated simultaneously, see HEW, *Report to Congress on Community Work and Training*.

93. HEW, *Report to Congress on Community Work and Training*. In spring 1967, WET aided nearly 65,000 individuals, but there were 1.2 million adults receiving assistance from AFDC. Senate, Committee on Finance, *Social Security Amendments of 1967*, 269, 307.

94. See "Guaranteed Income," *Congressional Quarterly Almanac* 23 (1967): 993–95.

95. Susan B. Carter et al., eds., *Historical Statistics of the United States: Earliest Times to the Present*, vol. 2, pt. B (Work and Welfare) (New York: Cambridge University Press, 2006), 799.

96. Lyndon B. Johnson, "Message from the President of the United States Transmitting Recommendations for the Welfare of Children," February 8, 1967, U.S. Congress, House of Representatives, 90th Cong., 1st sess., doc. no. 54, p. 8. See also Wilbur Cohen, "A Ten-Point Plan to Abolish Poverty," *Social Security Bulletin* 31, no. 12 (December 1968): 3–13.

97. Since 1964, approximately 150,000 recipients had enrolled in the work programs, but the total number of AFDC recipients had jumped by an additional 750,000. See Coll, *Safety Net*, 172, for 1964 figures, and Senate, Committee on Finance, *Social Security Amendments of 1967*, 296, for 1967 figures.

98. See, for example, Gilbert Y. Steiner, "Reform Follows Reality: The Growth of Welfare," *Public Interest* 34 (Winter 1974): 47–65.

99. "Remarks of the Honorable Wilbur D. Mills, Before the Annual Meeting of the Conference on Social Welfare, District II, Franklin, Arkansas," November 1, 1968. Wilbur Mills Papers Collection, Hendrix College, Conway, Ark. (hereafter WMPC), Box 420, Folder 24, 2–3.

100. Steiner, *The State of Welfare*, 43–44.

101. The Advisory Council on Public Welfare created under the 1962 amendments urged a redoubling of commitment to the services strategy. It also called for combining all the public assistance categories into one program with a uniform need-based standard for eligibility, and for using public assistance payments as a means to provide a guaranteed minimum income for all Americans. See *Congressional Quarterly Almanac* 22 (1966): 345.

102. *Wall Street Journal*, cited in Berkowitz, *Mr. Social Security*, 255. See also "No Reward for Violence," in "Washington Newsletter from Senator Russell B. Long," September 2, 1967, Russell B. Long Collection, Louisiana State University, Baton Rouge, La. (hereafter RBLC) Box 604, Folder 14, 1–2.

103. See Gareth Davies, *From Opportunity to Entitlement* (Lawrence: University of Kansas Press, 1999), 181.

104. Cited in Coll, *Safety Net*, 243.

105. For details of the committee plan, see *Congressional Quarterly Almanac* 23 (1967): 902.

106. *Congressional Quarterly Almanac* 23 (1967): 892–916.

107. Cited in Steiner, *State of Welfare*, 43. On how the committee's actions departed from past practice, see "Social Security Aid Raised; Welfare Pay Restricted," *Congressional Quarterly Almanac* 23 (1967): 892–916.

108. U.S. Congress, *Congressional Record—House*, August 17, 1967, pp. 23052–53.

109. See "Social Security Amendments of 1967, Public Law 90-248," *U.S. Statutes at Large*, LXXXI, 884, 894.

110. *Congressional Quarterly Almanac* 23 (1967): 902.

111. See, for example, statements by HEW Secretary John W. Gardner and Undersecretary Wilbur Cohen, Senate, Committee on Finance, *Social Security Amendments of 1967*, 211–18, 252–72.

112. Cited in Steiner, *State of Welfare*, 80.

113. Cited in Abramovitz, *Regulating the Lives of Women*, 340.

114. The racial overtones of Long's attacks were clear; he won notoriety for deriding the National Welfare Rights Organization (NWRO) and its members as "Black Broodmares, Inc." See Robert Mann, *Legacy to Power: Senator Russell Long of Louisiana* (New York: Paragon House, 1992), 269; and Daniel Patrick Moynihan, *The Politics of a Guaranteed Income* (New York: Random House, 1973), 336.

115. "Day Letter," Office of Senator Russell B. Long, September 21, 1967, RBLC, Box 604, Folder 20. See also Mann, *Legacy to Power*, 268–69.

116. See, for example, the floor amendments offered by Senators Robert Kennedy (D-N.Y.) and Fred Harris (D-Okla.) to limit the work requirement and to make AFDC-UP mandatory. Both amendments passed on close votes but were then eliminated in conference. In each case, Northern Democrats favored the amendment by more than three to one, and Southern Democrats opposed it by three to one. *Congressional Quarterly Almanac* 23 (1967): 58-S, 60-S.

117. *Congressional Quarterly Almanac* 23 (1967): 915–16.

118. Cited in "The Year in Congress," *NASW News*, February 1968, 8–9, excerpted in Bremner, *Children and Youth in America*, 564–66.

119. Steiner, *State of Welfare*, 48–50; see also Berkowitz, *Mr. Social Security*, 260–62.

120. Coll, *Safety Net*, 255–56.

121. *Congressional Quarterly Almanac* 25 (1969): 184.

122. "Social Security Amendments of 1967," excerpted in Bremner, *Children and Youth in America*, 563–64. For an overview of the WIN provisions, see U.S. Congress, Joint Publication, U.S. Senate, Committee on Finance, and U.S. House of Representatives, Committee on Ways and Means, *Summary of Social Security Amendments of 1967*, 90th Cong, 1st sess., December 1967, pp. 15–17. The WIN amendments included a plan for services, but they shifted the focus from counseling and other services aimed at rehabilitation and prevention to providing assistance in job search, placement, and training.

123. Gwendolyn Mink, *Welfare's End* (Ithaca, N.Y.: Cornell University Press, 1998), 50–60. Mink examines rulings by federal courts and the Supreme Court between 1968 and 1975 that curbed state and local discretion to set restrictive eligibility criteria. This made the entitlement to assistance available to a significantly increased percentage of AFDC's intended recipients.

124. Patterson, *America's Struggle*, 174.

125. Total outlays for in-kind benefits rose from $1.2 billion in 1965 to $10.8 billion in 1969, then doubled again by 1974. By the early 1970s, studies indicated that the support received by AFDC families in the form of in-kind aid and other services (often linked to AFDC receipt) more than doubled the resources they received through AFDC's cash benefit. Patterson, *America's Struggle*, 160.

Chapter 2. Welfarists Confront Workfarists

1. By the end of the decade, HEW secretary Robert Finch reported that the cost of AFDC "more than tripled since 1960" and that the "number of recipients has more than doubled." U.S.

Congress, Senate, Committee on Finance, *Hearings, Family Assistance Act of 1970*, 91st Cong., 2nd sess., April 29, 30, and May 1, 1970, pt. 1, 162–63.

2. Christopher Leman, *The Collapse of Welfare Reform* (Cambridge, Mass.: MIT Press, 1980), 73.

3. Martin Anderson, *Welfare: The Political Economy of Welfare Reform in the United States* (Stanford, Calif.: Hoover Institution Press, 1978), 4. For the party's positions on welfare, see, for example, "Republican Party Platform 1960" and "Republican Party Platform 1964," in John T. Woolley and Gerhard Peters, eds., *The American Presidency Project* (Santa Barbara: University of California, 1999–), http://www.presidency.ucsb.edu/platforms.php.

4. Anderson, *Welfare*, 4.

5. "Republican Platform 1968," in Wooley and Peters, *American Presidency Project*; see also Blanche Coll, *Safety Net* (New Brunswick, N.J.: Rutgers University Press, 1995), 257.

6. See, for example, M. Kenneth Bowler, *The Nixon Guaranteed Income Proposal* (Cambridge, Mass.: Ballinger, 1974); Daniel P. Moynihan, *The Politics of a Guaranteed Income* (New York: Random House, 1973); Vincent J. Burke and Vee Burke, *Nixon's Good Deed: Welfare Reform* (New York: Columbia University Press, 1974); Leman, *Collapse of Welfare Reform*; and Lester M. Salamon, *Welfare: The Elusive Consensus* (New York: Praeger, 1978).

7. See, for example, Steven M. Teles, *Whose Welfare?* (Lawrence: University Press of Kansas, 1998); James T. Patterson, *America's Struggle Against Poverty in the Twentieth Century* (Cambridge, Mass.: Harvard University Press, 2000); and Michael B. Katz, *In the Shadow of the Poorhouse* (New York: Basic Books, 1996). For an insightful study published after this research was conducted that highlights the relevance of the FAP struggles to enduring challenges of poverty and inequality, see Brian Steensland, *The Failed Welfare Revolution* (Princeton, N.J.: Princeton University Press, 2008).

8. Jamie Peck, *Workfare States* (New York: Guilford Press, 2001) and *Work-Place* (New York: Guilford Press, 1996). See also, for example, Joel F. Handler, *Social Citizenship and Workfare in the United States and Western Europe* (Cambridge: Cambridge University Press, 2004); and Bob Jessop, "Post-Fordism and the State," in Ash Amin, ed., *Post-Fordism* (Oxford: Blackwell, 1994).

9. This analysis draws in part on distinctions and typologies developed by Peck. See, in particular, his *Workfare States*, chapter 1. For other typologies, see Richard M. Titmuss, *Social Policy* (London: Allen and Unwin, 1974); Goran Therborn, "Welfare State and Capitalist Markets," *Acta Sociologica* 30 (1987): 237–54; and Gosta Esping-Anderson, *The Three Worlds of Welfare Capitalism* (Cambridge: Polity, 1990).

10. New Deal job creation programs to provide work for the unemployed ended in the early 1940s, and there was no permanent program of aid for the working poor. See, for example, Department of Health, Education, and Welfare, *Report to Congress on Community Work and Training Under Title IV of the Social Security Act as Amended by Section 409*, House Document 76, 90-1, January 1967, p. 1.

11. On Friedman's views, see Burke and Burke, *Nixon's Good Deed*, 140–141.

12. Milton Friedman, *Capitalism and Freedom* (Chicago: University of Chicago Press, 1962). See also Coll, *Safety Net*, 259; Moynihan, *Politics of Guaranteed Income*, 37; Patterson, *America's Struggle*, 181; and Robert A. Moffitt, "The Negative Income Tax and the Evolution of U.S. Welfare Policy," National Bureau of Economic Research, NBER Working Paper 9751, June 2003. Moffitt notes that in congressional hearings on FAP in 1969, Friedman objected to FAP's approach to implementing the negative income tax alongside existing assistance programs, rather than using it to replace them (7–8).

13. See Patterson, *America's Struggle*, 181–82. See also Irwin Garfinkel, "Negative Income Tax and Children's Allowances: A Comparison," *Social Work* 13, no. 4 (October 1968): 33–39; and Alan D. Wade, "The Guaranteed Minimum Income: Social Work's Challenge and Opportunity," *Social Work* 12, no. 1 (January 1967): 94–101.

14. Coll, *Safety Net*, 259.

15. Patterson, *America's Struggle*, 182; and Coll, *Safety Net*, 259.

16. See discussion in Patterson, *America's Struggle*, 183-84; and Coll, *Safety Net*, 260. In 1969, the Heineman Commission, created by Johnson to study the question of income guarantees, concluded: "Only when the poor are assured a minimum stable income can the other mechanisms in our fight against poverty—education, training, health and employment—begin to function adequately." President's Commission on Income Maintenance Programs, *Poverty amid Plenty* (Washington, D.C.: U.S. Government Printing Office, 1969), cited in Patterson, *America's Struggle*, 183.

17. Leman, *Collapse of Welfare Reform*, 74.

18. Polls indicated that 60 percent of the public opposed the idea. Patterson, *America's Struggle*, 184. Surveys of key members of Congress in 1967 and 1969 found both skepticism that a guaranteed income proposal would be taken up, and opposition to it. Leman, *Collapse of Welfare Reform*, 71. For a concise overview of positions on the issue, see *Congressional Quarterly Almanac* 23 (1967): 993-95.

19. For conflicting views within the Nixon camp over FAP and the South, see Kevin P. Phillips, *The Emerging Republican Majority* (New Rochelle, N.Y.: Arlington House, 1969), particularly 187-289; and Moynihan, *Politics of Guaranteed Income*, 376-79.

20. Leman, *Collapse of Welfare Reform*, 75.

21. The discussion in the following paragraphs draws upon the detailed chronology and analysis presented by journalists Vincent and Vee Burke, *Nixon's Good Deed*; Moynihan, *Politics of Guaranteed Income*; and memos circulated by administration officials.

22. For details of the proposals and arguments, see, for example, "Nixon Men Study Alternate Aids to the Poor: National Minimums or Guaranteed Income," *Wall Street Journal*, May 29, 1969.

23. See George P. Shultz, "Memorandum for the President" (undated, stamped as received by White House on May 7, 1969), Richard M. Nixon Presidential Materials Staff at Archives II, National Archives and Records Administration, White House Central Files, Subject: Welfare (hereafter RMNPMS), Box 60, 1.

24. See Salamon, *Elusive Consensus*, 68-69.

25. See Salamon, *Elusive Consensus*, 68.

26. For discussion of the English Poor Laws and their application in early U.S. poor relief, see, for example, Joel F. Handler and Yeheskel Hasenfeld, *We the Poor People: Work, Poverty, and Welfare* (New Haven, Conn.: Yale University Press, 1997), chapter 2, and Katz, *In the Shadow*, chapter 1.

27. On Speenhamland, see Frances Fox Piven and Richard A. Cloward, *Regulating the Poor*, (New York: Vintage Books, 1993), 29-32; and Fred Block and Margaret Somers, "In the Shadow of Speenhamland: Social Policy and the Old Poor Law," *Politics and Society* 31 (2003): 283-323. Steensland's *Failed Welfare Revolution* examines some of the same archival material from the Nixon administration to build an argument that draws on cultural factors to explain the defeat of guaranteed income proposals.

28. Martin Anderson, "A Short History of a 'Family Security System,'" April 14, 1969, RMNPMS, Box 60, 2-3.

29. Anderson, "A Short History," 14, RMNPMS, Box 60, 3-5.

30. Daniel P. Moynihan, "Memorandum for the President," April 22, 1969, 1-2, RMNPMS, Box 60.

31. Moynihan, "Memorandum," RMNPMS, 1-2.

32. Paul W. McCracken, "Memorandum for the President," April 24, 1969, 1-2, RMNPMS, Box 60. McCracken chaired the Council of Economic Advisers.

33. Shultz, "Memorandum," RMNPMS, 1.

34. Shultz, "Memorandum," RMNPMS, 2.

35. Shultz, "Memorandum," RMNPMS, 2.

36. "Family Security System," Draft Report of the Committee on Welfare of the Council for Urban Affairs (undated; stamped as received by White House on April 27, 1969), 15–16, RMNPMS, Box 60.

37. Shultz, "Memorandum," RMNPMS, 2.

38. See Leman, *Collapse of Welfare Reform*, 76.

39. Leman, *Collapse of Welfare Reform*, 58–69, 113–34.

40. Richard M. Nixon, "Welfare Reform: Shared Responsibility," August 8, 1969. *Vital Speeches of the Day* 35, no. 22 (September 1, 1969): 675.

41. Nixon, "Welfare Reform," 675.

42. Nixon, "Welfare Reform," 675.

43. Nixon, "Welfare Reform," 675.

44. Nixon, "Welfare Reform," 675.

45. See Moynihan, *Politics of Guaranteed Income*, chapters 3 and 4.

46. The discussion of public and press reactions to FAP in this and the following paragraphs is based on excerpts and commentary in Moynihan, *Politics of Guaranteed Income*, 251–53.

47. Cited in Moynihan, *Politics of Guaranteed Income*, 268.

48. Moynihan, *Politics of a Guaranteed Income*, 250.

49. Support came from the National Association of Manufacturers: Coll, *Safety Net*, 270. Moynihan reported to Nixon that early conversations with business leaders about the FAP proposal (before it was unveiled) were promising. Daniel P. Moynihan, "Memorandum for the President," April 23, 1969, RMNPMS, Box 60.

50. U.S. Congress, House, Committee on Ways and Means, *Hearings, Social Security and Welfare Proposals*, 91st Cong., 1st sess., October 15–November 13, 1969, pt. 5, p. 1067. On Chamber of Commerce lobbying, see, for example, "Senate Panel Stalls Welfare-Reform Bill over Minor Problems; Chances Still Good," *Wall Street Journal*, May 4, 1970.

51. Testimony before the Senate Finance Committee, January 20, 1972, excerpted in *Congressional Quarterly Almanac* 28 (1972): 900.

52. *Congressional Quarterly Almanac* 28 (1972): 900.

53. Cited in Burke and Burke, *Nixon's Good Deed*, 131.

54. For over a year, the administration was unable to secure the backing of the National Governors Council, or even a majority of governors. Leman, *Collapse of Welfare Reform*, 79; Coll, *Safety Net*, 270.

55. Cited in Burke and Burke, *Nixon's Good Deed*, 131.

56. Cited in Robert Mann, *Legacy to Power: Senator Russell Long of Louisiana* (New York: Paragon House, 1992), 305.

57. This article, along with the liberal and conservative reactions discussed in the following paragraphs, is cited in Burke and Burke, *Nixon's Good Deed*, 133–34.

58. See Peter Edelman, *Searching for America's Heart* (Boston: Houghton Mifflin, 2001), 111.

59. For the UAW statement, see House, Committee on Ways and Means, *Hearings, Social Security and Welfare Proposals*, pt. 6, pp. 1875–1928. Meany is cited in Burke and Burke, *Nixon's Good Deed*, 140.

60. See, for example, the statement of Clinton Fair, Legislative Representative, AFL-CIO, U.S. Congress, Senate, Committee on Finance, *Hearings, Family Assistance Act of 1970*, 91st Cong., 2nd sess., August 24–September 10, 1970, pp. 1727–31.

61. See House, Committee on Ways and Means, *Hearings, Social Security and Welfare Proposals*, pt. 3, pp. 699–704.

62. Moynihan, *Politics of Guaranteed Income*, 307–8.

63. The poverty threshold for a single-parent (female-headed) household with three children was $3,715 in 1969. U.S. Census Bureau, "Poverty Thresholds 1969," https://www.census.gov/hhes

/www/poverty/data/threshld/thresh69.html. The median family income in the United States in 1970 was $9,870. U.S. Census Bureau, "Median Family Income Up in 1970," Series P60, no. 68, May 20, 1971.

64. Moynihan, *Politics of Guaranteed Income*, 334. For the NWRO's proposal, see House, Committee on Ways and Means, *Hearings, Social Security and Welfare Proposals*, pt. 3, pp. 1013–23.

65. *Congressional Quarterly Almanac* 26 (1970): 1036.

66. Senate, Committee on Finance, *Family Assistance Act of 1970*, August 24–September 10, 1970, p. 1771.

67. U.S. Congress, *Congressional Record—House*, June 22, 1971, pp. 21343–44.

68. U.S. Congress, Senate, Committee on Finance, *Report to Accompany H.R. 17550: Social Security Amendments of 1970*, 91st Cong., 2nd sess., December 11, 1970, "Additional Views of Mr. Ribicoff," 415–26. See also remarks by Senator Percy (R-Ill.), calling for attention to barriers to employment for the poor, including a dearth of affordable childcare and discrimination by employers. U.S. Congress, *Congressional Record—Senate*, October 4, 1972, pp. 33689–91.

69. Senate, Committee on Finance, *Family Assistance Act of 1970*, August 24–September 10, 1970, p. 1767.

70. Testimony before the Senate Finance Committee, January 28, 1972, excerpted in *Congressional Quarterly Almanac* 28 (1972): 901–2.

71. *Congressional Quarterly Almanac* 26 (1970): 1038–39.

72. See House, Committee on Ways and Means, *Hearings, Social Security and Welfare Proposals*, pt. 5, pp. 1536–40; see also Coll, *Safety Net*, 270.

73. See, for example, the statement of Clarence Mitchell, director of the Washington Bureau of the NAACP and legislative chairman of the LCCR. Senate, Committee on Finance, *Family Assistance Act of 1970*, August 24–September 10, 1970, pp. 2096–97.

74. Cited in Moynihan, *Politics of Guaranteed Income*, 266–67.

75. Moynihan, *Politics of Guaranteed Income*, 375–77.

76. Cited in Burke and Burke, *Nixon's Good Deed*, 163–64.

77. See Chapter 3 for a discussion of Mills's role in the FAP debate. His support for FAP was a surprise to many. Even after the bill passed his committee, most of his colleagues expected him to vote against it on the House floor. "Nixon's Proposals for Welfare Reform Win Tentative Approval from Key House Panel," *Wall Street Journal*, February 27, 1970.

78. See Senate, Committee on Finance, *Family Assistance Act of 1970*, pt. 1, April 29, April 30, and May 1, 1970.

79. On debates within the administration on the notch problem, see "Lack of Consensus Among Nixon Aides Threatens Passage of Welfare Reform," *Wall Street Journal*, June 9, 1970; see also Leman, *Collapse of Welfare Reform*, 80.

80. The revised proposal tapered and reduced benefits linked to FAP, and increased penalties for recipients who refused to work. See U.S. Congress, Senate, Committee on Finance, *H.R. 16311: The Family Assistance Act, Revised and Resubmitted to the Committee on Finance by the Administration*, Committee Print, June 1970.

81. On administration concerns about Long's delays, see John G. Veneman, "Memorandum to the President," September 3, 1970, RMNPMS, Box 61.

82. Leman, *Collapse of Welfare Reform*, 81.

83. The new bill passed the House easily, 288–132, in June 1971. See *Congressional Quarterly Almanac* 27 (1971): 35-H.

84. Salamon, *Elusive Consensus*, 94–95; see also Burke and Burke, *Nixon's Good Deed*, 149.

85. Salamon, *Elusive Consensus*, 95.

86. *Congressional Quarterly Almanac* 27 (1971): 519–21.

87. For a description of the alternatives, see U.S. Congress, *Congressional Record—Senate*, October 4, 1972, pp. 33624–35.

88. Salamon, *Elusive Consensus*, 95-96.
89. See Burke and Burke, *Nixon's Good Deed*, 6; and Moynihan, *Politics of Guaranteed Income*, 534.
90. Salamon, *Elusive Consensus*, 96. Representatives Mills (D-Ark.) and John Byrnes (R-Ill.) played this leadership role in the House.

Chapter 3. Building Workfare

1. Robert Mann, *Legacy to Power: Senator Russell Long of Louisiana* (New York: Paragon House, 1992), 272.
2. "Remarks by Senator Russell B. Long (D-La.) before the 1971 Conference of the Southwest Region, American Public Welfare Association," March 24, 1971, Russell B. Long Collection, Louisiana State University (hereafter RBLC), Box 69, Folder 8, 34.
3. For examples of accounts that move quickly from the 1960s to the 1980s, see Michael B. Katz, *In the Shadow of the Poorhouse* (New York: Basic Books, 1996); Charles Noble, *Welfare as We Knew It* (New York: Oxford University Press, 1997); and Harrell R. Rodgers, Jr., *Poverty in a New Era of Reform* (Armonk, N.Y.: M. E. Sharpe, 2006). "Stalemate" is from the title of the chapter on this era in James T. Patterson, *America's Struggle Against Poverty in the Twentieth Century* (Cambridge, Mass.: Harvard University Press, 2000). For works that take a broader view of political and social developments in the 1970s and after, see, for example, David Brian Robertson, ed., *Loss of Confidence: Politics and Policy in the 1970s* (University Park: Pennsylvania State University Press, 1998); and Paul Pierson and Theda Skocpol, eds., *The Transformation of American Politics: Activist Government and the Rise of Conservatism* (Princeton, N.J.: Princeton University Press, 2007).
4. On WIN II, see, for example, Walter I. Trattner, *Poor Law to Welfare State* (New York: Free Press, 1994), 347; and Michael B. Katz, *The Price of Citizenship: Redefining the American Welfare State*, updated edition (Philadelphia: University of Pennsylvania Press, 2008), 65-65. On SSI, Theda Skocpol treats the Nixon reform period, which would include SSI and the origins of the EITC, as part of a window for policy reform opened by the War on Poverty and the Great Society, despite fundamental differences in the purposes of reform. See "Targeting Within Universalism," in Theda Skocpol, *Social Policy in the United States* (Princeton, N.J.: Princeton University Press, 1995), 250-74. For a clear statement of the position that SSI was a consolation prize, see Patterson, *America's Struggle*, 190. Trattner, *Poor Law to Welfare State*, 351, makes the argument that SSI was a largely administrative change. Regarding the EITC, there is little discussion of the program in Patterson, *America's Struggle*; Katz, *Shadow of the Poorhouse*; Blanche D. Coll, *Safety Net: Welfare and Social Security, 1929-1979* (New Brunswick, N.J.: Rutgers University Press, 1995); or Trattner, *Poor Law to Welfare State*. There are, of course, important exceptions. On the political development of SSI, see, for example, Jennifer L. Erkulwater, *Disability Rights and the American Social Safety Net* (Ithaca, N.Y.: Cornell University Press, 2006), particularly chapter 3; Martha Derthick, *Agency Under Stress* (Washington, D.C.: Brookings Institution, 1990); and Edward D. Berkowitz, *Robert Ball and the Politics of Social Security* (Madison: University of Wisconsin Press, 2003), 207-13. On the EITC, see, for example, Christopher Howard, *The Hidden Welfare State* (Princeton, N.J.: Princeton University Press, 1997), and "Protean Lure for the Working Poor," *Studies in American Political Development* 9 (Fall 1995): 404-36; and Dennis R. Ventry, Jr., "The Collision of Tax and Welfare Politics: The Political History of the Earned Income Tax Credit, 1969-99," *National Tax Journal* 53, no. 4 (December 2000): 983-1026.
5. This typology is set out by Lester M. Salamon, *Welfare Reform: The Elusive Consensus* (New York: Praeger, 1978), 104-5.

6. Labor standards in the 1933 National Industrial Recovery Act, the 1935 Wagner Act, and the 1938 Fair Labor Standards Act (which included the federal minimum wage) addressed the conditions of the working poor, but they were not income support programs.

7. The workfarist turn in public assistance also contributed to a broader conservative ascendance that began in the 1970s and has drawn the attention of scholars in recent years. See, for example, Bruce J. Schulman and Julian E. Zelizer, *Rightward Bound: Making America Conservative in the 1970s* (Cambridge, Mass.: Harvard University Press, 2008); Lisa McGirr, *Suburban Warriors: The Origins of the New Right* (Princeton, N.J.: Princeton University Press, 2001); and Rick Perlstein, *Before the Storm: Barry Goldwater and the Unmaking of the American Consensus* (New York: Hill and Wang, 2001).

8. In some cases (such as WIN II), their actions reflected long-standing views; in others (such as SSI), they were shaped by changing regional interests; and in still others (such as the EITC), they reflected efforts to stave off change. Institutionally, Long had significant autonomy due to his seniority and position in the Senate, and Mills was influenced by the culture of professionalism on fiscal matters that characterized the House Ways and Means Committee, on which he had served for decades. For a discussion of the Long and Talmadge family legacies, see V. O. Key, Jr., *Southern Politics in State and Nation* (New York: Alfred A. Knopf, 1949).

9. See, for example, Michael K. Brown, "Ghettos, Fiscal Federalism, and Welfare Reform," in Sanford F. Schram, Joe Soss, and Richard C. Fording, eds., *Race and the Politics of Welfare Reform* (Ann Arbor: University of Michigan Press, 2003), 60.

10. See, for example, U.S. Congress, *Congressional Record—Senate*, August 6, 1971, p. 30544. See also Gwendolyn Mink, *Welfare's End* (Ithaca, N.Y.: Cornell University Press, 1998), 50–60. Mink discusses Long's failed 1970 attempt to introduce at the federal level several state-level restrictive practices that had been struck down by the courts.

11. See "The 'New South': Changing but Still Conservative." Newer members were attuned to the changing political economy of the region and the new political culture of television-based campaigning. Their votes in Congress, however, differed little from those of their senior colleagues. *Congressional Quarterly Weekly Report*, June 11, 1971, pp. 1280–83.

12. Daniel P. Moynihan, *The Politics of a Guaranteed Income* (New York: Random House, 1973), 375–77. The same question hung over the second version of FAP in 1971. As Moynihan said at the University of North Carolina: "There will be much noise from the North insisting the program is not enough. This will make little difference in the outcome. The outcome will be decided by men of the South, now in Congress, who must summon the confidence that it is not too much." Moynihan had left the administration for Harvard University in December 1970. He sent a copy of the speech to Wilbur Mills, thanking Mills for his work on FAP. "Commencement Address," Daniel P. Moynihan, at the University of North Carolina at Greensboro, June 6, 1971, 7. Wilbur D. Mills Congressional Collection, Hendrix College, Conway, Ark. (hereafter WDMCC), Box 200, Folder 6, 9.

13. "Family Security System," draft report of the Committee on Welfare of the Council for Urban Affairs (undated; stamped as received by White House on April 27, 1969), esp. 8–9, Richard M. Nixon Presidential Materials Staff at National Archives II, White House Central Files, Subject: Welfare (hereafter RMNPMS), Box 60. Moynihan was in a complicated position to make this case publicly. He was attacked by liberals for the 1965 report on the black family he wrote as a Johnson administration official, and he was accused by conservatives of misleading Nixon into supporting FAP. On the latter point, see Edward L. Morgan, "Memorandum for John Ehrlichman, Family Assistance Plan: President's Meeting with the Senate Finance Republicans, 20 July 1970," July 16, 1970, RMNPMS, Box 61, 1.

14. Finch said: "This exclusion [of the working poor] also has begun to take on ominous and socially polarizing racial overtones, for AFDC recipients, those who are helped, are about

50-percent nonwhite while the working poor, those who are excluded, are 70-percent white." U.S. Congress, House, Committee on Ways and Means, *Hearings, Social Security and Welfare Proposals*, 91st Cong., 1st sess., pt. 1, October 15–16, 1969, p. 121.

15. Georgia governor Lester G. Maddox was characteristically blunt: "You're not going to be able to find anyone willing to work as maids or janitors or housekeepers if this bill goes through, that I promise you." "Welfare Reform: The Southern View," *Wall Street Journal*, December 15, 1970.

16. Cited in Moynihan, *The Politics of a Guaranteed Income*, 377. Despite Moynihan's criticism of Phillips and other political strategists identified with Nixon's "Southern strategy" to win conservative white votes and break the electoral dominance of the Democratic Party in the South, it is clear that some of the White House officials who favored FAP were familiar with the arguments that it would boost black political power in the South, thereby challenging the white (Democratic) political establishment. See points excerpted by Nixon aide John Ehrlichman from Richard Armstrong's article in *Fortune*. John D. Ehrlichman, Memorandum for the President, July 7, 1970, RMNPMS, Box 61, 1–2.

17. Vincent J. Burke and Vee Burke, *Nixon's Good Deed* (New York: Columbia University Press, 1974), 146–47.

18. Richard Armstrong, "The Looming Money Revolution Down South," *Fortune* 81, no. 6 (June 1970): 66. Armstrong cited census figures showing that 52 percent of FAP beneficiaries would be Southerners.

19. There were discrepancies and variations in the estimates over time. See, for example, *Congressional Quarterly Almanac* 26 (1970): 1037; and U.S. Congress, Senate, Committee on Finance, *Hearings, Family Assistance Act of 1970*, 91st Cong., 2nd sess., Part II, July 21–August 18, 1970, pp. 1077–78.

20. *Congressional Quarterly Almanac* 26 (1970): 1037. Elliot Richardson, who became HEW secretary in June 1970, argued that if only half of those eligible for FAP participated in the program (as was the case with AFDC at the time), then the increase in rolls was likely to be only half as large as critics projected. See Senate, Committee on Finance, *Family Assistance Act of 1970*, pt. 2, July 21–August 18, 1970, pp. 627–28.

21. Burke and Burke, *Nixon's Good Deed*, 147.

22. Letter to Representative Mills from the President of Allied Food Stores, Inc., Little Rock, Arkansas, October 1972. WDMCC, Box 197, Folder F1. Mills's response, in the same folder, said in part, "Like you, we are concerned about the problems which companies such as yours have with labor problems—and we agree that unemployed men, with no physical disabilities, should not receive welfare assistance." Constituents backing Long's position on FAP, because of the threat it posed to the structure of employment in the state, included the head of the Louisiana Department of Agriculture. RBLC, Box 144, Folder 22.

23. U.S. Congress, Senate, Committee on Finance, *Committee Print: H.R. 16211: The Family Assistance Act of 1970 (Revised and Resubmitted)*, 91st Cong., 2nd sess., June 1970, p. 25.

24. "Welfare Reform," *Wall Street Journal*, December 15, 1970. A primary concern of opponents, the article added, "is what all that money would do to the low-cost domestic labor supply."

25. Cited in Burke and Burke, *Nixon's Good Deed*, 149–50. Many observers shared Kevin Phillips's expectation that this trend "cannot help but push whites into the alternative major party structure—that of the GOP." Kevin P. Phillips, *The Emerging Republican Majority* (New Rochelle, N.Y.: Arlington House, 1969), 287.

26. "Welfare Reform," *Wall Street Journal*, December 15, 1970.

27. "Welfare Reform," *Wall Street Journal*, December 15, 1970.

28. U.S. Congress, *Congressional Record—Senate*, October 4, 1972, p. 33676. His Finance Committee staff developed an extensive study examining what it saw as the detrimental work incentive and labor market impacts of a range of liberal welfare expansion proposals in comparison to

his own workfare plan. U.S. Congress, Senate, Committee on Finance, *Confidential Committee Print, Staff Data on Programs for Families Headed by an Employable Adult*, 92nd Cong., 2nd sess., April 24, 1972.

29. U.S. Congress, House, Committee on Ways and Means, *The President's Proposals for Welfare Reform and Social Security Amendments, 1969*, 91st Cong., 1st sess., Committee Print, October 1969, p. 104.

30. Cited in Bowler, *Nixon Guaranteed Income Proposal*, 89.

31. Cited in Bowler, *Nixon Guaranteed Income Proposal*, 97. Broyhill was a Southern Republican.

32. House, Committee on Ways and Means, *Social Security and Welfare Proposals*, 321.

33. Burke and Burke, *Nixon's Good Deed*, 149.

34. Of the thirteen states that had no state minimum wage, seven were in the South. House, Committee on Ways and Means, *Social Security and Welfare Proposals*, 320.

35. Burke and Burke, *Nixon's Good Deed*, 149.

36. See *Congressional Quarterly Almanac* 26 (1970): 16-H, and *Congressional Quarterly Almanac* 27 (1971): 35-H.

37. Burke and Burke, *Nixon's Good Deed*, 147–48.

38. Nixon to Representative George Bush (unsigned), October 23, 1970, RMNPMS, Box 61, 1.

39. Burke and Burke, *Nixon's Good Deed*, 147.

40. Cited in Burke and Burke, *Nixon's Good Deed*, 187.

41. See U.S. Committee on Economic Security, *Report to the President* (Washington, D.C.: U.S. Government Printing Office, 1935), 36.

42. Talmadge suggested renaming FAP, to call it the "Welfare Expansion Bill." *Wall Street Journal*, June 9, 1970.

43. Senate, Committee on Finance, *Family Assistance Act of 1970*, pt. 1, April 29, April 30, and May 1.

44. Cited in Moynihan, *Politics of a Guaranteed Income*, 473.

45. The exchange went as follows: Senator Talmadge: "So he could do a little casual labor on somebody's yard from time to time and maybe sell a little heroin or do a little burglary and he would be in pretty good shape, wouldn't he?" Mr. Veneman: "He would be in about the same shape as under the present program." Senate, Committee on Finance, *Family Assistance Act of 1970*, April 29, April 30, and May 1, 223.

46. Senate, Committee on Finance, *Family Assistance Act of 1970*, April 29, April 30, and May 1, 230.

47. *Congressional Quarterly Almanac* 27 (1971): 865.

48. Cited in Leman, *Collapse of Welfare Reform*, 85–86.

49. On the initiation of federally backed state work and training programs in 1962 after ADC-UP's creation, see Department of Health, Education, and Welfare, *Report to Congress on Community Work and Training Under Title IV of the Social Security Act as Amended by Section 409*, House Document 76, 90-1, January 1967, pp. 3–4.

50. See *Congressional Quarterly Almanac* 27 (1971): 865; see also Leman, *Collapse of Welfare Reform*, 85–86; and Coll, *Safety Net*, 248–52.

51. See, for example, Nancy E. Rose, *Workfare or Fair Work* (New Brunswick, N.J.: Rutgers University Press, 1995), 102–3. In a special report on WIN, the Senate Finance Committee concluded that "it has in fact had very little impact on welfare rolls." U.S. Congress, Senate, Committee on Finance, *Committee Print: Material Related to Work and Training Provisions of Administration Revision of H.R. 16311*, 91st Cong., 2nd sess., August 1970, p. 10.

52. Coll, *Safety Net*, 249; and Rose, *Workfare or Fair Work*, 103.

53. Patterson, *America's Struggle*, 170; and Rose, *Workfare or Fair Work*, 103.

54. Title XIV (Aid to the Permanently and Totally Disabled) was added in 1950.

55. Historian Blanche Coll writes: "The liberalizing amendments [in 1956 and 1958] found their greatest justification in the group of needy adults who could not work because they were old or disabled, a group that would be cared for eventually by OASDI [Old Age, Survivors, and Disability Insurance]. Long would just as soon have left the ADC program off his list of increases, and he certainly wasn't alone." Coll, *Safety Net*, 181–82.

56. This discussion draws in part on Erkulwater's detailed study of the politics of SSI's passage (*Disability Rights*, chapter 3) and her earlier doctoral dissertation, "The Forgotten Safety Net: The Expansion of Supplemental Security Income," Department of Political Science, Boston College, May 2001.

57. In 1970, for example, there were approximately 9,650,000 AFDC recipients; Old Age Assistance, by far the largest of the programs included in SSI, had some 2,082,000 beneficiaries. Coll, *Safety Net*, 172.

58. Their different interests in pursuing the measure are examined in Erkulwater, "Forgotten Safety Net," 168–83; see also Derthick, *Agency Under Stress*, chapter 5.

59. The April 1970 FAP bill passed by the House included an income floor for these groups, as did the legislation reported out by the Senate Finance Committee. The House and Senate proposals were not reconciled in conference that year, however.

60. U.S. Congress, House, Committee on Rules, *Hearings on the Family Assistance Act of 1970*, 91st Cong., 2nd sess., April 7, 13, and 14, 1970, p. 104.

61. Mills made his preference clear: "Old-Age and Survivors Insurance has come relatively slowly to predominantly agricultural areas, since many occupations in which people in these areas are engaged were not in covered employment until recent years.... An Old-Age and Survivors Insurance payment... is a more satisfactory way for people to receive income on a regular basis than is a welfare payment." "Speech—Welfare Association Meeting," Little Rock, Ark., November 30, 1961, WDMCC, Box 776, Folder 10, pp. 11–12. Long, in contrast, regularly touted the increases he secured for his favored categories of public assistance recipients—namely, "aged, blind and disabled persons." "Statement of Honorable Russell B. Long, Chairman, Senate Committee on Finance, Before the Police Jury Association of Louisiana in Lafayette, Louisiana," April 10, 1972, RBLC, Box 231, Folder 40, pp. 15 and 17. In fact, he worried that the continued link to AFDC risked implicating these "deserving groups" in the "welfare mess." *Congressional Record—Senate*, August 6, 1971, pp. 30543–44.

62. M. Kenneth Bowler, *The Nixon Guaranteed Income Proposal* (Cambridge, Mass.: Ballinger, 1974), 111–13.

63. *U.S. News and World Report*, March 15, 1971, 44.

64. House, Committee on Rules, *Family Assistance Act of 1970*, 106–9 and 134–37.

65. Cited in Bowler, *Nixon Guaranteed Income Proposal*, 112.

66. House, Committee on Rules, *Family Assistance Act of 1970*, 161.

67. U.S. Congress, House, Committee on Ways and Means, *Report on H.R. 1, Social Security Amendments of 1971*, 92nd Cong., 1st sess., House Report 92-231, May 26, 1971, p. 4.

68. Quoted in Bowler, *Nixon Guaranteed Income Proposal*, 142.

69. U.S. Congress, Senate, Committee on Finance, *Hearings on Tax Credits to Stimulate Job Opportunities in Rural America*, 91st Cong., 1st sess., May 21 and 22, 1969, p. 1.

70. For an extensive discussion of these developments, see Jill Quadagno, "From Old-Age Assistance to Supplemental Security Income," in Margaret Weir, Ann Shola Orloff, and Theda Skocpol, eds., *The Politics of Social Policy in the United States* (Princeton, N.J.: Princeton University Press, 1988). The figure cited here is from page 255.

71. Burke and Burke, *Nixon's Good Deed*, 197.

72. From the end of the 1930s to the beginning of the 1970s, Louisiana's OAA program grew from the twentieth to the third largest in the nation, measured by the overall number of recipi-

ents (only California and Texas had larger programs). U.S. Congress, Senate, Committee on Finance, *Social Security Amendments of 1972. Report to Accompany H.R. 1*, 92nd Cong., 2nd sess., September 26, 1972, pp. 400–403. Unlike other Southern programs, Louisiana's also paid relatively high benefits, increasing its burden on the state. Michael K. Brown, *Race, Money, and the American Welfare State* (Ithaca, N.Y.: Cornell University Press, 1999), 124–25, 199.

73. Erkulwater, "Forgotten Safety Net," 170.
74. Erkulwater, "Forgotten Safety Net," 179.
75. Cited in Mann, *Legacy to Power*, 305.
76. See Erkulwater, "Forgotten Safety Net," 183–92; and Derthick, *Agency Under Stress*, chapter 5.
77. Cited in Erkulwater, "Forgotten Safety Net," 194.
78. Burke and Burke, *Nixon's Good Deed*, 188–204.
79. Cited in Erkulwater, "Forgotten Safety Net," 191.
80. *Congressional Quarterly Almanac* 28 (1972): 899–914.
81. Patterson, *America's Struggle Against Poverty in the Twentieth Century*, 189.
82. Leman, *Collapse of Welfare Reform*, 89.
83. Patterson, *America's Struggle*, 191.
84. Cited in Erkulwater, "Forgotten Safety Net," 193.
85. See Senate Committee on Finance, *Report to Accompany H.R. 1*, 12–13.
86. Gilbert L. Crouse, "Trends in AFDC and Food Stamp Benefits: 1972–1994," ASPE Research Notes, Office of the Assistant Secretary for Planning and Evaluation, U.S. Department of Health and Human Services, May 1995. Rebecca Blank notes that from 1970 to 1993, the median monthly state benefit for a mother with three children dropped from $792 to $435 in constant dollars. Rebecca Blank, *It Takes a Nation: A New Agenda for Fighting Poverty* (Princeton, N.J.: Princeton University Press, 1997), 100.
87. The average federal SSI payment for individuals increased from $95.11 in 1974 to $325.26 in 1994, due almost entirely to indexation. U.S. Congress, House, Committee on Ways and Means, *1998 Green Book*, 105th Cong., 2nd sess., May 19, 1998, pp. 263–64.
88. In the early 1980s and mid-1990s, SSI faced some reductions, but the cuts in SSI met more resistance and were more limited. See *Congressional Quarterly Almanac* 38 (1982): 478; *Congressional Quarterly Almanac* 52 (1996): 6–15; and "Welfare: Legal Immigrants to Benefit Under New Budget Accord," *New York Times*, July 30, 1997.
89. By 2004, federal EITC payments were approximately $34 billion; the TANF block grant was $16.5 billion. Ron Haskins, *Work over Welfare* (Washington, D.C.: Brookings Institution Press, 2006), 342.
90. Most studies of the EITC focus on its impact as a targeted tax credit, addressing issues such as design, compliance, efficiency costs, and labor market effects. See, for example, Saul D. Hoffman and Laurence S. Seidman, *Helping Working Families* (Kalamazoo, Mich.: Upjohn Institute, 2003) and *The Earned Income Tax Credit* (Kalamazoo, Mich.: Upjohn Institute, 1990); and Bruce D. Meyer and Douglas Holtz-Akin, eds., *Making Work Pay* (New York: Russell Sage, 2001). For studies that chart the EITC's history, tracing its roots to FAP, see Christopher Howard, "Happy Returns: How the Working Poor Got Tax Relief," *American Prospect* (March 1994); Howard, *Hidden Welfare State*, 67; and Howard, "Protean Lure," 404–36; see also Ventry, "Collision," 22. Scholars writing on welfare reform, meanwhile, largely disregard the EITC in their analysis of AFDC's transformation. See, for example, Patterson, *America's Struggle*; Katz, *Shadow of the Poorhouse*. Even those writing directly on workfare often neglect the EITC's emergence or expansion; see Peck, *Workfare States*.
91. Senate Committee on Finance, *Family Assistance Act of 1970*, April 29, 1970, p. 1.
92. Senate Committee on Finance, *Family Assistance Act of 1970*, April 29, 1970, p. 2.

93. Cited in Mann, *Legacy to Power*, 300.

94. Senate, Committee on Finance, "Press Release: 1 May 1970," H.R. 16311—*The Family Assistance Act of 1970*, 2. See also, Mann, *Legacy to Power*, 301.

95. Mann, *Legacy to Power*, 301.

96. See Ventry, "Collision," 23.

97. *Congressional Quarterly Almanac* 26 (1970): 1036.

98. Long's legislation (introduced again in 1973) would allow a tax deduction for wages paid to household and domestic workers. The idea, he explained, was both to draw poor women off of welfare and into domestic work, and to provide domestic labor for middle-income women who wanted to spend more time working. RBLC, Box 231, Folder 32, 4; and Box 614, Folder 13, 9.

99. See, for example, Bowler, *Nixon Guaranteed Income Proposal*, 89.

100. John G. Veneman, "Memorandum for the President," September 3, 1970, RMNPMS, Box 61, 3.

101. *Congressional Quarterly Almanac* 27 (1971): 519.

102. *Congressional Quarterly Almanac* 27 (1971): 521.

103. Cited in "The Family Assistance Plan—A Chronology," *Social Service Review* 46, no. 4 (December 1972): 607.

104. *Congressional Quarterly Almanac* 28 (1972): 905; Ventry, "Collision," 22; Howard, *Hidden Welfare State*, 67.

105. See Martin Anderson, *Welfare* (Stanford, Calif.: Hoover Institution Press, 1978).

106. U.S. Congress, *Congressional Record—Senate*, September 30, 1972, p. 33011.

107. Senate Committee on Finance, *Report to Accompany H.R. 1*, 85.

108. Mann, *Legacy to Power*, 303. See also U.S. Congress, Senate, Committee on Finance, *Welfare Reform: Guaranteed Job Opportunity—Explanation of Committee Decisions*, 92nd Cong., 2nd sess., April 28, 1972.

109. *Congressional Quarterly Almanac* 28 (1972): 905.

110. U.S. Congress, *Congressional Record—Senate*, September 30, 1972, p. 33011.

111. The three proposals were FAP, Long's workfare plan, and a welfarist alternative offered by Senator Ribicoff. For a description of the proposals and the debate, see U.S. Congress, *Congressional Record—Senate*, October 4, 1972, pp. 33624–35.

112. Many moderates and liberals, however, defended the tax credit, often employing Long's logic. Senator Walter Mondale (D-Minn.) argued, for example, that it would "bring a lot of relief to decent, hard-working American families who today, if they looked at the figures realistically, could say, 'Better stop working; our government has decided to tax me back on welfare.'" *Congressional Quarterly Almanac* 29 (1973): 579.

113. Howard argues persuasively that the ambiguity of the measure—its appeal to different policymakers for different reasons—eased its passage. Howard, "Protean Lure," 411–13.

114. James R. Storey, "The Earned Income Tax Credit: A Growing Form of Aid to Low-Income Workers," *CRS Report for Congress*, Congressional Research Service, updated December 6, 1996, p. 3.

115. Howard, *Hidden Welfare State*, 70–71.

116. U.S. Congress, Senate, Committee on Finance, *Report to Accompany H.R. 2166*, 94th Cong., 1st sess., Senate Report 94-36, March 17, 1975, p. 33. Howard, *Hidden Welfare State*, 71, says the effect was to reduce the potential beneficiaries to seven million.

117. In 1993, President Clinton pushed for and won passage of a very limited EITC benefit for childless low-income workers as well.

118. *Congress and the Nation* 5 (1977–1980): 688.

119. Those for whom jobs were not available or who were not expected to work (including the elderly, disabled, and blind, as well as single parents of children under the age of seven) would receive a federal grant providing an income "floor" of $4,200. For recipients who were employ-

able but not working, the federal payment would be $2,300. *Congress and the Nation* 5 (1977–1980): 688.

120. *Congress and the Nation* 5 (1977–1980): 688.

121. *Congressional Quarterly Almanac* 33 (1977): 472.

122. *Congressional Quarterly Almanac* 34 (1978): 601. *Congressional Quarterly* also noted that the rising tax revolt, which had started in California that year, made legislators cautious.

123. Cited in Storey, "Earned Income Tax Credit," 5. For an analysis of the broader political impact of the Revenue Act of 1978, particularly its role in reversing the progressivity of the tax code through reducing capital gains taxes and raising payroll taxes, see Jacob C. Hacker and Paul Pierson, *Winner-Take-All Politics*, (New York: Simon and Schuster, 2011), 99–100 and 133–34.

124. In developing its welfare reform plan, the Carter administration proposed major expansions of the EITC—including indexing it for inflation, adjusting it for family size, raising the minimum benefit by more than 50 percent, and extending its reach by nearly doubling the income cutoff. The EITC provision emphasized the tilt toward private-sector job creation in PBJI; the EITC would not be available for those in newly created public-sector jobs. *Congressional Quarterly Almanac* 34 (1978): 601. The EITC provision was also seen as a way to help win Long's support: an "apparent concession to Senator Long," reported *The New York Times*, "was the President's recommendation for a significant expansion of the so-called earned income tax credit system." Cited in Howard, "Protean Lure," 415.

125. On the politics of PBJI, see, for example, Gordon L. Weil, *The Welfare Debate of 1978* (White Plains, N.Y.: Institute for Socioeconomic Studies, 1978).

126. *Congressional Quarterly Almanac* 33 (1977): 472.

127. *Congressional Quarterly Almanac* 34 (1978): 601.

128. "Long and Dole Announce Welfare Reform Bill," Press Release, Office of Senator Long, June 20, 1979. RBLC, Box 625, Folder 18. Long wanted to go further: "I would favor making all federal laws and regulations relating to AFDC purely advisory with the states having complete discretion to design and implement their own family welfare programs." But his judgment was that "Congress is not ready for such sweeping change." "Remarks by Senator Russell B. Long to the National Council of Public Welfare Administrators, October 24, 1979." RBLC, Box 625, Folder 85.

129. *Congressional Quarterly Almanac* 34 (1978): 601.

130. *Congressional Quarterly Almanac* 34 (1978): 603.

131. In 1978, CETA supported more than 700,000 full-time jobs held by adults and another million summer jobs held by teenagers—before the public service employment spending was scaled back by Carter in 1980. See Weir, *Politics and Jobs*, 118–19; and Gordon Lafer, *The Job Training Charade* (Ithaca, N.Y.: Cornell University Press, 2002), 21, 163.

132. The House failed to override the veto by five votes (277–145). Of the twenty-two Democrats who voted to support Ford and sustain the veto, eighteen were from the South. "House Sustains Veto of Emergency Jobs Bill," *Congressional Quarterly Almanac* 31 (1975): 793–99.

133. Liberal lawmakers also won passage in the House of a labor law reform that would strengthen workers' ability to protect job security and resist cuts in wages and benefits through collective bargaining. In the fall of 1978, however, the measure was abandoned after falling two votes short of the sixty votes needed to limit debate in the Senate. See, for example, Gary M. Fink, "Labor Law Revision and the End of the Postwar Labor Accord," in Kevin Boyle, ed., *Organized Labor and American Politics, 1984–1994* (Albany: State University of New York Press, 1998).

Chapter 4. The Political Economy of Work and Welfare

1. See Paul Osterman and Beth Shulman, *Good Jobs America: Making Work Better for Everyone* (New York: Russell Sage Foundation, 2011), 16–17.

2. The failure to update policies and programs—in the face of changing social and economic conditions that diminish their reach and effectiveness—can be understood as a case of welfare state retrenchment by "drift" or "disjuncture." See Jacob S. Hacker, "Privatizing Risk Without Privatizing the Welfare State," *American Political Science Review* 98, no. 2 (May 2004): 243–60; and Gosta Esping-Andersen, *Social Foundations of Postindustrial Economies* (Oxford: Oxford University Press, 1999).

3. For a discussion of the failure of full-employment policies in the post–New Deal period, and the consequences for U.S. employment policies, see, for example, Margaret Weir, *Politics and Jobs* (Princeton, N.J.: Princeton University Press, 1992); Margaret Weir, "Wages and Jobs: What Is the Public Role?" in Weir, ed., *The Social Divide* (Washington, D.C.: Brookings Institution Press, 1998); Stephen Kemp Bailey, *Congress Makes a Law* (New York: Vintage, 1950); Robert M. Collins, *The Business Response to Keynes, 1929–1964* (New York: Columbia University Press, 1981); Theda Skocpol, "The Limits of the New Deal System and the Roots of Contemporary Welfare Dilemmas," in Margaret Weir, Ann Shola Orloff, and Theda Skocpol, eds., *The Politics of Social Policy in the United States* (Princeton, N.J.: Princeton University Press, 1988); and Gary Mucciaroni, *The Political Failure of Employment Policy, 1945–1992* (Pittsburgh: University of Pittsburgh Press, 1990).

4. See, for example, Arthur Altmeyer, *The Formative Years of Social Security* (Madison: University of Wisconsin Press, 1966), 28.

5. U.S. Committee on Economic Security, *Report to the President of the Committee on Economic Security* (Washington, D.C.: U.S. Government Printing Office, 1935), 3.

6. See Weir, *Politics and Jobs*, particularly chapter 2; and Skocpol, *Social Policy in the United States*, chapters 6 and 7.

7. Weir, *Politics and Jobs*, 41–43.

8. For decades after enactment of the federal minimum wage under the 1938 Fair Labor Standards Act (FLSA), conservatives of both parties would use this congressional wage-setting authority to carve out differential treatment for regions and industries and to limit minimum wage increases. See Daniel P. Gitterman, *Boosting Paychecks* (Washington, D.C.: Brookings Institution Press, 2010), 42–62.

9. On the defunding of the NRPB in 1943, see Weir, *Politics and Jobs*, 44–45.

10. See, for example, Collins, *Business Response to Keynes*, chapters 2 and 3, on the range of reactions by business to New Deal economic and social policies, including the role played by some business leaders in developing specific New Deal policies. See also Peter Swenson, "Arranged Alliance: Business Interests in the New Deal," *Politics and Society* 25 (March 1997): 66–116.

11. Elizabeth A. Fones-Wolf, *Selling Free Enterprise* (Urbana: University of Illinois Press, 1994), 2.

12. By 1937, NAM was spending more than half its budget on public relations, including weekly radio programs, paid advertisements, films, public speakers, press services, and school displays. Fones-Wolf, *Selling Free Enterprise*, 2. The discussion in this paragraph is drawn in part from Fones-Wolf, particularly the introduction and chapter 1.

13. For provisions of the defeated full employment bill of 1945, as well as its enacted successor, the Employment Act of 1946, see Anne Scitovsky, "The Employment Act of 1946," *Social Security Bulletin* 9, no. 3 (March 1946): 25–29, 56.

14. Weir, *Politics and Jobs*, 46.

15. Collins, *Business Response to Keynes*, 100–110.

16. See Nelson Lichtenstein, "From Corporatism to Collective Bargaining," in Steve Fraser and Gary Gerstle, eds., *The Rise and Fall of the New Deal Order, 1930–1980* (Princeton, N.J.: Princeton University Press, 1990), 122–52.

17. See, for example, Collins, *Business Response to Keynes*, 17; and Mucciaroni, *Political Failure of Employment Policy*, chapter 2. While social Keynesians urged large-scale public investment

and social spending as part of a strategy to ensure robust growth, commercial Keynesians advocated smaller fiscal and monetary adjustments and more limited macroeconomic intervention.

18. See *Congressional Quarterly Almanac* 34 (1978): 273–79.

19. Even those facing systemic discrimination within the labor market saw improvements in their work conditions and living standards in these years. See Lawrence Mishel, Jared Bernstein, and John Schmitt, *The State of Working America 1998/1999,* Economic Policy Institute (Ithaca, N.Y.: Cornell University Press, 1999), 45.

20. Rebecca M. Blank, *It Takes a Nation* (Princeton, N.J.: Princeton University Press, 1997), 54–55. See also Susan Mayer and Christopher Jencks, "War on Poverty: No Apologies, Please," *New York Times*, November 9, 1995.

21. Blank, *It Takes a Nation*, 54 and 56. For a discussion of the model's predictions and actual poverty levels through 1997, see Mishel, Bernstein, and Schmitt, *State of Working America 1998/1999*, 292–93.

22. Blank, *It Takes a Nation*, 53–54.

23. Blank, *It Takes a Nation*, 54.

24. For poverty, unemployment, and growth figures, see U.S. Census Bureau, "Historical Poverty Tables—People," Table 2, https://www.census.gov/hhes/www/poverty/data/historical/people.html; U.S. Department of Labor, Bureau of Labor Statistics (hereafter BLS), "Seasonally Adjusted Unemployment Rate," http://data.bls.gov/cgi-bin/surveymost?ln; and U.S. Bureau of Economic Analysis, "Percentage Change from Preceding Period in Real Gross Domestic Product," http://www.bea.gov/iTable/index_nipa.cfm.

25. Blank, *It Takes a Nation*, 55.

26. Blank, *It Takes a Nation*, 56; U.S. Congress, House, Committee on Ways and Means, *1998 Greenbook: Background Material and Data on Programs Within the Jurisdiction of the Committee on Ways and Means*, 105th Cong., 2nd sess., May 19, 1998, pp. 1234 and 1303; and U.S. Census Bureau, Historical Poverty Tables, Table 2.

27. See, for example, Barry Bluestone and Bennett Harrison, *The Great U-Turn* (New York: Basic Books, 1988); Frank Levy, *Dollars and Dreams* (New York: Russell Sage Foundation, 1988); Katherine S. Newman, *Falling from Grace* (New York: Vintage, 1988); and Paul Osterman, *Securing Prosperity* (Princeton, N.J.: Princeton University Press, 1999). For an early discussion of debates over the U.S. welfare state in the post-1970s economy, see, for example, Fred L. Block, Richard A. Cloward, Barbara Ehrenreich, and Frances Fox Piven, *The Mean Season* (New York: Pantheon Books, 1987).

28. For a historical discussion of some of the poverty-related issues raised here and a different definition of "doors" and "floors," see James T. Patterson, *America's Struggle Against Poverty in the Twentieth Century* (Cambridge, Mass.: Harvard University Press, 2000). For a contemporary analysis of the relationship between labor market developments and social provision, see Jacob S. Hacker, *The Great Risk Shift* (New York: Oxford University Press, 2006).

29. As many analysts have demonstrated, the aim of providing equitable social protections to all willing workers was never fully realized due to patterns of exclusion and discrimination in both labor markets and government policies. See, for example, Frank Levy, *New Dollars and Dreams: American Incomes and Economic Change* (New York: Russell Sage Foundation, 1998).

30. In the mid- to late 1990s (as AFDC was being replaced by TANF), 87.9 percent of adult AFDC/TANF recipients were female. Single women with children were the largest group of EITC recipients as well (39.4 percent of recipients, receiving 52.9 percent of overall benefits). In terms of race and ethnicity, by the mid-1990s the AFDC/TANF population was 37.2 percent African American, 35.6 percent White, and 20.7 percent Hispanic. The EITC's recipient population was 24 percent African American among single-parent recipients (the largest group) and 7.7 percent among married couples (the second largest group). The median age of female AFDC/TANF recipients was approximately thirty years, with nearly a quarter of the women (24 percent) between

the ages of twenty and twenty-four. The median age for EITC recipients was approximately thirty-six years. Among AFDC/TANF recipients for whom educational attainment was known, 43.5 percent had not completed high school. Among EITC recipients, 63.6 percent of single recipients had a high school degree or less (as did 71.5 percent of married recipients). For EITC characteristics, see Bruce D. Meyer and Douglas Holtz-Eakin, eds., *Making Work Pay* (New York: Russell Sage Foundation, 2001), 3–4. For AFDC, see Administration for Children and Families, "Characteristics and Financial Circumstances of AFDC Recipients FY 1995," September 1, 1995, http://archive.acf.hhs.gov/programs/ofa/character/FY95/index95.html, Tables 10, 22, 25, and 45; and (for educational attainment) Office of Family Assistance, Administration for Children and Families, U.S. Department of Health and Human Services, "Percent Distribution of TANF Adult Recipients by Educational Level, October 1997–September 1998," National Emergency TANF Datafile, Table 17 (as of May 28, 1999). For characteristics of the low-wage workforce (in more recent years), see Lawrence Mishel, Jared Bernstein, and Sylvia Allegretto, *The State of Working America 2006/2007*, Economic Policy Institute (Ithaca, N.Y.: Cornell University Press, 2007), 305.

31. The reports are compiled and released every two years by the Economic Policy Institute in Washington, D.C., and are published by Cornell University Press.

32. BLS, "Seasonally Adjusted Unemployment Rate." See also Mishel, Bernstein, and Schmitt, *State of Working America 1998/1999*, 220–21. The unemployment rate did not drop below 7 percent until December 2013. BLS, "The Employment Situation: December 2013," January 10, 2014, http://www.bls.gov/news.release/archives/empsit_01102014.pdf.

33. More than 13 percent experienced unemployment at some point during 2008, a year when the annual unemployment rate was 5.8 percent, for example. BLS, "Work-Experience Unemployment Rate, 2008," The Editor's Desk, January 6, 2010, http://www.bls.gov/opub/ted/2010/ted_20100106.htm.

34. See, for example, Mary Jo Bane and David Ellwood, *Welfare Realities* (Cambridge, Mass.: Harvard University Press, 1994).

35. For a discussion of the new BLS category and who it covers, see, for example, Steven E. Haugen, "Measures of Labor Underutilization from the Current Population Survey," BLS Working Paper 424, March 2009.

36. See David Leonhardt, *New York Times*, January 20, 2009. In August 2013, four years into the recovery, the rate was 13.7 percent, meaning that more than 21 million Americans, about one in seven people in the labor market, were underemployed. BLS, "The Employment Situation: August 2013," September 6, 2013, Table A-15 (Alternative Measures of Labor Underutilization), http://www.bls.gov/news.release/archives/empsit_09062013.pdf.

37. Like the unemployed, who were the focus of early New Deal planning, the underemployed are in many cases unable to realize what FDR called the "right to a useful and remunerative job" or the "right to earn enough to provide adequate food and clothing and recreation," both of which he believed were "accepted as self-evident" as part of "a new basis of security and prosperity." Franklin D. Roosevelt, "State of the Union Message to Congress," January 11, 1944, in John T. Woolley and Gerhard Peters, eds., *The American Presidency Project* (Santa Barbara: University of California, 1999–).

38. U.S. Census Bureau, "Household Data, Annual Averages," from the Current Population Survey, September 2009, 197–200, http://www.bls.gov/cps/cpsa2009.pdf.

39. U.S. Census Bureau, "Household Data, Annual Averages," from the Current Population Survey, September 2009 and September 2014, Table 24. See also Economic Policy Institute, "Ten Facts About the Recovery," July 6, 2011.

40. BLS, "Employment Situation: July 2014," Table A-4; see also Blank, *It Takes a Nation*, 58.

41. Underemployment rates for black and Hispanic workers were regularly twice as high as those for whites across this period. Lawrence Mishel, Josh Bivens, Elise Gould, and Heidi Shierholz, *The State of Working America*, 12th ed. (Ithaca, N.Y.: Cornell University Press, 2012), 351.

Underemployment rates for those who did not complete high school were 26.4 percent in mid-2013, nearly four times as high as for those with a bachelor's degree. See "Underemployment Highest for Those with Least Education," Economic Policy Institute, updated August 26, 2014, "http://www.stateofworkingamerica.org/charts/underemployment-education/.

42. Jared Bernstein, "Wage Growth Slows Despite Employment Gains," Quarterly Wage and Employment Series: 1999/2, Economic Policy Institute, May 30, 2000, Table 4, http://www.epi.org/publication/qwes_second99_qwes/.

43. BLS, Labor Force Statistics from the Current Population Survey, "Of Total Unemployed, Percentage Unemployed 15 Weeks and Over," LNU03008517, http://data.bls.gov/pdq/SurveyOutputServlet. BLS, "Employment Situation: July 2014," Table A-12.

44. BLS, "Work Experience of the Population in 1997," Table 4, http://www.bls.gov/news.release/history/work_112598.txt; U.S. Census Bureau, "Household Data, Annual Averages," Current Population Survey, September 2008, Table 31, http://www.bls.gov/cps/cpsa2008.pdf.

45. See, for example, Katherine V. W. Stone, *From Widgets to Digits* (New York: Cambridge University Press, 2004).

46. See Mary E. O'Connell, "Coming Unfringed: The Unraveling of Job-Based Entitlements," *American Prospect* 13 (Spring 1993): 55–63.

47. See BLS, "Employee Tenure in 2008," September 26, 2008, Table 1, http://www.bls.gov/news.release/archives/tenure_09262008.pdf; and Mishel, Bernstein, and Schmitt, *State of Working America 1998/1999*, 230–31.

48. BLS, "Employee Tenure in 2008," September 26, 2008, Tables 1 and 6; see also Mishel, Bernstein, and Allegretto, *State of Working America 2006/2007*, 305.

49. From 1979 to 2006, the percentage of men aged forty-five to fifty-four who had been in their current jobs ten years or more dropped from 58.4 to 44.8. For women, the percentage rose slightly from 35.4 in 1979 to 37.5 by 2006. BLS, "Employee Tenure in 2008," Table 2; and Lawrence Mishel, Jared Bernstein, and Heidi Shierholz, *The State of Working America 2008/2009*, Economic Policy Institute (Ithaca, N.Y.: Cornell University Press, 2009), 259.

50. BLS, "Worker Displacement, 2005–2007," August 20, 2008, Table 8.

51. BLS, "Worker Displacement, 2007–2009," August 26, 2010, Table 8, and "Worker Displacement, 2011–2013," August 26, 2014, Table 8.

52. Lawrence Mishel, Jared Bernstein, and Sylvia Allegretto, *The State of Working America, 2004/2005*, Economic Policy Institute (Ithaca, N.Y.: Cornell University Press, 2005), 275.

53. Mishel, Bernstein, and Allegretto, *State of Working America 2008/2009*, 260; and BLS, "Worker Displacement, 2005–2007,"August 20, 2008, Table 1. In the second half of the 1990s, the percentage of those displaced who were still out of work when interviewed dropped to one-quarter, before rising again to its previous level.

54. BLS, "Worker Displacement, 2007–2009," August 26, 2010, Table 7, http://www.bls.gov/news.release/archives/disp_08262010.pdf. The loss in pay was reported by workers who had been displaced from year-round, full-time jobs held for at least three years who had subsequently been reemployed in year-round, full-time positions.

55. See, for example, Sharon R. Cohany et al., "Counting the Workers," in Kathleen Barker and Kathleen Christensen, eds., *Contingent Work: American Employment Relations in Transition* (Ithaca, N.Y.: Cornell University Press, 1998), 51.

56. These employer-provided social protections, backed by federal tax expenditures, are an integral part of the U.S. welfare state. See Christopher Howard, *The Hidden Welfare State* (Princeton, N.J.: Princeton University Press, 1997); Marie Gottschalk, *The Shadow Welfare State* (Ithaca, N.Y.: Cornell University Press, 2000); and Jacob S. Hacker, *The Divided Welfare State* (New York: Cambridge University Press, 2002). Hiring contingent workers allows employers to pay less and provide fewer health and pension benefits, but also to "shed responsibility for income tax withholding, social security and employment tax benefits, and related employment costs."

Stanley D. Nollen and Helen Axel, "Benefits and Costs to Employers," in Barker and Christensen, *Contingent Work*, 128–29.

57. Mishel, Bernstein, and Shierholz, *State of Working America 2008/2009*, 252–53. See also BLS, "Contingent and Alternative Work Arrangements, February 2005," July 27, 2005, http://www.bls.gov/news.release/pdf/conemp.pdf.

58. Mishel, Bernstein, and Schmitt, *State of Working America 1998/1999*, 247–48. See also BLS, "Employed persons by full- and part-time status, reason, and sex, annual averages, 1968–2013."

59. BLS, "Employed persons by full- and part-time status"; BLS, "The Employment Situation: September 2009," Tables A-5 and A-6, http://www.bls.gov/news.release/archives/empsit_10022009.pdf; and BLS, "Employment Situation: June 2012," Summary Table A and Table A-8.

60. Mishel, Bernstein, and Schmitt, *State of Working America 1998/1999*, 248–50; Mishel, Bernstein, and Shierholz, *State of Working America 2008/2009*, 255–56; and BLS, "Employment Situation: June 2012," Table B-1.

61. Cohany, "Counting the Workers," 60.

62. Author's analysis of data in BLS, "Contingent and Alternative Employment Arrangements, February 1997," December 2, 1997, Table 5, http://www.bls.gov/news.release/history/conemp_020398.txt. See also Mishel, Bernstein, and Schmitt, *State of Working America 1998/1999*, 243.

63. Mishel, Bernstein, and Schmitt, *State of Working America 1998/1999*, 127.

64. Blank, *It Takes a Nation*, 55.

65. Jared Bernstein and Lawrence Mishel, "Wages Gain Ground," Economic Policy Institute, February 2, 1999.

66. Carmen DeNavas-Walt, Bernadette D. Proctor, and Jessica C. Smith, U.S. Census Bureau, *Income, Poverty, and Health Insurance Coverage in the United States: 2008* (Washington, D.C.: U.S. Government Printing Office, 2009). For the incomes of working-age families, see Elise Gould and Heidi Shierholz, "A Lost Decade," Economic Policy Institute, September 16, 2010, Figure G, updated September 14, 2011. For most working-age people, wages are the largest source of income.

67. In 1979, 4.2 percent of the full-time workforce earned hourly wages 25 percent or more below the poverty level. By 1989, 13.4 percent earned these wages. This figure fell during the 1990s, but by 2007, still stood at 9.4 percent, nearly double the rate of 1979, before dropping during the recession to 7.9 percent in 2009, as many low-wage workers simply lost their jobs. Mishel, Bernstein, and Shierholz, *State of Working America 2008/2009*, 140. See also Economic Policy Institute, "Wage Data: Poverty Level Wages," http://www.stateofworkingamerica.org/data.

68. Mishel, Bernstein, and Shierholz, *State of Working America 2008/2009*, 136 and 138.

69. Mishel, Bernstein, and Schmitt, *State of Working America 1998/1999*, 3. See also Mishel, Bernstein, and Shierholz, *State of Working America 2008/2009*, 102.

70. Mishel, Bernstein, and Schmitt, *State of Working America 1998/1999*, 8. See also Mishel, Bernstein, and Shierholz, *State of Working America 2008/2009*, 101.

71. Mishel, Bernstein, and Schmitt, *State of Working America 1998/1999*, 23.

72. BLS, "The Employment Situation: November 1998," 1, http://www.bls.gov/news.release/history/empsit_12041998.txt.

73. Overall, family incomes grew at an annual rate of just 0.1 percent. Mishel, Bernstein, and Shierholz, *State of Working America 2008/2009*, 46. (On work hours, see page 92.) For households headed by those under 65, median income actually fell by $1,951 between 2000 and 2007. Office of Management and Budget, *A New Era of Responsibility* (Washington, D.C.: U.S. Government Printing Office, February 2009), 8, http://www.whitehouse.gov/sites/default/files/omb/assets/fy2010_new_era/A_New_Era_of_Responsibility2.pdf.

74. DeNavas-Walt, Proctor, and Smith, U.S. Census Bureau, *Income, Poverty, and Health Insurance Coverage in the United States: 2008* (Washington, D.C.: U. S. Government Printing Office, 2009), 5; *Income, Poverty, and Health Insurance Coverage in the United States: 2009*, 5; *Income, Poverty, and Health Insurance Coverage in the United States: 2010*, 6; and DeNavas-Walt and Proctor, *Income, Poverty, and Health Insurance Coverage in the United States: 2013*, 23.

75. Although the percentage of less-educated workers (high school or less) has declined, they still composed almost 40 percent of the workforce (39.4 percent) in 2007. Mishel, Bernstein, and Shierholz, *State of Working America 2008/2009*, 170, 162.

76. Wages stagnated for African American men (moving up 0.4 percent from 2000 to 2007) and edged up slightly for women (up 1.7 percent). Mishel, Bernstein, and Shierholz, *State of Working America 2008/2009*, 177.

77. Mishel, Bernstein, and Shierholz, *State of Working America 2008/2009*, 184, and Mishel et al., *State of Working America*, 12th ed., 327–29. See also Office of Management and Budget, *A New Era of Responsibility*, 1; and BLS, "Tomorrow's Jobs," *Occupational Outlook Handbook*, 2008–9 edition (Washington, D.C.: Bureau of Labor Statistics, 2009). On the replacement of medium- and higher-paying jobs with lower-paying ones in the wake of the 2007–9 recession, see National Employment Law Project, "The Low-Wage Recovery and Growing Inequality," August 2012, http://www.nelp.org/page/-/Job_Creation/LowWageRecovery2012.pdf?nocdn=1.

78. Mishel, Bernstein, and Shierholz, *State of Working America 2008/2009*, 210 and Mishel, Bernstein, and Allegretto, *State of Working America 2006/2007*, 191. See also House, Committee on Ways and Means, *2008 Greenbook*, Appendix D, 27–31; and David Cooper, "Raising the Minimum Wage to $10.10 Would Lift Wages for Millions and Provide a Modest Economic Boost," Economic Policy Institute, December 13, 2013, Figure C.

79. EITC use was slow to respond to increased need during the 2001 recession (as during other downturns). But program use then increased significantly in the early 2000s, in part because fewer low-wage workers than in the late 1990s were experiencing wage gains adequate to move their incomes above the EITC-eligible level. Alan Berube, "The New Safety Net," *The Brookings Institution, Survey Series*, February 2006, 3–6, http://www.brookings.edu/metro/pubs/eitc/20060209_newsafety.pdf.

80. Operationally, the safety-net assumption also builds on the three preceding assumptions: access to job-based social protections presumes employment availability, security, and adequate and rising wages.

81. See, for example, Hacker, *Divided Welfare State*, and Gottschalk, *Shadow Welfare State*, chapter 3.

82. For those in the lowest wage quintile, the decrease from 1979 to 2006 was 13.9 percent (from 37.9 to 24.0). For high school graduates, the drop was 18.4 points (from 66.6 to 51.2 percent); college graduates saw a less severe decline of 12.1 points (from 79.6 to 67.5 percent). Mishel, Bernstein, and Shierholz, *State of Working America 2008/2009*, 149; and Elise Gould, "A Decade of Declines in Employer-Sponsored Health Insurance Coverage," Economic Policy Institute, February 23, 2012, Table 3. As Gould notes, the percentage of Americans covered by their own or someone else's employer-provided insurance (such as a spouse or parent) dropped steadily over the first decade of the 2000s, from 69.2 percent to 58.6 percent. The 2010 Affordable Care Act was projected to extend health insurance coverage to 25 million additional Americans once fully implemented. For a summary of the act's provisions and projected impacts, see Henry J. Kaiser Family Foundation, "Summary of the Affordable Care Act," April 23, 2013, http://kff.org/health-reform/fact-sheet/summary-of-the-affordable-care-act/.

83. Mishel, Bernstein, and Shierholz, *State of Working America 2008/2009*, 150. See also Mishel et al., *State of Working America*, 12th ed., 201.

84. Mishel, Bernstein, and Shierholz, *State of Working America 2008/2009*, 148. See also Mishel, Bernstein, and Schmitt, *State of Working America 1999/1999*, 143 and 120.

85. See for example, Employee Benefits Security Administration, U.S. Department of Labor, "What You Should Know About Your Retirement Plan," August 2013, 3, 9, http://www.dol.gov/ebsa/publications/wyskapr.html.

86. See O'Connell, "Coming Unfringed." See also BLS, "Employee Tenure in 2014," September 18, 2014, Table 1, www.bls.gov/news.release/archives/tenure_09182014.pdf; and Mishel, Bernstein, and Schmitt, *State of Working America 1998/1999*, 230.

87. For a discussion of some of the limitations of the unemployment insurance program for low-income mothers and proposals for reform, see Joel F. Handler and Yeheskel Hasenfeld, *We the Poor People* (New Haven, Conn.: Yale University Press, 1997), 136–39.

88. House, Committee on Ways and Means, *2008 Greenbook*, Section 4, 4–5.

89. House, Committee on Ways and Means, *2008 Greenbook*, Section 4, 4–5. On the decline in benefit receipts in 2014 after the expiration of extended benefits and other state and federal cuts, see Josh Bivens, "Historically Small Share of Jobless People are Receiving Unemployment Insurance," Economic Policy Institute, September 24, 2014.

90. House, Committee on Ways and Means, *2004 Greenbook*. For data on employer-sponsored pension and health coverage by wage/income level, for example, see Section 13, pages 12 and 22. The racial disparity in job-related health insurance is also striking. In 2002, 74.3 percent of whites under age sixty-five had employment-based health insurance, while only 54 percent of African Americans and 44.5 percent of Hispanics were insured through their jobs (Section C, 36). For an analysis of how social insurance benefits have historically accrued at a lower rate for racial and ethnic minorities because of lower wages produced by patterns of discrimination in the labor market, see Wendell Primus and Kathryn Porter, "Strengths of the Safety Net," Center on Budget and Policy Priorities, July 1998.

Chapter 5. The Conservative Assault and the Liberal Retreat

1. See David W. Rohde, *Parties and Leaders in the Postreform House* (Chicago: University of Chicago Press, 1991), particularly chapters 2 to 4.

2. "1980 Republican Platform Text" and "1980 Democratic Platform Text," *Congressional Quarterly Almanac* 36 (1980): 59B–63B.

3. *Congressional Quarterly Almanac* 36 (1980): 13-B. Their strongest gains were in the South: for the first time in modern history, Republicans won more than half as many Southern seats as Democrats in the House (43–78) and nearly as many in the Senate (11–14). *Congressional Directory* (Washington, D.C.: U.S. Government Printing Office, 1932–82).

4. For a discussion of market fundamentalism, see Margaret R. Somers and Fred Block, "From Poverty to Perversity: Ideas, Markets, and Institutions over 200 Years of Welfare Debate," *American Sociological Review* 70 (April 2005): 260–87.

5. *Inaugural Addresses of the Presidents of the United States: Bicentennial Edition* (Washington, D.C.: U.S. Government Printing Office, 1989), 332.

6. See "White House Report," in The White House, Office of the Press Secretary, "America's New Beginning: A Program for Economic Recovery," February 18, 1981.

7. The logic was set out in proposed changes to the extended unemployment benefits program: "Individuals whose prospects for returning to their previous line of work are still not good after 3 months of unemployment would be expected to adjust to changed economic conditions by accepting a job that may not pay as much as their previous job. This change will speed the transition from jobs that are not opening up again to jobs in sectors where workers are in demand." The White House, "America's New Beginning," Section 1, 24.

8. See John Tamny, "The Essential George Gilder Explains How Economies Work," *Forbes*, June 16, 2013.

9. Cited in Kathleen M. Shaw, Sara Goldrick-Rab, Christopher Mazzeo, and Jerry A. Jacobs, *Putting Poor People to Work* (New York: Russell Sage Foundation, 2006), 25.

10. Charles A. Murray, *Losing Ground: American Social Policy, 1950–1980* (New York: Basic Books, 1984).

11. "Losing More Ground," *New York Times,* Opinion section, February 3, 1985.

12. Republicans and conservative Southern Democrats joined forces in opposition to extending unemployment benefits and increasing the minimum wage in the early 1970s, and in sustaining Nixon (1970) and Ford (1975) vetoes of Democratic job creation bills. *Congressional Quarterly Almanac* 26–31 (1970–75).

13. See, for example, *Congressional Quarterly Almanac,* "1980 Democratic Party Platform Text."

14. William Julius Wilson, *The Truly Disadvantaged: The Inner City, the Underclass, and Public Policy* (Chicago: University of Chicago Press, 1987). See, for example, Wilson's testimony in U.S. Congress, House, Select Committee on Children, Youth, and Family, *Hearings, A Domestic Priority: Overcoming Family Poverty in America,* 100th Cong., 2nd sess., September 22, 1988. See also Loic Wacquant and William Julius Wilson, "Poverty, Joblessness and the Inner City," in Phoebe H. Cottingham and David T. Ellwood, eds., *Welfare Policy for the 1990s* (Cambridge, Mass.: Harvard University Press, 1989), 70–102; and Shaw et al., *Putting Poor People to Work,* 25–26.

15. "The Obligation to Work and the Availability of Jobs: A Dialogue Between Lawrence M. Mead and William Julius Wilson," *Focus* 10, no. 2 (1987), Institute for Research on Poverty, University of Wisconsin–Madison, 11. See also Lawrence Mead, *Beyond Entitlement* (New York: Free Press, 1986), 3–4.

16. For an overview of his approach, see Lawrence M. Mead, ed., *The New Paternalism: Supervisory Approaches to Poverty* (Washington, D.C.: Brookings Institution Press, 1997), and Mead, *Beyond Entitlement.*

17. John A. Farrell, *Tip O'Neill and the Democratic Century* (Boston: Little, Brown and Company, 2001), 550.

18. Martin Tolchin, "The Troubles of Tip O'Neill," *New York Times*, Magazine section, August 16, 1981.

19. Farrell, *Tip O'Neill,* 544, 551.

20. *Congressional Quarterly Weekly Report,* June 13, 1981, 1023–26; see also Nicol C. Rae, *Southern Democrats* (New York: Oxford University Press, 1994), 89.

21. Cited in Rae, *Southern Democrats,* 89.

22. "Conservatives Hit New High in Showdown Vote Victories," *Congressional Roll Call, 97th Congress, 1st Session* (Washington, D.C.: Congressional Quarterly, 1982), 37–42. See also Farrell, *Tip O'Neill,* 550, 544–45, and 554; and Jim Wright, *Balance of Power* (Atlanta: Turner Publishing, 1996), 351.

23. Farrell, *Tip O'Neill,* 543, 551.

24. Thomas P. O'Neill, Jr., *Man of the House: The Life and Political Memoirs of Speaker Tip O'Neill* (New York: Random House, 1987), 341.

25. Farrell, *Tip O'Neill,* 548–49. See also Ronald Reagan, "Address Before a Joint Session of the Congress on the Program for Economic Recovery," February 18, 1981, in John T. Woolley and Gerhard Peters, eds., *The American Presidency Project* (Santa Barbara: University of California, 1999–), http://www.presidency.ucsb.edu.

26. Wright, *Balance of Power,* 342; see also Farrell, *Tip O'Neill,* 547. For the administration's case, see "Text of Reagan FY '82 Budget Revisions," *Congressional Quarterly Weekly Report,* March 14, 1981, 485.

27. See Thomas Byrne Edsall with Mary D. Edsall, *Chain Reaction* (New York: W. W. Norton, 1992), 140–53.

28. "'Welfare Queen' Becomes Issue in Reagan Campaign," *New York Times*, February 15, 1976.

29. "President Reagan's Economic Proposals," *Congress and the Nation* 6 (1981–84): 1039. SSI and six other programs that the administration characterized as a "social safety net" largely "escaped the deep budget cuts other programs suffered" that year. *Congressional Quarterly Almanac* 36 (1981): 461. In 1982, however, the administration proposed cuts in SSI spending of $1.1 billion over five years, some of which were adopted. *Congressional Quarterly Almanac* 37 (1982): 478.

30. Edwin L. Dale, spokesman for the Office of Management and Budget, cited in David E. Rosenbaum, "Study Shows Planned Welfare Cuts Would Most Hurt Poor Who Work," *New York Times*, March 20, 1981.

31. Cited in Farrell, *Tip O'Neill*, 556.

32. Farrell, *Tip O'Neill*, 558.

33. *Congressional Quarterly Weekly Report*, May 2, 1981, 743. See also Farrell, *Tip O'Neill*, 556.

34. Cited in Farrell, *Tip O'Neill*, 558. For the reactions of other Democrats, see, for example, "Budget Fight Shows O'Neill's Fragile Grip," *Congressional Quarterly Weekly Report*, May 9, 1981, 786.

35. *Congress and the Nation* 6 (1981–84): 892–93.

36. "House Ratifies Savings Plan in Stunning Reagan Victory," *Congressional Quarterly Weekly Report*, June 27, 1981, 1127–29. See also Wright, *Balance of Power*, 359; and Farrell, *Tip O'Neill*, 558–59.

37. *Congress and the Nation* 6 (1981–84): 892–93. See also Farrell, *Tip O'Neill*, 560.

38. In 1982, Reagan again proposed deep cuts in AFDC and food stamps. Congress scaled back but approved reductions in both. *Congressional Quarterly Almanac* 37 (1982): 476–79.

39. James T. Patterson, *America's Struggle Against Poverty in the Twentieth Century* (Cambridge, Mass.: Harvard University Press, 2000), 206.

40. *Congressional Quarterly Almanac* 36 (1981): 461.

41. Alan L. Feld, "The Economic Recovery Tax Act of 1981: Fairness in Rate Cuts in the Individual Income Tax," *Cornell Law Review* 68 (1983): 429.

42. Feld, "Economic Recovery Tax Act," 432; see also Daniel P. Gitterman, *Boosting Paychecks* (Washington, D.C.: Brookings Institution Press, 2010), 67.

43. See *Congress and the Nation* 6 (1981–84): 886.

44. As recently as 1979, a national minimum benefit level was included in Carter's scaled-back welfare reform bill, which passed in the House 222–184 but was never taken up in the Senate. *Congressional Quarterly Almanac* 34 (1978): 601.

45. For use of block grants in the Nixon administration, see Michael K. Brown, *Race, Money and the American Welfare State* (Ithaca, N.Y.: Cornell University Press, 1999), 317–21. On the Reagan administration's block grant strategy, see The White House, "America's New Beginning," 24–26.

46. Paul Pierson, *Dismantling the Welfare State? Reagan, Thatcher and the Politics of Retrenchment* (Cambridge: Cambridge University Press, 1994), 123. For Reagan's proposal to transfer control of AFDC and foods stamps to the states, see Ronald Reagan, "Address Before a Joint Session of the Congress Reporting on the State of the Union," January 26, 1982.

47. This analysis draws in part on Pierson, *Dismantling the Welfare State?*, 115–25.

48. U.S. Congress, Senate, Committee on the Budget, *Omnibus Budget Reconciliation Act of 1981: Report of the Committee on the Budget to Accompany S.1377*, 97th Cong., 1st sess., June 17, 1981, p. 437. The quote is from the section of the report prepared by the Committee on Finance.

49. Senators Long and Grassley (R-Iowa) supported and even offered amendments to strengthen the administration proposals, "which would allow AFDC recipients to work in return for their benefits." *Congressional Quarterly Weekly Report*, May 9, 1981, p. 797.

50. *Congressional Quarterly Almanac* 35 (1981): 461. The 1962 Public Welfare Amendments had authorized the secretary of Health, Education, and Welfare (later Health and Human Services) to waive specific requirements of the Social Security Act "in order to enable a State to carry out any experimental, pilot or demonstration project that the Secretary judges likely to assist in promoting the objectives of AFDC." These waivers were granted sparingly until the Reagan administration, and much more liberally then and after. U.S. Congress, House, Committee on Ways and Means, *1998 Greenbook: Background Material and Data on Programs Within the Jurisdiction of the Committee on Ways and Means*, 105th Cong., 2nd sess., 1998, p. 405.

51. Lawrence Mead, *The New Politics of Poverty: The Nonworking Poor in America* (New York: Basic Books, 1992), 168, 190.

52. The LIOAB assisted states in receiving waivers from federal AFDC regulations. For an in-depth discussion of the LIOAB and congressional Democrats' resistance to writing new waiver guidelines into legislation, see Steven M. Teles, *Whose Welfare?* (Lawrence: University Press of Kansas, 1998), 121–30.

53. David Ellwood and Mary Jo Bane, *Welfare Realities* (Cambridge, Mass.: Harvard University Press, 1994), 22–23; see also Judith M. Gueron, "Work and Welfare: Lessons on Employment Programs," *Journal of Economic Perspectives* 4, no. 1 (Winter 1990): 91–95.

54. Farrell, *Tip O'Neill*, 577–78.

55. Cited in Farrell, *Tip O'Neill*, 579.

56. Gordon Lafer, *The Job Training Charade* (Ithaca, N.Y.: Cornell University Press, 2002), 185.

57. *Congressional Quarterly Weekly Report*, November 14, 1981, pp. 2216–17.

58. Cited in Farrell, *Tip O'Neill*, 593.

59. Farrell, *Tip O'Neill*, 584. See also Robert Mann, *Legacy to Power: Senator Russell Long of Louisiana* (New York: Paragon House, 1992), 377; and Barry Bluestone and Bennett Harrison for the Congressional Joint Economic Committee, "The Great American Job Machine: The Proliferation of Low-Wage Labor in the American Economy," December 1986, http://files.eric.ed.gov/fulltext/ED281027.pdf.

60. Cited in Farrell, *Tip O'Neill*, 584–85.

61. Farrell, *Tip O'Neill*, 586, cites a briefing book produced by the White House Office of Policy Information, June 1, 1982.

62. Mann, *Legacy to Power*, 378.

63. Farrell, *Tip O'Neill*, 593. For Reagan's optimistic projections, see, for example, "Text of President Reagan's [November 10] Press Conference," *Congressional Quarterly Weekly Report*, November 14, 1981, pp. 2248–51.

64. See "New Job Training Legislation Awaits Senate, House Action," *Congressional Quarterly Weekly Report*, June 12, 1982, pp. 1405–6, which reports that Democrats on the House Education and Labor Committee argued that "the direct job creation approach is the most cost effective, timely and efficient means of stimulating employment during a recessionary period."

65. See Lafer, *Job Training Charade*, 177–78.

66. For the Reagan administration's case against CETA, see The White House, "America's New Beginning," Section 4, 26–27. For an overview of public service employment in the 1970s under the CETA program, see, for example, Donald C. Baumer and Carl E. Van Horn, *The Politics of Unemployment* (Washington, D.C.: Congressional Quarterly Press, 1995), particularly chapters 1, 3, 4, and 5.

67. Lafer, *Job Training Charade*, 177–78. For an overview of job training programs and politics, see Susan Kellam, "Worker Retraining: Do Displaced Workers Get Adequate Training for New Jobs?" *Congressional Quarterly Researcher*, January 21, 1994.

68. Lafer, *Job Training Charade*, 173.

69. Lafer, *Job Training Charade*, 186.

70. Lafer, *Job Training Charade*, 185–87.
71. See White House, "America's New Beginning," Section 4, 26–27.
72. "Text of Presidential News Conference [September 28, 1982]," *Congressional Quarterly Weekly Report*, October 2, 1982, p. 2455.
73. "House Passes $1 Billion Democratic Jobs Bill," *Congressional Quarterly Weekly Report*, September 18, 1982, p. 2292.
74. "S&L Aid, Jobs Bill Cleared," *Congressional Quarterly Weekly Report*, October 9, 1982, p. 2622.
75. House, Committee on Ways and Means, *1998 Greenbook*, 1007; and *2004 Greenbook*, 15–118; and "America's New Beginning," Section 4, 26–27. For a review of literature evaluating training programs from the 1970s to the 1990s, see David B. Mulhausen, "Do Jobs Programs Work? A Review Article," *Journal of Labor Research* 26, no. 2 (Spring 2005): 299–322.
76. On efforts by congressional Democrats in the 1960s and 1970s to create an ongoing program of public service employment, against the objections of the Johnson and Nixon administrations, see, for example, Margaret Weir, *Politics and Jobs* (Princeton, N.J.: Princeton University Press, 1992), 117–19. The 1980 Democratic platform said, "We pledge a $12 billion antirecession jobs program, providing at least 800,000 additional jobs." "Democratic Party Platform 1980," in Woolley and Peters, *The American Presidency Project*.
77. See Lafer, *Job Training Charade*, 186–87.
78. See Lafer, *Job Training Charade*, 188–89; and Shaw et al., *Putting Poor People to Work*, 100–101.
79. Farrell, *Tip O'Neill*, 598.
80. *Congressional Quarterly Almanac* 37 (1982): 469.
81. *Congressional Quarterly Almanac* 37 (1982): 461.
82. Cited in Danziger, "Fighting Poverty and Reducing Welfare Dependency," in Cottingham and Ellwood, *Welfare Policy*, 47–48.
83. *Congressional Quarterly Almanac* 37 (1982): 469.
84. Daniel Patrick Moynihan, *Family and Nation* (New York: Harcourt Brace Jovanovich, 1986), 156–57, notes that as governor of California, testifying against Nixon's Family Assistance Plan, Reagan had offered a proposal to eliminate the tax liability for workers whose earnings left them in poverty. The record of Reagan's major policy initiatives in his first term as president does not suggest that expanding the EITC was a priority for him at that time.
85. Jeffrey H. Birnbaum and Alan Murray, *Showdown at Gucci Gulch* (New York: Vintage, 1987), 23–31.
86. Cited in Birnbaum and Murray, *Showdown*, 40.
87. Moynihan, *Family and Nation*, 161.
88. Cited in R. Kent Weaver, *Ending Welfare as We Know It* (Washington, D.C.: Brookings Institution Press, 2000), 66.
89. Martin Anderson, *Welfare: The Political Economy of Welfare Reform in the United States* (Stanford, Calif.: Hoover Institution Press, 1978), 54–55, 238.
90. U.S. Department of the Treasury, "Tax Reform for Fairness, Simplicity and Economic Growth: The Treasury Department Report to the President," Treasury I, November 1984.
91. Christopher Howard, *The Hidden Welfare State* (Princeton, N.J.: Princeton University Press, 1997), 148–49; and Dennis R. Ventry, Jr., "The Collision of Tax and Welfare Politics," *National Tax Journal* 53, no. 4 (December 2000): 15.
92. "Reagan's May 28 Address on Tax Reform," *Congressional Quarterly Weekly Report*, June 1, 1985, 1074.
93. Robin Toner, "Major Help Found in Tax Bill for Low-Income Households," *New York Times*, August 22, 1986.
94. Danziger, "Fighting Poverty," 48.

95. Cited in Toner, "Major Help," *New York Times*, August 22, 1986.

96. Reagan had also been unable to privatize or make significant cuts in Social Security. For an analysis of the accomplishments and limits of his retrenchment efforts, see, for example, Pierson, *Dismantling the Welfare State*, particularly chapters 3 and 5.

97. Cited in U.S. Domestic Policy Council, *Up from Dependency: A New National Public Assistance Strategy* (Washington, D.C.: Department of Health and Human Services, 1986), 1.

98. For accounts stressing the FSA's bipartisan character, see, for example, Harrell R. Rodgers, Jr., *American Poverty in a New Era of Reform* (Armonk, N.Y.: M. E. Sharpe, 2006), 86–90; and Anne Marie Cammisa, *From Rhetoric to Reform?* (Boulder, Colo.: Westview, 1998), 57–58.

99. *Congressional Quarterly Almanac* 43 (1987): 546–47.

100. As a final concession, the House leadership allowed an amendment from Representative Mike Andrews (D-Tex.) that cut another $500 million from the measure. "After Struggle, House Passes Welfare Reform," *Congressional Quarterly Almanac* 43 (1987): 546–57.

101. Dole's amendment for the first time incorporated an individual federal work requirement for certain AFDC recipients (those in AFDC-UP), rather than a state requirement to establish work and training programs (which began with WIN). "After Years of Debate, Welfare Reform Clears," *Congressional Quarterly Almanac* 44 (1988): 349–64.

102. The work mandate remained in the final conference report, and House negotiators cut $1.1 billion from their incentives for states to provide higher benefits. *Congressional Quarterly Almanac* 44 (1988): 72–73H. For the debate and vote, see U.S. Congress, *Congressional Record— House*, July 7, 1988, pp. 16772–99.

103. See *Congressional Quarterly Almanac* 44 (1988): 349–64.

104. See Robert Reischauer, "The Welfare Reform Legislation, Directions for the Future," in Cottingham and Ellwood, *Welfare Policy for the 1990s*, 10–40. On congressional battles over the FSA, see *Congressional Quarterly Almanac*, "After Struggle," 546–57; and "After Years of Debate," 349–64.

105. This had been accomplished through increases in federal financial participation through the 1940s and 1950s, and through significant infusions of in-kind assistance in the 1960s and early 1970s.

106. Reischauer, "Welfare Reform Legislation," 22. See also Gilbert L. Crouse, "Trends in AFDC and Food Stamp Benefits: 1972–1994," ASPE Research Notes, Office of the Assistant Secretary for Policy Evaluation, U.S. Department of Health and Human Services, May 1995.

107. See *Congressional Quarterly Almanac* 44 (1988): 349. For regional variations, see *Statistical Abstract of the United States*, 110th ed. (Washington, D.C.: U.S. Bureau of the Census, 1990), 368.

108. *Congressional Quarterly Almanac* 43 (1987): 553.

109. Reischauer, "Welfare Reform Legislation," 31–35. See also Joel F. Handler, "The Transformation of Aid to Families with Dependent Children: The Family Support Act in Historical Context," *New York University Review of Law and Social Change* 16, no. 4 (Winter 1987–88): 457–534.

110. See Reischauer, "Welfare Reform Legislation," 28–29.

111. *Congressional Quarterly Almanac* 44 (1988): 364.

112. *Congressional Quarterly Almanac* 44 (1988): 360. At the time, only 6 percent of AFDC recipients were in AFDC-UP (for two-parent families), which was subject to the work requirement.

113. See, for example, Will Marshall, "Replacing Welfare with Work," Progressive Policy Institute, July 1994. PPI was a project of the Democratic Leadership Council. Marshall, PPI's founder and president, had served as the DLC policy director and was co-author of the book *Mandate for Change*. PPI reported that the Clinton presidential campaign drew extensively from the book.

114. Reischauer, "Welfare Reform Legislation," 28–29.

115. See Mead, *The New Politics of Poverty*, 129.
116. Cited in Hugh Heclo, "Poverty Politics," in Sheldon H. Danziger, Gary D. Sandefur, and Daniel H. Weinberg, eds., *Confronting Poverty* (Cambridge, Mass.: Harvard University Press, 1994), 405.
117. Cited in Heclo, "Poverty Politics," 402.
118. "Democratic Party Platform 1984," and "Democratic Party Platform 1988," in Woolley and Peters, *The American Presidency Project*.
119. Pierson, *Dismantling the Welfare State*, 215.
120. Cited in Heclo, "Poverty Politics," 416. For a fuller discussion of the Bush administration's waiver policies, see Teles, *Whose Welfare*, 130–34.
121. Heclo, "Poverty Politics," 412.
122. Many public assistance programs were cut significantly in the 1980s. One that grew was Medicaid: coverage expanded due to federal policy directives, although the expansion was almost entirely limited to children in poor families, rather than adults. See, for example, "Using Discontinuous Eligibility Rules to Identify the Effects of the Federal Medicaid Expansions on Low-Income Children," David Card and Lara D. Shore-Sheppard, *Review of Economics and Statistics* 86, no. 4 (August 2004): 752–66.
123. For O'Neill's comment on the bill, see "House Overwhelmingly OK's Tax Overhaul Bill," *Congressional Quarterly Weekly Report*, September 27, 1986, p. 2257. See also Toner, "Major Help."
124. President Eisenhower had sought and secured an increase as well, and Nixon signed one in 1974, after vetoing earlier increases passed by Congress. In 1977, President Carter and congressional liberals tried unsuccessfully to index the wage to inflation, a step that would have institutionalized the New Deal principle of a basic wage floor. "Minimum Wage," *Congressional Quarterly Researcher*, December 16, 2005, p. 1066.
125. Ellwood and Bane, *Welfare Realities*, 148–49.
126. Based on the legislative history, *Congressional Quarterly* noted in the mid-1980s that "the traditional target of minimum wage advocates . . . is a standard equal to roughly half of the average wage for non-supervisory private workers." *Congressional Quarterly Weekly Report*, March 7, 1987, p. 404. By 1989, the real value of the minimum wage reached its lowest point since 1956. Economic Policy Institute, Issue Guide, Minimum Wage, updated July 2, 2009, Figure A, http://www.epi.org/publication/tables_figures_data/. See also Gitterman, *Boosting Paychecks*, 67.
127. George E. Paulsen, *A Living Wage for the Forgotten Man* (Selingsgrove, Pa.: Susquehanna University Press, 1996), 94. Conservatives also objected to expanding the number of occupations covered by the wage, and to attempts to index it. "Minimum Wage," *Congressional Quarterly Researcher*, December 16, 2005, p. 1066.
128. Senate floor statement, March 25, 1987, upon the introduction of the Minimum Wage Restoration Act of 1987. "Raising the Minimum Wage," *Congressional Digest* 66, no. 8–9 (August–September 1987): 200. See also Representative George Miller, Letter to the Editor, *New York Times*, January 21, 1987.
129. "Minimum Wage Gets Maximum Attention," *Congressional Quarterly Weekly Report*, March 7, 1987, pp. 403–7; and Timothy B. Clark, "Raising the Floor," *National Journal* 19, no. 12 (March 21, 1987): 705; see also "Minimum Wage," *Congressional Quarterly Researcher*, December 16, 2005.
130. Clark, "Raising the Floor," 702.
131. See "Raising the Minimum Wage," *Congressional Digest* 66, no. 8–9 (August–September 1987): 224. The testimony was on June 10, 1987.
132. "Minimum Wage Gets Maximum Attention," *Congressional Quarterly Weekly Report*, March 7, 1987, p. 407. Conservatives also continued to make two familiar arguments against the minimum wage: first, that it would interfere in the contractual relationship between employer and employee; and second, that its cost would force employers to eliminate jobs.

133. Christopher Howard makes this argument persuasively in "Protean Lure for the Working Poor," *Studies in American Political Development* 9 (Fall 1995): 404–36.

134. See, for example, *Congress and the Nation* 8 (1989–1992): 611. Others proposed this tradeoff as well. The moderate Democratic case for the EITC as an alternative to a higher minimum wage or traditional welfare programs was set out by the Progressive Policy Institute. See Elaine Ciulla Kamarck and William A. Galston, "Putting Children First: A Progressive Family Policy for the 1990s," Progressive Policy Institute, September 27, 1990, 27. For a detailed analysis of the politics of the minimum wage fight and the role of the EITC within it, see "Paycheck Politics," *National Journal*, July 8, 1989, 1746–49.

135. For a concise statement of the argument that the minimum wage and the EITC are necessary complements, and that in the absence of an increased minimum wage, the EITC risks subsidizing the creation of low-wage jobs, see Barry Bluestone and Teresa Ghilarducci, "Making Work Pay: Wage Insurance for the Working Poor," Public Policy Brief, no. 28, Jerome Levy Economics Institute, Bard College, 1996.

136. "Conservative Coalition Forming: Bill to Boost Minimum Wage Faces Rough Sailing in House," *Congressional Quarterly Weekly Report*, April 16, 1988, p. 1012.

137. "Minimum-Wage Impasse Finally Ended," *Congressional Quarterly Almanac* 45 (1989): 333–40.

138. Republicans sought measures that softened the perception that they favored the wealthy during the tax battles of 1989 and 1990, and both congressional Democrats (led by Representative Downey) and President Bush proposed EITC increases in the context of battles over expanding federal childcare programs. *Congress and the Nation* 8 (1989–1992): 95. For a discussion of the childcare debates and how this fueled the EITC's expansion, see Howard, "Protean Lure," and "Family Fights," *National Journal*, June 6, 1990, 1333–37.

139. Oren M. Levin-Waldman, *The Case of the Minimum Wage: Competing Policy Models* (Albany: State University of New York Press, 2001), 128.

140. Lafer, *Job Training Charade*, 8.

141. Lafer, *Job Training Charade*, 15.

Chapter 6. The New South and the New Democrats

1. See, for example, R. Kent Weaver, *Ending Welfare as We Know It* (Washington, D.C.: Brookings Institution Press, 2000); Ann Marie Cammisa, *From Rhetoric to Reform?* (Boulder, Colo.: Westview, 1998); and Peter Edelman, "The Worst Thing Bill Clinton Has Done," *Atlantic Monthly*, March 1997, 43–58.

2. See, for example, Bruce Reed, Memorandum for the President, "What You've Achieved in Domestic Policy," November 29, 2000, William J. Clinton Presidential Library, Little Rock, Arkansas (hereafter WJCPL), Bruce Reed Files, Box 17, Folder 5.

3. See, for example, *Congressional Roll Call 1993, 103rd Congress, First Session* (Washington, D.C.: Congressional Quarterly, Inc., 1994): 22C–30C, for a discussion of changes in both parties in the context of socioeconomic developments in the South.

4. See Gavin Wright, *Old South, New South* (New York: Basic Books, 1986), particularly chapter 8; and James C. Cobb, *The Selling of the South*, 2nd ed. (Urbana: University of Illinois Press, 1993), particularly chapters 6 and 7.

5. Bruce J. Schulman, *From Cotton Belt to Sunbelt* (Durham, N.C.: Duke University Press, 1994), 219; see also *Halfway Home and a Long Way to Go: The Report of the 1986 Commission on the Future of the South* (Research Triangle Park, N.C.: Southern Growth Policies Board, 1986).

6. Schulman, *Cotton Belt to Sunbelt*, 156, and Cobb, *Selling of the South*, 94–96. For an extended discussion, see Cobb, particularly chapters 7 and 8.
7. Schulman, *Cotton Belt to Sunbelt*, 214.
8. Schulman, *Cotton Belt to Sunbelt*, 159, 214–16. See also Earl Black and Merle Black, *Politics and Society in the South* (Cambridge, Mass.: Harvard University Press, 1987), 314.
9. Cited in Dan Balz and Ronald Brownstein, *Storming the Gates: Protest Politics and the Republican Revival* (Boston: Little, Brown, 1996), 203.
10. Nicol C. Rae, *Southern Democrats* (New York: Oxford University Press, 1994), 90; and "Blue Dog Coalition Heydays," *Congressional Quarterly Weekly Report*, January 19, 1989, 112.
11. Cited in Rae, *Southern Democrats*, 72.
12. Cited in Rae, *Southern Democrats*, 72.
13. See the annual "Vote Studies: Conservative Coalition," published in *Congressional Roll Call* from 1957 to 1998, which chronicled the changing ideological and demographic profiles of the Southern contingent.
14. "Business progressivism" has a long history in the South; see, for example, Cobb's discussion of George Tindall's 1963 article, "Business Progressivism: Southern Politics in the Twenties," in *Selling of the South*, 3–4.
15. Black and Black, *Politics and Society in the South*, 296–97.
16. Sidney Blumenthal, *The Clinton Wars* (New York: Farrar, Straus and Giroux, 2003), 35.
17. See Schulman, *Cotton Belt to Sunbelt*, particularly chapters 7 and 8.
18. *Halfway Home*, 7.
19. Schulman, *Cotton Belt to Sunbelt*, 159.
20. *Halfway Home*, 7. See also Schulman, *Cotton Belt to Sunbelt*, 173.
21. Black and Black, *Politics and Society in the South*, 166–67.
22. *Halfway Home*, 7–8.
23. Schulman, *Cotton Belt to Sunbelt*, 217.
24. Schulman, *Cotton Belt to Sunbelt*, 211–12, writing about the case of North Carolina. See also Cobb, *Selling of the South*, chapter 5, "Too Busy to Hate."
25. Black and Black, *Politics and Society in the South*, 315.
26. Balz and Brownstein, *Storming the Gates*, 64–65.
27. For this and other typologies of Democratic Party factions in the 1980s and 1990s, see Balz and Brownstein, *Storming the Gates*, 65–66, and Rae, *Southern Democrats*, 20–23.
28. See, for example, "Private vs. Public Sector: Reagan and Mondale at Odds over Jobs, Unions, Pay Issues," *Congressional Quarterly Weekly Report*, October 13, 1984, p. 2652. See also Balz and Brownstein, *Storming the Gates*, 66–67.
29. Cited in John A. Farrell, *Tip O'Neill and the Democratic Century* (Boston: Little, Brown, 2001), 562. See also Thomas P. O'Neill, Jr., *Man of the House* (New York: Random House, 1987), 350, for O'Neill's reflections on efforts by Rep. David McCurdy (D-Okla.) to generate a candidate to oppose him as speaker.
30. Balz and Brownstein, *Storming the Gates*, 68. For another analysis of the shift, see Robert Kuttner, *The Life of the Party* (New York: Viking, 1988).
31. See William Galston and Elaine Ciulla Kamarck, "The Politics of Evasion: Democrats and the Presidency," Progressive Policy Institute, Washington, D.C., September 1989.
32. Balz and Brownstein, *Storming the Gates*, 69–71. See also Rae, *Southern Democrats*, 116; and Kenneth S. Baer, *Reinventing Democrats* (Lawrence: University Press of Kansas, 2000), 110.
33. Balz and Brownstein, *Storming the Gates*, 71.
34. See Will Marshall and Martin Schram, eds., *Mandate for Change* (New York: Berkley Books, 1993), ix; and Baer, *Reinventing Democrats*, 7.
35. Marshall and Schram, *Mandate for Change*, ix.
36. Baer, *Reinventing Democrats*, 82–83. See also Rae, *Southern Democrats*, 89, 113–14.

37. Cited in Baer, *Reinventing Democrats*, 82; see also 111. The number of DLC members is from Marshall and Schram, *Mandate for Change*, ix.

38. See, for example, Mark Schmitt, "When the Democratic Leadership Council Mattered," *American Prospect*, February 10, 2011.

39. Baer, *Reinventing Democrats*, 53–54. In the 1980 and 1984 elections, Democrats won the fewest congressional districts in the South to date in the modern era (78 and 82). Republicans won the most (43 and 47), and nearly matched Democrats in the Senate (11–14 and 12–14). *Congressional Directory* (Washington, D.C.: U.S. Government Printing Office, 1932–84).

40. Balz and Brownstein, *Storming the Gates*, 67. See also Earl Black and Merle Black, *The Rise of Southern Republicans* (Cambridge, Mass.: Harvard University Press, 2002), especially chapter 7, "Reagan's Realignment of White Southerners."

41. Stanley B. Greenberg, *Middle Class Dreams* (New York: Times Books, 1995), 203.

42. Greenberg, *Middle Class Dreams*, 203–5.

43. Baer, *Reinventing Democrats*, 111, 121.

44. Democratic Leadership Council (DLC), "New Orleans Declaration," statement endorsed at the Fourth Annual DLC Conference, March 1, 1990. DLC, "Key Document," www.dlc.org.

45. DLC, "New Orleans Declaration."

46. See, for example, Lyndon B. Johnson, "Annual Address to Congress on the State of the Union," January 4, 1965, in John T. Woolley and Gerhard Peters, eds., *The American Presidency Project* (Santa Barbara: University of California, 1999–), http://www.presidency.ucsb.edu.

47. DLC, "The New Democrat Credo," January 1, 2001, cited in Daniel DiSalvo, "The Death and Life of New Democrats," *The Forum* 6, no. 2 (2008): 5.

48. DLC, "New Orleans Declaration." See also Baer, *Reinventing Democrats*, 168–70.

49. See Galston and Kamarck, "Politics of Evasion," and William Galston, "Incomplete Victory: The Rise of the New Democrats," in Peter Berkowitz, ed., *Varieties of Progressivism in America* (Stanford, Calif.: Hoover Institution Press, 2004), 75.

50. William Galston and Elaine Kamarck, "Five Realities That Will Shape 21st Century Politics," in *Blueprint: Ideas for a New Century*, September 1998, cited in Baer, *Reinventing Democrats*, 257.

51. Galston, "Incomplete Victory," 74.

52. Galston and Kamarck, *Politics of Evasion*, 14, 2, 6. The authors argued that overcoming the exclusion of minorities from voting rights was "a continuing moral imperative of our time," 10. But the DLC's approach was criticized by some liberals for quietly reinscribing the racially-charged divide between the poor and the middle and working classes, particularly given existing social cleavages forged by the rhetoric and policies of the Reagan years.

53. Greenberg, *Middle Class Dreams*, vii, 36–37. See also Balz and Brownstein, *Storming the Gates*, 72.

54. Greenberg, *Middle Class Dreams*, 36–37.

55. This "racial sentiment," Greenberg concluded, "had disfigured white middle-class perceptions of the Democratic party, government, and the American Dream." Greenberg, *Middle Class Dreams*, 42, ix.

56. Greenberg, *Middle Class Dreams*, vii–ix.

57. Greenberg, *Middle Class Dreams*, 281–82.

58. Baer, *Reinventing Democrats*, 169, describing the views of Doug Ross.

59. Rae, *Southern Democrats*, 117–18. Reed served as a speechwriter for Senator Gore in the mid- to late 1980s. He was the issues director for the Clinton campaign of 1992, and later director of Clinton's Domestic Policy Council. From 2001 to 2010 he was president of the DLC.

60. Robert J. Shapiro, "Work and Poverty: A Progressive View of Minimum Wage, Earned Income Tax Credit," Public Policy Institute. The PPI paper made a strong case for relying instead on the Earned Income Tax Credit. See Baer, *Reinventing Democrats*, 139.

61. See James P. Ziliak, "Filling the Poverty Gap, Then and Now," Department of Economics and Center for Poverty Research, University of Kentucky, September 2003, Appendix Tables 2, 3, and 11, for detailed data on the Southern safety net, including program participation and spending over time.

62. For the DLC's approach to these issues, see, for example, "Beyond Affirmative Action," in the DLC magazine, *The New Democrat*, May 1, 1995.

63. Bill Clinton, "Address to the Democratic National Committee," Los Angeles, September 20, 1991. Cited in Greenberg, *Middle Class Dreams*, 212.

64. Cited in Baer, *Reinventing Democrats*, 163.

65. Baer, *Reinventing Democrats*, 195. The quote is from Paul Starobin, "An Affair to Remember," *National Journal*, January 16, 1993, 120.

66. Cited in Baer, *Reinventing Democrats*, 164.

67. Theda Skocpol, *Boomerang: Clinton's Health Security Effort and the Turn Against Government in U.S. Politics* (New York: W. W. Norton, 1996), 24–25, 28.

68. James T. Patterson, *America's Struggle Against Poverty in the Twentieth Century* (Cambridge, Mass.: Harvard University Press, 2000), 218–22.

69. Cited in Skocpol, *Boomerang*, 37.

70. Governor Bill Clinton and Senator Al Gore, *Putting People First: How We Can All Change America* (New York: Times Books, 1992), 6–7.

71. Clinton and Gore, *Putting People First*, 15, 165.

72. Clinton and Gore, *Putting People First*, 179. See also Edelman, "Worst Thing," 44.

73. Balz and Brownstein, *Storming the Gates*, 76.

74. Balz and Brownstein, *Storming the Gates*, 76.

75. Clinton faced sustained challenges only from neoliberal Paul Tsongas and former California governor Jerry Brown.

76. Cited in John B. Judas and Ruy A. Teixeira, *The Emerging Democratic Majority* (New York: Scribner, 2002), 29.

77. Balz and Brownstein, *Storming the Gates*, 77–78.

78. See Rae, *Southern Democrats*, 129, and Balz and Brownstein, *Storming the Gates*, 101. Among Democrats in the newly-elected House, Southerners were outnumbered nearly two to one (173–85).

Chapter 7. Showdown and Settlement

1. See White House, Office of Management and Budget (OMB), *Vision of Change for America*, February 17, 1993, 1, for how campaign themes were expressed in policy proposals.

2. Reed served on the White House Domestic Policy Council; William Galston worked as deputy assistant to the president for domestic policy in the first Clinton administration. Elaine Kamarck served as Gore's top domestic policy adviser. Stanley Greenberg continued to serve as a pollster and political adviser to the president. From and Marshall did not join the administration, but they remained involved in welfare reform, including in working with congressional allies to shape the debate.

3. "Address by the President to the Democratic National Convention," United Center, Chicago, Illinois, August 29, 1996.

4. For components of Clinton's long-term investment plan, see OMB, *Vision of Change*, 135–38. Clinton's health security initiative, had it succeeded, also would have improved conditions facing the working poor.

5. George Hager, "Key Democrats Seek Jobs Plan as Early Clinton Priority," *Congressional Quarterly Weekly Report*, January 30, 1993, 212–13.

6. OMB, *Vision of Change*, 21.

7. Samuel Rosenberg, *American Economic Development Since 1945* (New York: Palgrave Macmillan, 2003), 281–83.

8. OMB, *Vision of Change*, 10.

9. Robert B. Reich, *Locked in the Cabinet* (New York: Knopf, 1997), 63. Leon Panetta headed the Office of Management and Budget; Alice Rivlin was his deputy.

10. Governor Bill Clinton and Senator Al Gore, *Putting People First: How We Can All Change America* (New York: Times Books, 1992), 177.

11. Rosenberg, *American Economic Development*, 281–83. DLC analysts later applauded the president for "reject[ing] traditional fiscal stimulus in favor of restraint and deficit reduction." William Galston, "Incomplete Victory," in Peter Berkowitz, ed., *Varieties of Progressivism in America* (Stanford, Calif.: Hoover Institution Press, 2004), 79.

12. Greenspan, Reich wrote, "haunts every budget meeting, though his name never comes up directly" (Reich, *Locked in the Cabinet*, 64).

13. Robert Reich, Memorandum to the President, "The Underlying Moral Question this Election Year," cited in *Locked in the Cabinet*, 292–93.

14. The "investments embedded in the proposal," Reich lamented, "are afterthoughts." Reich, *Locked in the Cabinet*, 64, 71. For Harkin's concerns about splitting the package, see *Congressional Quarterly Weekly Report*, February 20, 1993, p. 365.

15. *Congressional Quarterly Weekly Report*, April 24, 1993, pp. 1001–3.

16. Rosenberg, *American Economic Development*, 283.

17. See Margaret Weir, "Wages and Jobs: What Is the Public Role?" in Margaret Weir, ed., *The Social Divide: Political Parties and the Future of Activist Government* (Washington, D.C.: Brookings Institution Press, 1998), 268–311; and Alan Brinkley, "Liberals and Public Investment: Recovering a Lost Legacy," *American Prospect*, March 21, 1993.

18. Reich, "Working Principles," *American Prospect*, November 1, 2000. An August 1993 memo from Reich to Clinton was leaked to the *Wall Street Journal*, provoking an outpouring of conservative opposition. Clinton subsequently told Reich that he intended to delay the minimum wage fight until after passing health care legislation. He worried that a proposed hike "now would be a lightning rod for conservatives." Reich, *Locked in the Cabinet*, 122.

19. See James R. Storey, "The Earned Income Tax Credit," Congressional Research Service, December 5, 1996, 9–11; and "Excerpts from Clinton's News Conference in the Rose Garden," *New York Times*, May 15, 1993.

20. *Congressional Quarterly Weekly Report*, June 26, 1993, p. 1636.

21. See "Tax Policy," *Congress and the Nation* 9 (1993–96): 83–93.

22. U.S. Congress, House, Committee on Ways and Means, *1998 Greenbook: Background Material and Data on Programs Within the Jurisdiction of the Committee on Ways and Means*, 105th Cong., 2nd sess., May 19, 1998, 411, 872.

23. Reich, *Locked in the Cabinet*, 194–95, 226–27. Robert Rubin replaced Bentsen as Treasury secretary in December 1994.

24. Reich, *Locked in the Cabinet*, 237. See also Todd Purdum, "President Will Seek a Higher Minimum Wage, Senior Aides Say," *New York Times*, January 24, 1995. Clinton aides characterized the proposed increase in part as an incentive for welfare recipients to work.

25. Robert Marshall Wells and Karen Foerstel, "Clinton Proposes Increase in Minimum Wage," *Congressional Quarterly Weekly Report*, February 4, 1995, p. 371.

26. See U.S. Department of Labor, Office of the Chief Economist, "Making Work Pay: The Case for Raising the Minimum Wage," March 1996.

27. Reich, *Locked in the Cabinet*, 239–40.

28. For the administration's response to the DLC, see U.S. Department of Labor, "Making Work Pay," March 1996.

29. See U.S. Congress, Joint Economic Committee, *Hearing: Evidence Against a Higher Minimum Wage*, 104th Cong., 1st sess., pt. 1, February 22, 1995, as well as the "Hearing Excerpt" statement by Vice Chairman Jim Saxton (R-N.J.).

30. See Oren M. Levin-Waldman, *The Case of the Minimum Wage: Competing Policy Models* (Albany: State University of New York Press, 2001), 131. See also Jerold Waltman, *The Politics of the Minimum Wage* (Champaign: University of Illinois Press, 2000), 89, 102.

31. Reich, *Locked in the Cabinet*, 237.

32. See Reich, *Locked in the Cabinet*, 317.

33. See, for example, Richard W. Stevenson, "Clinton Signs a Bill Raising Minimum Wage by 90 Cents," *New York Times*, August 21, 1996.

34. U.S. Department of Labor, "Making Work Pay," and U.S. Census Bureau, "Poverty Thresholds 1997."

35. For an analysis of the EITC's limits, see Anne E. Alstott, "Why the EITC Doesn't Make Work Pay," *Law and Contemporary Problems* 73 (Winter 2010): 284–313.

36. Bruce Reed, Memorandum for the President, "The Politics of Welfare Reform," May 30, 1994, William J. Clinton Presidential Library, Little Rock, Ark. (hereafter WJCPL), Bruce Reed Files, Box 21, Folder 6, 5.

37. The 1988 platform, for example, called for "an indexed minimum wage that can help lift and keep families out of poverty." "Democratic Party Platform 1988," in John T. Woolley and Gerhard Peters, eds., *The American Presidency Project* (Santa Barbara: University of California, 1999–), http://www.presidency.ucsb.edu/platforms.php.

38. See David T. Ellwood, draft letter to Senator Moynihan, January 31, 1994, WJCPL, Bruce Reed Files, Box 13, Folder 8; and David T. Ellwood, Mary Jo Bane, and Wendell Primus, "Memorandum for Bruce Reed," written for a meeting in May 1993, WJCPL, Bruce Reed Files, Box 20, Folder 6. A liberal reform plan premised on making the FSA work was introduced by Representative Robert Matsui (D-Calif.). Ronald Brownstein, "Latest Welfare Reform Plan Reflects Liberals' Priorities," *Los Angeles Times*, May 20, 1994.

39. Dan Balz and Ronald Brownstein, *Storming the Gates: Protest Politics and the Republican Revival* (Boston: Little, Brown, 1996), 90.

40. Balz and Brownstein, *Storming the Gates*, 91. See also David T. Ellwood to President William Jefferson Clinton, Confidential, November 14, 1995, WJCPL, Bruce Reed Files, Box 19, Folder 7, page 1.

41. See Balz and Brownstein, *Storming the Gates*, 90. Liberal objections were on display at an August 1993 hearing; see *Congressional Quarterly Almanac* 49 (1993): 374.

42. See Morton Kondracke, *Roll Call*, February 24, 1994. See also Balz and Brownstein, *Storming the Gates*, 266–68; and Kathleen M. Shaw et al., *Putting Poor People to Work* (New York: Russell Sage Foundation, 2006), 27–29.

43. Charles Murray, "The Coming White Underclass," *Wall Street Journal*, October 29, 1993. For the administration's internal reaction to Murray and others, see Bruce Reed, Memorandum for Mack McLarty, "William Bennett Article on Ending Welfare for Out-of-Wedlock-Births," February 6, 1994; see also Memorandum for the President, "Welfare Reform and Senator Moynihan," December 13, 1993, WJCPL, Bruce Reed Files, Box 16, Folder 7.

44. "Republican Party Platform," 1932–88, in Woolley and Peters, *American Presidency Project*.

45. For a discussion of the debates within the Republican Party, see Ron Haskins, *Work over Welfare* (Washington, D.C.: Brookings Institution Press, 2006).

46. Talent's plan to "deny all AFDC and food stamp benefits to unwed mothers under age 21 and to their children" was introduced in the Senate as well, by Lauch Faircloth (R-N.C.). *Congressional Quarterly Almanac* 50 (1994): 364. Reed argued that with Republicans "at war with one another," Clinton had a new opportunity to "dominate the debate" by focusing on "work and

responsibility." See Reed, "Politics of Welfare Reform," 1, 4; and Joe Goode and Stan Greenberg, "Memorandum to The Welfare Reform Group, RE: Welfare Reform—Priorities and Funding," May 20, 1994, WJCPL, Bruce Reed Files, Memos to the President, OA 18943, Box 21, Folder 6.

47. *Congressional Quarterly* noted that Clinton "galvanized public opinion on the issue during his 1992 presidential campaign, pushing both parties to the right with his centrist ideas. Then, by playing down welfare reform during his first two years in office, he created a political vacuum that Republicans are now exploiting." "GOP Welfare Plan: Self-Help and Leave It to the States," *Congressional Quarterly Weekly Report,* February 25, 1995, p. 613. For a discussion of the political positioning on welfare reform, see R. Kent Weaver, *Ending Welfare as We Know It* (Washington, D.C.: Brookings Institution Press, 2000), particularly chapters 9 to 12.

48. House Ways and Means Committee, *1998 Greenbook*, 465. See also Robin Rogers-Dillon, *The Welfare Experiments: Politics and Policy Evaluation* (Stanford, Calif.: Stanford Law and Politics, 2004), 153; and Shelly Arsenault, "Welfare Policy Innovation and Diffusion: Section 1115 Waivers and the Federal System," *State and Local Government Review* 32, no. 1 (2000): 49–60.

49. Cited in Rogers-Dillon, *Welfare Experiments*, 11.

50. Cited in Michael B. Katz, *In the Shadow of the Poorhouse* (New York: Basic Books, 1996), 311. The White House political staff also focused on the waiver issue. See, for example, Georgia Governor Zell Miller, "Memorandum to Rahm Emanuel, Assistant to the President and Director of Political Affairs," June 14, 1993; and Rahm Emanuel, "Memorandum for Carol Rosco," June 16, 1993, WJCPL, Bruce Reed Files, Box 13, Folder 4. Reed and Emanuel developed extensive plans for using waivers as part of the legislative and communications effort on welfare reform. See Rahm Emanuel and Bruce Reed, Memorandum for the Chief of Staff, "Welfare Reform Strategy," March 30, 1995, WJCPL, Bruce Reed Files, Box 21, Folder 3.

51. Rogers-Dillon, *Welfare Experiments*, 6–7, 20; Katz, *In the Shadow*, 311.

52. "Technical Report: Explaining the Decline of Welfare Receipt, 1993–1996," Council of Economic Advisors, May 9, 1997, 1, 4–5.

53. Peter Edelman, "The Worst Thing Bill Clinton Has Done," *Atlantic Monthly*, March 1997, 44.

54. Rosenberg, *American Economic Development*, 284–85.

55. Cited in Reich, *Locked in the Cabinet*, 155–56.

56. See "Welfare Reform Meeting, OEOB, Room 324, April 14, 1993," WJCPL, Bruce Reed Files, Box 20, Folder 5. Getting agreement, even among the group's co-chairs, was sometimes difficult. See Reed's notes on a meeting at HHS, November 12, 1993, that he titles "Welfare Hell." WJCPL, Bruce Reed Files, Box 26, Folder 5.

57. Liberals objected to the two-year time limit and to a provision that allowed states to restrict benefits to recipients who had additional children. Senator Robert Dole (R-Kans.) called the Clinton plan "the end of welfare reform as we know it." "Welfare Reform Takes a Back Seat," *Congressional Quarterly Almanac* 50 (1994): 364–65.

58. Reich, *Locked in the Cabinet*, xv; and Edelman, "Worst Thing," 44.

59. See the testimony by Donna E. Shalala, Secretary of Health and Human Services, U.S. Congress, House, Committee on Ways and Means, *Hearings: Welfare Reform Proposals*, 103rd Cong., 2nd sess., pt. 1, July and August 1994, 30–34.

60. Some of Clinton's liberal allies were uneasy about the administration's early statements: "Getting poor people into jobs and keeping them there is the goal, not simply cutting them off from welfare. But the campaign phrase has taken on a life of its own, and I don't have a good feeling about where that life might end." Reich, *Locked in the Cabinet,* 156.

61. Will Marshall, Ed Kilgore, and Lyn A. Hogan, "Work First: A Proposal to Replace Welfare with an Employment System," Progressive Policy Institute, March 2, 1995.

62. See "Mainstream Forms Task Force; Cites Goals for Welfare Reform," press release, Mainstream Forum, October 20, 1993, and letter to Clinton, signed by seventy-seven U.S.

representatives, dated October 19, 1993. WJCPL, Bruce Reed Files, Box 17, Folder 3. See also Bruce Reed, Memorandum for the President, "Welfare Reform Damage Control," February 17, 1994, Box 21, Folder 7; and Memorandum for Christine Varney, "McCurdy and Welfare Reform," October 20, 1993, Box 17, Folder 3.

63. See Rahm Emanuel and Bruce Reed, Memorandum for Leon Panetta, "Welfare Reform Strategy," December 2, 1994, on how to "take back the initiative" on welfare after the 1994 elections. WJCPL, Bruce Reed Files, Box 37, Folder 6.

64. *Congressional Directory* (Washington, D.C.: U.S. Government Printing Office, 1954–96).

65. Balz and Brownstein, *Storming the Gates*, 203.

66. Balz and Brownstein, *Storming the Gates*, 207–8. See also Peter Applebome, "The 1994 Elections: The South; The Rising G.O.P. Tide Overwhelms the Democratic Levees in the South," *New York Times*, November 11, 1994.

67. In the nearly sixty years since the Social Security Act, Southerners had chaired the House Ways and Means Committee in thirty-six years, and the Senate Finance Committee in forty-nine. In 1995, the Finance Committee was chaired by Robert Packwood (R-Ore.), then William Roth (R-Del.). *Congressional Directory*, 1930–96. See also Balz and Brownstein, *Storming the Gates*, 204–5.

68. Rosenberg, *American Economic Development*, 286.

69. "GOP Welfare Plan: Self-Help, and Leave It to the States," *Congressional Quarterly Weekly Report*, February 25, 1995, pp. 613–18.

70. *Congressional Quarterly Weekly Report*, September 23, 1995. See also *Congress and the Nation* 9 (1993–96): 87–88.

71. See Baer, *Reinventing Democrats*, 9. The administration defended spending in areas like job training and education as a way to prepare people to meet their own economic needs. Balz and Brownstein, *Storming the Gates*, 351. For the case for "militant centrism," see Rahm Emanuel, Don Baer, and Bruce Reed, Memorandum for the Chief of Staff, "Defining a Centrist Presidency," October 20, 1994. WJCPL, Bruce Reed Files, Box 17, Folder 3.

72. This was clearly a priority for Southern Republicans such as Armey and Gingrich, who pushed the approach in the Contract with America and in legislation in 1995. Southern Democratic support for devolution and defense of state discretion dated to the New Deal and earlier.

73. U.S. Department of Health and Human Services, Administration for Children and Families, Office of Family Assistance, "Characteristics and Financial Circumstances of AFDC Recipients FY 1995," Table 34.

74. In nine states in the South, the average credit received was above the national average as well. Internal Revenue Service, *Sources of Income Bulletin* 14, no. 4 (1996): 106–58.

75. William G. Whittaker, "The Fair Labor Standards Act: Continuing Issues in the Debate," Congressional Research Service, CRS Report for Congress, May 28, 2008, p. 26.

76. Balz and Brownstein, *Storming the Gates*, 288–89. See also "Inside Congress: Republican Contract," *Congressional Quarterly Weekly Report*, February 25, 1995, pp. 580–85.

77. *Congressional Quarterly Weekly Report*, February 25, 1995, pp. 613–18.

78. *Congressional Quarterly Weekly Report*, February 25, 1995, pp. 613–18; March 25, 1995, pp. 872–75. For the conservative view that policy should prioritize inducing behavioral changes among welfare recipients over granting additional flexibility to the states, see Robert Rector, "Implementing Welfare Reform and Restoring Marriage," in Stuart M. Butler and Kim Holmes, eds., *Priorities for the President* (Washington, D.C.: The Heritage Foundation, 2001), 4.

79. "Long and Dole Announce Welfare Reform Bill," press release, Office of Senator Long, June 20, 1979, Russell B. Long Collection, Louisiana State University, Baton Rouge, Louisiana, Box 625, Folder 18.

80. The time limits idea had originated in part with David Ellwood years earlier. He had suggested that long-term welfare reliance could be tackled through a combination of work supports

and job guarantees with a time limit on assistance. Ellwood urged Clinton to reject the Republican version of time limits in 1995. See David T. Ellwood to President William J. Clinton, Confidential, November 14, 1995, WJCPL, Bruce Reed Files, Box 19, Folder 7, page 3.

81. Balz and Brownstein, *Storming the Gates*, 288.

82. *Congressional Quarterly Weekly Report*, March 25, 1995, pp. 872–75. Several Republican governors supported the House legislation but complained about the block grant allocations and federal mandates. See letters sent by Ohio Governor George Voinovich to Majority Leader Dole (March 27, 1995), and by Illinois Governor Jim Edgar (March 16, 1995) and New Jersey Governor Christine Todd Whitman (March 17, 1995) to Speaker Gingrich. WJCPL, Bruce Reed Files, Box 13, Folder 7.

83. Jeffrey Katz, "House Passes Welfare Bill," *Congressional Quarterly Weekly Report*, March 25, 1995, p. 872.

84. Only one Republican (Representative Connie Morella of Maryland) opposed final passage. Katz, "House Passes Welfare Bill," 872. Representative Deal, sponsor of the Democratic alternative, switched to the Republican Party later in the spring.

85. "Welfare Bill Clears Under Veto Threat," *Congressional Quarterly Almanac* 51 (1995): 7-35 to 7-52.

86. David T. Ellwood, "Memorandum," to Bruce Reed, Subject: Presidential Letter, March 20, 1995, WJCPL, Bruce Reed Files, Box 33, File 4.

87. Fax marked "To: Rahm," from the Department of Health and Human Services/Assistant Secretary for Planning and Evaluation/Human Services Policy (DHHS/ASPE/HSP), May 9, 1995, WJCPL, Bruce Reed Files, Box 14, Folder 8.

88. Clinton saw the recommendation and noted his agreement on the copy returned to Reed. Bruce Reed and Rahm Emanuel, "Memorandum for the President: Welfare Reform Update," May 26, 1995, WJCPL, Bruce Reed Files, Memos to the President, OA 18943, Box 21, Folder 3, 1.

89. See Donna E. Shalala, Memorandum for the President, "Block Granting Income Security Programs," January 10, 1995, WJCPL, Bruce Reed Files, Box 31, Folder 5.

90. Edelman, "Worst Thing," 45. See Edelman for a more detailed analysis of Clinton's strategic options and choices.

91. See "Welfare Bill Clears Under Veto Threat," *Congressional Quarterly Almanac* 51 (1995): 7-35 to 7-52; and Edelman, "Worst Thing," 45.

92. "Most Democrats voted for it reluctantly," *Congressional Quarterly Almanac* reported. "Welfare Bill Clears Under Veto Threat," *Congressional Quarterly Almanac* 51 (1995): 7-48.

93. As late as June, Republicans were still pursuing a strategy of linking welfare and Medicaid, in order to force a Clinton veto. See "Committee Gives Partisan Vote to Welfare, Medicaid Plans," *Congressional Quarterly Weekly Report*, June 19, 1996, p. 1877.

94. Edelman, "Worst Thing," 46.

95. Edelman, "Worst Thing," 46; Richard S. Morris, *Behind the Oval Office* (New York: Random House, 1997), 297. See also "GOP's New Welfare Strategy Has Democrats Reassessing," *Congressional Quarterly Weekly Report*, July 13, 1996, pp. 1969–70.

96. Trent Lott, *Herding Cats: A Life in Politics* (New York: Regan Books, 2005), 124.

97. Lott, *Herding Cats*, 131.

98. Lott, *Herding Cats*, 131–35.

99. Lott, *Herding Cats*, 135. Despite the negotiations, Lott said he never quite knew where Clinton stood on the welfare reform legislation, and whether that would change. "Today he says he'll sign it," Lott reported. "I don't know what his position will be tomorrow." See "Conferees May Determine Fate of Overhaul Bill," *Congressional Quarterly Weekly Report*, July 20, 1996, p. 2050.

100. Lott, *Herding Cats*, 136–38.

101. "GOP's New Welfare Strategy," *Congressional Quarterly Weekly Report*, July 13, 1996, p. 1969.

102. "Talking Points, Welfare Reform Meeting, June 6, 1996," WJCPL, Bruce Reed Files, Box 19, Folder 3.

103. The administration set out its position on the House and Senate bills in its "Statement of Administration Policy" letters from Jacob J. Lew, Acting OMB Director, to House Rules Committee Chairman Gerald Solomon (R-N.Y.) on July 16, 1996, and Senate Budget Committee Chairman Pete Domenici (R-N. Mex.) on July 18, 1996. WJCPL, Bruce Reed Files, Box 19, Folder 2. Policies providing vouchers to children whose parents had exceeded time limits had already been adopted in Louisiana to accompany the state's two-year time limit. See fax from Senator John Breaux (D-La.) to Bruce Reed with July 1996 *Times Picayune* article on the Louisiana law, and note to Reed: "Seems like [Louisiana] has already done a lot of what POTUS' bill does!" John Breaux to Bruce Reed, July 24, 1996, WJCPL, Bruce Reed Files, Box 19, Folder 3.

104. Cited in Morris, *Behind the Oval Office*, 301.

105. Morris, *Behind the Oval Office*, 302.

106. George Stephanopoulos, *All Too Human* (Boston: Little, Brown, 1999), 420.

107. Todd S. Purdum, "Clinton Recalls His Promise, Weighs History, and Decides," *New York Times*, August 1, 1996. See also John F. Harris and John E. Yang, "Clinton to Sign Bill Overhauling Welfare," *Washington Post*, August 1, 1996.

108. Purdum, "Clinton Recalls His Promise." See also Reich, *Locked in the Cabinet*, 320–21.

109. Robert Pear, "Millions Affected: After the President Acts, More in Party Back Measure in House," *New York Times*, August 1, 1996. More than three times as many House Democrats voted for the conference report—after Clinton signaled his support—as had voted for the House measure earlier in the month.

110. "After 60 Years, Most Control Is Passing to the States," *Congressional Quarterly Weekly Report*, August 3, 1996, p. 2196. See also *Congressional Quarterly Almanac* 52 (1996): 6-3 to 6-24. The Dole campaign quote is from *New York Times*, August 23, 1996.

111. Morris, *Behind the Oval Office*, 300.

112. Edelman, "Worst Thing," 44; see also Reich, *Locked in the Cabinet*, 321.

113. Sidney Blumenthal, *The Clinton Wars* (New York: Farrar, Straus and Giroux: 2003), 146.

114. Edelman, "Worst Thing," 46.

115. On Clinton's approach to welfare as governor, see Bill Clinton, *My Life* (New York: Alfred A. Knopf, 2004), 329–30.

116. Cited in Rogers-Dillon, *Welfare Experiments*, 149.

117. Stephanopoulos, *All Too Human*, 420.

118. See Barbara Vobejda and Judith Havemann, "Two HHS Officials Quit over Welfare Changes," *Washington Post*, September 12, 1996. See also E. J. Dionne, Jr., "Resigning on Principle...," *Washington Post*, September 17, 1996; and "Acts of Principle," *New York Times*, Opinion section, September 13, 1996.

119. For a comparison of TANF (as amended in 1997) with AFDC, see Vee Burke, "New Welfare Law: Comparison of New Block Grant Program with Aid to Families with Dependent Children," Congressional Research Service, CRS Report for Congress, 96–720, EPW, updated October 7, 1997, research.policyarchive.org/315.pdf.

120. See "Welfare Overhaul: After 60 Years, Most Control Sent to States," *Congressional Quarterly Almanac* 52 (1996): 6-3 to 6-24.

121. See *Congress and the Nation* 9 (1997–2001): 486–90.

122. See Gordon Lafer, *The Job Training Charade* (Ithaca, N.Y.: Cornell University Press, 2002), 196. For discussion of the "human capital development" model, see Shaw et al., *Putting Poor People to Work*, 22–25. On the defining features of work-first programs, see Will Marshall, "Replacing Welfare with Work," Policy Briefing, Progressive Policy Institute, Washington, D.C., July 1994, 8. On how some state officials were driven to this approach in part by fiscal realities and evolving federal expectations, see Jamie Peck, *Workfare States* (New York: Guilford Press, 2001), 187.

123. The trend reached beyond welfare recipients to a broader population of low-wage and other employees by the late 1990s. See Shaw et al., *Putting Poor People to Work*, particularly chapter 3 (on work-first dynamics in welfare reform, including state caseload reduction incentives) and chapters 5 and 6 (on broader workforce development programs).

124. Will Marshall, "Replacing Welfare with Work," 4–5. Program results compiled by other analysts showed that programs providing genuine education and skills building delivered more promising outcomes: participants in such programs earned relatively higher wages than those who were simply assisted with job referrals or other work-first services. For those who completed at least the equivalent of a year's postsecondary education through college or other credentialing programs, the improvements in income were particularly striking. See Shaw et al., *Putting Poor People to Work*, 5–6. On congressional revisions to JTPA to prohibit short-term job-readiness exercises rather than serious skills training, see Lafer, *Job Training Charade*, 196; and Susan Kellam, "Parties Hope Job Training Bill Will Spin Political Gold," *Congressional Quarterly Weekly Report*, May 16, 1992, p. 1334.

125. Cited in Peck, *Workfare States*, 193. See also "Comments on Draft Discussion Paper by Working Group on Welfare Reform, Family Support and Independence," Memo from Larry Mead to Mary Jo Bane, David Ellwood, Bruce Reed, January 24, 1994, WJCPL, Bruce Reed Files, Box 56, Folder 8.

126. Lawrence M. Mead, *Beyond Entitlement* (New York: Free Press, 1986), 64–65. See also Shaw et al., *Putting Poor People to Work*, 28.

127. Will Marshall, "Replacing Welfare With Work," 10.

128. Lafer, *Job Training Charade*, 196. Shaw et al., *Putting Poor People to Work*, also examines the policy shift in training programs to meet the presumed needs of employers in their discussion of the Workforce Investment Act.

129. See, for example, Rosenberg, *American Economic Development*, 309–11. Mangum, Mangum, and Sum report that low-wage workers in the United States experience less mobility than their counterparts in most advanced industrial countries, typically remaining in the low-wage sector five years longer than workers in Germany, France, Italy, the United Kingdom, Denmark, and Sweden. Garth L. Mangum, Stephen L. Mangum, and Andrew M. Sum, *The Persistence of Poverty in the United States* (Baltimore: Johns Hopkins University Press, 2003), 50–51.

130. Lafer, *Job Training Charade*, 197–98.

Chapter 8. The New World of Workfare

1. U.S. Department of Labor, Bureau of Labor Statistics (BLS), "Seasonally Adjusted Unemployment Rate," http://data.bls.gov/cgi-bin/surveymost?ln; U.S. Bureau of Economic Analysis, "Percentage Change from Preceding Period in Real Gross Domestic Product," http://www.bea.gov/iTable/index_nipa.cfm.

2. See, for example, David E. Rosenbaum, "Clinton Promises to Protect Middle Class on Taxes," *New York Times*, October 31, 1992; and R. A. Zaldivar, "In Debate over Middle-Class Policies, Definition Becomes Key," *Philadelphia Inquirer*, January 15, 1995.

3. Bruce Reed, Memorandum for the President, "What You've Achieved in Domestic Policy," November 29, 2000, William J. Clinton Presidential Library, Little Rock, Ark. (hereafter WJCPL), Bruce Reed Files, Box 17, Folder 5.

4. Steven Greenhouse, "Will the Safety Net Catch Economy's Casualties," *New York Times*, Week in Review section, November 16, 2008.

5. "Address by the President to the Democratic National Convention," United Center, Chicago, Illinois, August 29, 1996. See also Robert B. Reich, *Locked in the Cabinet* (New York: Knopf,

1997), 326; and "News Conference: Clinton Says Welfare Bill Is 'Real Step Forward,'" *Congressional Quarterly Almanac* 52 (1996): D17-D19.

6. Governor Bill Clinton and Senator Al Gore, *Putting People First* (New York: Times Books, 1992), 165.

7. Steven M. Gillon, *The Pact* (New York: Oxford University Press, 2008), 192. See also Trent Lott, *Herding Cats* (New York: HarperCollins, 2005), 143.

8. Reich, *Locked in the Cabinet*, 347.

9. Michael Waldman, *POTUS Speaks* (New York: Simon and Schuster, 2000), 180.

10. Todd S. Purdum, "Ickes, Longtime Clinton Ally, to Quit as No. 2 Chief of Staff," *New York Times*, November 12, 1996; Ickes was the son of FDR's interior secretary. Rahm Emanuel and Bruce Reed, already on staff, were promoted to leading political and policy positions.

11. Sidney Blumenthal, *The Clinton Wars* (New York: Farrar, Straus and Giroux, 2003), 237; see also Elizabeth Drew, *Whatever It Takes* (New York: Viking, 1997), 257.

12. Gillon, *The Pact*, 194, 197. See also Lott, *Herding Cats*, 143.

13. Drew, *Whatever It Takes*, 143.

14. Gillon, *The Pact*, 196; see also Blumenthal, *Clinton Wars*, 269.

15. Lott, *Herding Cats*, 143.

16. "Provisions: What the Budget Bill Does," *Congressional Quarterly Weekly Report*, December 13, 1997, pp. 3082–91; and "Provisions: Inside the Tax-Cutting Bill," *Congressional Quarterly Weekly Report*, September 27, 1997, pp. 2331–38. Among other tax credits, the education initiatives included a new HOPE tuition tax credit.

17. Jeffrey L. Katz, "Reconciliation: Panel's Democrats Lose Efforts to Change Welfare Proposal," *Congressional Quarterly Weekly Report*, June 14, 1997, p. 1373; and "What the Budget Bill Does," *Congressional Quarterly Weekly Report*, December 13, 1997, pp. 3082–91. SSI eligibility for some legal immigrants already in the country and eligible for assistance was restored in the final version of the legislation, and time-limited eligibility for food stamps was restored for some legal immigrants in subsequent years. Liberals also wanted to restore greater public assistance eligibility for legal immigrants, and to rewrite the rules on work requirements to allow more welfare recipients to pursue an education in lieu of other work-related activity; they were not successful in incorporating these provisions.

18. The spending cut bill passed the House by 270–162 on June 25, 1997; the tax cut bill passed 253–179 on June 26, 1997.

19. Al From, "The Balanced Budget Deal: Critical for the Country, Crucial for Our Party," *DLC Update*, May 6, 1997.

20. Waldman, *POTUS Speaks*, 182.

21. David Espo, "Gephardt Calls for Policy Changes," Associated Press, December 3, 1997; see also Richard L. Berke, "Gephardt Criticizes Politics of Small Ideas, White House Fumes," *New York Times*, December 3, 1997.

22. BLS, "Seasonally Adjusted Unemployment Rate." See also Lawrence Mishel, Josh Bivens, Elise Gould, and Heidi Shierholz, *The State of Working America*, 12th ed. (Ithaca, N.Y.: Cornell University Press, 2012), 29.

23. See Thomas Gabe, "Welfare, Work, and Poverty Status of Female-Headed Families with Children: 1987–2011," Congressional Research Service, CRS Report for Congress, January 9, 2013, 23.

24. Bill Clinton, "Remarks at Midwestern Technology Corporation of St. Louis in St. Louis, Missouri," *Weekly Compilation of Presidential Documents* 33, no. 33 (1997): 1229–32. For Clinton's equally positive assessment of the reform a decade later, see Bill Clinton, "How We Ended Welfare, Together," *New York Times*, August 22, 2006.

25. Waldman, *POTUS Speaks*, 188; see also Blumenthal, *Clinton Wars*, 312.

26. Waldman, *POTUS Speaks*, 188.

27. Blumenthal, *Clinton Wars*, 312–13.

28. This description is based on the accounts of two participants in the discussions, Waldman and Blumenthal. See also Reich's exchange with Clinton on these issues, Reich, *Locked in the Cabinet*, 347.

29. See Richard S. Morris, *Behind the Oval Office* (New York: Random House, 1997), 301–2.

30. Gillon, *The Pact*, 213–14.

31. Gillon, *The Pact*, 218–19.

32. For details on Clinton's plan, elaborated in spring 1999, see *Saving Social Security Now and Meeting America's Challenges for the 21st Century*, http://clinton2.nara.gov/WH/SOTU99/sss.html. Many conservatives as well as liberals viewed Clinton's plans for individual accounts as "partial privatization." See, for example, Michael D. Tanner, "Clinton Wanted Social Security Privatized," Cato Institute Commentary, July 13, 2001.

33. Gillon, *The Pact*, 224.

34. Glenn Kessler and Eric Pianin, "The Budget's Brick Wall; Spending Hikes, Tax Cuts Collide with Social Security," *Washington Post*, April 7, 2000.

35. In early 1998, estimates of the ten-year surplus were between $660 billion and $1.1 trillion. By mid-2000, the ten-year estimate had risen to $4.19 trillion ($1.87 trillion excluding Social Security funds). See Clay Chandler and John M. Berry, "What to Do with a Surplus," *Washington Post*, March 17, 1998; and John F. Harris and Eric Pianin, "Surplus Estimate Is Doubled; Clinton Offers GOP Deal to End 'Logjam,'" *Washington Post*, June 27, 2000. Clinton's budget request for 2000 "asked for $213 billion in new spending over five years," yet Clinton "wrapped himself in the cloak of fiscal discipline by insisting that most of the projected surplus—about $827 billion over the next five years—be dedicated to buying down the debt." *Congress and the Nation* 10 (1997–2001): 36, 72.

36. *Congressional Quarterly Weekly Report*, March 23, 2000, 643–46.

37. See comments by Jeff Faux, cited in Kessler and Pianin, "The Budget's Brick Wall."

38. Martin Feldstein, "Social Security Reform and Fiscal Policy in the Clinton Administration," remarks prepared for Harvard University Conference, "Economic Policy in the 1990s," June 29, 2001, http://www.nber.org/feldstein/amecpol90.html.

39. Bureau of Labor Statistics, "Seasonally Adjusted Unemployment Rate," "Number Unemployed for 15 Weeks and Longer," and "Median Weeks Unemployed," http://data.bls.gov/cgi-bin/surveymost?ln.

40. U.S. Census Bureau, "Historical Poverty Tables—People," Table 2, https://www.census.gov/hhes/www/poverty/data/historical/people.html.

41. U.S. Census Bureau, "Historical Poverty Tables—People," Table 3.

42. Jared Bernstein and Jeff Chapman, "Falling Through the Safety Net," Economic Policy Institute, April 17, 2003, 4–6.

43. See, for example, Peter Edelman, *Searching for America's Heart* (Boston: Houghton Mifflin, 2001), 146; and Gabe, "Welfare, Work, and Poverty Status," 22.

44. David Nather, "Welfare's Next Overhaul," *Congressional Quarterly Weekly Report*, March 17, 2001, 585.

45. Anjetta McQueen, "Economic Downturn May Thwart Welfare Bill Aiming to Reduce Poverty as Lawmakers Lean Toward Status Quo," *Congressional Quarterly Weekly Report*, January 26, 2002, p. 248.

46. Anjetta McQueen, "Proposals to Adjust Welfare System Will Hew Closely to the Center," *Congressional Quarterly Weekly Report*, February 2, 2002, p. 301.

47. Liberals and moderates pushed for a $6 billion funding increase in childcare supports for working welfare recipients over five years, but conservatives held the line at $1 billion. For details, see "Welfare Reauthorization: Overview of the Issues," Congressional Research Service, CRS Issue Brief for Congress, July 1, 2005, https://opencrs.com/document/IB10140/2005-07-01;

and "TANF Grants Extended Through 2010," *Congressional Quarterly Almanac* 61 (2005): 10-7 to 10-8.

48. Clea Benson, "States Scramble to Adapt to New Welfare Rules," *Congressional Quarterly Weekly Report,* June 25, 2007, pp. 1907–8.

49. See, for example, Ann Lordeman, "The Workforce Investment Act," Congressional Research Service, March 2, 2006, http://assets.opencrs.com/rpts/RS22396_20060302.pdf.

50. The increase barely restored the purchasing power lost since the last increase ten years earlier. See Lawrence Mishel, "Declining Value of the Federal Minimum Wage Is a Major Factor Driving Inequality," Economic Policy Institute, February 21, 2013, 2, http://www.epi.org/publication/declining-federal-minimum-wage-inequality.

51. Bush's proposal to allow individuals to divert a portion of their Social Security taxes into individual retirement accounts never made headway in Congress. *Congress and the Nation* 12 (2005–8): 862.

52. *Congress and the Nation* 10 (1997–2001): 23–24.

53. *Congressional Quarterly Almanac* 64 (2008): B-8. Pelosi became speaker in 2003.

54. In the 1992 elections, Democrats won 62 percent of the House seats from the South; in 2008, they won 44 percent of those seats; by 2012 it was just 27.5 percent—less than one-third the level of the 1950s and early 1960s. *Congressional Quarterly Almanac* 65 (2009): A-3, and author's calculations.

55. See Robert Dreyfuss, "How the DLC Does It," *American Prospect,* December 19, 2001; and Michael Lind, "Obama: Last of the 'New Democrats'?" *Salon.com,* October 30, 2012, http://www.salon.com/2012/10/30/obama_last_of_the_new_democrats.

56. David Nather, "Democrats on a Mission to the Middle," *Congressional Quarterly Weekly Report,* December 4, 2006, p. 3224.

57. Dreyfuss, "How the DLC Does It."

58. Ed Kilgore, "Requiem for the DLC," *New Republic,* February 9, 2011.

59. Martin Dupuis and Keith Boeckelman, *Barack Obama: The New Face of American Politics* (Westport, Conn.: Praeger, 2008), 99–100.

60. Barack Obama, *The Audacity of Hope* (New York: Crown, 2006), 176–88.

61. Obama, *Audacity of Hope,* 178.

62. See Andrea Louise Campbell, "Paying America's Way," in Theda Skocpol and Lawrence R. Jacobs, eds., *Reaching for a New New Deal* (New York: Russell Sage Foundation, 2011), 388, 390. Cited in Richard C. Fording and Joseph L. Smith, "Barack Obama's 'Fight' to End Poverty: Rhetoric and Reality," *Social Science Quarterly* 93, no. 5 (2012): 1161. See also Obama for President, *Change We Can Believe In* (New York: Three Rivers Press, 2008), 198; and Kathleen Hennessey, "Obama Emphasizes New Aspects of Life Story," *Los Angeles Times,* April 24, 2012.

64. Jeffrey Jones, "Americans Hopeful Obama Can Accomplish Most Key Goals," *Gallup.com,* November 12, 2008, http://www.gallup.com/poll/111853/americans-hopeful-obama-can-accomplish-most-key-goals.aspx. See also the discussion in Fording and Smith, "Barack Obama's 'Fight,'" 1180.

65. John Cranford, "Renegotiating Social Contracts," *Congressional Quarterly Weekly Report,* January 19, 2009, p. 118.

66. *Congressional Quarterly Almanac* 65 (2009): 3.

67. For a discussion of the role of race in Obama's approach to poverty issues, see Fording and Smith, "Barack Obama's 'Fight,'" 1178.

68. Cited in Dupuis and Boeckelman, *Barack Obama,* 114. Later in the same interview (with *The American Prospect*), Obama said, "I share all the aims of Paul Wellstone or Ted Kennedy ... but I'm more agnostic, much more flexible on how we achieve those ends."

69. Cited in Michael Grunwald, *The New New Deal: The Hidden Story of Change in the Obama Era* (New York: Simon and Schuster, 2012), 32.

70. Obama for President, *Change We Can Believe In*, 56.
71. Obama, *Audacity of Hope*, 156–57.
72. Obama for President, *Change We Can Believe In*, 38–39.
73. Obama, *Audacity of Hope*, 157–58. As an Illinois state senator, Obama said: "I am not a defender of the status quo with respect to welfare. Having said that, I probably would not have supported the federal legislation, because I think it had some problems. But I'm a strong believer in making lemonade out of lemons." State of Illinois, 90th General Assembly, Senate Transcript, May 31, 1997, 42.
74. On the politics of the Affordable Care Act, including the role of moderate and conservative Democrats in eliminating the "public option" provision backed by liberals, see, for example, Kimberly J. Morgan and Andrea Louise Campbell, *The Delegated Welfare State* (New York: Oxford University Press, 2011), 227–35; Lawrence R. Jacobs and Theda Skocpol, *Health Care Reform and American Politics* (New York: Oxford University Press, 2012), particularly chapters 1 to 4; and Paul Starr, *Remedy and Reaction: The Peculiar American Struggle over Health Care Reform* (New Haven: Yale University Press, 2013), particularly chapters 6, 7, and 9.
75. The question of *why* the Obama administration failed to seize this opportunity remains a subject of debate. Likely factors included his commitment to fiscal restraint, his decision to devote extensive political capital to major health care reform, and the obstructionist strategies of congressional Republicans. For analysis of the limits and possibilities of policy change under Obama, see Lawrence R. Jacobs and Desmond S. King, "Varieties of Obamaism: Structure, Agency, and the Obama Presidency," *Perspectives on Politics* 8, no. 3 (September 2010): 793–802; and Theda Skocpol, *Obama and America's Political Future* (Cambridge, Mass.: Harvard University Press, 2012).
76. Grunwald, *New New Deal*, 101–2. Lew later became secretary of the Treasury when Geithner departed; Sperling and Furman also moved up, into positions vacated by Summers and Romer.
77. See Alan S. Blinder and Mark Zandi, "How the Great Recession Was Brought to an End," July 27, 2010, https://www.economy.com/mark-zandi/documents/end-of-great-recession.pdf. They estimated that emergency fiscal and monetary measures added 8.4 million jobs to the American economy by 2010. See also Congressional Budget Office, *Estimated Impact of the American Recovery and Reinvestment Act on Employment and Economic Output from October 2012 to December 2012*, February 2013, 1, http://www.cbo.gov/publication/43945.
78. Grunwald, *New New Deal*, 7.
79. Cited in Ron Suskin, *Confidence Men* (New York: HarperCollins, 2011), 154.
80. Suskin, *Confidence Men*, 154. See, for example, Paul Krugman, "Franklin Delano Obama?" *New York Times*, November 8, 2008: "My advice to the Obama people is to figure out how much help they think the economy needs, then add 50 percent."
81. Ryan Lizza, "The Obama Memos," *New Yorker*, January 30, 2012. See also Grunwald, *New New Deal*, 110–12.
82. Blinder and Zandi estimated that tax cuts may be half as effective as spending in terms of stimulus. See Blinder and Zandi, "How the Great Recession Was Brought to an End," 16. For the Congressional Budget Office estimates of the multiplier effect associated with specific tax cuts or spending increases in the Recovery Act, see Congressional Budget Office, "Estimated Impact of the American Recovery and Reinvestment Act," 6.
83. Jonathan Alter, *The Promise* (New York: Simon and Schuster, 2010), 116–17.
84. Urban-Brookings Tax Policy Center, *Tax Stimulus Report Card: Conference Bill,* February 13, 2009, 2, http://www.taxpolicycenter.org/UploadedPDF/411839_conference_reportcard.pdf.
85. Alter, *Promise*, 84–85.
86. Grunwald, *New New Deal*, 64.

87. Cited in Grunwald, *New New Deal*, 95; see also 83.

88. See, for example, Skocpol, *Obama and America's Political Future*, 20, on the implications for the act's effectiveness.

89. Grunwald, *New New Deal*, 97–98.

90. Grunwald, *New New Deal*, 133. For a discussion of how these policy areas related to Obama's long-term reform agenda, see Grunwald's chapter 2, "The Four Pillars." Obama's agenda for economic reform included ending the Bush tax cuts, and pursuing targeted investments to maintain U.S. competitiveness, but no major labor market reforms (Grunwald, *New New Deal*, 51–56.) See also Office of the Press Secretary, The White House, *Remarks of President Barack Obama, Address to Joint Session of Congress*, February 24, 2009.

91. The stimulus would include temporary spending for some of Obama's campaign pledges. See Campbell, "Paying America's Way," 395.

92. Grunwald, *New New Deal*, 333.

93. Romer later wrote, "I desperately wish we'd been able to design a public employment program that would have directly hired many unemployed workers, especially young people." Christina Romer, "The Fiscal Stimulus, Flawed but Valuable," *New York Times*, October 20, 2012. See also Alter, *Promise*, 86; and Grunwald, *New New Deal*, 122–23.

94. See Congressional Budget Office, "Estimated Impact of the American Recovery and Reinvestment Act," 3.

95. See, for example, Adam Nagourney, "Bracing for a Backlash over Wall Street Bailouts," *New York Times*, March 15, 2009.

96. Arloc Sherman, "Poverty and Financial Distress Would Have Been Substantially Worse in 2010 Without Government Action, New Census Data Show," Center on Budget and Policy Priorities, November 7, 2011, 4, http://www.cbpp.org/cms/?fa=view&id=3610.

97. The Recovery Act provisions for the EITC, the Child Tax Credit, unemployment benefits, TANF, the Supplemental Nutrition Assistance Program (food stamps), child care for low-income families, Head Start, and public housing totaled $95.7 billion. (This does not include the measure's temporary increase in Medicaid reimbursements to the states, estimated at $86.6 billion.) "Tax Cuts and Spending Increases in the Conference Agreement," *Congressional Quarterly Weekly Report*, February 16, 2009, pp. 354–55. For other assessments of the act's poverty-reduction components, see Sherloc, "Poverty and Financial Distress," and Kristin S. Seefeldt and John D. Graham, *America's Poor and the Great Recession* (Bloomington: Indiana University Press, 2013), particularly 85–90.

98. States used $1.3 billion of this for TANF-related subsidized employment programs, a tenfold increase in spending. About half of those employed were adults placed in year-round positions, and half were youth (up to age twenty-four), in year-round or summer employment positions. Mary Farrell, Sam Elkin, Joseph Broadus, and Dan Bloom, *Subsidizing Employment Opportunities for Low-Income Families: A Review of State Employment Programs Created Through the TANF Emergency Fund*, Office of Planning, Research, and Evaluation, Administration for Children and Families, U.S. Department of Health and Human Services, OPRE Report 2011-38 (2011), ES-6, http://www.mdrc.org/publication/subsidizing-employment-opportunities-low-income-families.

99. See Office of Management and Budget, *A New Era of Responsibility: Renewing America's Promise* (Washington, D.C.: U.S. Government Printing Office, 2009); http://www.whitehouse.gov/sites/default/files/omb/assets/fy2010_new_era/A_New_Era_of_Responsibility2.pdf. The budget also called for making permanent the Making Work Pay tax credit.

100. "Conference Agreement," *Congressional Quarterly Weekly Report*, February 16, 2009, 354–55.

101. Sherman, "Poverty and Financial Distress." The study uses a poverty measure recommended by the National Academy of Sciences (and increasingly used by researchers as well as government officials). Among other differences with the official poverty measure, it incorporates the effects of in-kind assistance and refundable tax credits on poverty levels.

102. National Employment Law Project, "Modernizing Unemployment Insurance: Federal Incentives Pave the Way for State Reforms," May 2012, http://nelp.3cdn.net/a77bc3b5988571ee4b_dfm6btygh.pdf. Many of the reforms built on proposals made by the congressionally-mandated Advisory Council on Unemployment Compensation of the mid-1990s.

103. See John J. Topoleski, "Trade Adjustment Assistance for Workers (TAA) and Reemployment Trade Adjustment Assistance (RTAA)," Congressional Research Service, September 24, 2010, http://digitalcommons.ilr.cornell.edu/cgi/viewcontent.cgi?article=1624&context=key_workplace.

104. Studies have suggested that more than twenty million government and nonmanufacturing (service) workers are in occupations that can be offshored (three times as many as are in offshorable manufacturing positions). Yet in fiscal year 2011, a modest 98,000 workers were certified for TAA benefits, and 66 percent of these were from traditional manufacturing occupations. U.S. Department of Labor, "Trade Adjustment Assistance for Workers, Fiscal Year 2011 Report to the Committee on Finance of the Senate and Committee on Ways and Means of the House of Representatives," 7–8, http://www.doleta.gov/tradeact/docs/AnnualReport11.pdf.

105. See David H. Bradley and Ann Lordeman, "Funding for Workforce Development in the American Recovery and Reinvestment Act (ARRA) of 2009," Congressional Research Service, February 19, 2009, http://assets.opencrs.com/rpts/R40182_20090219.pdf.

106. Neil Ridley and Evelyn Ganzglass, "Responding to the Great Recession: How the Recovery Act Boosted Training and Innovation in Three States," Center for Law and Social Policy, February 2011, 1–4, http://www.clasp.org/resources-and-publications/files/Responding-to-the-Great-Recession-ARRA-and-WIA-2011.pdf.

107. Skocpol, *Obama and America's Political Future*, 161.

108. Suzanne Mettler, "Obama and the Challenge of Submerged Policies," 131, in Skocpol, *Obama and America's Political Future*. See also Suzanne Mettler, *The Submerged State* (Chicago: University of Chicago Press, 2011).

109. See Fording and Smith, "Barack Obama's 'Fight,'" 1179.

110. Alter, *Promise*, 131. Public opinion polls continued to express skepticism toward antipoverty programs in the aftermath of the recession. Asked to identify the single most important cause of poverty, a plurality (24 percent) said "too much government welfare that prevents initiative." This was followed by "lack of job opportunities" (18 percent), "lack of good educational opportunities" (13 percent), and "breakdown of families" (13 percent). Erin McClam, "Many Americans Blame 'Government Welfare' for Persistent Poverty, Poll Finds," *NBCNews.com*, June 6, 2013, http://www.nbcnews.com/feature/in-plain-sight/many-americans-blame-government-welfare-persistent-poverty-poll-finds-v18802216.

111. For some provisions, the below-the-radar policy design had an economic rationale. Economists argued that dispersing the Making Work Pay tax credit across a year's worth of weekly paychecks—rather than in a single, more visible payment—would increase the likelihood that the money would be spent rather than saved, creating a greater stimulus effect. See, for example, Mettler, *Submerged State*, 48–49.

112. Romer, "Fiscal Stimulus."

113. Mettler, "Submerged Policies," 135.

114. Mettler, "Submerged Policies," 142.

115. Cited in Grunwald, *New New Deal*, 297. See also U.S. Bureau of Economic Analysis, "Percentage Change from Preceding Period in Real Gross Domestic Product."

116. BLS, "Seasonally Adjusted Unemployment Rate."

117. Projected to extend health care coverage to twenty-five million uninsured Americans, the Affordable Care Act signed in March 2010 included provisions aimed at increasing coverage among low- and middle-income non-elderly Americans. For a description of the ACA, see

"Summary of the Affordable Care Act," Henry J. Kaiser Family Foundation, April 23, 2013, http://kff.org/health-reform/fact-sheet/summary-of-the-affordable-care-act/. For estimates on coverage and costs of its provisions, see "Effects on Health Insurance and the Federal Budget for the Insurance Provisions in the Affordable Care Act—May 2013 Baseline," Congressional Budget Office, May 14, 2013. A 2012 Supreme Court ruling that the ACA's Medicaid expansion was optional for the states meant that fewer people than expected would be covered. A significant number of working-poor Americans (in states opting not to expand Medicaid) were likely to find themselves in a coverage gap—unable to qualify for Medicaid coverage under their existing state rules because their earnings are too high (or for other reasons), but unable to qualify for subsidized premiums in the law's new health insurance exchanges because their earnings are too low. See, for example, Virginia Young, "For People in the Gap, Health Insurance Exchange Won't Help," *St. Louis Post-Dispatch,* August 24, 2013.

118. See Campbell, "Paying America's Way," 401; and Skocpol, *Obama and America's Political Future,* 58. See also Theda Skocpol and Vanessa Williamson, *The Tea Party and the Remaking of American Conservatism* (New York: Oxford University Press, 2012). While policymakers focused increasingly on the debt in 2009 and 2010, public opinion polls indicated that nearly three times as many people rated unemployment as the nation's top concern, and equal numbers expressed support for increased spending to spur growth as for cutting spending to reduce the deficit (47 percent each). "Deficit Concerns Rise, but Solutions Are Elusive," Pew Research Center, March 10, 2010, http://www.pewresearch.org/2010/03/10/deficit-concerns-rise-but-solutions-are-elusive.

119. Grunwald, *New New Deal,* 331–37. The Works Progress Administration was created in 1935 and provided employment to more than eight million people before it ended in 1943.

120. Grunwald, *New New Deal,* 334–35.

121. Pelosi lost thirty-eight Democrats on the vote, but prevailed 217–212. "House Passes $154 Billion Jobs Bill," *Congressional Quarterly Almanac* 65 (2009): 7–11. See also Robert Kuttner, *Debtors' Prison* (New York: Alfred A. Knopf, 2013), 63.

122. The White House, Office of the Press Secretary, "Remarks by the President in State of the Union Address," January 27, 2010. See also Kuttner, *Debtors' Prison,* 65–66.

123. John McArdle, "GOP Makes Record Gains in Recapturing a Majority," *Congressional Quarterly Weekly Report,* November 8, 2010, pp. 2547–51.

124. Skocpol, *Obama and America's Political Future,* 5.

125. See Richard E. Cohen and Joseph J. Schatz, "Jobs Plan Faces GOP Resistance," *Congressional Quarterly Weekly Report,* September 19, 2011, pp. 1930–32.

126. See John Irons, "Testimony before the Congressional Progressive Caucus, Ad Hoc Hearing on Job Creation," Economic Policy Institute, November 17, 2011, http://www.epi.org/publication/testimony-congressional-progressive-caucus.

127. Jonathan Alter, *The Center Holds* (New York: Simon and Schuster, 2013), 164.

128. See, for example, Matt Bai, "Obama vs. Boehner: Who Killed the Debt Deal?" *New York Times,* March 28, 2012; and Kuttner, *Debtors' Prison,* 65–66.

129. Paul Krugman, *End This Depression Now* (New York: W. W. Norton, 2012), 143.

130. The effectiveness of the bully pulpit (and Obama's use of it) remains a subject of scholarly debate; see, for example, Larry M. Bartels, "A New Deal Fantasy Meets Old Political Realities," and Theda Skocpol, "Making Sense of America's Political Maelstrom," in Skocpol, *Obama and America's Political Future.* See also Lawrence R. Jacobs, "The Public Presidency and Disciplinary Presumptions," *Presidential Studies Quarterly* 43, no. 1 (March 2013): 16–34.

131. Skocpol, *Obama and America's Political Future,* 36–37. Although the administration released a report defending its record on aiding poor and middle-class families and its proposed jobs program, these arguments rarely entered the larger public debate on the economy and social policy. See The White House, *Creating Pathways to Opportunity,* October 2011, http://www

.whitehouse.gov/sites/default/files/revised_creating_pathways_to_opportunity_report_10_14_11.pdf.

132. "Transcript: Ryan's Response to State of the Union," *CNN.com*, January 26, 2011, http://www.cnn.com/2011/politics/01/25/sotu.response.ryan; see also Alter, *Center Holds*, 314.

133. See, for example, U.S. Congress, House, Committee on Oversight and Government Reform, *The Stimulus: Two Years Later, Hearing Before the Subcommittee on Regulatory Affairs, Stimulus Oversight and Government Spending*, 112th Cong., 1st sess., February 16, 2011.

134. The budget also included $2 trillion in high-end tax cuts for individuals and businesses. Carl Hulse, "House Approves Republican Budget Plan," *New York Times*, April 15, 2011; see also U.S. Congress, House, Budget Committee, "Summary of the Fiscal Year 2012 Budget Resolution," April 5, 2011, http://budget.house.gov/uploadedfiles/keyfactssummary.pdf.

135. In the assessment of the *New York Times* editorial board, Gingrich "made racial resentment an integral part of his platform as a conservative challenger to Mitt Romney." "Preaching Division in South Carolina," *New York Times*, Opinion section, January 17, 2012.

136. Cited in Alter, *Center Holds*, 188.

137. Jonathan Weisman, "House Passes GOP Budget Plan, Mostly Along Party Lines," *New York Times*, March 29, 2012; also cited in Alter, *Center Holds*, 317.

138. The White House, Office of the Press Secretary, "Remarks by the President at the Democratic National Convention," September 7, 2012.

139. Alter, *Center Holds*, 323.

140. See "Full Transcript of the Mitt Romney Secret Video," *MotherJones.com*, September 19, 2012, http://www.motherjones.com/politics/2012/09/full-transcript-mitt-romney-secret-video.

141. Alter, *Center Holds*, 316.

142. Alter, *Center Holds*, 316.

143. See, for example, Molly Ball, "Blue Dogs Are Dwindling," *NationalJournal.com*, November 16, 2012, http://www.nationaljournal.com/congress-legacy/blue-dogs-are-dwindling-20121116; and Mike Lillis, "New Dems Hope to be a Force in 113th Congress," *The Hill*, November 17, 2012.

144. See "Ryan Plan Gets 69 Percent of Its Budget Cuts from Programs for People With Low or Moderate Incomes," Center on Budget and Policy Priorities, April 8, 2014; Theodore Schleifer, "G.O.P. Congressman's Plan to Fight Poverty Shifts Efforts to States," *New York Times*, July 25, 2014; and Jackie Calmes, "Obama Budget Opens Rift for Democrats on Social Benefits," *New York Times*, April 10, 2013. For Obama's actions, see Eduardo Porter, "Inequality in America: The Data Is Sobering," *New York Times*, July 30, 2013; and The White House, Office of the Press Secretary, "Remarks by the President on Economic Mobility," December 4, 2013, "Remarks by the President on the Economy," July 24, 2013 (Knox College), and "President Barack Obama's State of the Union Address," January 28, 2014.

145. See, for example, Michael D. Shear, "After Push by Obama, Minimum-Wage Action Is Moving to the States," *New York Times*, April 3, 2014; and "The What-Might-Have-Been Budget," Opinion section, *New York Times*, March 4, 2014. Stymied in Congress, the administration took a number of smaller steps through executive action, which included raising the minimum wage for some federal contractors to $10.10, and a series of initiatives to address the challenges of the long-term unemployed. (See The White House, Office of the Press Secretary, "Executive Order—Minimum Wage for Contractors," February 12, 2014; and "NELP Applauds Administration Effort to Boost Hiring of Long-Term Unemployed," National Employment Law Project, October 15, 2014.) On the support of some congressional Republicans (such as Paul Ryan) for increasing the EITC, see Schleifer, "G.O.P. Congressman's Plan," *New York Times*, July 25, 2014.

146. BLS, "Seasonally Adjusted Unemployment Rate." See also Mishel et al., *State of Working America*, 29.

147. Total EITC recipients rose from 12.5 million in 1990 to 19.3 million in 2000; federal spending on the credit rose from $7.5 billion to $32.3 billion. U.S. Congress, House, Committee on Ways and Means, *2004 Greenbook: Background Material and Data on Programs within the Jurisdiction of the Committee on Ways and Means*, Section 13, 41.

148. By the mid-1990s, these expenditures approached $50 billion annually, a tenfold increase from the mid-1980s. Roughly half of this increase was driven by the growth of the EITC; expansions of Medicaid were the second largest contributor. David T. Ellwood, "Anti-Poverty Policies for Families in the Next Century: From Welfare to Work—and Worries," *Journal of Economic Perspectives* 14, no. 1 (Winter 2000): 189.

149. Carmen DeNavas-Walt, Bernadette D. Proctor, and Jessica C. Smith for the U.S. Census Bureau, *Income, Poverty, and Health Insurance Coverage in the United States: 2010*, Current Population Reports, P60-239 (Washington, D.C.: U.S. Government Printing Office, 2011), 4. The share of the population experiencing poverty for at least two months in 2009, 23.1 percent, was more than one and a half times the official poverty rate for that year (14.3 percent).

150. Figure 4 and Table 6 in DeNavas-Walt et al., *Income, Poverty, and Health Insurance Coverage in the United States: 2010*, 14, 19.

151. "Older, Suburban and Struggling, 'Near Poor' Startle the Census," *New York Times*, November 18, 2011.

152. "The Low-Wage Recovery and Growing Inequality," National Employment Law Project, data brief, August 2012, 1, http://nelp.3cdn.net/8ee4a46a37c86939c0_qjm6bkhe0.pdf.

153. Catherine Rampell, "Part-Time Work Becomes Full-Time Wait for Better Job," *New York Times*, April 19, 2013.

154. "Family Net Worth Drops to Level of Early '90s, Fed Says," *New York Times*, June 11, 2012.

155. Mishel et al., *State of Working America*, 71.

156. David Cay Johnston, "When the Cupboard Is Bare," *New York Times*, November 11, 2008; Trymaine Lee, "Families with Children in City Shelters Soar to Record Levels," *New York Times*, December 23, 2008. See also Michael Cooper, "Deep Recession Sharply Altered U.S. Jobless Map," *New York Times*, September 26, 2011.

157. Sherman, "Poverty and Financial Distress," 4.

158. Expansions of the EITC and Child Tax Credit were extremely modest compared with program expansions in the late 1990s and were not permanent; increases in SNAP (food stamp) benefits were also short-lived. Expansions in unemployment insurance and Medicaid coverage in the stimulus bill and Affordable Care Act were dependent on action by the states, and many states, particularly in the South, opted not to enact them or to do so in extremely limited ways. A minimum wage increase (to $7.25 per hour in mid-2009, the third installment of a 2007 law) provided a slight earnings boost for those at the bottom of the wage scale.

159. BLS, "Worker Displacement: 2007–2009," August 26, 2010, http://www.bls.gov/news.release/archives/disp_08262010.pdf.

160. Standardized eligibility and federal funding offered the capacity for a quick expansion of assistance during the downturn, and the effective delivery of those additional resources to a high percentage of eligible individuals and families. Federal funding streams proved particularly advantageous at a time when many state-led and -financed programs were threatened by state budget crises. See, for example, Peter Katel, "Straining the Safety Net," *Congressional Quarterly Researcher*, July 2009, 660.

161. U.S. Census Bureau, PowerPoint presentation for press conference on release of DeNavas-Walt et al., *Income, Poverty and Health Insurance Coverage in the United States: 2010*, September 13, 2011, 25, https://www.census.gov/newsroom/releases/pdf/2010_Report.pdf.

162. Carmen DeNavas-Walt, Bernadette D. Proctor, and Jessica C. Smith, for the U.S. Census Bureau, *Income, Poverty, and Health Insurance Coverage in the United States: 2009*, Current Population Reports, P260-238 (Washington, D.C.: U.S. Government Printing Office, 2010), 62, Table B.

See also "A Lost Decade: Poverty and Income Trends Paint a Bleak Picture for Working Families," Economic Policy Institute, September 16, 2010, Figure C, http://www.epi.org/publication/lost-decade-poverty-income-trends-continue. The poverty rate for working-age Americans reached 12.9 percent in 2009, the highest level since these numbers were first tracked in 1966.

163. "Forced to Early Social Security, Unemployed Pay a Steep Price," *New York Times,* June 9, 2012.

164. Kristin Seefeldt, Gordon Abner, Joe A. Bolinger, Lanlan Xu, and John D. Graham, "At Risk: America's Poor During and After the Great Recession," White Paper, School of Public and Environmental Affairs, Indiana University, Bloomington, 2012, 22–23.

165. Sherman, "Poverty and Financial Distress," 4. Jason DeParle and Robert M. Gebeloff, "The Safety Net: Living on Nothing but Food Stamps," *New York Times,* January 3, 2010. Federal spending for food stamps reached $78 billion in 2011. Congressional Budget Office, "The Supplemental Nutrition Assistance Program," April 2012, http://www.cbo.gov/sites/default/files/cbofiles/attachments/04-19-SNAP.pdf.

166. See, for example, Ellyn Ferguson, "Who Needs Food Aid?" *Congressional Quarterly Weekly Report,* October 15, 2012, pp. 2059–61. In the SNAP program, states are given some discretion to determine how assets such as a vehicle are valued in determining whether a household qualifies for aid.

167. See Seefeldt, "At Risk," 21, on the growth of the program; and Sherman, "Poverty and Financial Distress," 4, on poverty reduction effects.

168. See Katel, "Straining the Safety Net," 649; Josh Bivens, "Historically Small Share of Jobless People are Receiving Unemployment Insurance," Economic Policy Institute, September 25, 2014; and Dionne Searcey and Jonathan Weisman, "Hiring Surges; Jobless Rate Falls to 5.9%," *New York Times,* October 4, 2014.

169. In 2010, for example, only 7.2 percent of EITC benefits for working families with two children went to those in deep poverty (with incomes under 50 percent of the poverty line—about $11,000). Internal Revenue Service, *Statistics of Income,* 2009, http://www.irs.gov/pub/irs-soi/09sprbul.pdf.

170. EITC recipients and payments actually declined in the recession years of 1980 and 1981, expanded in the 1990 recession, and barely budged in the recession year 2001. See Internal Revenue Service, *Statistics of Income,* various years; and House, Committee on Ways and Means, *2004 Greenbook,* Section 13, 41.

171. Internal Revenue Service, *Statistics of Income,* 2008–2010; DeNavas-Walt et al., *Income, Poverty and Health Insurance Coverage: 2009,* 56, Table B-1; and Sherman, "Poverty and Financial Distress," 4.

172. From 2007 to 2008 (the first full year of the recession), the number of TANF recipients actually dropped to a historic low for TANF (from 3.96 million to 3.78 million). U.S. Department of Health and Human Services, Administration for Children and Families, Archives, "Caseload Data, 2000–2008," updated April 3, 2010, http://archive.acf.hhs.gov/programs/ofa/data-reports/caseload/caseload_recent.html. Nationally, the TANF caseload rose a modest 16 percent from the start of the recession at the end of 2007 through December 2010, then began to fall again, despite continued high rates of unemployment and poverty. LaDonna Pavetti, Ife Finch, and Liz Schott, "TANF Emerging from the Downturn a Weaker Safety Net," Center on Budget and Policy Priorities, March 1, 2013, 3, http://www.cbpp.org/cms/index.cfm?fa=view&id=3378.

173. Some 68 percent of poor families with children received AFDC/TANF aid in 1996; by 2010 only 27 percent did. Danilo Trisi and LaDonna Pavetti, "TANF Weakening as a Safety Net for Poor Families," Center on Budget and Policy Priorities, March 13, 2012, http://www.cbpp.org/cms/?fa=view&id=3700. See also "Chart Book: TANF at 18," Center on Budget and Policy Priorities, revised August 22, 2014, and "Temporary Assistance for Needy Families: Fewer Eligible

Families Have Received Cash Assistance Since the 1990s, and the Recession's Impact on Caseloads Varies by State," U.S. Government Accountability Office, GAO-10-164, February 23, 2010, http://www.gao.gov/products/GAO-10-164.

174. This follows a long-term trend of declining benefits in AFDC: from 1970 to 1996, average benefits fell by 20 percent overall in real terms (and by more than 40 percent in two-thirds of the states). Ife Finch and Liz Schott, "The Value of TANF Cash Benefits Continued to Erode in 2012," Center on Budget and Policy Priorities, March 28, 2013, 1, 3, and 7, http://www.cbpp.org/cms/?fa=view&id=3943.

175. Keith Gunnar Bentele, "Evaluating the Performance of the U.S. Social Safety Net in the Great Recession," Center for Social Policy, University of Massachusetts–Boston, Paper 62, April 2012, 7.

176. Bentele, "Evaluating the Performance," 3, 9.

177. Jeongsoo Kim, Shelley K. Irving, and Tracy A. Loveless, "Dynamics of Economic Well-Being: Participation in Government Programs, 2004 to 2007 and 2009: Who Gets Assistance?" *Current Population Reports*, P70-131, U.S. Census Bureau, Washington, D.C., July 2012, p. 2, http://www.census.gov/prod/2012pubs/p70-130.pdf. In addition to public assistance, many of these families also benefited from the Child Tax Credit, which went into effect in 1998, was increased (to a credit maximum of $1,000) in 2001, and was made partly refundable (to make lower earners eligible) in 2003. The 2009 Recovery Act temporarily extended that eligibility to even lower earners.

178. Kathleen Short, "The Supplemental Poverty Measure: 2013," U.S. Census Bureau, Current Population Reports, P60-251, October 2014.

179. See, for example, Roberton Williams and Elaine Maag, "The Recession and the Earned Income Tax Credit," Urban Institute, December 2008, http://www.urban.org/Uploaded PDF/411811_recession_and_EITC.pdf. For EITC recipients whose earnings qualify for the maximum benefit (those with annual earnings ranging from about $9,500 to $23,000 in 2014), a drop in wages means that their EITC benefits will stay the same. For those with earnings below this, a decline in wages will mean a drop in EITC benefits as well, compounding the loss in earnings rather than compensating for it. See Center on Budget and Policy Priorities, "Policy Basics: The Earned Income Tax Credit," updated January 31, 2014, http://www.cbpp.org/cms/?fa=view&id=2505, for a calculator of EITC benefits.

180. See, for example, Tim Padgett, "Why Would a Governor Spurn Stimulus Money?" *Time Magazine*, March 13, 2009; and Robert Pear, "States' Policies on Health Care Exclude Some of the Poorest," *New York Times*, May 24, 2013. The Joint Center for Political and Economic Studies released a poll in May 2013 indicating that public support for the expansion was solid in many of the states whose governors were opposed.

Conclusion

1. See, for example, statements by then-DLC chair Bill Clinton that the New Democratic approach "plainly rejects the old ideologies and false choices they impose. Our agenda isn't liberal or conservative. It is both, and it is different." Al From, "Hey, Mom, What's a New Democrat?" *Washington Post*, June 6, 1993.

2. Particularly after the region's rapid growth between the 1960s and the 1980s, observers reached bold conclusions: "The contemporary South, many commentators maintained, skipped the intermediate stage in America's passage from rural to urban to suburban nation, from agrarian to industrial to service economy, but rejoined America's post-industrial mainstream," writes Bruce J. Schulman, *From Cotton Belt to Sunbelt* (Durham, N.C.: Duke University Press, 1994), 219.

3. See, for example, "The New Progressive Declaration: A Political Philosophy for the Information Age," particularly 26–28, and Robert J. Shapiro, "Restoring Upward Mobility in the Knowledge Economy," 183–99, in Will Marshall, ed., *Building the Bridge: 10 Big Ideas to Transform America* (Lanham, Md.: Rowman and Littlefield, 1997).

4. In the first decade of the twenty-first century, liberal lawmakers pushed for additional childcare funding for welfare recipients rather than fundamental reforms to TANF, for example. See Congressional Research Service, CRS Issue Brief for Congress, "Welfare Reauthorization," updated December 22, 2005, http://digital.library.unt.edu/ark:/67531/metadc83875/?q=welfare%20reauthorization%20december%202005. The Obama administration took a partial—but temporary—step toward restoring the link between TANF spending and increased need by including a $5 billion TANF Emergency Contingency Fund in the Recovery Act. Congressional Research Service, "American Recovery and Reinvestment Act of 2009 (P.L. 111–5): Summary and Legislative History," April 20, 2009, 31–32. The fund expired in September 2010 and was not renewed.

5. See, for example, Winifred Bell, *Aid to Dependent Children* (New York: Columbia University Press, 1965), 107. The pattern was evident in OAA as well as ADC; see Jill Quadagno, *The Transformation of Old Age Security* (Chicago: University of Chicago Press, 1988).

6. See, for example, James C. Cobb, *The Selling of the South*, 2nd ed. (Urbana: University of Illinois Press, 1993), particularly chapter 10.

7. *Halfway Home and a Long Way to Go: The Report of the 1986 Commission on the Future of the South* (Research Triangle Park, N.C.: Southern Growth Policies Board, 1986), 5.

8. *Halfway Home*, 4.

9. *Halfway Home*, 9.

10. The recommendations include uniform eligibility standards and minimum benefit levels for AFDC. *Halfway Home*, 17–18, 23.

11. Although more than half the states have created EITC programs to supplement the federal program, few Southern states have done so. Of twenty-five states with programs on the books as of mid-2014, only three were in the South. "Tax Credits for Working Families: Earned Income Tax Credit," National Conference of State Legislatures, updated July 31, 2014.

12. For a discussion of the relationship between Southern and national economic development in an era of globalization, see, for example, Michael Dennis, *The New Economy and the Modern South* (Gainesville: University of Florida Press, 2009), particularly chapter 1.

13. Writing about the national labor market at the end of the 1990s, Theda Skocpol cited findings by John Schwartz that "two-thirds of workers who start at subpar wages are unable to lift themselves to a decent wage even after a decade of full-time work." Theda Skocpol, *The Missing Middle: Working Families and the Future of American Social Policy* (New York: W. W. Norton, 2000), 5.

14. James P. Ziliak, "Filling the Poverty Gap: Then and Now," National Poverty Center Working Paper Series, #03-8, November 2003, University of Michigan, 31 and Table 11.

15. LaDonna Pavetti, Ife Finch, and Liz Schott, "TANF Emerging from the Downturn a Weaker Safety Net," Center on Budget and Policy Priorities, March 1, 2013, 22–23.

16. Schulman, *Cotton Belt to Sunbelt*, 218.

17. Robert Mann, *Legacy to Power* (New York: Paragon House, 1992), 305.

18. See Steven Ruggles, "The Effects of AFDC on American Family Structure, 1940–1990," *Journal of Family History* 22, no. 3 (July 1997): 309, 312.

19. By the 2000s, most aid through the three main cash support programs—the EITC, SSI, and AFDC/TANF—was conditioned on work. In contrast, more than 90 percent of aid from these programs was provided as a need-based entitlement in the late 1970s. For spending levels in these programs over time, see IRS *Statistics of Income*, annual reports, 1976 to 1999, http://www.irs.gov/uac/SOI-Tax-Stats-SOI-Bulletins; Susan B. Carter, Scott Sigmund Gartner, Michael R. Haines,

Alan L. Olmstead, Richard Sutch, and Gavin Wright, eds., *Historical Statistics of the United States*, vol. 2, part B: *Work and Welfare* (New York: Cambridge University Press, 2006); and *Budget of the United States Government, Fiscal Year 2009* (Washington, D.C.: Office of Management and Budget, 2008).

20. See Judith N. Shklar, *American Citizenship* (Cambridge, Mass.: Harvard University Press, 1991).

21. Paul Osterman and Beth Shulman, *Good Jobs America: Making Work Better for Everyone* (New York: Russell Sage Foundation, 2011), 17.

22. See Robert Kuttner, *Obama's Challenge* (White River Junction, Vt.: Chelsea Green, 2008), 146.

23. See Joel F. Handler and Yeheskel Hasenfeld, *Blame Welfare, Ignore Poverty and Inequality* (New York: Cambridge University Press, 2007), 251–52. Nine of the fifteen occupations projected to add the most openings from 2001 to 2010 had earnings that were low or very low. U.S. Bureau of Labor Statistics (BLS), "Occupational Employment Projections to 2010," November 2001, cited in "Future Job Market," *Congressional Quarterly Researcher*, January 11, 2002, 4. For more recent projections, see C. Brent Lockard and Michael Wolf, "Occupational Employment Projections to 2020," *Monthly Labor Review*, January 2012, Table 1, http://www.bls.gov/opub/mlr/2012/01/art5full.pdf.

24. See Lawrence Mishel, "Declining Value of the Federal Minimum Wage Is a Major Factor Driving Inequality," Economic Policy Institute, February 21, 2013, http://www.epi.org/publication/declining-federal-minimum-wage-inequality.

25. See Paul Osterman, "Job Quality in the U.S.: The Myths That Block Action," in Chris Warhurst, Françoise Carré, Patricia Findlay, and Chris Tilly, eds., *Are Bad Jobs Inevitable?* (London: Palgrave Macmillan, 2012), 57. On the misclassification of workers, see also Janice Fine and Jennifer Gordon, "Unpacking the Logics of Labour Standards Enforcement," in Warhurst et al., eds., 195.

26. Osterman and Shulman, *Good Jobs*, 32, 73–74.

27. The resulting "truncated policy menu" focused narrowly on policies to improve education (to help some individuals escape the low-wage workforce), and policies such as the EITC (to sustain those unable to escape it). Paul Osterman, "Job Quality in the U.S.," in Warhurst et al., *Are Bad Jobs Inevitable?* 47.

28. Osterman and Shulman, *Good Jobs*, 16.

29. National Employment Law Project, "The Low-Wage Recovery and Growing Inequality," August 2012, 1, http://www.nelp.org/index.php/content/content_about_us/tracking_the_recovery_after_the_great_recession.

30. U.S. Government Accountability Office, *Unemployment Insurance: Low-Wage and Part-Time Workers Continue to Experience Low Rates of Receipt*, GAO-07-1147 (Washington, D.C.: U.S. GAO, 2007), 3. For data on health and pension benefits, see Lawrence Mishel, Jared Bernstein, and Heidi Shierholz, *The State of Working America 2008/2009* (Ithaca, N.Y.: Cornell University Press, 2009), 149–50.

31. David T. Ellwood, "Anti-Poverty Policies for Families in the Next Century: From Welfare to Work—and Worries," *Journal of Economic Perspectives* 14, no. 1 (Winter 2000): 187–98.

32. See Gareth L. Magnum, Stephen L. Magnum, and Andrew M. Sum, *The Persistence of Poverty in the United States* (Baltimore: Johns Hopkins University Press, 2003), 75.

33. See, for example, Peter Edelman, *Searching for America's Heart* (Boston: Houghton Mifflin, 2001), 146. In 2013, 6.3 percent of Americans (19.8 million) had incomes at 50 percent or more below the poverty level. U.S. Bureau of the Census, "Historical Poverty Tables—People," Table 22, https://www.census.gov/hhes/www/poverty/data/historical/people.html.

34. These families receive little assistance other than food stamps and Medicaid. See Pamela J. Loprest, "Disconnected Families and TANF," OPRE Brief #2, Urban Institute and U.S. Depart-

ment of Health and Human Services, Administration for Children and Families, Office of Planning, Research and Evaluation, November 2011, http://www.acf.hhs.gov/sites/default/files/opre/disconnected.pdf.

35. U.S. Internal Revenue Service, "Earned Income Credit," Publication 596, 2013.

36. Keith Gunnar Bentele, "Evaluating the Performance of the U.S. Social Safety Net in the Great Recession," Center for Social Policy, University of Massachusetts Boston, Paper 62, April 2012, pp. 3, 9.

INDEX

Abbott, Grace, 20, 258n14, 262n14
ADC. *See* Aid to Dependent Children
Advisory Committee on Public Employment and Relief, 18–20
Advisory Council on Public Welfare, 266n101
AFDC. *See* Aid to Families with Dependent Children
Affordable Care Act (ACA), 223, 253, 307n74; coverage under, 285n82, 309n117; state implementation of, 312n158. *See also* health insurance
African Americans, 11, 25, 163; affirmative action policies and, 168, 169; FAP and, 60–61; job-related benefits for, 122–23, 286n90; Mondale and, 172; New Democrats and, 173; self-employed, 115; underemployment of, 71, 110, 282n41; unemployment rate among, 109–10; wages of, 119. *See also* civil rights movement
Aid to the Blind (AB), 5, 18, 22, 28, 33, 80, 83, 135, 263n35
Aid to Dependent Children (ADC), 16–34, 265n66, 266n85
Aid to Families with Dependent Children (AFDC), 92–95, 105; AFDC-UP program and, 35–36, 49, 149; block-grant proposals and, 197–99, 202, 203, 206; during Carter years, 92; during Clinton years, 160, 187, 194, 195, 198–208; creation of, 8, 16, 19–21, 33; EITC and, 10, 77, 99–100, 161, 194–96, 244–45; FAP and, 51, 53–56, 62–65, 96; FSA and, 150; during Johnson years, 35–41, 47; Mills on, 36–37, 40, 77, 81; during Nixon years, 44–48, 53–54; during Reagan years, 131, 135, 137–39, 152; SSI and, 80, 85, 195, 276n57; TANF and, 239, 248–49, 281n30, 313nn173–74; WIN II and, 77–79

Aid to the Permanently and Totally Disabled (APTD), 18, 263n35, 275n54. *See also* disabled, aid to
Alter, Jonathan, 229, 307n83, 310n127
Altmeyer, Arthur, 19, 262n8
American Jobs Act, 231–32
American Recovery and Reinvestment Act, 224–30; cost of, 308n97; tax cuts in, 307n82
Anderson, Martin, 43, 50–51, 63, 89, 146, 268n3
Archer, Bill, 27, 184, 193, 194, 198, 213
Armey, Dick, 185, 189, 193
Atwater, Lee, 164

Babbitt, Bruce, 169
Baer, Kenneth, 169, 292n32
Baker, James, 132
Balanced Budget Act of 1997, 212–15, 217
Ball, Robert, 31, 83, 265n74
Balz, Dan, 192–93, 294n9
Bane, Mary Jo, 189, 191, 206, 282n34
Bartels, Larry M., 260n30, 310n130
Begala, Paul, 213
Bell, Winifred, 24, 63n39
Bennett, Robert, 185
Bennett, William, 188
Bentsen, Lloyd, 27, 76, 149; in Clinton administration, 180, 182, 184; as Dukakis's running mate, 168
Berkowitz, Edward, 263n35, 265n63, 272n4
Bernstein, Jared, 224, 231, 281n19, 305n42
Biden, Joseph, 224
Black, Earl and Merle, 163–64, 166, 294n8, 295n40
Blank, Rebecca, 104, 105, 277n86
Blinder, Alan S., 104, 307n77, 307n82
block grants, 197–99, 202, 203, 206, 232–34; for TANF, 206, 219, 277n89

Blue Dog Democrats, 163, 213, 217, 220, 231, 234
Blumenthal, Sidney, 204, 294n16
boll weevil Democrats, 133, 136-37, 141, 163, 169
Boren, David, 183
Bowles, Erskine, 213, 231; on Social Security reform, 216
Bradley, Bill, 145, 146
Breaux, John, 169, 170, 246; Clinton administration and, 183
Brock, William, 157
Brown, Josephine, 17, 18, 21, 261n3
Brown, Michael K., 258n16, 273n9
Brownstein, Ronald, 192-93, 294n9, 298n38
Broyhill, Joel, 73
Bryan, Richard, 183
Bureau of Family Services, 26
Bureau of Labor Statistics, 109
Bureau of Public Assistance, 22, 25, 26
Burke, Vincent and Vee, 76, 268n6
Burns, Arthur, 48, 50
Burton, Phil, 133
Bush, George H. W., 244; as president, 153-54, 157-59, 168; as representative, 76; as vice president, 135
Bush, George W., 210, 218-21, 244, 306n51
business progressivism, 163, 294n14
Byrd, Harry F., 27, 30, 72
Byrd, Robert, 40
Byrnes, John, 78, 81

Campbell, Andrea Louise, 260n33, 306n62
Carter, Jimmy, 92-96, 152-53, 166-67, 279n124
CETA. *See* Comprehensive Employment and Training Act
Chappell, Marisa, 260n34
Child Tax Credit (CTC), 227, 236, 253, 312n158, 314n177
Children's Health Insurance Program (CHIP), 214
Chiles, Lawton, 90, 169
civil rights movement, 11, 70, 162, 169, 178; AFDC and, 35-37; FAP and, 54, 60-61; WIN and, 39, 40. *See also* African Americans
Clay, William, 93
Clinton, Bill, 180-209, 241, 244, 245; DLC and, 166, 169-72, 175-78, 194, 314n1; as governor, 149, 160-61, 175, 179, 189; on minimum wage, 176, 183-86, 215, 297n18; presidential campaign of, 175-78, 296n75; second term of, 210-18; Southern Growth Policies Board and, 247; welfare reform of, 45-46, 126, 149, 176-78, 187-212, 246
Cloward, Richard, 57, 269n27
Cochran, Thad, 193
Cohen, Wilbur, 29, 31, 265n68
Coll, Blanche, 40, 276n55
Committee on Economic Security (CES), 17-20, 29, 100
Community Work and Training (CWT) programs, 33, 35, 266n92
Comprehensive Employment and Training Act (CETA), 95, 137, 279n131; JTPA and, 142, 144, 155
Conservative Democratic Forum (CDF), 133, 163, 169
contingent work, 71, 106, 112, 114-15, 251, 283n56
Contract with America, 189, 193, 200
Council of Economic Advisors, 104, 190, 224
Cuomo, Mario, 177

Deal, Nathan, 198
DeLauro, Rosa, 185
DeLay, Tom, 193
Dellums, Ronald, 60
Democratic Leadership Council (DLC), 161, 166-75; balanced budget support by, 214; George W. Bush and, 220-21; Clinton and, 166, 169-72, 175-78, 194, 314n1; Conservative Democratic Forum versus, 169; end of, 244; minimum wage and, 185; Obama and, 223; welfare reform and, 187, 192, 196, 207-8, 246
Democrats: Blue Dog, 163, 213, 217, 220, 231, 234; boll weevil, 133, 136-37, 141, 163, 169; New, 166-80, 212-14, 221, 242; Reagan, 172, 220
Dirksen, Everett, 40
disabled, aid to, 23, 28, 33, 107, 121; APTD and, 18, 263n35, 275n54; FAP and, 57; OASDI and, 276n55, 276n61; Social Security Act and, 5, 18; SSI and, 76, 80-85, 135, 195, 248; WIN and, 68. *See also* Aid to the Permanently and Totally Disabled
DLC. *See* Democratic Leadership Council

Dole, Robert, 27, 149, 193; as presidential candidate, 200, 201, 204; welfare reform bill of, 198–99, 291n101
domestic workers, 25, 73, 74, 88, 274n24, 278n98
Doughton, Robert, 15, 20, 21, 27
Downey, Thomas, 152
Drew, Elizabeth, 213, 304n11
Dukakis, Michael, 167, 168, 172, 178

Earned Income Tax Credit (EITC), 8, 10, 76–77, 86–96, 146; AFDC and, 10, 77, 99–100, 161, 194–96, 244–45; during George H. W. Bush years, 158, 215; during George W. Bush years, 218; during Carter years, 92–95, 279n124; during Clinton years, 183–86, 193–96, 209, 236, 278n117; creation of, 11, 46–49; criticisms of, 248–49, 252–54; FSA and, 152, 155, 157; impact on poverty of, 12, 261n39; job availability and, 111–12; Russell Long and, 83, 85–94, 98, 146, 157; minimum wage and, 155, 186, 293n135; New Democrats and, 173, 176, 183; during Nixon years, 45, 67–69; during Obama years, 227, 234, 235, 239–40, 312n158; passage of, 67–69, 91, 244; PBJI and, 93; during Reagan years, 127, 128, 131, 140, 145–48, 290n84; TANF and, 253–54, 277n89, 281n30
Economic Opportunity Act of 1964, 34–35
Economic Recovery Tax Act of 1981, 137–38, 145
Edelman, Peter, 191, 200, 204, 206, 270n58, 293n1
Ehrenreich, Barbara, 257n9, 258n10, 281n27
Ehrlichman, John, 48
Eisenhower, Dwight D., 28, 264n59, 292n124
EITC. *See* Earned Income Tax Credit
Ellwood, David T., 189, 191, 199, 206, 282n34, 287n14, 312n48
Emanuel, Rahm, 199, 200, 203, 224, 299n50, 304n10
Emergency Jobs and Unemployment Assistance Act, 95
entitlement programs. *See* New Deal welfarism
Erkulwater, Jennifer, 80, 272n4, 276n56

Fair Labor Standards Act (FLSA), 6, 101, 156, 250, 251, 273n6, 280n8
Family Assistance Plan (FAP), 44–74, 244, 246; AFDC and, 51, 53–56, 62–65, 96; congressional voting on, 74–75, 88, 90; EITC and, 86, 90–91; failure of, 62–67, 73–76, 83, 90; Long on, 62, 64, 67, 72–76, 86–90, 249; Mills on, 62, 67, 81, 271n77, 274n22; Moynihan on, 48, 51–52, 70–73, 273nn12–13; Reagan's view of, 139; SSI and, 82, 84; WIN II versus, 67–71, 77–78
Family Support Act (FSA), 148–57, 160, 187, 191, 197
FAP. *See* Family Assistance Plan
Federal Emergency Relief Administration (FERA), 17–18, 20–21
Feldstein, Martin, 218
Finch, Robert, 48, 71, 77; AFDC and, 267n1, 273n14; SSI and, 83
FLSA. *See* Fair Labor Standards Act
Foley, Tom, 187
food stamp program, 42, 234, 253, 312n158; during Carter years, 92; during Clinton years, 184, 193, 298n46; during Nixon years, 63, 86; during Obama years, 226–27, 232–34, 237–40; during Reagan years, 137, 145
Ford, Gerald R., 91, 95, 279n132
Fording, Richard K., 260n35, 273n9, 306n63
Friedman, Milton, 46, 268n12
From, Al, 168–70, 172, 175, 180; on welfare reform, 187, 192, 296n2
FSA. *See* Family Support Act
Full Employment and Balanced Growth Act, 95–96, 102, 143
full employment policies, 95, 101–2, 144, 153, 167, 280n13
Furman, Jason, 224, 307n76

Galston, William, 171, 173, 295n52, 296n2
Geithner, Timothy, 224, 230
George, Walter F., 26
Gephardt, Richard, 145, 146, 168, 169; on Gingrich, 213; on minimum wage, 184–85; on New Democrats, 214; on welfare reform, 187
Gilbert, Neil, 259n26
Gilder, George, 130
Gilens, Martin, 258n18

Gingrich, Newt, 7, 127, 179; block-grant proposal of, 197; on Obama, 233; as Speaker of the House, 193, 201, 213; on welfare reform, 189
Goldberg, Chad Alan, 259n20
Gordon, Linda, 20, 260n35
Gore, Al, Jr., 168, 170, 178; presidential campaign of, 220; on Social Security reform, 216; as Vice President, 180, 202–4, 246
Gore, Al, Sr., 63
Gottschalk, Marie, 259n24
Gramm, Phil, 133, 136, 162, 193
Grassley, Charles E., 27, 228n49
Great Depression, 101, 103, 141, 210; Obama on, 222; Reagan on, 157; Roosevelt and, 2–3, 16–17, 229; unemployment during, 16, 110
Great Recession, 1–4, 123; aftermath of, 235–41, 248–49; economic stimulus plans for, 221–35; poverty rate during, 2, 261n41; TANF and, 254, 313n172; unemployment during, 110, 120, 210
Great Society programs, 15, 28, 34–35, 41, 103, 171, 250; New Democrats' view of, 161, 171, 173; Nixon's view of, 44; Reagan's view of, 127, 129, 134, 145
Greenberg, Stanley, 172–73, 295n55, 296n2
Greenspan, Alan, 182, 297n12
Grunwald, Michael, 224, 231, 306n69
Grusky, David B., 260n31
guaranteed income proposals, 35, 46–49, 54–56, 71–76, 84, 89, 269n27

Hacker, Jacob S., 259n24, 260nn28, 31, 279n23
Handler, Joel F., 259nn20,25–26, 291n29
Harkin, Tom, 183
Harris, Fred, 39, 59, 63, 267n116
Harrison, Pat, 20, 27
Hart, Gary, 167, 168
Hasenfeld, Yeheskel, 259nn20, 25
Head Start program, 227
Health, Education, and Welfare (HEW) Department, 30–32, 40, 47–49, 55, 82, 289n50
Health and Human Services (HHS) Department, 189–91, 199, 205
health insurance, 101, 191; employer-provided, 121–24, 252–53, 283n56; racial and ethnic disparities in, 122, 123, 286n90; welfare reform and, 62–63, 176, 194, 200, 202, 297n18. *See also* Affordable Care Act
Heineman Commission, 269n16
Hispanics, 110, 122–23, 163, 282n41, 286n90
Hoey, Jane, 22, 25–26, 263n31, 264n50
Hopkins, Harry, 17, 261n2
housing assistance, 41, 60, 86, 135, 217, 227, 233
Howard, Christopher, 91, 259n24, 260n28, 272n4, 277n90
Humphrey, Hubert, 43
Humphrey–Hawkins bill, 95–96, 102, 143
Hutchinson, Asa, 189

Ickes, Harold, 213, 304n10

Jackson, Jesse, 168
Jansson, Bruce, 259n22
Jessop, Bob, 259n26
Job Opportunity and Basic Skills Training (JOBS) program, 151, 191
job training, 29, 92–95, 137, 279n131; community work and, 33, 35, 212, 266n92; FAP and, 51–52; postsecondary education and, 303n124; special wage for, 158
Job Training Partnership Act (JTPA), 142–44, 147–48, 155, 159; revisions to, 303n124; successor to, 207–8
Johnson, Lyndon B., 15, 28, 34–41, 244; on guaranteed income, 47; WIN and, 67
Johnston, Bennett, 142
JTPA. *See* Job Training Partnership Act

Kamarck, Elaine, 171, 173, 295n52, 296n2
Katz, Michael B., 259n27, 268n7
Katznelson, Ira, 258n16, 260n35
Kemp, Jack, 134
Kennedy, Edward M. "Ted," 95, 156, 184–85, 200
Kennedy, John F., 15, 41, 103, 244; ADC program and, 28–34, 265n66
Kennedy, Robert F., 39, 267n116
Kerr, Robert, 39
Kerry, John, 220
Keynesian economics, 100–102, 230, 231, 280n17. *See also* New Deal welfarism
Kilpatrick, James, 57
Kricheli-Katz, Tamar, 260n31

Kristol, William, 188
Krugman, Paul, 260n31, 307n80, 310n129

Lafer, Gordon, 143, 158–59, 208, 279n131
Landrum, Phil, 72
Latta, Delbert, 13
Leath, Martin, 133, 163
Levin-Waldman, Oren, 158, 293n139
Lew, Jack, 224, 307n76
Lewis, John, 163
Lieberman, Robert, 258n16
Livingston, Bob, 193
Long, Gillis, 133, 169, 174
Long, Russell B., 11, 26–28, 39–40, 247, 273n8; on AFDC, 40, 279n128, 288n49; block-grant proposal of, 198; Clinton and, 184, 246; on EITC, 83, 85–94, 98, 146, 157, 194; on FAP, 62, 64, 67, 72–76, 86–90, 249; on National Welfare Rights Organization, 267n114; on PBJI, 93; Reagan tax cuts and, 142; retirement of, 149, 161; on SSI, 81–84; on WIN II, 67–70, 72–73
Lott, Trent, 193, 201–2, 213, 301n96
Low Income Opportunity Advisory Board (LIOAB), 140, 289n52

Mack, Connie, 193
Mainstream Forum, 192, 202
Making Work Pay tax credit, 226, 229, 237
Mansfield, Michael, 66, 265n84
Marshall, Will, 174, 180, 192, 207, 291n113, 296n2, 303n124
McCain, John, 260n37
McCarthy, Eugene, 63
McCurdy, David, 192
McGovern, George, 64, 171
Mead, Lawrence, 132, 207, 287nn15–16, 289n51
Meany, George, 40, 58
Medicaid, 3, 84, 103, 252, 253; AFDC and, 42, 62; during Clinton years, 193, 194, 200, 202; during Obama years, 232–33, 240, 312n158; during Reagan years, 292n122
Medicare, 84, 103; during Clinton years, 183, 194, 213, 216–17; during Obama years, 233
Mettler, Suzanne, 229–30, 260n33
Michel, Robert, 193
Mills, Wilbur, 15, 27, 161, 246, 273n8, 276n61; on ADC, 26–28, 30, 33, 266n85; on AFDC, 36–37, 40, 77, 81; on FAP, 62, 67, 81, 271n77, 274n22; on SSI, 81, 83, 84; on WIN II, 67–70, 77
minimum wage, 155, 250, 315n13; during George H. W. Bush years, 157–59; during George W. Bush years, 219; during Clinton years, 176, 183–86, 215, 236, 297n18; EITC and, 155, 186, 293n135; Fair Labor Standards Act and, 280n8; New Democrats and, 173, 174; during Nixon years, 60, 74, 292n124; during Reagan years, 128, 131, 156–57; during Roosevelt years, 98, 101
Mink, Gwendolyn, 267n123, 273n10
Mondale, Walter, 145, 167, 172, 278n112
Morgan, Kimberly J., 250n33
Morris, Dick, 201, 203, 204
Moynihan, Daniel Patrick, 27, 199, 290n84; FAP and, 48, 51–52, 61, 70–73, 273nn12–13; FSA and, 149, 152
Murray, Charles, 130, 188, 189, 298n43
Myles, John, 260n28

Nadasen, Premilla, 260n34
Nathan, Richard, 48
National Association of Manufacturers (NAM), 101, 270n49, 280n12
National Association of Social Workers (NASW), 40, 47
National Commission on Fiscal Responsibility and Reform, 231
National Resources Planning Board, 101
National Welfare Rights Organization (NWRO), 58–60, 62–64, 267n114
negative income tax, 46–47, 89, 268n12. *See also* Earned Income Tax Credit
neoliberal Democrats, 167–68
New Deal welfarism, 5–7, 40, 97–107, 131–32, 243, 251–52; assumptions of, 99, 106–25, 144, 282n37; during Clinton years, 161, 187, 197–208, 211, 217; definition of, 262n16; Keynesian economics and, 100–102, 230, 231, 280n17; New Democrats and, 167, 170, 171, 173; new social contract versus, 249–55; during Nixon years, 44–45, 49, 55, 68; during Obama years, 221–23, 229, 235, 244; origins of, 15–26; during Reagan years, 127, 129, 134, 145, 148, 152, 154; SSI and, 80–81. *See also* Social Security Act
New Democrats, 166–80, 212–14, 221, 242
New Economy, 171, 220, 242–43, 251
New South, 70, 72, 162–79, 242–43, 258n15

Nickles, Don, 193
Nixon, Richard, 45–55, 60–62, 166, 244, 246; George H. W. Bush and, 76; campaign of 1968 of, 43–44; Russell Long on, 249; minimum wage under, 60, 74, 292n124; SSI and, 83–84. *See also* Family Assistance Plan (FAP)
Nunn, Sam, 169, 170

Obama, Barack, 210–12, 221–41, 244–45, 260n37, 307n73
Obey, David, 181
Office of Economic Opportunity (OEO), 47
Old Age, Survivors, and Disability Insurance (OASDI/Social Security), 5, 17, 38, 84, 107, 193, 214–18, 234, 237–38, 276n55, 276n61.
Old Age Assistance (OAA) program, 23, 121, 263n35, 276n72; creation of, 17–18; limitations of, 20, 47; SSI and, 8, 80–85, 276n57
Old Age Insurance (OAI) program. *See* Old Age, Survivors, and Disability Insurance
Omnibus Budget Reconciliation Act (OBRA): of 1981, 136–40, 144, 145; of 1993, 183, 184
O'Neill, Thomas Philip, Jr., "Tip," 132–36, 141, 144–45, 155, 167, 287n24
Orszag, Peter, 224, 225, 230
Osterman, Paul, 251, 258n8, 281n27, 316n25

Panetta, Leon, 136; in Clinton administration, 180, 182, 184, 203–4
part-time workers, 71, 106, 109, 114–15, 251, 283n56
Patterson, James T., 259n22
PBJI. *See* Program for Better Jobs and Income
Peck, Jamie, 44, 259n26
Pelosi, Nancy, 220, 231
pensions. *See* retirement plans
Perkins, Ellen, 26
Perkins, Frances, 17
Perot, Ross, 178
Personal Responsibility and Work Opportunity Reconciliation Act (PRWORA), 204–6, 210–12
Phillips, Kevin, 71, 269n19
Pierson, Paul, 259n27, 260nn31–32, 272n4, 279n123
Piven, Frances Fox, 57, 259nn25–26, 281n27
Polanyi, Karl, 50–52
poor laws, 45, 49–50, 262n10, 269n27

poverty rates, 103, 218; calculation of, 308n101; EITC and, 12–14, 117, 261n39; among elderly, 238; European, 12, 13; during Great Recession, 2, 261n41; trends in, 261nn40–41; wage levels and, 117–20, 284n67
Primus, Wendell, 205, 206, 286n90
Program for Better Jobs and Income (PBJI), 92–95, 279n124
Progressive Policy Institute, 174, 291n113
PRWORA. *See* Personal Responsibility and Work Opportunity Reconciliation Act
public assistance. *See* Social Security Act

Quadagno, Jill, 258n16, 260n28, 263n34, 315n5
Quayle, Dan, 142, 143

Rangel, Charles, 27, 147
Reagan, Ronald, 7, 103, 126–56, 244, 245; EITC under, 127, 128, 131, 140, 145–48, 290n84; inaugural speech of, 129; reelection of, 167, 169
Reagan Democrats, 172, 220
Recovery Act of 2009. *See* American Recovery and Reinvestment Act
Rector, Robert, 188, 300n78
Reed, Bruce, 174, 180, 295n59, 296n2, 304n10; on waivers, 299n50; on welfare reform, 187, 199, 200, 203, 211, 298n46
Reese, Ellen, 259n19, 260n34
Reich, Robert, 176, 180, 182–83, 191, 297n12
Reischauer, Robert, 150, 291n104
retirement plans, 22, 24, 121–24, 252–53; civil service, 112; contingent workers and, 283n56; minority workers and, 122, 123, 286n90; privately managed, 216–17, 306n51
Ribicoff, Abraham, 30–33, 60, 64, 75
Richardson, Elliott, 59
Rivlin, Alice, 180, 182
Robb, Charles, 169, 170
Roemer, Buddy, 149
Rogers-Dillon, Robin, 190, 299n48
Romer, Christina, 224, 226, 229–31, 308n93
Romney, Mitt, 233, 260n37
Roosevelt, Franklin D., 15–17, 100–101, 156, 173, 243; on economic rights, 282n37; Obama on, 222, 223; Romer on, 226, 229

Roth, William V., 27, 134
Rubin, Robert, 180, 182, 184
Ryan, Paul, 232–34

Salamon, Lester, 66, 268n6
Santorum, Rick, 233
Schram, Sanford F., 260n35, 273n9
Schulman, Bruce, 165, 166, 249, 273n7, 293n5
Shalala, Donna, 180, 199
Shaw, Clay, 198
Shklar, Judith N., 259n20
Shriver, Sargent, 47
Shulman, Beth, 258n8
Shultz, George, 51–52, 58, 65
Simpson, Alan, 231
Skocpol, Theda, 259n24, 263n34, 272n3, 296n67, 306n62, 307nn74–75, 315n13
Smith, Anne Marie, 260n34
social insurance. *See* Social Security Act
Social Security Act, 5–7, 47, 101–3, 243, 250, 258n14; Clinton and, 215–19; creation of, 16–22, 100; Obama and, 232, 234–38; public assistance programs of, 2–5, 15–26; Public Welfare Amendments to, 29, 32–33, 35–36, 41, 86, 289n50; social insurance programs of, 5, 16–19, 97–102, 261n7; SSI and, 80, 83–84. *See also* New Deal welfarism
Social Security program. *See* Old Age, Survivors, and Disability Insurance
Soss, Joe, 260n35, 273n9
Southern Growth Policies Board, 164–66, 247
Speenhamland public assistance system (U.K.), 50–51
Sperling, Gene, 212, 224, 307n76
SSI. *See* Supplemental Security Income
State of Working America reports, 107–8
Steiner, Gilbert, 34, 264n59, 265n76, 266n98
Stenholm, Charles, 133
Stephanopoulos, George, 203, 205–6, 302n106
stimulus legislation of 2009. *See* American Recovery and Reinvestment Act
Stockman, David, 133, 136, 140, 146
Street, Deborah, 260n28
Summers, Larry, 224, 225, 230
Supplemental Nutrition Assistance Program (SNAP), 227, 238, 312n158. *See also* food stamp program

Supplemental Security Income (SSI), 8, 76, 135, 248–49; AFDC and, 80, 85, 195, 276n57; for disabled, 76, 80–85, 135, 195, 248; FAP and, 82, 84; inflation indexation of, 277n87; naming of, 83–84; passage of, 67–69, 80–85, 244, 276n55; Social Security and, 80, 83–84

Talent, Jim, 189, 298n46
Talmadge, Herman, 72, 161, 246; on AFDC recipients, 77, 275n45; WIN II and, 66–69, 76–79, 207, 267n122
TANF. *See* Temporary Assistance for Needy Families
Tanner, John, 202
tax policy, 250; during Bush years, 218; during Clinton years, 183, 186, 190, 193; during Obama years, 225–26, 229, 232, 307n82; during Reagan years, 133, 134, 142, 145–48, 152
Teles, Steven M., 259n24
Temporary Assistance for Needy Families (TANF), 3, 86, 206, 209; AFDC and, 239, 248–49, 281n30, 313nn173–74; block grants for, 206, 219, 277n89; during George W. Bush years, 218–19; EITC and, 253–54, 277n89, 281n30; during Obama years, 227, 238–40, 254, 313n172
temporary workers, 106, 114–15
Thurmond, Strom, 31, 164, 265n75
Tindall, George, 249
Trade Adjustment Assistance (TAA) program, 228, 309nn103–4
Tsongas, Paul, 167, 296n75

Ullman, Al, 27, 74, 91–94
underemployment, 107, 109–11, 282nn36–37, 315n13; among contingent workers, 114–15, 251, 283n56; among minorities, 71, 110, 282n41
unemployment insurance, 2, 103, 116, 250; eligibility for, 258n11; during Obama years, 110, 112, 120, 210, 227–28, 238–39; during Reagan years, 137; as social safety net, 107, 121, 124, 252
unemployment rates, 108–9; during Great Depression, 16, 110; among minorities, 109–10; during Obama years, 230–32, 236–37; during Reagan years, 141–42

unionization, 58, 106; in Southern states, 162, 164, 195, 249
"Up From Dependency" report, 148
Urban Affairs Council, 52, 273n13

Van Voorhis, Rebecca A., 259n26
Veneman, John, 48, 88; on AFDC, 77, 275n45; on SSI, 83–84
Volcker, Paul, 140
Voting Rights Act of 1965, 72, 163, 295n52

Wagner Act, 101, 273n6
waivers, 139–40, 189–90, 299n50; and AFDC, 148, 197, 289n52; and FSA, 151
Waldman, Michael, 212, 214–16
War on Poverty. *See* Great Society programs
Weaver, Kent R., 259n24
Weir, Margaret, 100, 263n34, 280n3
Whittington, Will, 102
Williams, John, 62
Williams, Lawrence, 57

Wilson, James Q., 188
Wilson, William Julius, 131, 287nn14–15
Winter, William, 247
Witte, Edwin, 19, 20, 261n6
Work Experience and Training (WET) program, 29, 35, 266n92
work incentive (WIN) program, 37–41, 244, 245; Byrne on, 81; Long on, 67; during Nixon years, 44, 49; Reagan's reforms of, 135, 139, 151–52; Talmadge amendments to (WIN II), 66–69, 76–79, 207, 267n122
workfare state, 1, 212, 235, 240, 245, 249; and workfare, definition of, 4, 6, 44–45, 65, 262n16
Workforce Investment Act (WIA), 207, 214–15, 228, 303n128
Works Progress Administration (WPA), 101
Wright, Jim, 134, 137, 287n22

Zandi, Mark, 307nn77,82

ACKNOWLEDGMENTS

I am indebted to many colleagues and friends, too numerous to thank individually, for their support and contributions to this project. Many offered comments and suggestions on parts of the project along the way. A few who read multiple chapters (sometimes more than once) deserve particular thanks. Rogers Smith, Steve Skowronek, and David Cameron provided valuable guidance and reactions at an early stage. Michael Brown, Dan Wirls, Kent Eaton, and Ken Sharpe offered a range of perceptive and constructive ideas and insights at key junctures. Rick Valelly, Chris Howard, and Marie Gottschalk were tremendously generous with their time, observations, and suggestions. And Peter Agree, editor-in-chief at Penn Press, was unfailingly enthusiastic about the project as it evolved. I am grateful too for the keen editorial eye of Pamela Haag.

At the University of California, Santa Cruz, I have benefited not only from the support of colleagues, but also from lively exchanges with students in a series of seminars and classes on social policy and economic inequality. The library staff at UCSC's McHenry Library provided indispensable assistance in tracking congressional hearings and executive branch reports. The archivists at several other collections provided expert guidance to the material I sought on various research trips, and a number went out of their way to make my research both productive and enjoyable. I thank in particular the staff at the Wilbur D. Mills Archive, William J. Clinton Presidential Library, Louisiana State Archives, Russell B. Long Collection, Gerald R. Ford Presidential Library, Franklin D. Roosevelt Presidential Library, and the National Archives. The UCSC Academic Senate and Division of Social Sciences provided research funds to facilitate these trips. Finally, I owe my deepest gratitude to Bill, for everything.

Parts of this work were presented at the American Political Science Association meetings in 2011 (Seattle), 2007 (Chicago), 2006 (Philadelphia), and 2005 (Washington, D.C.); at the Western Political Science Association meetings in 2011 (San Antonio), 2008 (San Diego), and 2006 (Albuquerque); and at the 2006 Policy History Conference (Charlottesville). Part of Chapter 1 is a revised version of "Democratic Divisions in the 1960s and the Road to Welfare Reform," *Political Science Quarterly* 126 (Winter 2011–12): 579–610. Chapter 3 is a revised version of "The Institutional Origins of 'Workfarist' Social Policy," *Studies in American Political Development* 21 (Fall 2007): 203–29. Chapter 4 is a revised version of "Doors, Floors, Ladders, and Nets: Social Provision in the New American Labor Market," *Politics and Society* 41 (March 2013): 29–72.